Also of Interest

† Available in hardcover and paperback.

Biology
and the
Social Sciences

About the Book and Editor

Biology and the Social Sciences: An Emerging Revolution
edited by Thomas C. Wiegele

Exciting new developments in behavioral biology are creating an intellectual revolution in the study of human behavior and are causing social scientists to reassess the ways in which they approach their disciplines. This book examines how these new findings are likely to transform and shape anthropology, sociology, economics, and political science in the coming decade. The book begins with an overview of the rapidly changing relationship between biological and social studies. In successive sections, well-known social scientists, biologists, and philosophers address the theoretical challenges involved in incorporating material from sociobiology, ecology, genetics, and psychophysiology into their own disciplines' approaches to the analysis of human behavior. The concluding chapters examine specific methodological problems and related issues.

Thomas C. Wiegele is director of the Center for Biopolitical Research and professor of political science at Northern Illinois University. His recent book *Biopolitics: Search for a More Human Political Science* (Westview) explored the impact of a biological perspective on the discipline of political science.

Biology
and the
Social Sciences
An Emerging Revolution

edited by
Thomas C. Wiegele

Westview Press / Boulder, Colorado

Copyright © 1982 by Westview Press, Inc.

Published in 1982 in the United States of America by
  Westview Press, Inc.
  5500 Central Avenue
  Boulder, Colorado 80301
  Frederick A. Praeger, Publisher

Library of Congress Cataloging in Publication Data
Main entry under title:
Biology and the social sciences.
   Includes index.
   1. Sociobiology — Addresses, essays, lectures.   2. Social sciences — Addresses, essays, lectures.
I. Wiegele, Thomas C.
GN365.9.B54   304.5   81-14808
ISBN 0-86531-201-X   AACR2
ISBN 0-86531-202-8 (pbk.)

Printed and bound in the United States of America

To the memory of my father,
Joseph Wiegele, an honorable man

Contents

Acknowledgments

Numerous people contributed in various ways to the production of this book. Most important was the work of Susan V. Kisiel, my research assistant, who did a good deal of interdisciplinary digging to locate many of the selections in the volume. She also was most helpful in sorting through many of the bibliographic and administrative details that are so necessary in producing an anthology. I salute her for her good cheer and well-organized perseverance.

Several individuals at Northern Illinois University have been very supportive of me in this and other projects that I have undertaken over the past several years. Dr. James D. Norris, dean of the College of Liberal Arts and Sciences, and Dr. Dean Jaros, dean of the Graduate School, are fine scholars and administrators who have been more than understanding of the research enterprise. I am grateful for their counsel and wisdom. Dr. M. Ladd Thomas, chairman of the Department of Political Science, has provided good humor and many acts of kindness during the recent past. Two colleagues with whom I am in daily contact, Dr. Paul J. Kleppner, director of the Office of Social Science Research, and Dr. L. Douglas Dobson, director of the Program in Applied Policy Research, have always been ready to come to my aid in moments of near desperation. I am also grateful for the kind encouragement and advice of Dr. Robert H. Blank, chairman of the Department of Political Science at the University of Idaho, who spent a year in residence at the Center for Biopolitical Research. The center's first two postdoctoral fellows, Drs. Donna Day Baird and Joseph Losco, provided useful insights regarding the relationship between biology and the social sciences.

This volume would not have been possible without the encouragement, concern, and optimism of Lynne C. Rienner and Miriam Gilbert of Westview Press. The careful editing of Jeanne E. Remington, also of Westview, is much appreciated. Thanks also to Carolyn Jablonski and Carmen Velez for their diligent proofreading of the entire text.

Joan Flaherty and Patrick Conte provided helpful administrative support in the production of several aspects of the work.

Typing was efficiently done by Mary Narvaez, Eileen O'Shaughnessy, Barbara Parot, Joan Smith, and Lisa Yuen.

Finally, my wife, Mary, has been consistently supportive over many years. That support has always been given selflessly and honestly, and I am grateful for it.

T.C.W.

The Contributors

Janice I. Baldwin, Department of Sociology, University of California, Santa Barbara

John D. Baldwin, Department of Sociology, University of California, Santa Barbara

David P. Barash, Department of Psychology, University of Washington, Seattle

Jerome H. Barkow, Department of Sociology and Social Anthropology, Dalhousie University

Kenneth E. Boulding, Institute of Behavioral Science, University of Colorado

Napoleon A. Chagnon, Department of Anthropology, Pennsylvania State University

William H. Durham, Department of Anthropology, Stanford University

Lee Ellis, Division of Social Science, Minot State College, North Dakota

Piotr Fedoseev, Vice-President, USSR Academy of Sciences

Charles Frankel (deceased), Philosophy and Public Affairs, Columbia University

Jack Hirshleifer, Department of Economics, University of California, Los Angeles

John H. Kunkel, Department of Sociology, University of Western Ontario

Gerhard Lenski, Department of Sociology, University of North Carolina, Chapel Hill

R. C. Lewontin, Department of Biology, Harvard University

Roger D. Masters, Department of Government, Dartmouth College

Allan Mazur, Department of Sociology, Syracuse University

Steven A. Peterson, Division of Social Science, Alfred University

Glendon Schubert, Department of Political Science, University of Hawaii–Manoa

Albert Somit, Department of Political Science, and President, Southern Illinois University, Carbondale

Pierre L. van den Berghe, Department of Sociology, University of Washington, Seattle

John C. Wahlke, Department of Political Science, University of Arizona, Tuscon

S. L. Washburn, Department of Anthropology, University of California, Berkeley

Thomas C. Wiegele, Center for Biopolitical Research and Department of Political Science, Northern Illinois University

Edward O. Wilson, Museum of Comparative Zoology, Harvard University

Part 1
Introduction

1

Is a Revolution Brewing in the Social Sciences?

Thomas C. Wiegele

The purpose of this volume is to pull together the key sources in the existing literature dealing with the impact of biology on the social sciences. In its present totality, I believe that this literature demonstrates that an intellectual revolution is indeed brewing in the social sciences. This revolution, put simply, is a challenge to the general but not exclusive notion within the social sciences that human social behavior is caused by some combination of learning and environmental factors. Biologically oriented social scientists, while recognizing the importance of both learning and environmental influences, have argued that social behavior is much more complex and that the biological attributes of the human organism and evolutionary processes must be taken into account if we are to understand human behavior more accurately. Such an orientation, as will be seen throughout this book, is encouraging social scientists to rethink commonly accepted definitions of human nature.

The biological challenge to the social sciences should not be considered in rigidly revolutionary terms, i.e., as an explosive event that has forced the development of the social sciences onto a distinctly new path. Rather, this has been a slow, emerging revolution that has been underway, almost unnoticed, for at least a decade. As a result, we are in the relatively early stages of the transformation of the social sciences into biologically sensitive disciplines. Thus, the work produced so far is uneven, frequently tentative, and, as is so often the case in the social sciences, noncumulative. Nevertheless, the fact that such scholarship has not developed in an orderly fashion should not in any way be interpreted as meaning that the work is not serious or significant.

Many will view the subject matter of this volume as highly controversial, and perhaps it is. But it is controversial only among "traditional" social scientists. The natural sciences have long recognized the influences of biological factors on social behavior. The debate regarding a biological orientation, nevertheless, has provoked and will continue to provoke a good deal of

3

scholarly exchange. But that should not concern us because arguments are the stuff of intellectual progress.

It will become clear as the reader progresses through the volume that there does not appear to be a commonly accepted definition of biology. Many writers equate sociobiology with biology; others view additional subfields within the biological sciences as more appropriate for bridge building with the social sciences. A more comprehensive perspective would use the phrase "life sciences" as the most appropriate terminology, thus allowing for a much more broadly based biological orientation that could include not only sociobiology but, for example, ecology, psychophysiology, and medicine. Casting the net more widely strikes me as a more sensible approach because there are different levels of analysis and methodological approaches within the social sciences themselves; and, as we shall see in a moment, specific biological orientations lead the social science researcher to circumscribe the arena of inquiry to specific sets of questions. Significantly, a life science approach would allow for the incorporation of behavioral medicine into the study of human social activity. Social scientists with an applied orientation will find the area of medicine, which they have left unexplored, to be an extremely useful body of knowledge.

The preceding paragraph serves as an introduction to my own disappointment with those social scientists who focus much too narrowly on one element of biology — sociobiology — to the exclusion of many other life science factors, methodologies, and perspectives. Nevertheless, I believe that it is inevitable that this will change as we eventually get into more empirically oriented, biologically based scholarship.

What the reader will find in this volume, therefore, is a strong, though not exclusive, emphasis on sociobiological approaches to social scientific analysis. The meaning of sociobiology and the intellectual direction to which it beckons should be clarified at the outset. In an oft-quoted definition, Wilson (1980: 295) has written that "sociobiology is defined as the systematic study of the biological basis of social behavior and the organization of societies in all kinds of organisms including human beings." This definition will be examined at great length in the readings, but sketching out several concepts in sociobiology might be useful at this point. The "central theorem of sociobiology," as explained by Barash (1977: 63), is that "when any behavior under study reflects some component of genotype, animals should behave [so] as to maximize their inclusive fitness." Barash (1977: 81) ties this to social behavior by indicating that inclusive fitness refers to an organism's "net genetic representation in succeeding generations, including other relatives in addition to offspring." Sociobiology taps the intellectual roots of natural selection in Darwinian evolutionary theory, i.e., the idea that some genetic attributes are favored in the contests of organisms and their environments for survival and successful reproduction.

We should also be aware of the junction in the road between sociobiology and many other life science orientations. White (1978: 282) has pointed out that "sociobiological theory shows a concern for ultimate as against proximate causes that is not wholly appropriate for the social sciences." To explain human social behavior in ultimate terms, the analyst must confront the broad sweep of evolutionary developments rooted in time immemorial, while in dealing with proximate causation, the social scientist works with much shorter units of time, occasionally as short as milliseconds in experimental research. Each of these orientations represents a significantly different intellectual style and investigative strategy, and each has a different effect on the study of human social behavior. As stated above, until recently social scientists have been much more interested in sociobiology than they have in other life science approaches, and this has involved them in discussions of ultimate causation and the general impact of evolutionary processes.

What has been the value of this interest in ultimate causation? Losco (forthcoming) has explored how a sociobiological orientation might contribute to advancing knowledge within the social science disciplines. He sees three possibilities: "(1) ultimate accounts may be able to provide satisfying explanations of behavior for the social sciences on their own, rendering proximate explanations obsolete; (2) ultimate accounts may straightforwardly identify particular proximate causes with which social scientists can build behavioral models; (3) ultimate explanations may be useful in the more limited sense of providing a means for rejecting proximate hypotheses which are grossly out of synchronization with evolutionary theory." Although all of these points have been subjected to much discussion, often quite heated, in the literature of sociobiology as well as that of the social sciences, it is probably safe to say that there are relationships between sociobiology and the other life sciences, between ultimate and proximate causation, that are worth discovering and exploiting for both biologists and social scientists. At the very least, however, we ought to be self-conscious of the directions in which we are moving. White (1978: 282), in a pointed challenge, says it well: "Like a good doctor, the social scientist must, in addition to being conversant with the general principles of his science, also be able to apply them to suit the individual case before him."

Social scientists who have adopted a biological orientation in their work are often confronted with the charge that they are reducing the study of human behavior to "simple biological structures." This charge is frequently made, but I do not believe that it can be substantiated. Biologically sensitive social scientists argue that human behavior is coming to be recognized as far more complex than previously thought, and that explanations that do not combine biological factors with learning and environmental variables will simply not represent the power of understanding that is possible with present-day scholarship. Masters (1980) points out that "social science is . . . unlikely to be reduced to a simplistic, monist system based on molecular genetics." He advances three reasons for this judgment, centered on knowledge from the scientific as well as the social arenas: (1) the diversity of motivational and behavioral systems at the individual level; (2) the process of cultural evolution at the social level; and (3) the hierarchical structuring of complex systems resulting from evolutionary processes and embedded in the human gene pool.

Related to the reductionist argument is the assertion that a biological orientation in the study of human social behavior is antihumanistic. Caplan (1980: 38) states the issues clearly:

> Perhaps it is not really a gap in understanding that now separates the practitioners of scientific research from those in the humanities. Rather, the trouble may be that each group knows all too well what the other is doing on the far side of the divide. Humanists correctly perceive current efforts to "scientize" the humanities with insights from biology and other sciences as an attempt to reduce or eliminate large areas of the humanities such as ethics, politics, and aesthetics. The threat to the autonomy and existence of these central humanistic domains is often explicit. Similarly, those in the sciences resent the efforts of humanists to erect conceptual moats around subjects such as ethics and political theory. They see such attempts at restriction as inimical to the very enterprise of science.

I believe that a truly profound understanding of human nature must ultimately include both biological and nonbiological considerations. Wilson (1978: 13) has emphasized that "social scientists cannot afford to ignore . . . [the] rapidly tightening principles" of biology, but he also is quick to add that "the social sciences are potentially far richer in content" than the life sciences. In our attempts to understand human behavior, the most truly humanistic orientation is one that attempts to *integrate* the multiplicity of factors that contribute to this understanding. Anything less than this falls short of a truly humanistic mark, whether it is done from a sociohumanistic perspective or a natural science perspective. Thus, the blending of these two intellectual cultures can only lead us to a more humanistic understanding of human nature. Furthermore, it should be noted that biology will not destroy the humanities and the social sciences, as some would have us believe, but rather breathe life into them — an invigoration that is sadly overdue.

The remainder of this volume is divided into six parts: an overview section that lays out many observations on the relationship between biology and the social sciences generally, four parts dealing with the specific disciplines of anthropology, economics, political science, and sociology, and a concluding part that is both general and critical. Each reading was selected on the basis of whether it contributed to an understanding of the *relationship* between biology and the social sciences or between biology and particular disciplines. This strategy, of course, yields a very specific type of article. Not included in the volume are those many pieces of empirical work that have gone beyond the nature of the relationship and into the actual testing of the kinds of hypotheses proposed by many of the authors here. On the basis of the present volume, therefore, an inference should *not* be made that this collection represents the extent of the published work in biology and the social sciences. Much scholarship has already been produced and a major part of it is cited by the contributors to this book.

Some readers may question the decision to exclude psychology from the list of social sciences. This field was originally included but was set aside for two reasons. First, psychology is usually considered as a disciplinary bridge between the natural sciences and the social sciences. As such, it is not a social science in the same sense as anthropology, economics, political science, or sociology. More importantly, however, subfields of psychophysiology and biopsychology have long been a part of psychology and the question of whether biology might be relevant to psychology is therefore moot. On the other hand, it is true that some psychologists have been interested in sociobiology (e.g., see Campbell, 1975).

Although it is correct to assume that the general import of the volume is to support the development of a relationship between biology and the social sciences, I have not tried to stack the cards by arbitrarily eliminating all contrary material. Some very strong critical commentary has been included, and indeed, if a biosocial thrust is to progress, the probing questions raised by these authors must be addressed.

There is no question that a firm base of scholarship combining biological perspectives with the study of human social behavior already exists. The past decade of work has demonstrated that biosocial science represents a serious, perhaps revolutionary, intellectual challenge to "normal" social science. That base is about to expand dramatically with the publication of numerous books during the next few years.

Other developments are likely to continue at a more accelerated pace. The professional conventions of the disciplines are hosting more and more panels with a biosocial orientation, and specialized conferences are taking place with increased frequency. Political science has apparently led the way with the founding, during 1980, of the Association for Politics and the Life Sciences, which represents a continuing and serious commitment to the study of a biological political science. It is likely that the 1980s will witness the birth of graduate programs to train students in biologically oriented social science research and policy analysis.

I will end this brief essay by stating the hope that social scientists not become overly concerned with the boundaries of the disciplines in which they received their primary training. Those boundaries should be ever-changing and actively moving in unexplored directions. Without such movement the social sciences risk becoming stagnant, arrogant, inward looking, and protective.

As social scientists pursuing truth we should not be annoyed if other disciplines, especially the life sciences, attempt to contribute to an understanding of human social behavior. We do not "own" any niche in the world of discovery.

References

Barash, D. P. (1977) *Sociobiology and Behavior.* New York: Elsevier Press.

Barlow, G. W., and J. Silverberg. (1980) *Sociobiology: Beyond Nature/Nurture?* Boulder, Colo.: Westview Press.

Campbell, D. T. (1975) "On the Conflicts Between Biological and Social Evolution and Between Psychology and Moral Tradition." *American Psychologist,* December.

Caplan, A. L. (1980) "Of Mice and Men: The Human Sciences and the Humanities." *Hastings Center Report,* December.

Losco, J. (forthcoming) "Proximate and Ultimate Explanation: How Is Sociobiology Relevant to the Social Sciences?" *Journal of Social and Biological Structures.*

Masters, R. D. (1980) "Biology and the Social Sciences." unpublished manuscript.

White, E. (1978) "Sociobiology and Politics." *Political Science Reviewer,* Vol. 8.

Wilson, E. O. (1978) *On Human Nature.* Cambridge, Mass.: Harvard University Press.

Wilson, E. O. (1980) "A Consideration of the Genetic Foundation of Human Social Behavior," in Barlow and Silverberg, *Sociobiology: Beyond Nature/Nurture?* Boulder, Colo.: Westview Press.

Part 2
The General Relationship Between Biology and the Social Sciences

Introduction to Part 2

In this section, which provides a general overview of the relationship between biology and the social sciences, two of the authors have differing degrees of positive commitment to the establishment of such a relationship. A third expresses serious reservations.

Van den Berghe argues that technical and intellectual developments in biology are forcing social scientists "to take biology seriously." Indeed, van den Berghe asserts that although it will be difficult, a rapprochement between biology and the social sciences is inevitable. A key to understanding van den Berghe is his sharp commentary on past (and by implication contemporary) social scientific inquiry. He writes that "social scientists became increasingly concerned with abstract formal structures rather than with processes; with reified collectivities rather than with interacting individuals; with mentalistic constructs, ideologies, and symbolic systems rather than with observable behavior; and with statistical manipulation of aggregated data rather than with careful study of ongoing social processes. Human beings as organisms were seen as mere carnal vectors for culture and for social structures."

Van den Berghe exhorts his social science colleagues to "return to their biological roots" if they are at all serious about scientific inquiry. He suggests that the paradigm of sociobiology appears to be a worthwhile arena from which to gather testable hypotheses about human social behavior and he provides numerous examples for the reader. He sternly lays the responsibility for the disjuncture between biology and the study of human social behavior squarely on the shoulders of the social science community and he challenges the latter to demystify human behavior.

Wilson, a biologist, develops the concept of disciplines and antidisciplines, and in doing so he provides examples from cell biology/biochemistry and ecology/population biology. This is done by way of preface to his major point, which is that "biology is the antidiscipline of the social sciences." Wilson readily admits that his position will not be "congenial to the prevailing view in the social sciences and humanities that human social life is the nearly exclusive product of cultural determinism, constrained only by the most elementary and unstructured biological drives." Nevertheless, he surveys the social sciences (unfortunately neglecting political science) in general terms in order to illustrate the importance and necessity of a biological perspective.

In a final section on the limits of reductionism, Wilson argues that "the full phenomenology of social life cannot be predicted from a knowledge of the genetic programs of the individuals alone." Thus, while "biology is the key to human nature and social scientists [therefore] cannot afford to ignore its emerging principles," it must be underscored, says Wilson, that "the social sciences are potentially far richer in content. Eventually they will absorb the relevant ideas of biology and go on to beggar them by comparison."

Although van den Berghe and Wilson are generally hopeful that a fruitful collaboration can develop between biology and the social sciences, Frankel is at best skeptical and at worst highly critical of such a development. Frankel's critique, while cast in terms of an argument against the tenets espoused by Wilson, is nevertheless applicable to many of the basic positions advanced by those who advocate a closer intellectual relationship between biology and the social sciences. Importantly for Frankel, "propositions about the hypothalamus and the limbic system do not contain terms like 'love,' 'hate,' 'good,' or 'bad.' They cannot, therefore, be the only premises we need to produce psychological or moral statements containing such terms. Nor can we do without such terms, for they have been developed to deal with discernable aspects and qualities of human experience which the language of molecular biology and biochemistry cannot adequately characterize." Included in Frankel's critical commentary are the writings of Charles Darwin. Here Frankel adopts a philosophical/theological stance and assails Darwin for his views on creation and the antiteleological orientation in his thought.

Although Frankel admits that "as a science, sociobiology is new and probably important," he also feels that biology cannot explain the subtleties and nuances of the human spirit. "We are not machines," Frankel insists, "to be taken apart or put together again. We are organisms with a long history in our genes, and in our habits and sentiments."

T.C.W.

2

Bridging the Paradigms: Biology and the Social Sciences

Pierre L. van den Berghe

After a half century of drifting apart from the natural sciences, the social sciences are forced once more to take biology seriously. Inevitable though the rapprochement may be, it will not happen easily. The social sciences grew in the late nineteenth century out of the same intellectual movement that launched biology into its modern phase with Darwin and Mendel. Indeed, early sociology and anthropology were strongly inspired by biology and by evolutionary theory and asked all the right and important questions about human societies. Unfortunately, the biology of the time was not advanced enough to save the social sciences from giving some of the wrong answers. Unsavory associations of early evolutionary thinking in social science with social Darwinism, racism, imperialism, and laissez faire capitalism led to a revulsion against biology among social scientists.

From the 1930s through the 1960s, the dominant current in sociology and anthropology was one of dogmatic environmentalism, extreme cultural relativism, antireductionism, and antievolutionism. There were, to be sure, countercurrents. Anthropology developed various brands of cultural evolutionism on its own. Behaviorism was not antireductionist nor culturally relativistic, but it certainly was environmentalist in the extreme and stressed ontogeny at the cost of almost complete neglect of phylogeny. As a general statement, it is no exaggeration to say that the mainstream of the social sciences in economics, political science, sociology, and anthropology was characterized by an almost complete oblivion of the organic basis of behavior.

Human behavior could be understood, it was widely believed, without any reference to the fact that humans are animals. Among the behavioral sciences, psychology and anthropology both retained an interest in human anatomy and physiology, but at the cost of internal fragmentation within these

Reprinted with permission from M.S. Gregory, A. Silvers, and D. Sutch (eds.), *Sociobiology and Human Nature*. San Francisco: Jossey-Bass, 1978, pp. 33–52. Footnotes have been eliminated.

13

disciplines. Neither developed a consensually accepted paradigm of human behavior. Social scientists became increasingly concerned with abstract formal structures rather than with processes; with reified collectivities rather than with interacting individuals; with mentalistic constructs, ideologies, and symbolic systems rather than with observable behavior; and with statistical manipulation of aggregated data rather than with careful study of ongoing social processes. Human beings as organisms were seen as mere carnal vectors for culture and for social structures.

The era of cultural determinism in social science left a stifling intellectual legacy. During the last half century, biology has made enormous strides while the social sciences have remained largely stagnant. Indicative of this are the inordinate publication lags in social science journals: It is not uncommon for a period of eighteen months or more to elapse between submission of an article and its publication. Social scientists tolerate this because their enterprise is so uncumulative that claims for priority seldom arise. They manipulate great masses of dubious data but make few findings; they use a lot of jargon but their so-called concepts and theories are largely reiterations of old ideas, pretentious platitudes, or, worse yet, pompous nonsense. They are, however, very good at quoting classics, seeking academic ancestors, and establishing intellectual pedigrees. Their textbooks are tiresome commentaries on the gospels according to "Saints" Marx, Durkheim, Weber, and Pareto and on the epistles of "Saints" Parsons and Lévi-Strauss. During their half century of lofty isolation from the natural sciences, the social sciences have become, in short, a scholastic tradition rather than an evolving scientific discipline.

Some social scientists have given up the pretense of doing science and claim affiliation with the humanities. They should be free to pursue their worthy calling unhindered. Here, however, I shall address the majority of social scientists who continue to claim affiliation with the scientific community, and I shall suggest to them that unless their disciplines return to their biological roots their claims to scientific status are going to become increasingly tenuous. More specifically, I shall suggest that the paradigm of sociobiology, while still very much in the formative stage, is the most promising. Finally, I shall make a few suggestions on how the present chasm between biology and the social sciences can be bridged.

Before turning to that ambitious agenda, let me first briefly draw attention to the intellectual obstacles that social scientists erect between themselves and their comprehension of biological evolutionary thinking. The burden of establishing the rapprochement is squarely on the social scientists. It is they who have to rejoin the scientific fraternity. It is they who will have to throw off their self-imposed intellectual blinkers. Let me briefly examine a few of these:

Resistance to Reductionism. In the natural sciences, reductionism is widely accepted as the only game in town. In the social sciences, it is a dirty word. In their attempt to establish their *raison d'être* as separate disciplines, the social sciences have constantly reiterated that human social phenomena are not reducible to any of the "lower" levels of the organization of matter, that society is a reality *sui generis* that can only be understood in terms of its own laws, that collectivities are more than the sum of their members, and so on. The high priest of the antireductionist dogma was Emile Durkheim, but Spencer also made his contribution to it by declaring society to be like an organism — indeed, a "superorganism." Some minor currents in the social sciences, notably behaviorism, remained reductionist, but most "schools" did not.

Reification of the Group. Some social scientists, notably Radcliffe-Brown and a whole school of British anthropologists, have defined social structures as networks of individual relationships. Many, perhaps most, manage to speak of societies, cultures, groups, organizations, social structures, norms, values, and so on with little if any reference to individual actors. When pushed, they will admit that societies are made up of live people, but many assume that much of what they try to understand can best be approached at the *group* level of analysis and is not reducible to individual behavior. Again, there are notable exceptions within the social sciences, such as classical economists, game theorists, exchange theorists, and behaviorists, who make no such assumption — but even in the aggregate they do not define the field.

Biologists, of course, overwhelmingly make the assumption that the individual organism or even ultimately the gene is the main unit of selection, rather than the group. There are group selectionists in biology too (for example, Wynne-Edwards, 1962), and biologists sometimes slip into careless, teleological-sounding language from which one could infer group selectionist thinking. However, the general strategy is to try to explain evolution at the lowest possible level of organization of matter, rather than at the highest, and this strategy has been overwhelmingly successful. It may well be that the human species is exceptional in this respect, but, if it is, social scientists after a century have yet to make the kind of theoretical strides with their group level of analysis that biologists have with individual natural selection through differential reproduction.

Dualistic Thinking. Many social scientists are afflicted with the mental malady of dichotomization. They are by no means unique in this, and possibly the human mind itself is programmed to think in terms of binary oppositions. Modern scientific thinking, however, is largely monistic in its conceptions of the universe. Concretely, the dualistic thinking of social scientists has led them to conceive of nature and nurture, of heredity and environment, as pairs of opposites. Many have implicitly assumed that, because they are dogmatic environmental determinists, biologists must be rigid genetic determinists. They have, therefore, great difficulty in understanding that natural selection theory is based on the selective effect of environmental pressures on genotypes. For biologists, the heredity-environment dichotomy is only a low-level heuristic device to disentangle causative factors in specific evolutionary processes — most assuredly not a way of stating general problems nor an issue on which to take a polemical stance. A biologist considers any stance on the relative importance of heredity and environment in the determination of human conduct as analogous to asking "What is more important in determining the nature of a coin — the head or the tail?"

Emphasis on Conscious Motivation. No doubt because humans *have* achieved a considerable measure of self-consciousness and because people often try to explain their conduct self-consciously, social scientists often assume that nearly all of human behavior must be explained in terms of conscious purpose. Some, following Durkheim, even go as far as to assume that human groups or organizations have collective consciousness and goals that transcend the individual consciousness of their members. Since biologists deal with organisms that, as far as we know, are not self-conscious, volition is not part of their conceptual arsenal; but biologists, being human, sometimes inadvertently slip into teleological and voluntaristic phraseology, as when they speak of the "purpose" of evolution. What to the biologist is a sloppy metaphor is the stock in trade of the social scientist. Perhaps the most common ground for rejecting a biological approach to human behavior is the presumably unique self-consciousness of human beings. Because humans are self-conscious organisms, it is argued, their behavior is *in principle* not comparable to that of other animals. The statement usually stops at the level of the assertion, its demonstration being held to be superfluous because of its "self-evident" validity.

Emphasis on Verbal Behavior. The problem with an emphasis on verbal behavior is similar to the problem of consciousness. Because humans, to the best of our knowledge, are the only animals on this planet to use spontaneously, inevitably, and universally a complex communication system made up of symbols with arbitrary meanings, it is no wonder that social scientists should have become fascinated with verbal behavior and all its ideological and religious derivations. Whole brands of social psychology (symbolic interactionism, phenomenology, and ethnomethodology) come close to equating human behavior with symbolic communication. Other social scientists know that the relationship between verbal and nonverbal behavior is complex and problematic and that we do not all act as we say we do. However, verbal or written accounts of behavior are often much more easily, quickly, and inexpensively collected than rigorous observations of nonverbal behavior. Therefore, data about human behavior are typically several steps away from the actual behavior. We all too often rely on second- or third-hand reports or recollections about behavior, contaminated by selective perception, defective recall, deliberate deception, erroneous inference, ascription of motives, and many other factors that make interpretation of human behavior so difficult.

We have little solid human ethology.

Emphasis on Structure at the Expense of Process. The failure of emphasizing structure at the expense of process is not unique to the social sciences, but it is characteristic of disciplines that lack a good general theory and yet seek to reduce the bewildering diversity of the world around them to a more manageable order. Biology, too, began to taxonomize on the basis of morphological structure before it could successfully explain and predict. The social sciences are still largely at the stage of description, classification, taxonomy, and empirical generalization. Since structures are often far easier to describe and classify than are processes, the structural emphasis of the social sciences is almost inevitable. Understanding process presupposes good theory, something the social sciences have only very patchily developed so far.

Interplay of Observer and Observed. The problem raised by the interplay of observer and observed also is not unique to the social sciences, but it is far more serious when observer and observed belong to the same species and are conscious of each other's actions. One of the consequences of the Heisenberg effect in social science is that a theory or a prediction has the potential of bringing forth its own negation or, conversely, of becoming a self-fulfilling prophecy. A social science theory can and often does become a political ideology used to direct political action. The Heisenberg effect thus both limits the scope of theory construction about human behavior and heightens the level of passion in scientific discourse by directly or indirectly affecting the material (and reproductive) interests of both observer and observed. The rejection of sociobiology (and of evolutionary theory in general) typically reaches fever pitch only when applied to humans. The grounds for rejection are often patently ideological rather than scientific. Modern opponents of sociobiology often think as the Victorian cleric did of Darwin's theory of natural selection: They pray that it is not true, or they hope that, if true, at least it will not become generally known.

Sociobiology is peculiarly threatening not only to social scientists but also to the generality of thinking laypersons (including some biologists) because it has an enormous potential for *demystifying* human behavior. For reasons suggested later, we evolved as a species so uniquely equipped for deceit that we have a seemingly unlimited capacity to deceive ourselves. Therefore, we can be expected to resist strenuously any attempt to strip off the multiple layers of elaborate ideological cant under which we hide our motivations.

Perhaps the most fundamental, persistent, and long-lasting debate in social science has concerned the role of beliefs versus interests in the conduct of human affairs. "Idealists," on the one hand, are those who think that humans behave in certain ways because they have come to accept norms and values taught them by their culture and that without such norms and values social existence would be unthinkable. "Materialists," on the other hand, believe that selfish interests dictate human behavior and that norms and values are either convenient conventions for everyone's benefit (such as driving on the right-hand side of the road) or the result of extraordinarily elaborate forms of deceit.

Most surprising is that the debate should continue when the overwhelming empirical evidence supports the materialist thesis. The few, limited bodies of prototheory that "work" in social science (by the usual scientific canons of parsimony, predictiveness, reproducibility, and so on) are those that are predicated on the selfish pursuit of self-interest: classical economics, behaviorism, Marxist class theory, exchange theory, and game theory. The many competing "theories"—such as symbolic interactionism, functionalism, or ethnomethodology—are not only far more recondite and less parsimonious but they are also largely unsupported by fact. The only thing that postpones their demise is that their proponents are sufficiently attuned to their own self-interests as to couch their "models" in essentially *untestable* terms. Only one social science, economics, has unequivocally accepted the selfish view of human social behavior as the net outcome of individual decisions to maximize gains and minimize losses. Not surprisingly, it is the only social science with a generally accepted theoretical paradigm, one good enough to warrant the regular employment of its practitioners by large corporate and governmental decision makers.

By sociobiology, I mean, very broadly, the application of Darwinian evolutionary theory to the behavior of animals, including humans. I am using the label that Wilson in *Sociobiology: The New Synthesis* (1975) helped establish to describe the convergence on a general paradigm of behavior that grew out of several decades of work by behavior and population geneticists, ethologists, paleontologists, physiological psychologists, and many other specialists. But that paradigm only began to crystallize in the mid-1960s and to make an impact on the social sciences in the mid-1970s. The very label *sociobiology* has evoked passionate rejection, even among some biologists, but the simple fact remains that, well over a century after its publication, Darwin's theory remains the only viable explanation for the evolution of life on this planet. It explains behavior as well as morphology, and there is no reason to invoke special creation for our own species.

This is not the place to attempt a summary of sociobiology, for two are already available, at different levels: an easily accessible introduction for laypersons (Barash, 1977) and the lengthier and somewhat more technical work already mentioned (Wilson, 1975a). The basic theoretical literature can still be surveyed in a fairly limited number of recent publications (Alexander, 1971, 1974, 1975; Campbell, 1972; Emlen and Oring, 1977; Hamilton, 1964, 1967, 1972; Maynard Smith, 1964, 1971; Orians, 1969; Trivers, 1971, 1972, 1974; Williams, 1975). Human applications of sociobiology are, of course, by far the most controversial and are still quite tentative, but the literature on the topic is suddenly exploding (Campbell, 1975; Dawkins, 1976; Greene, in press; Hartung, 1976; Mazur, 1973; Parker, 1976; Shepher, 1971; van den

Berghe, 1974; van den Berghe and Barash, 1977). The fundamental question regarding human behavior and evolution is whether self-consciousness, symbolic language, technology, and all that we mean by culture make our species so qualitatively different from all other species as to exclude us from the scope of biological evolution, at least as far as measurable change in historical times is concerned. Many social scientists have, explicitly or implicitly, taken the position that, for all practical intents and purposes, our biological heritage is of only marginal consequence in determining our behavior and that we change and adapt overwhelmingly by a cultural evolution that is Lamarckian in nature and largely operates at the level of group selection.

Sociobiology, be it noted, is *not* the antithesis of the culturally determinist position just outlined. Sociobiologists are quite happy to recognize that the human species is unique in *some* important respects. So, for that matter, is every species; otherwise it would not be a species. Humans, in short, are not unique in being unique. Nor do sociobiologists deny the importance of human consciousness and culture and the effect these have in greatly accelerating processes of human adaptation to and modification of the environment. But sociobiologists see these human attributes as the outcome of a continuing process of biological evolution and therefore as inseparable from and incomprehensible without biological evolution. There are some discontinuities but also many continuities between human and nonhuman behavior; the phylogeny of higher vertebrates clearly continues to be an essential framework for understanding human behavior. Many higher vertebrates also adapt to changing environments by social transmission of learned behavior. There is only one process of evolution. Heredity and environment, nature and nurture, the inborn and the learned — each set shows only two faces of the same interactive reality. This is as true for us as for other animals, even though our species evolved an impressive bag of tricks in dealing with our environment.

Sociobiology, then, is not a rigid genetic determinism or a simplistic instinct theory. It allows for every species evolving in its own way in meeting environmental challenges. The more complex the organism is neurologically, the more flexible its repertoire of behavioral responses and the greater its capacity for learning from its own experience. What social scientists have been saying about the conscious, purposive nature of human behavior, the complex levels of social organization made possible by symbolic communication, the high degree of environmental control made possible by modern technology, the extreme rapidity of culturally induced change, and all the other things that make us, as far as we know, unique on this planet is all undeniable. The place of social scientists as specialists in one species that happens to be uniquely dear to us is thus assured. If the social sciences are ever to achieve scientific status, however, they cannot continue to dangle in an evolutionary vacuum, isolated from the natural sciences.

Sociobiology does not challenge the separate existence of the social sciences;

it merely invites them to become integrated in a theoretical framework that for over a century has been overwhelmingly successful in explaining the diversity of life on this planet. The framework is broad enough that it can easily accommodate even that argumentative animal, the social scientist.

In principle, then, there is no major difficulty in bridging the paradigm of evolutionary biology with several of the major lines of thinking in the social sciences, especially with the ones mentioned earlier: economics, exchange theory, game theory, behaviorism, and, at the "macro" level, Marxism—and even some brands of functionalism. Much of what social scientists have been saying about humans has suffered from the limitations already outlined but has nonetheless been true. Now is the time to broaden the relevance of these truths by putting us right back where we belong, as one of some two million species on this fragile little biosphere of ours. Only then will our distinctive humanity come into proper perspective.

Bridging the paradigms will be the task of a generation. Let me just make a few tentative suggestions of how this can be done. The most basic question that can be asked about human social behavior is, "Why are we social?" Some species are much more social than others, and forms of sociality also vary considerably from species to species. Among vertebrates, *Homo sapiens* is one of the more social species, but we fall far short of many invertebrate species (such as the social insects) in degree of social integration of our societies. Yet human sociality is based on more complex mechanisms and leads to more complexly differentiated societies than any other known species.

Animals band together in cooperative groups to the extent that this behavior contributes to their individual fitness (that is, reproductive success). Specifically, there are two main ways in which sociality can increase fitness: by affording protection against predators (as, for example, is clearly the case with primates and ungulates) or by affording advantages in locating, gathering and exploiting resources (mainly food), as is true of the social insects. There are also circumstances in which the clumping of resources can lead to great population densities, but mere aggregations of animals, however large, do not constitute societies unless there is *cooperative* behavior.

For primates, sociality is primarily a question of defense against predators. The problem is especially acute among the more terrestrial species, such as baboons and macaques. For hominids, predator defense may have played some role in early evolution, but it probably ceased being the *major* problem a million or more years ago. As has been repeatedly suggested, it was the ecological adaptation of early hominids to hunting and scavenging large game that required a sexual division of labor with extensive cooperation between males and females, paternal investment in provisioning the young, and inter-male cooperation in hunting (Washburn and De Vore, 1961). But this was only the starting point of our sociality, for we gradually developed an ability to gang up against each other, both among closely related species of early hominids and within the ancestral line of *Homo sapiens*. We became, in short, our own predators, organized for intergroup aggression (Bigelow, 1969). Males learned to steal women, and we all learned increasingly efficient ways of wiping each other out and even of eating each other. We cooperated, in part, to kill or displace our conspecifics in competition for resources. The most successful hunting primate became both hunter and hunted, and so we remain to this day.

If such was our general evolutionary scenario, as the fossil record strongly suggests, through what specific mechanisms did we develop our complex kind of sociality? I would like to suggest that three main mechanisms evolved in succession and now continue to operate side by side to produce even the most complex of contemporary human societies: (1) kin selection, (2) reciprocity, and (3) coercion.

Kin selection. Kin selection is undoubtedly the oldest mechanism to have developed, appearing in insects that evolved hundreds of millions of years before we did. We share kin selection with all social organisms and like thousands of other social species, we are nepotistic; that is, we tend to favor kin over nonkin and to favor close kin over distant kin. We may be relatively unique in being *conscious* of our nepotism, but other animals are also nepotistic, presumably without any awareness that they are. Consciousness of kin relatedness is thus not a necessary condition of nepotism. Natural selection happens through the differential reproduction of different alleles of the same genes, which is to say that the relative success of alleles is contingent on the reproductive success of their carriers. The gene is the ultimate unit of natural selection, but each gene's reproduction is dependent on its "survival machine," the organism in which it happens to be at any given time (Dawkins, 1976).

Genes that predispose their carriers to be nepotistic will be selected for, since their duplication hinges on the reproduction of all their carriers. If biologically related individuals can be made to cooperate and thus enhance each other's fitness, then the particular alleles of the genes they share will have a competitive advantage over those carried by nonnepotistic relatives. Or, seen from the perspective of an individual organism, each individual reproduces its genes directly through its own reproduction and indirectly through the reproduction of its relatives to the extent that it shares genes with them. In simple terms, each organism may be said to have a 100 percent genetic interest in itself; a 50 percent interest in its parents, offspring, and full siblings; a 25 percent interest in half siblings, grandparents, grandchildren, uncles, aunts, nephews, and nieces; a 12.5 percent interest in first cousins, half nephews, greatgrandchildren; and so on.

If other factors are held constant, these degrees of relatedness will predict the extent of nepotism or "altruism." Relatives, to the extent that they are related, can be expected to help increase each other's fitness even at some cost to their own fitness. Theoretically, the altruistic transaction between relatives will take place if its cost-benefit ratio (to altruist and recipient respectively) is smaller than their coefficient of relatedness. In less abstract terms, nepotism is a function both of the degree of relatedness in the organisms involved and of their relative need, which in the last analysis translates into their ability to convert resources into reproduction. Parents of postreproductive age, for instance, can be expected to be more altruistic toward reproductive children than vice versa, even though their coefficient of relatedness is identical (one half in both cases).

The evidence for human nepotism is overwhelming. All human societies have been organized on the basis of kinship and marriage, and, until the rise of more complex societies in the last few thousand years, the structure of relationships created by mating and reproductive ties constituted the backbone of the social organization of all human societies. Even in the most complex industrial societies, nepotism continues to operate, along with other mechanisms of sociality to which we shall turn presently.

There is unfortunately no space here to elaborate on the application of kin selection theory to human kinship, but I have done so elsewhere (van den Berghe and Barash, 1977). Clearly, I am not suggesting a simple, mechanistic application of the model to human societies. Nor do I deny that cultural evolution has given rise to a range of elaboration and modifications on that basic biological model. Different cultures prescribe different treatment of the same category of relatives, and the same culture often prescribes different treatment of equally related kin (for example, parallel and cross cousins). Some of these ostensibly cultural differences are themselves partly explainable in terms of kin selection theory, because they relate to such factors as probability of paternity. The lower the probability of paternity, for example, the more closely related matrilineal kinsmen become, compared to the *mean* relatedness of patrilineal kin, real or putative. Of course, even the simplest human societies are not organized *solely* on the basis of kin selection.

Reciprocity. Reciprocity has long been a central concern of social scientists from Durkheim and Mauss to Blau and Lévi-Strauss. Reciprocity can be said to be the basis of a relationship when there is a conscious expectation that beneficent behavior will be returned. It can occur between any two individuals, whether kin related or not; but the more closely related two individuals are the less likely reciprocity is to be a necessary and important element of the interaction. In other words, unrelated individuals who cannot benefit by interacting on the basis of kin selection will depend much more heavily on reciprocity for enhancing their mutual interests than will kin, who can benefit both by kin selection and reciprocity.

Since reciprocity is based on conscious expectation that favors will be returned, it presupposes two conditions: long-term memory and recognition of individual members of one's interacting group. These conditions, in turn, probably exist only in the neurologically more complex higher vertebrates (birds and mammals). The neurological capacity for reciprocity is a relatively late development in animal sociality, and the extent to which it operates in nonhuman species has only begun to be investigated. It seems likely that reciprocity will be found in primates, but it is far more developed in humans than in any other known species, and it has probably played an important role in human sociality for hundreds of thousands of years, certainly ever since the development of symbolic language.

While reciprocity has been enormously elaborated on by human cultures, it too grew out of natural selection. The prototype of reciprocal behavior may well have been the male-female bond, which is essentially a cooperative arrangement to raise joint offspring to the mutual benefit of both parents. It may be that only in humans can this partnership become fully deliberate and conscious (with its elaborate ritualization in marriage), but female deception of the male to induce him to invest in offspring other than his own is not a human monopoly. Female langurs (Indian monkeys) go into false estrus when pregnant at the time a new male takes over a harem; female hamadryas baboons (a species where there is rigid polygynous pair bonding) hide from "their" males when having sneak copulation with other males. Such deceit mechanisms in nonhumans, while probably not fully conscious, give at least some indication of the evolutionary origin of reciprocity in pair mating.

The fundamental problem with reciprocity is, of course, cheating or freeloading. Assuming the universal attraction of getting something for nothing, reciprocity quickly breaks down unless there are fairly reliable ways of detecting cheaters and debarring them from further interactions. But mechanisms of detection in turn invite more subtle forms of deceit. Unless freeloaders are subtle about it, they will quickly be found out. Reciprocity, once it began to play a significant role in our hominid ancestors and to spread beyond the male-female relationship, probably became in its own right an important selective pressure for further intellectual development. Ever more subtle forms of cheating called for increasingly sophisticated methods of detection. Recent examples would be the counterfeiting of paper money or the use of computers to commit crimes. The more humans or protohumans came to rely on reciprocity in addition to kin selection as an important basis of sociality, the more it paid them to be smart. And being smart meant in good part an ability to *out*smart their partners.

Deceit, that ubiquitous feature of human interaction, probably has a fairly long evolutionary history. We clearly are highly hypocritical animals. Still, effective lying is a fine art not within the reach of everyone, since we have also evolved very subtle ways of detecting liars. The ultimate form of deception then becomes self-deception. This is where our elaborate systems of morality and ideology come in: The relentless pursuit of self-interest is usually disguised under some profession of benevolence, which is all the more effective for being sincerely believed by the speaker.

What of trust, then? Is not trust, rather than deceit, the basis of human sociality? Some would have us believe so; but what do we really mean by trust? Unless we are fools, we do *not* trust strangers. We only trust those with whom we have had good previous experience *and* those with whom we anticipate a continuing relationship. This means, in effect, that we only trust people if we are involved with them in continuing systems of reciprocity where there is a fairly reliable way of detecting, excluding, and punishing cheaters. We do not "trust" the stranger to give us a good $20 bill; we "trust" law enforcement agencies to throw counterfeiters in jail. The one major exception to the wisdom of universal mistrust is behavior toward our relatives. We often implicitly trust our close kin because we sense that, with them, kin selection reinforces reciprocity.

Even close relatives will occasionally cheat us, but they are much less likely to do so than nonkin. In fact, they can only be expected to do so when a single act of deceit is likely to bring about such overwhelming benefits as to overcome all the anticipated benefits of kin selection in the future. The faking of wills and the devious maneuvering surrounding rich relatives in their dotage would be examples of such conditions where deceit between relatives is rampant and where trust is therefore most likely to be very fragile.

Coercion. Coercion is not a human monopoly either, but there too we have pride of place. Reciprocity is nice as far as it goes, but it suffers from a gravely limiting condition: By definition, there has to be something in it for everybody. At the very least, everyone has to *think* he or she is getting something out of the exchange. Otherwise there is no point to it. Unfortunately, animals also compete for finite resources where the outcome is a zero-sum game: A's gain is B's loss. Animals regulate resource competition through some combination of dominance orders and territoriality. The former determines order of access to resources, while the latter divides the habitat into mutually exclusive patches monopolistically exploited by a single individual or subgroup within a population. Clearly, the establishment of both territories and dominance orders involves tests of strength and therefore aggression. Individual coercion between adults or of young animals by adults is quite common in many social species. Some species of primates, for example, engage in such mild forms of coercion as displacement behavior: The dominant animal displaces a subordinate for no other immediate reason than to reinforce its dominance. Others fight openly over access to key resources, such as females in estrus. A few, such as savannah baboons, even form coalitions of two or three adult males to exclude or displace other males from access to females, and a recent study suggests that reciprocity rather than kin selection may be the basis of who associates with whom in ganging up on other males (Packer, 1977).

Nevertheless, humans are coercive on a scale and in a manner quite unmatched in other animals. Human coercion (and aggression) is a group enterprise, a conscious, premeditated one. The same intelligence that enabled humans to evolve complex systems of reciprocity as a means of extending the scope of our sociality beyond the confines of kin selection also gave us the capacity to use reciprocity for purposes of coercion and thus to evolve warfare and intraspecific parasitism. Once our species had become clever enough to cooperate on the basis of reciprocity for the purpose of garnering resources such as game, the development of intergroup aggression to eliminate competitors and steal women was around the evolutionary corner. Group coercion is reciprocity for purposes of intraspecific aggression and parasitism. In a species where coalitions for reciprocal benefit can be easily formed, it is inevitable that they will be formed against conspecifics. Plunder is always tempting if I can call on enough of my partners to ensure a cheap victory over my competitors. The incidence of warfare and other forms of aggression is therefore a function of the ease with which balances of power can be disrupted. The latter can be done either through better organization or through better technology.

For all but the last few thousand years of hominid evolution, intergroup aggression was a modest, small-scale affair. Bands of hunters clashed with each other, but ecological constraints on population density were such that numbers were small and, what is more, fairly evenly balanced. Given an approximately equal level of technology and group size, the odds for success were roughly even, and therefore aggression was only moderately attractive. If, to those limiting conditions, one adds the absence of stored resources worth stealing, other than human meat and women, the attraction of plunder was also limited. One only came to blows if a particularly good opportunity for a quick kill with minimum risk of retribution arose, but such occasions were not common.

The real "take-off" point for the development of human coercion and intraspecific parasitism on a massive and organized scale was the domestication of plants and animals for food. This meant both the beginning of surplus production and much bigger population densities and thus bigger societies. With ecological constraints on societal size greatly relaxed, intersocietal competition put a premium on ever larger and more tightly organized societies, and this is where coercion took a quantum jump. No longer did loosely organized small bands simply raid each other, kill a few men, and steal a couple of women. Now much larger and better organized groups started conquering each other's land for keeps and exploiting each other's labor.

States, ruling classes, slavery, professional soldiers, courts, and all the other paraphernalia of organized coercion began to gain prominence, and soon the race was on. Ever bigger, ever more tyrannically organized societies fought ever bigger battles with each other for ever growing stakes. The rationale for internal tyranny was defense against external aggression, but the more states grew in size and power, the more coercive and parasitic their ruling classes became in relation to their own subject populations. The more internally coercive societies had a competitive edge over the stateless societies. They were, on the whole, larger and better organized for aggression. Once control over the means of organized violence became the monopoly of a small group of specialists, the machinery was, quite naturally, used for internal coercion as well as external aggression.

Conclusion

What I have done is little more than restate a well-known scenario of human evolution in a reductionist framework that stresses the following elements:

The first is a view of culture as an outgrowth of a particular line of biological evolution that is fully comprehensible only within that broader evolutionary framework. Culture is our species' way of adapting fast to changing conditions, including those of our own making. In recent millennia, it has become by far our most important way of adapting, but culture does not wipe the biological slate clean. We remain the kind of animal that our entire phylogeny has made us: a highly, but not infinitely, adaptable one.

The second is a view of human sociality as based on three main mechanisms that gained importance in clear evolutionary sequence: (1) kin selection, a blind, unconscious mechanism of gene selection through differential reproduction that we share with thousands of other species; (2) reciprocity, a more or less conscious mechanism that we may share to a limited extent with some of the more intelligent higher vertebrates but that we developed to a far greater extent than any other known form of life; and (3) coercion, a special kind of reciprocity that enables the organized few to exploit the less organized many. Coercion is reciprocity for the few at the expense of the many. All three of these mechanisms continue to underlie our sociality, although their relative weight increasingly moved from kin selection to reciprocity and from reciprocity to coercion. All three grew out of our particular line of biological evolution, but all three assume a wide range of cultural expressions.

Third is a view of collective human phenomena as the net outcome of competing individual interests. Each individual is predicted to behave consciously or unconsciously in ways that will maximize his or her gains and minimize losses. Individual interests include passing on one's genes, directly or indirectly through relatives, but in humans some interests have become at least partially divorced from reproduction. Many social scientists have asserted that collectivities have emergent properties not reducible to those of their constituent members. None has yet demonstrated that "social laws" are anything but the kind of statistical regularities such as can be expected when one aggregates any kind of individual data. For purposes of summary description, it is often handy to deal with aggregated data and to speak of collectivities as if they were independent agents. Large bureaucratic organizations in industrial societies, for example, often seem to have a quasi-organic life of their own, but closer examination reveals the complex interplay of individual interests; the supposedly collective values, norms, and goals are typically the expression of the interests of the few individuals in control.

The human being is a sufficiently special kind of animal and sufficiently dear to all of us to assure the social sciences a permanent place in our scientific establishment. But if the social sciences are to progress they must demystify human behavior. There is evidence that, because of the central role of deceit in the conduct of human affairs, we are singularly resistant to theories that demystify human behavior. Such may be the main basis of opposition to reintegrating the social sciences into a theoretical framework that accounts for the evolution of all life forms on this planet. But demystify we must if we are to reach an adequate understanding of our own behavior. Given our rapidly growing ability to destroy ourselves and our habitat, it is urgent that we improve our level of self-consciousness about our behavior.

Our dilemma is that if we continue to behave as we have in the past we shall greatly hasten our inevitable disappearance from this planet. In the long run, as John Maynard Keynes remarked, we are all dead; but as far as our species is concerned behavioral change can mean the difference between five hundred years and five billion years. Sociobiology predicts that we shall continue to reproduce, consume resources, and destroy each other with abandon because we are programmed to care only about ourselves and our relatives. So far, there is little evidence to show that sociobiology is wrong. The ultimate challenge of humanity is to prove sociobiology wrong, not by assertion but through self-conscious change in our behavior. Far from being an apology for the status quo, sociobiology is a challenge for change. The more we learn about the kind of animal we are, the more self-conscious our behavior will become; and the more self-conscious we are, the more effectively we can change in the direction we choose.

References

Alexander, R.D. (1971) "The Search for an Evolutionary Philosophy of Man." *Proceedings of the Royal Society of Victoria* 84, 99–120.

———. (1974) "The Evolution of Social Behavior." *Annual Review of Ecology and Systematics* 5, 325–383.

———. (1975) "The Search for a General Theory of Behavior." *Behavioral Science* 20, 77–100.

Barash,D.P. (1977) *Sociobiology and Behavior*. New York: Elsevier.

Bigelow, R. (1969) *The Dawn Warriors*. Boston: Little, Brown.

Campbell, B. (ed.) (1972) *Sexual Selection and the Descent of Man, 1871-1971*. Chicago: Aldine.

Campbell, D.T. (1975) "On the Conflicts Between Biological and Social Evolution and Between Psychology and Moral Tradition." *American Psychologist* 30 (12), 1103-1126.

Dawkins, R. (1976) *The Selfish Gene*. New York: Oxford University Press.

Emlen, S.T., and L.W. Oring. (1977) "Ecology, Sexual Selection and the Evolution of Mating Systems." *Science* 197, 215-223.

Greene, P. (in press) "Promiscuity, Paternity and Culture." *American Ethnologist*.

Hamilton, W.D. (1964) "The Genetical Evolution of Social Behaviour." *Journal of Theoretical Biology* 7, 1-52.

———— . (1967) "Extraordinary Sex Ratios." *Science* 156, 477-488.

———— . (1972) "Altruism and Related Phenomena, Mainly in Social Insects." *Annual Review of Ecology and Systematics* 3, 193-232.

Hartung, J. (1976) "On Natural Selection and the Inheritance of Wealth." *Current Anthropology* 17 (4), 607-622.

Maynard Smith, J. (1964) "Group Selection and Kin Selection." *Nature* 201 (4924), 1145-1147.

———— . (1971) "What Use Is Sex?" *Journal of Theoretical Biology* 30, 319-335.

Mazur, A. (1973) "A Cross-Species Comparison of Status in Small Established Groups." *American Sociological Review* 38, 513-530.

Orians, G.N. (1969) "On the Evolution of Mating Systems in Birds and Mammals." *American Naturalist* 103, 589-603.

Packer, C. (1977) "Reciprocal Altruism in *Papio Anubis*." Nature 265, 441-443.

Parker, S. (1976) "The Precultural Basis of the Incest Taboo." *American Anthropologist* 73 (2), 285-305.

Shepher, J. (1971) "Mate Selection Among Second-Generation Kibbutz Adolescents and Adults." *Archives of Sexual Behavior* 1 (4), 293-307.

Trivers, R.L. (1971) "The Evolution of Reciprocal Altruism." *Quarterly Review of Biology* 46 (4), 35-57.

———— . (1972) "Parental Investment and Sexual Selection," in B. Campbell (ed.), *Sexual Selection and the Descent of Man*. Chicago: Aldine.

———— . (1974) "Parent-Offspring Conflict." *American Zoologist* 14 (1), 249-264.

van den Berghe, P.L. (1974) "Bringing Beasts Back In." *American Sociological Review* 39 (6), 777-788.

———— and D.P. Barash. (1977) "Inclusive Fitness and Human Family Structure." *American Anthropologist* 79, 809-823.

Washburn, S.L., and De Vore, I. (1961) "Social Behavior of Baboons and Early Man." *Viking Fund Publication in Anthropology* 31, 91-105.

Williams, G.C. (1975) *Sex and Evolution*. Princeton, N.J.: Princeton University Press.

Wilson, E. O. (1975) *Sociobiology: The New Synthesis*. Cambridge, Mass.: Harvard University Press.

Wynne-Edwards, V.C. (1962) *Animal Dispersion in Relation to Social Behavior*. New York: Hafner.

3

The Concepts of Disciplines and Antidisciplines

Edward O. Wilson

> The opposite of a correct statement is a false statement. But the opposite of a profound truth may well be another profound truth.
>
> — *Niels Bohr*

For every discipline in its early stages of development there exists an antidiscipline. For many-body physics, particle physics; for chemistry, many-body physics; for molecular biology, chemistry; for cellular biology, molecular biology; and so forth. With the word *antidiscipline* I wish to emphasize the special adversary relation that exists initially between the studies of adjacent levels of organization. This relationship is also creative, and with the passage of a great deal of time it becomes fully complementary.

In this article I will argue that biology has now moved close enough to the social sciences to become their antidiscipline. Hitherto biology has affected the social sciences largely through technological manifestations such as the benefits of medicine, the mixed blessings of genetics, and the specter of population growth. Although of great practical importance, these matters are wholly trivial with reference to the conceptual foundation of the social sciences. The conventional academic treatments of "social biology" and "social issues of biology" present some formidable intellectual challenges, but they are not concerned with the core of social theory. Many scholars judge this core to be the deep structure of human nature, an essentially biological phenomenon that is also the primary focus of the humanities.

If it is true that biology is the antidiscipline of the social sciences, the past failure of the social sciences to develop a common body of theory is under-

Reprinted with permission from *Daedalus,* September 1977, pp. 127–140. The format of the citations has been revised and footnotes have been eliminated. "Biology and the Social Sciences" was the original title of this article.

standable. The reason is that the relevant branches of biology — neurobiology and sociobiology — are only now becoming mature enough to attain a juncture with the social sciences. Although it would be premature to say that biology can revolutionize the social sciences, at least to the extent that chemistry has revolutionized biology, it would be equally premature to say that it cannot.

This proposition is well worth examining. To that end I will first describe precedents from the history of biology, then turn to some developments within the individual social sciences that suggest a growing susceptibility to biological explanation. Finally, acknowledging my obligation as a student of the antidiscipline, I will attempt to define the obviously strong limitations of biological reductionism.

Disciplines and Antidisciplines

In general, the practitioners of a given discipline in its early, natural-history phase are concerned with the discovery and classification of phenomena. They stress novelty and particularity. In terms of the classic thematic dualities of science (Holton, 1973), their explanations are characteristically holistic, emphasizing pattern and form over units of construction. In the early phase, specialists are also likely to be dualistic in philosophy, questioning whether their phenomena are directly subject to the laws of the remainder of science (see Northrup, 1947). And in later stages, having been converted, they are still more concerned with what Victor Weisskopf (1967) has called extensive as opposed to intensive research, the use of existing theory to explain the widest possible range of phenomena as opposed to the search for fundamental laws.

Members of the antidiscipline are likely to be monistic with reference to the discipline and dualistic with reference to their own subject. Having chosen as their primary subject the units of the lower of the paired levels of organization, they believe that the next discipline above can be reformulated by their laws. Their interest is relatively narrow, abstract, and exploitative, lacking the totemic attachment to phenomenology displayed by the most devoted students of the discipline above. Thus P. A. M. Dirac, speaking of the theory of the hydrogen atom, could say that its consequences would unfold as mere chemistry, whereas the biochemist Franz Hofmeister responded to the recent great advances in cell structure by recommending (in 1901) that biologists pay more attention to enzymes.

It is easy to see why each discipline is also an antidiscipline. A tense creative interplay is inevitable because the devotees of adjacent levels of organization are committed to different methodologies when they focus on the upper level. By today's standards a broad scholar can be defined as one who is a student of three subjects: his discipline, the lower antidiscipline, and the subject to which his specialty stands as antidiscipline. A well-rounded cellular neurophysiologist, for example, is deeply involved in the microstructure and behavior of single cells, but he also understands the molecular basis of electrical and chemical transmission, and he hopes to explain enough of neuron systems to help account for the more elementary patterns of animal behavior (for example, see Kandel, 1976).

Cell Biology and Biochemistry

In the late 1800s cell biology and biochemistry grew at an accelerating pace. Their relationship during this period was very complicated, but it can be broadly characterized as fitting the schema just described. The cytologists were excited by the mounting evidences of an intricate cell architecture. They had also deduced the mysterious choreography of the chromosomes during cell division, setting the stage for the emergence of modern genetics and experimental developmental biology. Many biochemists, on the other hand, remained skeptical of the idea that so much structure exists. They emphasized the possibility of artifact production by the chemical reactions used in cytological preparations and stood apart from the debate then raging over whether protoplasm is homogeneous, reticular, granular, or foamlike. Their interest lay in the more "fundamental" issues of the chemical nature of protoplasm, especially the newly formulated enzyme theory of life.

In general, biochemists judged the cytologists too ignorant of chemistry to grasp the basic processes, whereas the cytologists considered the methods of the chemists inadequate to characterize the structures that diagnose the living cell. The renewal of Mendelian genetics and subsequent progress in chromosome mapping did little at first to effect a synthesis. Biochemists, seeing no immediate way to encompass classical genetics, by and large ignored it.

Both sides were essentially correct. Biochemistry has now explained so much of the cellular machinery by its own terms as to justify its most extravagant early claims. But in achieving this feat (mostly during the past thirty years) it was partially transformed into the new discipline of molecular-biology—biochemistry that entails particular spatial arrangements and movements of large molecules. Cytology forced the development of a special kind of chemistry and the employment of a wide array of powerful new methods, including electrophoresis, chromatography, density-gradient centrifugation, and X-ray crystalography. At the same time cytology metamorphosed into modern cellular biology. Aided by electron microscopy, it converged in language and outlook toward molecular biology. Finally, classical genetics, by switching from *Drosophila* to the ultrafast-breeding and far more simply constructed bacteria and viruses, has incorporated much of biochemistry to become molecular genetics.

Progress over a large part of biology was fueled by competition among the various attitudes and themata derived from biology and chemistry—the discipline and its antidiscipline. Joseph Fruton (1976), a biochemist who has paid close attention to this Hegelian interplay, has suggested that inevitably "such competition is attended by tensions among the participants. I venture to suggest that this competition and these tensions are the principal source of the vitality of biochemistry and are likely to lead to unexpected and exciting novelties in the future, as they have in the past."

Ecology and Population Biology

Modern ecology has had a troubled history. As recently as ten years ago it was painfully unfashionable in many American universities. An anecdote will illustrate how serious the situation had become. The Department of Biology at Harvard University was at that time increasingly dominated by molecular and cellular biology, and there appeared to be little chance of adding new faculty members specializing on populations or ecosystems. One afternoon I proposed departmental membership for a distinguished ecologist who had been appointed by another school within the university. One of the molecular geneticists, a new Nobel laureate, said, "Are they out of their minds?" When I asked what he meant, he responded that anyone who hired an ecologist must be out of his mind. After the meeting one of my senior colleagues in evolutionary biology suggested that I not refer explicitly to ecology in the future, because it had become a "dirty word." The ecologist was invited much later, after the molecular and cellular biologists had formed independent administrative units.

Ecology is almost embarrassingly fashionable now, and I should add at once that the several ecologists subsequently added to the Department of Biology are on very cordial terms with all their colleagues. But the lesson learned at Harvard and at other universities with similar experiences was, I believe, that few scientists are willing to share resources with those whose research is more than one level of organization removed. Populations and communities, the central concern of ecology, are separated from molecules and cells by an entire level, that of the organism. In an environment ruled by competitive research, profit can be extracted only from the discipline and antidiscipline.

The problem with ecology, however, was more than lack of sympathy from molecular and cellular biologists. The difficulty came ultimately from ecology's focus on the highest level of biological organization, the community, and the weakness of its connections to fundamental population biology. Without quite realizing it, ecology was an orphan discipline. By the 1950s theoretical population genetics, one of the logical antidisciplines, had grown into a technically formidable, even arcane subject. Its models were derived from the distinctive chromosomal mechanics of Mendelian heredity, and it dealt almost exclusively with the interplay of the Darwinian operators — selection, mutation pressure, gene flow, genetic drift, and meiotic drive. Ecology was reduced to the single parameter of the selection coefficient. By a remarkable piece of bad luck, experiments and field studies were concentrated on *Drosophila*. Fruit flies are superb insects for rapid genetic and demographic analysis in the laboratory, but they are singularly hard to find and to study in their natural habitats. Much of what is known of their ecology was deduced from their appearance at food traps. Partly as a result of this historical accident, population genetics remained apart from ecology.

Similarly, with the single exception of pure demography, the fundamental theory of population ecology had not advanced much beyond the principles advanced by Alfred Lotka, Vito Volterra, and R. A. Fisher in the 1920s and early 1930s. Ecology, consisting largely of analysis at the level of entire communities, developed as an ever more elaborate descriptive science. In some of its branches, such as biogeography and phytosociology, the systems of classification and quantitative description reached phantasmagoric extremes.

The time was obviously ripe for a new effort that would bring population genetics and population ecology together and cast them in their proper role as antidisciplines to community ecology. In the late 1950s and early 1960s a small group of younger population biologists (I confess to being a member) set about self-consciously to make such an effort. Several meetings were held to discuss the matter and to some extent to divide the labor. The undoubted leader was the late Robert H. MacArthur, whose work on complex community phenomena was exceptional in its originality and discrimination of important problems (see Wilson, 1973). MacArthur's (1957) seminal contribution was his . . . analysis of the population-abundance frequency curve of a community of bird species. Descriptive ecologists had accumulated a large amount of information on this subject but had done little more than fit empirical curves to it. MacArthur used the data to test a series of competing hypotheses based on models of various forms of interaction among species populations, a process which up to that time had been very difficult to study directly in nature. Although his method has had only limited success when applied to other biological communities, it validated postulational-deductive theory and demonstrated that leaps of the imagination can lay open the most complex ecological processes and give them new meaning.

The response of other ecologists to such renewed model building at the population level was predictably mixed. Many of those devoted to painstaking descriptive work refused to believe that general laws could be so cheaply bought. The patterns they discerned seemed too elaborate, the variables too numerous, and the mark of history too deep and idiosyncratic to make general models anything more than a clever illusion. A community of organisms is a tangled bank, to use Darwin's famous phrase in the closing paragraph of the *Origin of Species*, or a uniquely woven tapestry, in the metaphor of one of the recent critics. Prominent ecological schools still exist, comprised of ecosystems analysts, theoretical population ecologists, physiological ecologists, and so forth. It is cytology versus biochemistry all over again. But the history of this subject, if I have interpreted it correctly, is now entering the middle phase of the classic ontogeny. Broad areas of agreement are already apparent, and model building at the population level has become routine (see, for example, May, 1976).

The Social Sciences and Biology

Let us now return to the original proposition that biology is the antidiscipline of the social sciences. This assessment is not congenial to the prevailing view in the social sciences and humanities that human social life is the nearly exclusive product of cultural determinism, constrained only by the most elementary and unstructured biological drives. There is a strong tendency to think of our own species as entirely plastic and hence all but equipotent in the design of its social institutions. However, this conception will not stand close scrutiny. A comparison of the literally tens of thousands of other highly social species on Earth, from colonial coelenterates through the social insects to the most social of the birds and mammals, reveals that the sum of all the varieties of human social behavior occupies only a small envelope in the space of realized social arrangements (Wilson, 1975a).

Anthropocentrism is a disabling vice of the intellect. I am reminded of the clever way Robert Nozick (1974) deflated our sense of superiority to other animal species in order to make his principal argument for vegetarianism. If visitors from another planet happened to be far more intelligent and sensitive than ourselves, and applied our own criteria of relativity, they could proceed in good conscience to eat us. By the same token, and to our considerable chagrin, scientists among them might find us uninteresting as a social species — just another cultural-linguistic variant on the basic mammalian theme — and instead turn to study the more theoretically challenging societies of ants and termites.

It is this quality of specificity and restriction that biologists have in mind when they speak of genetic determinism. In order to define a genetic trait precisely it is necessary to compare two or more states of the same character. To say that blue eyes are inherited, without further qualification, is not meaningful, because everyone knows that blue eyes are the product of the interaction of genes and the largely physiological environment that brought final coloration to the irides. But to say that the difference between blue and brown eyes is based partly or wholly upon differences in genes is a meaningful statement by virtue of being testable and translatable into the laws of genetics.

Human social behavior can be evaluated in the same way, first by comparison with the systems of other species and then, with far greater difficulty and ambiguity, by studies of variation within the species. For example, certain general traits are shared with most other Old World primates, including size of intimate social groups on the order of 10–100; males larger than females, probably in relation to polygyny; a long period of socialization in the young, shifting in focus from the mother to age- and sex-peer groups; and social play strongly developed, with emphasis on role practice, mock aggression, and exploration. It is virtually inconceivable that primates, including human beings, could be socialized into the radically different repertories of insects, fish, birds, or antelopes; or that the reverse could be accomplished. Human beings, by conscious design, might well *imitate* such arrangements; but it would be a fiction played out on a stage, running counter to deep emotional responses and with no chance of persistence through as much as a single generation.

Homo sapiens is distinct from other primate species in ways that can be explained only as the result of a unique human genotype. Universal or near-universal traits include the facial expressions that denote basic emotions, and some other forms of paralinguistic communication; elaborate kinship rules that include incest avoidance; a semantic, symbolical language that develops in the young through a relatively strict timetable; close sexual and parent-offspring bonding; and others. Again, to socialize a human being out of such species-specific traits would be very difficult if not impossible, and almost certainly destructive to mental development. People might imitate the distinctive social arrangements of a white-handed gibbon or hamadryas baboon, but it seems extremely unlikely that human social systems could be stably reconstructed by such effort.

It is significant that not only do human beings develop a species-characteristic set of social behaviors, but that these behaviors are generally mammalian, and most specifically Old-World primate in character. Furthermore, even the species-specific traits are logically derivable in some cases from the inferred ancestral modes still displayed by a few related species. For example, the facial expressions and some nonlinguistic vocalizations can be plausibly derived in phylogenetic reconstructions (van Hooff, 1972). This is precisely the pattern to be expected if the human species was derived from Old-World primate ancestors (a fact) and still retains genetic constraints in the development of social behavior (a hypothesis).

An important quality of a genetic determinism is that it seldom entails the control of a single phenotype by a single gene. Polygenic inheritance is the rule, and the entity determined is not one trait but rather a range of possible phenotypes. For example, diabetes and schizophrenia possess moderate genetic components. The multiple genes underlying them produce a stronger tendency to develop the traits; they also prescribe the range of possible manifestations that are probable under specified environmental conditions. In a parallel way basic human social behaviors — including those as structured as male-group bonding, territoriality, and kinship rules — emerge as outermost phenotypes following behavioral development, the range and scope of which is constrained by the interaction of polygenes with the environment. With reference to this interaction, there is no reason to regard most forms of human social behavior as qualitatively different from physiological and nonsocial psychological traits.

Whatever the present social arrangements of our species, the biological foundation of human nature arose in populations that adapted to special environments. The prevailing hypothesis, which holds that the basic qualities were fashioned as an adaptation to a more predatory existence in open habitats, may or may not be correct in detail. The important point is that the emotional controls and the developmental pathways are considered to be structured in idiosyncratic ways that can be wholly understood only by retracing the ecological history of the species (King, 1977). That such a relationship exists in other social species can be readily demonstrated (Wilson, 1975a). This is why paleoanthropology, by reconstructing the Pleistocene African environment, has an important role to play in behavioral biology.

An unavoidable question is the extent to which social behavior varies genetically *within* the human species. This is a subject entirely removed from the distinctive properties of human behavior vis-à-vis that of other species. The evidence is strong that almost but probably not quite all differences among cultures are based on learning and socialization rather than on genes (Freedman, 1974). At the same time variation within populations is evidently great enough to create the potential for further human social evolution by population-wide genetic change. Studies comparing monozygotic twins with dizygotic same-sex twins suggest a genetic component in the variation of a large array of traits having an influence on the development of social behavior. These traits include verbal and number ability, word fluency, perceptual speed, memory, the timing of language acquisition, psychomotor skill, extroversion-introversion, homosexuality, and certain forms of neuroticism and psychosis (Ehrman and Parsons, 1976; McClearn and DeFries, 1973; Heston and Shields, 1968; Lennenberg, 1969; and Davis and Flaherty, 1976). Although not conclusive in themselves, such studies are strongly suggestive. Behavioral heritability is also enhanced by the undoubted existence of single, identifiable point mutations and chromosome aberrations, such as those causing the Lesch-Nyhan and Turner's syndromes, that alter various components of behavior differentially. Some geneticists have gone so far as to suggest that once the conditions make their appearance in spite of medical precautions, their study can permit the indirect genetic dissection of behavioral traits, in analogy to the technique used for nematodes and fruit flies.

My overall impression of the available information is that *Homo sapiens* is a typically animal species with reference to the quality and magnitude of the genetic diversity affecting behavior. If the comparison is correct, the psychic unity of humankind has been reduced in status from a dogma to a testable hypothesis. This is not an easy thing to say in the present political ambience of the United States, and it is regarded as punishable heresy in some sectors of the academic community. But the idea needs to be faced squarely if the social sciences are to be entirely honest. I cannot regard it as dangerous. Quite the contrary: the political consequences of its objective examination will be determined by our value system, not the reverse. It will be better for scientists to study the subject of genetic behavioral diversity than to maintain a conspiracy of silence out of good intentions and thereby default to ideologues.

Following this elementary excursion into genetic determinism, let us now consider how the various social sciences might be influenced by biological theory. In the brief sections to follow I have little more than scraps of information and impressions to offer. It is hoped that they will nevertheless suffice to provide a view of the reverse side of the social sciences as it has been glimpsed by a biologist approaching in that direction.

Anthropology

The central question of biological anthropology is the nature and strength of the coupling between cultural and biological evolution. Cultural evolution is Lamarckist and usually very fast; biological evolution is Darwinist and slower by at least an order of magnitude. Because the most rapid cultural changes track environmental fluctuations too brief in duration to influence directional genetic selection, cultural fitness can be expected to diverge frequently from genetic fitness (Richerson and Boyd, 1977). But the divergence must be limited in degree and duration, because ultimately the newly created social environment will be tracked and the gap narrowed by natural selection. If this modification of basic sociobiological theory is correct, there should be two detectable consequences. First, it will be learning rules rather than specific cultural forms that are inherited (Feldman and Cavalli-Sforza, 1976). And where the rules are most directly concerned with survival and reproduction, as in the case of sexual and parental bonding, incest avoidance, and xenophobia, they are likely to be the most rigid and structured. Marshall Sahlins (1976) has recently argued that the lack of clear correspondence between human kinship rules and the details of genetic kin selection theory disproves basic sociobiological theory as far as human beings are concerned. But this goes much too far. Kinship rules are central to social organization in most societies, and in aggregate they appear to enhance inclusive genetic fitness. Richerson and Boyd (1977) have suggested that four competing hypotheses can be posed for the explanation of kinship rules: detailed genetic control, rational strategizing, complete cultural determinism, and coupled cultural and genetic control. They conclude that the ethnographic facts are consistent only with the model of coupled cultural and genetic control.

The second expected consequence of coupling is that the genetic fitness conferred by particular cultural traits should be strongest in the oldest, culturally most stable societies. Thus it appears correct to focus attention on hunter-gatherer and persistent, preliterate herding and agricultural societies. This circumstance explains why anthropology has already become the social science closest to sociobiology. Explicit tests of sociobiological theory are being made in studies on polygyny, status, societal fissioning, territory, and warfare (Chagnon, 1976; and Durham, 1976).

It is probable that population biology will be simultaneously altered to accommodate the special problems of anthropology. In addition to the solution of the dual inheritance problem, there is a need for advances in the theory of group and kin selection to distinguish unilateral, "hard core" altruism from transactional, "soft-core" altruism. Also, the complexity of human population structures presents unique challenges to biology. Population boundaries are seldom sharp, often being confused by discordant linguistic, cultural, and historical-political patterns. Groups also shift rapidly in their loyalties, forming alliances in one year and dividing into quarreling factions the next. The present theory of population genetics and ecology is entirely inadequate to handle such complications (Wilson, 1975b).

Psychology and Psychoanalytic Theory

Just as anthropology has been burdened in the past by the doctrine of complete cultural determinism, conventional psychology has been burdened by general process learning theory. It was natural for Thorndike, Watson, and other pioneering psychologists to choose large animals, that is, birds and mammals, for their study objects, rather than insects and opisthobranch mollusks. Partly as a result of this choice, learning came to be accepted as the central process of behavior. Moreover, the learning process was viewed as being essentially equipotential: the same laws were theorized to apply to whatever learning process and organism are chosen. Thus Skinner (1938) could say, "The general topography of operant behavior is not important, because most if not all specific operants are conditioned. I suggest that the dynamic properties of operant behavior may be studied with a single reflex." It was believed that by placing animals in simplified laboratory environments, where stimulation can be rigidly controlled, the most general laws would emerge.

This is a powerful idea, with seductive precedents in the physical sciences, and it has resulted in substantial advances in the study of animal and human behavior. Nevertheless, general process learning theory has started to crumble. In its place is appearing the description of a melange of specialized learning phenomena that conform to no general law except, perhaps, evolution by natural selection. The full range of learning potential of each species appears to be separately programmed. According to the species, each animal is "prepared" to learn certain stimuli, counterprepared to learn others, and unprepared (neutral) with respect to still others. For example, adult herring gulls quickly learn to distinguish their newly hatched chicks but never their own eggs, which are nevertheless as visually diversified. Indigo buntings are prepared to learn the circumpolar constellations by which they orient their nocturnal migrations, but are counterprepared to learn other constellations. When chicks are shocked at their beaks while drinking water and simultaneously given a visual stimulus, they thereafter avoid the visual stimulus, but they do not learn to avoid an auditory stimulus presented the same way. The reverse is true when the shock is administered to the feet; that is, the chicks are prepared to learn sound but counterprepared to learn visual cues (Shettleworth, 1972). The timing of preparedness in the life cycle is also programmed and species-specific in ways that are readily interpreted as adaptations to the particular environments experienced by the species during their recent evolutionary pasts.

The hypothesis of learning rules as idiosyncratic evolutionary adaptations has seldom been examined with reference to the human species. It seems significant that phobias, which share some properties with imprinting in lower animals, are readily acquired against snakes, spiders, rats, and other potentially dangerous objects in mankind's ancient natural environment, but only rarely against such dangerous artifacts as knives and electrical outlets (Seligman, 1972). Language is acquired by small children through a progression of closely timed steps, involving distinctive vocalizations and phrase forms later replaced by adult language (Brown, 1973). It is difficult to believe that the rules of this most human of all learning events have not been shaped by natural selection.

Psychoanalytic theory appears to be exceptionally compatible with sociobiological theory, a fact already appreciated by some of the psychoanalysts themselves (for example, see Lifton, 1976). If the essence of the Freudian revolution was that it gave structure to the unconscious, the logical role of sociobiology is to reconstruct the evolutionary history of that structure. When Freud speculated in *Totem and Taboo* on the primal father, primal horde, and the origins of the incest taboo, he created a sociobiological hypothesis, but a poor one. The same is true of his insights into the conflict of self and society presented in *Civilization and Its Discontents*. Whether population biology and evolutionary theory can be used to restructure and objectively test some of psychoanalytic theory remains to be seen.

Economics

Classic economic theory restricted itself to the goods and services that can be measured by money and market pricing. In recent years new, less easily quantified parameters have entered the equations, including time, human capital, and environmental quality (Samuelson, 1976). A closer scrutiny is also being made of what Leibenstein (1976) has termed the X-efficiency factors, which include motivation, *esprit*, effort, persistence, and other psychological variables made mensurable. In a word, microeconomics has begun to incorporate social psychology. It is now widely appreciated that human beings do not behave as rationalizing economic machines. Macreoeconomic predictions of the future will almost certainly be based on the wiser perception of irrational elements in human nature.

To the extent that the new parameters of human irrationality are interpreted as an evolutionary product, the methods of economics will converge toward those of biology. Already, models in ecology and sociobiology have borrowed heavily from the graphical methods of economics. Optimization and decision theory are routinely used. The utility measure of biology is genetic fitness, and the enabling devices are anatomy, physiology, and behavior. I expect that once a method is developed for assessing the coupling of genetic and cultural evolution, the utility measures of economics and evolutionary biology will come to overlap broadly.

An interspecific comparative economics is also a possibility. During recent research on the evolution of division of labor in insect societies, George Oster and I (in preparation) have written a short book that resembles a textbook in microeconomics. Insect economics differs in several respects: the transactions among colony members are almost exclusively instead of merely partially instinctive (that is, "irrational"), the societies are mostly sterile and female, and (because of the haplodiploid genetic bias) unilateral altruism has far greater genetic utility than in human societies. The broad forms of the analyses are otherwise much the same. The point is that human economics is not really general economics, but rather the description of economic behavior in one mammalian species with a limited range of the biological state variables.

Sociology

By virtue of its loftier perch in the hierarchy of subject matter, sociology should be the queen of the social sciences. Yet I personally find it the most alien and least interesting. Part of the cause is revealed in the following statement by Durkheim (1938): "In a word, there is between psychology and sociology the same break in continuity as between biology and the physicochemical sciences. Consequently, every time that a social phenomenon is directly explained by a psychological phenomenon, we may be sure that the explanation is false." I suspect that this statement is as completely wrong for sociology as it proved to be for biology. Although few contemporary sociologists would uncritically accept *The Rules of Sociological Method*, Durkheim's dualism lives on by tradition. Sociological analysis seldom utilizes the known facts of social psychology to any depth, and evolutionary biology remains all but taboo. The specters of biologism and social Darwinism are still feared, entirely without justification. The situation is so extreme that I suspect that progress in the near future will be measured by the connections sociology makes with its antidisciplines. To the extent that it does not make these connections, it will remain an ad hoc, descriptive science.

Yet sociology is not destined to be cannibalized by the antidisciplines, any more than cytology was absorbed by biochemistry. The reason is that sociology is truly the subject most remote from the fundamental principles of individual behavior. Advanced literate societies, the main concern of sociology, are the most removed in character from the kinds of social and economic systems in which the genetic basis of human social behavior evolved. Having been jerrybuilt on the Pleistocene human biogram, they are the least stable, probably have the greatest discrepancies between genetic and cultural fitness, and hence are most likely to display emergent properties not predictable from a knowledge of individual psychology alone.

The Limits of Reductionism

Karl von Frisch once made a remarkable statement about his research. He said that the honeybee is like a magic well — the more you draw from it, the more there is to draw. Other students of social insects share this sense of seemingly infinite richness in the phenomena of colonial life. They have learned that a great deal of evolutionary novelty at the social level can be generated by only a small amount of genetic change at the level of the individual. A slight modification in one parameter of allometric pupal growth, for example, can produce a new array of castes; whereas an altered response to a pheromone can create a new mode of communication.

The full phenomenology of social life cannot be predicted from a knowledge of the genetic programs of the individuals alone. When the observer shifts his attention from one level of organization to the next, he expects to find obedience to all of the laws of the levels below. But upper levels of organization require specification of the arrangement of the lower units, which in turn generates richness and the basis of new and unexpected principles. The specification can be classified into three categories: combinatoric, spatial, and historical. Thus the ammonia molecule neutralizes its electric dipole moment and conserves the laws of nuclear physics by inverting the negatively charged nitrogen back and forth through the triangle of positively charged hydrogens at a frequency of 3×10^{10} per second. But this symmetry is broken in the case of sugar and other larger organic molecules, which are too large and complexly structured to invert themselves. They break but do not repeal the symmetry laws of physics (Anderson, 1972). This specification may not be of great interest to particle physicists, but its effects redound throughout organic chemistry and biology.

Primitive wasps, comprising early members of the order Hymenoptera, evolved the sex determination mechanism of haplodiploidy, whereby unfertilized eggs yield males and fertilized eggs yield females. This mechanism may have been a specific adaptation that permits females to choose the sex of the offspring according to the nature of the separate prey items they are able to subdue. But whatever the initial cause, haplodiploidy represented a historical accident that predisposed these insects to develop advanced forms of sociality. The reason is that it causes sisters to be more closely related genetically than mothers are to daughters, and so they find genetic profit in becoming a sterile caste specialized for the rearing of sisters. As an apparent result, social life among insects is almost limited to the phylogenetically advanced hymenopterans, namely the social wasps, social bees, and ants. Furthermore, most cases of insect social life can be classified either as matriarchies, in which queens control colonies of daughters, or as sisterhoods, in which sterile daughters control the egg-laying mothers. Many other strange effects flow from this genetic asymmetry. In addition, the hymenopterous societies have proved so successful that they dominate and alter much of the terrestrial ecosystems of the Earth (Wilson, 1971). Who could have guessed all of this from a knowledge of haplodiploidy?

The urge to be a reductionist is an understandable human trait. Ernst Mach (1942) captured it in the following definition: "Science may be regarded as a minimal problem consisting of the completest presentment of facts with the least possible expenditure of thought." This is the sentiment of a member of the antidiscipline, impatient to set aside complexity and get on with the search for more fundamental ideas. The laws of his subject are necessary to the discipline above, they challenge and force a mentally more efficient restructuring; but they are not sufficient for its purposes. Biology is the key to human nature, and social scientists cannot afford to ignore its emerging principles. But the social sciences are potentially far richer in content. Eventually they will absorb the relevant ideas of biology and go on to beggar them by comparison.

References

Anderson, P. W. (1972) "More is Different." *Science* 177, 393–396.

Brown, R. (1973) *A First Language.* Cambridge, Mass.: Harvard University Press.

Chagnon, N. A. (1976) "Fission in an Amazonian Tribe." *The Sciences* 16, 14–18.

Davis, B. D., and P. Flaherty (eds.). (1976) *Human Diversity: Its Causes and Social Significance.* Cambridge: Ballinger.

Durham, W. H. (1976) "Resource Competition and Human Aggression, Part I: A Review of Primitive War." *Quarterly Review of Biology* 51, 385–415.

Durkheim, E. (1938) *The Rules of Sociological Method.* 8th ed. Translated by S. A. Solovay and J. H. Mueller. New York: Free Press.

Ehrman, L., and P. A. Parsons. (1976) *The Genetics of Behavior*. Sunderland, Mass.: Sinauer.

Feldman, M. W., and L. L. Cavalli-Sforza. (1976) "Cultural and Biological Evolutionary Processes: Selection for a Trait under Complex Transmission." *Theoretical Population Biology* 9, 238–259.

Freedman, D. G. (1974) *Human Infancy: An Evolutionary Perspective*. New York: Wiley.

Fruton, J. S. (1976) "The Emergence of Biochemistry." *Science* 192, 327–334.

Heston, L. L., and J. Shields. (1968) "Homosexuality in Twins: A Family Study and a Registry Study." *Archives of General Psychiatry* 18, 149–160.

Holton, G. (1973) *Thematic Origins of Scientific Thought: Kepler to Einstein*. Cambridge, Mass.: Harvard University Press.

Kendall, E. R. (1976) *Cellular Basis of Behavior*. San Francisco: Freeman.

King, G. E. (1977) "Socioterritorial Units and Interspecific Competition: Modern Carnivores and Early Hominids." *Journal of Anthropological Research*.

Leibenstein, B. (1976) *Beyond Economic Man: A New Foundation for Economics*. Cambridge, Mass.: Harvard University Press.

Lennenberg, E. H. (1969) "On Explaining Language." *Science* 164, 635–643.

Lifton, R. J. (1976) *The Life of the Self: Toward a New Psychology*. New York: Simon and Schuster.

MacArthur, R. H. (1957) "On the Relative Abundance of Bird Species." *Proceedings of the National Academy of Sciences, United States* 43, 293–295.

Mach, E. (1942) *The Science of Mechanics*. 9th ed. LaSalle, Ill.: Open Court.

May, R. M. (ed.). (1976) *Theoretical Ecology: Principles and Applications*. Philadelphia: Saunders.

McClern, G. E., and J. C. DeFries. (1973) *Introduction to Behavioral Genetics*. San Francisco: Freeman.

Northrup, F. S. C. (1947) *The Logic of the Sciences and Humanities*. New York: Macmillan.

Nozick, R. (1974) *Anarchy, State, and Utopia*. New York: Basic Books.

Oster, G. F., and E. O. Wilson. *Caste and Ecology in the Social Insects*. In preparation.

Richerson, P. J., and R. Boyd. (1977) "A Dual Inheritance Model of the Human Evolutionary Process." *Journal of Theoretical Biology*.

Sahlins, M. (1976) *The Use and Abuse of Biology*. Ann Arbor: University of Michigan Press.

Samuelson, P. A. (1976) *Economics*. 10th ed. New York: McGraw-Hill.

Seligman, M. E. P., and J. L. Hager (eds.). (1972) *Biological Boundaries of Learning*. Englewood Cliffs, N.J.: Prentice-Hall.

Seligman, M. E. P. (1972) "Phobias and Preparedness," in Seligman and Hager (eds.) *Biological Boundaries of Learning*. Englewood Cliffs, N.J.: Prentice-Hall, 451–462.

Shettleworth, S. J. (1972) "Conditioning of Domestic Chicks to Visual and Auditory Stimuli," in Seligman and Hager (eds.) *Biological Boundaries of Learning*. Englewood Cliffs, N.J.: Prentice-Hall, 228–236.

Skinner, B. F. (1938) *The Behavior of Organisms: An Experimental Analysis*. New York: Appleton.

Van Hooff, J. A. R. A. M. (1972) "A Comparative Approach to the Phylogeny of Laughter and Smiling," in R. A. Hinde (ed.) *Non-Verbal Communication*. Cambridge:

Cambridge University Press, 209–241.

Weisskopf, V. F. (1967) "Nuclear Structure and Modern Research." *Physics Today* 20, 23–26.

Wilson, E. O. (1973) "Eminent Ecologist, 1973: Robert Helmer MacArthur." *Bulletin of the Ecological Society of America* 54, 11–12.

———— . (1975a) *Sociobiology: The New Synthesis.* Cambridge, Mass.: Harvard University Press.

———— . (1975b) "Some Central Problems of Sociobiology." *Social Science Information* 14, 5–18.

———— . (1971) *The Insect Societies.* Cambridge, Mass.: Harvard University Press.

4

The Social Sciences Cannot
Be Unified with Biology

Charles Frankel

There is a fairly simple logical reason why the social sciences and the humanities cannot be "unified" with biology in the terms that Wilson apparently contemplates. Propositions about the hypothalamus and the limbic system do not contain terms like "love," "hate," "good," or "bad." They cannot, therefore, be the only premises we need to produce psychological or moral statements containing such terms. Nor can we do without such terms, for they have been developed to deal with discernible aspects and qualities of human experience which the languages of molecular biology and biochemistry cannot adequately characterize. It is an old notion that a belief in the universal reign of physical laws implies that all explanations must be in the vocabulary of the natural sciences. To be sure, if the necessary physical conditions were not present, human beings would not have the plans, projects, ideas, and emotions that they do. These are, in this sense, physical events, and proper objects of study by the natural sciences. Yet this does not imply that they cannot also be studied quite independently of the natural sciences, or that nothing of significance will be revealed by such independent study.

Consider, for example, the ideas in Wilson's book, which presumably could be connected, if we had the requisite theoretical and practical information, to neuronal events in his brain cells. Would such an explanation of the physiological and chemical goings-on inside Wilson's head tell us anything about the logical content or merits of these ideas, or their relationship to the past and future of biological research, or their possible utility in assessing different forms of social organization? And when he says that "the mind . . . is an epiphenomenon of the neuronal machinery of the brain," does he mean to say that his ideas, even if they do not in themselves have characteristics such as

Reprinted by permission from Charles Frankel, "Sociobiology and Its Critics," *Commentary,* 68: 1 (July 1979), pp. 44–47. All rights reserved. This is an abbreviated version: the first five and one-half pages have been deleted.

spatial extension or mass, cannot be said to be the causes of anything in their own right? In a normal sense of the word "cause," they have demonstrably caused, for example, other people's anger. We could presumably trace the causal sequence leading to this anger through the glandular systems of Wilson's critics, but such an effort would tell us nothing about what is most pertinent—the particular extent of his ideas, the specific character of his critics' beliefs, and the distinctive quality of that emotion known as "anger." For this word does not have a synonym in the language of neurons, which describes only its physical conditions. It is the name for a recognizable feeling, aroused by and directed toward objects, persons, or ideas describable only in common-sense language and not in the language of neurophysiology.

We have normal modes of thinking and speaking about phenomena of human life like books, promises, marriage, constitutions, schools, the experience of listening to music, the rules and interests of the scientific community. Intelligible statements, capable of being called true or false, sensible or foolish, discerning or obtuse, can be made in these modes. If "scientific materialism" means that the progress of science will expose such modes of thinking and speaking as superstitions, then it proposes to abandon irreplaceable forms of responsible discourse on which much human knowledge and wisdom are founded. Happily, however, a belief that man is part of physical nature does not carry this logical implication. Indeed, if it did, it would be a self-vitiating belief.

If Wilson's conception of "scientific materialism" is out of synchronization with the language and perspectives of ordinary life, the same, I think, is true of his ethical philosophy. Our ethical principles are to be appraised in the light of their consequences for the human gene pool. Such an appraisal, to the extent that we are capable of making it, is of course important, but it is surely not the only relevant test of moral principles or social policies. A developed civilization has enterprises too varied and requirements too complex to permit any single set of considerations, even genetic ones, to monopolize moral judgment. Even if we knew more than we do about the actual effects of the moral ideas we employ on the future genetic constitution of the race, we could still not say what a *desirable* genetic result would be without invoking, in addition to this scientific information, an independent framework of social and moral norms. Although Wilson is obviously aware of the long debate over the propriety of using purely biological norms as a basis for ethics, I am not persuaded that his own version of evolutionary ethics is an improvement over nineteenth-century versions.

Indeed, it is bogged down in some old nineteenth-century issues. The central problem of sociobiology, he tells us, is how the individual organism, genetically predisposed to struggle for survival, can also carry "altruistic" genes that dispose it to sacrifice its individual existence for the group. This problem concerned Darwin, and Wilson's solution, though more elaborately developed, is not substantially different: kin-bonding is so important for survival that the genes that make for strong kin bonds and individual self-sacrifice tend to come through the evolutionary filter and to persist. But to argue that this is the "central" problem of sociobiology is to take it for granted that the polarity of individual vs. society is the inevitable place to begin when one tries to understand animal or human behavior. If nothing else, the data accumulated by Wilson himself about the inbred social orientation of the higher primates should cast doubt on the intellectual utility of such a point of departure. It owes more, it seems to me, to the old social-contract metaphor, now revived, than to materials intrinsic to the story of evolution.

Further, Wilson's materialism, which leads him, when speaking of human thoughts and feelings, to deflate them into "epiphenomena," leads him, when using moral terms like "altruism," to inflate them into words without cash value. The insect killed by the queen of the colony as it fertilizes her eggs is, in Wilson's parlance, behaving "altruistically." From that behavior to the conduct of the religious martyr or the battlefield hero we have, if we use his vocabulary, a single unbroken spectrum of individual self-sacrifice for the good of the community. But when "altruism" is used indifferently to characterize unconscious instinctual behavior and voluntary sacrifice by a creature conscious of the nature of death, it is not scientific information or a naturalistic philosophical perspective that we are receiving. It is, I fear, an object lesson in the abuse of words.

Yet these criticisms of the philosophical adornments which Wilson has added to his scientific endeavor still leave a central issue to be examined. When a wolf grovels before his conqueror or a peacock shows his feathers to a hen, they are not simply following a social custom. They are doing what they do as a result of natural selection and the transmission to them of certain biologically inherited traits. And human beings, too, grovel and strut and show their feathers. So the great question arises: what proportion of human behavior is physiological and genetic in its causes? How much of what we commonly explain as a product of history and convention, like monogamous marriage, private property, or organized warfare, is in reality bone of our bones and flesh of our flesh, and not subject to change except with extraordinary effort and unpredictable consequences?

This is the question which joins sociobiological research to moral and social concerns that are in the forefront of the contemporary consciousness. Yet, oddly enough, when Wilson addresses this question, his answers are usually so guarded or vague, or so fundamentally in accord with the dominant conventions, that it is a bit of a mystery why his critics have been so indignant. On the "nature-vs.-nurture" controversy, Wilson writes: "The evidence is strong that almost all differences between human societies are based on learning and

social conditioning rather than heredity. And yet perhaps not quite all." On
the social meaning of sex differences, he says:

> Here is what I believe the evidence shows: modest genetic differences exist be-
> tween the sexes; the behavioral genes interact with virtually all existing en-
> vironments to create a notable divergence in early psychological development;
> and the divergence is almost always widened in later psychological development
> by cultural sanctions and training. Societies can probably cancel the modest
> genetic differences entirely by careful planning and training, but the con-
> vergence will require a conscious decision based on fuller and more exact
> knowledge than is now available.

To take a final example, here is Wilson on the supposed proneness of man
to aggression:

> Aggression does not resemble a fluid that continuously builds pressure against
> the walls of its containers, nor is it like a set of active ingredients poured into an
> empty vessel. It is more accurately compared to a preexisting mix of chemicals
> ready to be transformed by specific catalysts that are added, heated, and stirred
> at some later time.

In other words, sometimes we are caused to be angry, and when the prov-
ocation is severe enough, our anger runs away with us. Why? That is the
nature of human beings. We would not act that way if our genes were different.

There is much of this sort of analysis in *On Human Nature:* conformity to
social norms is traced back to "conformist" genes; religion is explained by
reference to an aboriginal human impulse, "sacralization." It is a kind of explanation that comes perilously close to the medieval proposition that opium,
under proper conditions, can put us to sleep because it has dormitive powers.
For that matter, at least we know, within reasonable limits, what "dormitive"
means. When Wilson uses a word like "aggression," however, it covers a
gamut from destruction for the pleasure of destruction to the behavior of an
animal or human being whose vital interests are in collision with those of
others. *L'eléphant est un animal féroce; quand on l'attaque, il se défend.*

In brief, where currently controverted issues are concerned, Wilson's views
are usually conventional ideas in biological wrappings. On the whole, despite
the brouhaha he has caused, he leans to the view that social environment is the
primary agent in shaping human behavior. What separates him from the
critics with whom he shares that view is only the qualification that, while environment is responsible for most of our behavior, it is perhaps not responsible
for all.

Why, then, the brouhaha? One reason, undoubtedly, is that his critics are rendered anxious even by this small qualification. They would rather not have it expressed. It is obvious to them, as it is obvious to anyone, that human beings have characteristics which no society has created and to which all societies must respond or face trouble — needs for food, sexual drives, cycles of maturation and aging, requirements for warmth, communication, emotional support. It is probably obvious to most of Wilson's critics, too, that individuals differ in their tastes and capacities, and that, B. F. Skinner to the contrary notwithstanding, no environmental reforms can make everyone capable of creating a Sistine Chapel or even desirous of doing so. But they would prefer that such truths be treated with silence. The open mention of them, like the mention of sex in polite Victorian circles, can only incite wicked thoughts. Wilson, in their eyes, has opened a dangerous door: once opened, no one can know what new and more disturbing reservations may have to be entertained about the omnipotence of environmental influences. And Wilson, despite the innocuous character of most of his specific opinions about social issues, has nevertheless done something himself to arouse such fears. Not only has he brought together a great mass of arresting information about the genetically programmed social behavior of animals, but he offers a great plan for sociobiological research, a sweeping form of scientific materialism, and a good deal of talk about social planning that suggests, at least to eager critics, that there is a technocrat or a eugenicist hiding behind his conciliatory words.

But perhaps there is also something more. The ideology of sociobiology is separable from its scientific merits. But as an ideology, at least in Wilson's formulation, it occupies one piece of common ground with the ideology of its critics. What we have is a quarrel between adherents of a common faith. It is the faith that the old notion of Divine Design can be replaced by an almost equally encompassing notion of Human Design.

When Darwin produced massive amounts of data indicating that man and other primates had a common origin, he did not call attention to facts that no one before him had ever noticed. The similarities between monkeys and human beings had long been part of the common sense of mankind. Nor was it the idea that the human body and human nature were the products of a long process of development that essentially shocked the Victorian mind. There was a history of such speculation before Darwin, as there was also a history of argument that the destiny of man, like that of the animals, was to struggle grimly for survival. Darwin himself took this idea from a Christian minister, Thomas Malthus.

It was two other implications of the Darwinian theory that made the greatest trouble. One was the indication that there was no separate Creation for man, no moment in the history of the evolutionary process when the laws of development ceased their operation and man, miraculously, was invested with a soul. The other was the profoundly antiteleological thrust of Darwin's thought. There were no preordained ends to the evolutionary process; there were, indeed, no ends at all, only temporary terminations which were themselves new beginnings. Nature had no direction; it could not even be said to be a fumbling experimenter, seeking new and better forms for living things. And while human beings had ideals and goals, and these could be seen as the instruments used by the species to control its destiny, such ideals and goals were themselves products of the evolutionary process and freighted with the experience through which the species had gone. The dumb inert past — out of human control and largely beyond human memory — controlled the behavior of human beings and the shape of human nature and human institutions. Human thoughts about the future were at best minor elements in the history of the race.

Darwin himself was disturbed by this implication of his theory, and wrote Charles Peirce inviting the American philosopher to give his attention to the problem of how the human mind can function as an agent in human evolution. That it can so function is attested by history, not least the history of human creativeness since Darwin: social insurance, public-health measures, the revolution in communications, the progress in surgery, nuclear energy, are a few of the human artifices that have profoundly affected the character of human life, and the nature of the human future, including the composition of the human gene pool. It is clearly a mistake to say that mankind does not have some power over its destiny.

But the picture of the human condition which emerges from the Darwinian theory remains untouched at its core. Man is an animal most of whose doings are not the product of conscious thought, whether his or nature's. He can come to know more about himself and the universe he inhabits. His nobility lies in his effort to master his fate. But he understands and masters it, when he does, at the edges. His reconstruction of his environment, and of his own behavior and nature, is piecemeal at best, and can be nothing more. A great rational pattern, an encompassing idea of justice and goodness, cannot be successfully imposed on the natural or the human scene. These scenes are clutters of accident. A causal order can be discerned by man in some parts of the clutter, but that causal order is not what the human heart would like.

Religious people have had their own ways of rejecting this picture, or of absorbing it into their faiths. They speak of God's purposes as inscrutable, or limited to another and immaterial world. But many of those who think of themselves as having wholly accepted the Darwinian scheme have also found this aspect of the evolutionary story too bitter to swallow. Consciously or unconsciously, they have sought to think their way around it by returning purpose to the universe in the shape of a supremely masterful human reason. At one extreme, that reason can reshape man's environment and make a new animal of him. At the other extreme, that reason can grasp man's genetic structure, and learn enough to shape his evolution to his heart's desire. This denaturalized humanism is the common thread that runs through the evangelical materialisms and positivisms of the nineteenth century, and as the quarrels over sociobiology reveal, it persists in the twentieth century, and joins many in the hereditarian camp to many in the environmentalist.

The distinction between "hereditarians" and "environmentalists" is not a distinction between "conservatives" and "liberals," or "Left" and "Right." Kant and Noam Chomsky, two men of the "Left," have argued for preordained structures in the human mind. Hume and Burke, usually called "conservatives," have argued for the great influence of custom and convention. Indeed, at the extremes, neither "hereditarians" nor "environmentalists," neither Wilson nor his opponents, are quite evolutionary enough in their thinking. On both sides, they ignore or underestimate the significance of that great area of human life which is controlled by the custom that is second nature, and which is the product of evolutionary experience, though it may leave no genetic deposit in its wake. Mankind lives within institutions—markets, legal systems, families, states, etc.—which are the products of history. They have not been conscious inventions, although at times conscious intelligence has figured in the process of remodeling them. But more frequently they have been changed by quite unintellectual forces, and we are living with the consequences, sometimes fortunate, very frequently unfortunate. Yet we cannot begin *de novo*. Try to think of remaking the world as though such structures did not exist, or had not shaped our ideas, character, and passions, and the human mind fails or sinks into forms of madness.

As a science, sociobiology is new, and probably important. As the basis for an intelligent philosophy, it belongs to that stream of thought to which people of various political dispositions have belonged—Erasmus, Rousseau, Diderot, John Stuart Mill, Freud—to name only a few. It reminds us of what the evangelistic fever about an idea tends to make us forget: that human beings have a certain physiology; that their bodies usually control their minds; that they have certain drives, and go through certain arcs of development, which are biological in origin. Societies shape these drives and affect these patterns of development profoundly. But just as there are a hundred ways of shaping shoes but the human foot remains there to pay the price, so, for each form of social orientation or control, there is a human cost. This is not a new thought, but it is a useful one. We are not machines to be taken apart or put together again. We are organisms with a long history in our genes, and in our habits and sentiments.

But as a social ideology, sociobiology breathes something of the same spirit that B. F. Skinner's *Walden Two* does. It is regrettable that a field of inquiry that can offer so much passionately interesting information, and that has the potential to teach a reasonable philosophical modesty, should also be overlaid with the vision of still another brave, new world. But as Edward Wilson might remind us, this is what tends to happen to ideas when an animal with the human genetic predispositions gets hold of them. Whether or not such an explanation holds, it is certainly what happens regularly on the present intellectual scene.

Part 3
Anthropology

Introduction to Part 3

Anthropologists, with a disciplinary history in physical anthropology, are not strangers to the incorporation of biological and medical factors into explanations of human social behavior. As implied in the general introduction to this volume, it is precisely this type of interdisciplinary orientation that could advantageously be adopted in all of the social sciences. The "new" sociobiology, however, has raised some intriguing questions for students of cultural anthropology. In general, Part 3 will reflect on these questions, examining the impact of sociobiology on cultural anthropology. As will be seen in the writings of other social scientists, the biological perspective represents a major intellectual controversy for anthropologists.

In Chapter 5 Barkow observes that sociobiology has the capability to order behavioral information about many species and he indicates that much of this knowledge cannot be explained by any other theoretical constructs. So enticing is this ordering ability, developed essentially from animal studies, that Barkow proposes that it be applied to the exploration of human social behavior. But in applying it to our species, he cautions, we must take great care: "The two chief problems involve (1) the uncertainty of sociobiological prediction and (2) the uniqueness of hominid ecological adaptation."

Barkow discusses issues relating to these two problems when he tackles the question of whether human cultural forms are consistent with sociobiological theory. In this regard he examines evolution, psychobiology, and cultural mechanisms.

Rejecting the notion that sociobiology is simply a fad, Barkow urges his anthropological colleagues to master the literature of contemporary evolutionary biology. Having done that, he says, anthropologists will be able to join with biologists in studying human social behavior.

The basic thesis of the Durham selection is that "models for the evolution of human social behaviors should explicitly integrate both the genetic and the cultural inheritance mechanisms." This observation constitutes the basis for Durham's coevolutionary theory in which biological *and* cultural evolution favor "those attributes which increase, or at least do not decrease, the ability of individual human beings to survive and reproduce in their natural and social environments."

In advancing a coevolutionary theoretical perspective, Durham observes that "human beings are not just passively receptive" to conditioning by culture. It is likely that they have developed what he calls "selective biases" that predispose them to "acquire those aspects of the phenotype which past experience and some degree of prediction suggest to be most advantageous for personal inclusive fitness."

In a more clearly biological framework, Durham argues that it will be important for anthropologists to pay particular attention to the functioning and evolution of the human brain, as this will be critical in relating biology to the study of culture. Indeed, "the organic evolution of that organ would mean a bias in favor of the selective retention of more rather than less cultural traits."

Durham concludes by suggesting that a coevolutionary perspective combining biological and cultural factors will probably result in renewed research at the individual level of analysis. In this regard, areas of interest to anthropologists should include medical anthropology, demography, nutrition, migration, and aggression. A biological point of view should open up new research orientations in these areas.

The basic sympathies of Barkow and Durham to sociobiology are strongly challenged by Washburn, who is skeptical about using animal studies to provide knowledge regarding human social behavior. His discussion of the behavior of apes, for example, is highly critical of animal data.

Washburn's strongest criticism of a sociobiologically oriented anthropology is that it pays insufficient attention to human language ability. "Language," he says, "is the behavior that distinguishes human social behavior from the social behavior of other primates." Indeed, in a harsh reference to human ethology, Washburn asserts that that field can be defined as "the science that pretends humans cannot speak."

Though Washburn develops many criticisms of the sociobiological approach, he nevertheless predicts that the interest and enthusiasm of scholars for sociobiology "will lead to the development of a biologically and socially based behavioral science." But this new social science, he says, will not resemble the discipline that E.O. Wilson envisioned in the third chapter of this book.

To conclude this Part, Chagnon reflects on the current state of anthropology regarding orientations toward biological models of human behavior. He remarks that it is somewhat surprising that hostility should run so deep, especially since anthropologists have always had some biological interests. Nevertheless, he focuses on the major cleavage in the discipline between physical and cultural anthropology which, he asserts, has produced long-standing professional suspicions. Indeed, the idea of a "holistic" discipline is largely a myth that has been fostered by the authors of introductory textbooks. To bridge this gap Chagnon calls for new research initiatives within the framework of evolutionary biology *and* traditional anthropology to empirically test the natural selection hypotheses of sociobiology.

T.C.W.

5

Culture and Sociobiology

Jerome H. Barkow

Anthropologists have long been concerned with the evolution of human behavior—one thinks immediately of the influential compilations by Montagu
(1962), Roe and Simpson (1958), Tax (1960), and Washburn (1961). Nor has
interest in human behavioral evolution abated—glance at Fox's (1975)
Biosocial Anthropology; King's (1975) careful reconstructions of early hominid
territoriality; the collection of studies of human language origins edited by
Harnad, Steklis, and Lancaster (1977); or the very large number of works
reviewed by Fox and Fleising (1976). Though the light shed on early human
behavior by the fossil record and comparative ethology remains rather dim,
the debate continues.

But this anthropological debate *is* in that light, the light of the fossil record.
It centers on the nature of early hominid ecological adaptation: were our
ancestors hunters, gatherers, scavengers, etc.? Did they evolve in terms of
groups which were highly aggressive toward one another, or is intergroup aggression a modern phenomenon having to do with the development of
agriculture? Such questions are asked in the context of evolutionary biology,
of course, but the stress is on *selective pressures involving adaptation to environment.*

The sociobiologists, on the other hand, focus strongly on *selective pressures
predicted by theory*, on the implications of the maximization-of-inclusive-fitness
axiom for the pure theory of behavioral evolution. They are not, after all, experts in human behavior and have a strong tendency to assume that they and
we already understand the nature of hominid behavioral adaptation to environment (but see Trivers, 1971). As will be discussed shortly, the
sociobiologists' problems stem not from their theory but from its premature
application to human beings, an application which has paid scant attention to
the uniqueness of the human ecological niche.

The strength of sociobiology derives not from its insights into human

Reproduced by permission of the author and the American Anthropological Association from
American Anthropologist, 80 (1): 5–20, 1980. The chapter has been slightly condensed and the footnotes have been deleted.

behavior (not so far, at least) but from its ability to order diverse facts about numerous other species, facts which are almost inexplicable in terms of any other theory. Regardless of how fashionable it may be in some circles to criticize sociobiology, it is important to remember that it fits species from seahorses to lemurs, from termites to gulls; can we fail to apply it to human behavior? Evolutionary biology's applicability to every species but our own is unchallenged; how do we claim that it is irrelevant to our own species (as does Sahlins, 1976) without camping out with the anti-evolutionary Creationists for whom man and beast must forever be separated by the latter's lack of a soul? If the occasional lapses into "nothing-butism" of the sociobiologists are to be lamented, those who would reduce the new evolutionary biology to no more than a resurgence of the dark pseudobiology of the Nazis or the influence of capitalism on biological thought are equally at fault. Nor can it be charged (as we will see below in the section on "Mechanisms") that sociobiology is necessarily tied to outmoded ideas of the rigid genetic determination of behavior. Sociobiology can and must be applied to our species, but *carefully* applied. The two chief problems involve (1) the uncertainty of sociobiological prediction and (2) the uniqueness of hominid ecological adaptation.

The Nature of Sociobiological Explanation

Sociobiology resembles early Freudian thought. Both are paradigms (cf. Kuhn, 1962), that is, widely applicable frameworks rather than simple theories to be proven or disproven. Both can lead to controversial theories of human nature. Both—and this is the most important point—postulate complex covert processes the outward manifestation of which can be highly variable. One branch of sociobiology, Trivers' "parental investment theory," provides a good illustration of this last difficulty.

Trivers (1972) sets out to explain sexual dimorphism, both behavioral and morphological, in terms of intrasexual selection. The female, having more energy invested in an ovum than does a male in a sperm cell and having more of her reproductive capacity potentially at risk in any given fertilization, will be much more "coy" about permitting copulation than the male. Maximization of inclusive fitness demands that the female be more selective than the male in her choice of partners. All things being equal, males will therefore maximize *their* inclusive fitness by competing for partners. Since some of this competition is likely to be agonistic in nature, larger males will tend to prevail. Thus, there is intrasexual selection for large size among males but not among females. Particular ecological considerations can rule out agonistic competition among males (see Wilson, 1975:334), but, in general, wherever sexual dimorphism does exist it will be the male which is larger.

Unfortunately, a recent news article in *Science* (over Kolata's [1977] byline) provides a contradiction: in a certain species of bats, the females are larger than the males! Do we then throw out parental investment theory, so powerful a contribution to modern zoology that *Science* considered a possible contradiction to its predictions worthy of a news article? No. Closer examination revealed that this particular species of bat was under considerable predator pressure and it was often necessary for the female to take to the air, along with her fetuses or her pups. Her greater size permitted her to escape while carrying her offspring. Thus, predator pressure cancelled out any external manifestation of the tendency toward smaller females predicted by parental investment theory. The latter has therefore not been invalidated but merely shown to have been incomplete in this particular application. One must know the full behavioral repertoire of a species and the details of its ecological adaptation before one can apply sociobiology to it.

This is because sociobiology is a theory of selective pressures generated by intraspecific competition among organisms each of which is seen as striving to maximize its genetic representation in the next generation. But such competition is only *one* source of selective pressure: the external environment still exists! Thus, a sociobiological explanation of the behavior of *any* species which fails to take into account other selective pressures, i.e., ecological pressures, is likely to be wrong. Such errors do not and cannot falsify sociobiological theory, however, for that theory is one of selective pressures, and the existence of such pressures is not contradicted by their lack of genotypic-phenotypic manifestation. As in the case of the bats, ecological pressure may be preventing their expression or altering it. Evolution, as Simpson (1953) pointed out many years ago, always involves compromise among many, often conflicting, selective pressures.

In the case of the bats, the apparent contradiction led to the gathering of additional data. Therefore, the theory can be said to have served the purpose of theory, i.e., ordering existing data and leading to the discovery of new facts. What if there had been no predator in the bats' ecology? I am confident that the zoologists would have decided that their understanding of bat ecology was still incomplete. They would not have immediately thrown out Trivers.

But Sahlins (1976) does. He argues that *human* behavior simply does not fit the predictions of the sociobiologists. Take the existence of unilineal descent groups. For example, why should ego invest more heavily in patrilateral kin than matrilateral kin, when his average coefficient of consanguinity (relatedness, or proportion of shared genes) to these two kin sets is equal? Another case: Why should ego give up his/her own child in order to adopt someone else's? These behaviors make no apparent sense in terms of sociobiology but do occur cross-culturally.

The sociobiologist must reply that these behaviors may indeed be consistent with his theories, had we sufficient ecological knowledge to apply them properly. Favoring patrilateral kin over matrilateral kin might lead to the formation of groups of agnates capable of defending scarce resources against enemies, thereby maximizing the inclusive fitness of all lineage members. Similarly, faced with the task of explaining widespread adoption, the sociobiologist might hypothesize that here was a solidarity-generating mechanism, which, by preventing internecine warfare, maximized the fitness of all participants by "reciprocal altruism" (Trivers, 1971). Perhaps an individual who refuses to adopt is ostracized and finds himself at an economic disadvantage, or perhaps no one will aid his/her offspring. I do not present these conjectures as final refutations of Sahlins' criticisms but as illustrations of the improbability of so easily overthrowing the sociobiological paradigm. Just as he did in the case of the bat, the sociobiologist faced with human behavioral apparent contradictions to his theories concludes not that his framework is invalid but that his data are inadequate.

Two additional and more powerful examples of sociobiological versatility: Kurland (in press), developing an idea suggested by Alexander (1974), asks why an individual should invest in his sister's children rather than in his own. In answer, Kurland invokes the concept of "paternity certainty." Your wife's children share 1/2 of your genes, *provided you are their father*. Your actual relatedness to them will therefore be 1/2 times the probability that you are indeed your (jural) children's father, i.e., times the average paternity certainty for your society. Let us say that this figure is 1/3: you are therefore related to your own children by $(1/2)(1/3) = (1/6)$ (see note 3). Your relatedness to your "full" sister, in theory 1/2, is at least 1/4 (representing your common mother) plus 1/4 (your putative common father) times the paternity certainty of 1/3, totalling $1/4 + (1/4)(1/3) = 1/3$. Since you thus share 1/3 of your genes with your sister and she provides 1/2 the genes of her children, you are related to her children by $(1/2)(1/3) = 1/6$. In this situation, sociobiology predicts you will invest equally in both sister's children and your own, all things being equal, since you are related to both sets of children by 1/6. In societies in which paternity certainty falls under 1/3, you should invest more heavily in sister's children than your own; if paternity certainty is more than 1/3, you should favor your wife's children. Kurland notes that, just as we would expect, matrilineal societies tend to have low paternity certainty and to place little stress on female fidelity; patrilineal societies tend to have high paternity certainty and place greater stress on female chastity and fidelity. Men invest in their sister's children where there is matrilineality and in their own children when patrilineality prevails. In other words, the avunculate makes sense in terms of sociobiology! Whatever individuals' *conscious* motives, they act *as if* they had performed the above calculations.

The following is a final example of a challenge to sociobiology. In conversation with Daniel G. Freedman of the University of Chicago, Freedman pointed out to me that the fertility of the Western nations has been decreasing in recent years and may even approach "zero population growth"; how can limiting one's offspring be consistent with sociobiology's maximization-of-inclusive-fitness axiom? Here, again, sociobiology can readily explain away an apparent contradiction to its dicta.

Evolutionary wisdom has to do with adaptation to former and not present environments. During our phylogenesis, it was apparently adaptive for individuals to limit the total number of their offspring in order to maximize parental investment in each of them. Such a pattern is quite common under ecological conditions in which total living space or resources are limited or in which without parental care no offspring will survive and is known as "K-selection" (Wilson, 1975:337–339). There are even cases (e.g., wild turkeys) in which inclusive fitness is maximized by having no offspring at all in order to invest in a brother's offspring (Wilson, 1975)! Apparently, our own ancestors lived with an ecology in which it maximized inclusive fitness to limit offspring and at times even to have none. We therefore still have these capabilities, and those of us in Western nations and in the European portion of the U.S.S.R. are exercising them, even though it may be that by so doing we could be decreasing our respective inclusive fitnesses. Even if we are, such a situation would in no way put sociobiology in question. As environments change, behaviors once adaptive frequently become maladaptive. Selection either decreases the frequency of the maladaptive behavior in the population, or else the species (or local group) becomes extinct. The only thing clear in the current situation is that once, at least, our capacity to restrict reproduction — a capacity shared by !Kung women (Lee, 1972) — maximized inclusive fitness.

Culture and Biology: One System or Two?

If sociobiology is indeed sufficiently flexible to be applied to human behavior without automatic contradiction, we still do not know precisely *how* to so apply it. Perhaps the ecological approach which saved sociobiology for the bats will serve human beings. But what *is* the ecological adaptation of *Homo sapiens*?

Human beings adapt to environment in terms of a socially transmitted system of behavior and meanings called "culture." The neurological capacity for this system apparently evolved in response to a rapidly changing ecology in which maximum behavioral flexibility won out over more stable ("wired in") behavioral mechanisms. The system includes accumulated knowledge about both the exploitation of environmental resources and the form of social organization. It has the unique and emergent property of itself evolving.

It is the fact that cultures, too, evolve, that so complicates the application of sociobiology to human beings. What can the relationship be between ongoing processes of sociocultural evolution and the biological evolution which is the concern of the sociobiologists? Sahlins (1976) would answer, none! He accurately reflects prevailing social science opinion in arguing that biological evolution did produce, back in the dim past, the general and universal capabilities of our species, but that today *culture* patterns behavior. Let us return briefly to that past to see why culture-biology interaction is not as simple as Sahlins would have it.

Evolution of Cultural Capacity

It is now well accepted (e.g., Barkow, 1973, 1975; Durham, 1976a; Geertz, 1964) that we evolved in a "feedback reciprocal relation" (Dobzhansky, 1963) between biological and cultural evolution which generated our "capacity for culture" (Spuhler, 1959). Presumably, the initial impetus for this feedback was the drying trend of the Pliocene, forcing our ancestors from the forests to the savanna in spite of the latter's greater predator pressures. Presumably, too, these early ancestors had just enough "cultural capacity" (perhaps at the level of the modern chimpanzee) to permit them to adapt somewhat more efficiently than did other individuals. They would have had more offspring than did their fellows, so that the next generation would therefore have had a slightly greater psychobiological capacity for culture. This greater ability would have permitted greater cultural invention and more dependence on culture for survival, thereby again resulting in selection for greater cultural capacity, once again permitting the further elaboration of cultural adaptive strategies, and once again increasing selective pressures for cultural capacity, in a vicious circle. Unfortunately, this positive feedback cycle did *not* continue *ad infinitum*.

During most of this process, the more culture we had, the more psychobiological capacity for culture we evolved, leading to more culture, and so on. Culture and the capacity for culture developed neck-and-neck. Yet, culture won the race. *Biological evolution slowed down just as cultural evolution speeded up* (Barkow, 1977b).

This decrease in the rate of biological evolution was purely a technical matter. More efficient technology led to greater population size and mobility, thereby increasing gene flow and ending the "Sewall Wright effect" of genetic drift. Simultaneously, population movement may have sparked a great surge in cultural evolution. Technology became more productive, social units grew larger and more complexly organized, the Neolithic replaced the Paleolithic, farmers replaced hunter-gatherers, tribes replaced bands, and states replaced tribes. Recent human history has seen an enormous acceleration of the rate of cultural evolution, primarily fueled by technological innovation. The remaining pockets of Paleolithic peoples are being rapidly absorbed or destroyed by large-scale societies. Whatever effects these changes have had on our genetic makeup as a species, it seems apparent that biological evolution could not have "tracked" its former Siamese twin: the two systems of evolution must be at least partially independent. We cannot (yet) have been genetically adapted to our present high technology society.

Psychobiology and Contemporary Cultures

Perhaps it is unnecessary for us to *have been* genetically adjusted to our present cultures: perhaps we already *are* so adjusted. That original feedback between biological and cultural evolution generated in us a host of behavioral predispositions and abilities ("biogrammar," as Tiger and Fox [1971] term it), and they are presumably still with us, still constraining sociocultural development in a manner which might make the theories of the sociobiologists retain their relevance even for cultural behavior. After all, a number of political scientists have long been stressing the continuity between human behavior and that of other animals, discussing the validity of inferences drawn from the study of other species and often arguing convincingly that our political behavior, at least, still reflects our general primate characteristics (Beck, 1975; Masters, 1975, 1976a, 1976b; Wilhoite, 1976; and especially a recent collection, Somit, 1976). I myself have argued (1973, 1975) that our social institutions may be profitably viewed as patterned expressions of general primate behavioral traits and that our various systems of prestige and status, in particular, represent the rearrangement of primate social hierarchy tendencies by that feedback process between biological and cultural evolution discussed above. Similarly, I have argued (1976) that human intrapsychic structure bears striking similarities to the (presumed) attention structure of our terrestrial primate ancestors.

For sociobiology, then, our evolutionary history must mean that our biogrammar includes traits selected for because they (once, at least) tended to maximize their carriers' inclusive fitness in a *cultural context*. To the extent that our psychobiology continues to constrain and influence cultural evolution, we should expect some culturally patterned behaviors to tend to maximize fitness (and so to be consistent with sociobiological theory). But, remembering that we were selected for great behavioral flexibility, we are also likely to maximize fitness in different ways in different cultures. (Note that I am deferring discussion of the mechanisms by which such behavioral predispositions might generate social forms consistent with sociobiological prediction until the section on "Mechanisms." At the moment, it is necessary only to underline that there is no reason to posit the existence of rigid, genetically encoded "instincts" to explain such congruence.)

We are left with theoretical grounds for asking whether our cultural forms *are* consistent with sociobiological theory. That is, do our cultures enable us (as individuals) to maximize our inclusive fitness? The two most recent and thorough discussions of the relationship between biological and sociocultural

evolution, those of Durham (1976c) and of Richerson and Boyd (1977), conclude that, on the whole, the cultural behavior of individuals is indeed consistent with their efforts to maximize their respective inclusive fitnesses, although
Durham also admits that, under external constraint, individuals may act
against their own fitness interests. Durham (1976b) even makes a strong case
for primitive warfare actually being in the fitness interests of its individual participants, despite appearances to the contrary. Kurland's analysis of the avunculate, previously discussed, also suggests that far more of human behavior
may be consistent with sociobiology than we may expect.

But the consistency of our cultural forms with the maximization-of-
inclusive-fitness axiom of sociobiology is, in the end, an empirical question. If
this consistency seems unlikely in our own very new, high-technological and
near zero-population-growth society, it may yet be true for those peoples
whose cultures have apparently altered little in many centuries. There has
been some empirical research in Iran (Irons, 1975, 1976), Botswana (Blurton
Jones and Sibley, 1977) and Nigeria (Barkow, 1977c) exploring this possibility. These studies do seem to show that, at least at times, individuals who
follow certain prescribed norms of behavior may thereby maximize their inclusive fitness. But, as Durham (1976a:97) emphasizes, this kind of research is
uncommonly difficult. The studies cited represent the birth of a new literature
rather than final conclusions ready for the textbooks.

Before we leave the topic of sociocultural-biological evolutionary interaction, fairness requires the presentation of at least one opposing view. (After
all, Jean Jacques Rousseau's dictum that civilization is bad for people retains
many adherents.) F.T. Cloak (1975, 1976) has explored the possibility that
cultural evolution may be so independent of its biological counterpart that some
cultural traits can actually reduce the inclusive fitness of their bearers. For
Cloak, the basic unit of both biological and cultural evolution is the "instruction." The "message" a gene carries is an instruction. But cultures are also
composed of molecular traits consisting of instructions. Both biological and
cultural evolution involve nothing but the differential propagation of instructions: soma and society are merely an instruction's way to make more instructions. They are epiphenomena. Evolution is not about the survival of the individual carrier of an instruction or about his culture; it is about instructions
competing with each other to increase their (respective) frequencies.

To adapt Cloak's arguments, one might visualize a conquest state which advances by conquering neighboring peoples. The tendency to conquer would
be the "instruction" in question. As long as there were weak neighboring
peoples to be conquered and assimilated, the instruction would propagate
itself successfully. This process would continue regardless of its effect on the
"health" of the state as a whole or on its individual citizens. The citizen-soldiers
might well suffer a considerable loss in fitness — war is bad for one's health, as

the slogan has it—but this consideration would be irrelevant to cultural evolution, since the casualties could always be made up with new recruits from conquered peoples.

The point is not whether such conquest states actually have existed or whether the fitness of their citizen-soldiers is or is not reduced. The point is that Cloak's ideas permit the painting of an extreme case in which sociocultural and biological evolution are clearly seen to be independent. Sociocultural evolution is here pictured as *reducing* the inclusive fitness which *biological* evolution presumably always maximizes. We thus have theoretical grounds for expecting that cultural patterns may at times oppose inclusive fitness yet continue to be propagated. As is the case with so many questions derived from sociobiology, the hypothesis begs for empirical research.

Ideas About Mechanisms

Human behavioral predispositions may be constraining cultural evolution, and this constraint may be in the direction of maximizing inclusive fitness. This is because as long as both biological and cultural systems of evolution were linked in a reciprocal feedback process, any cultural instruction which increased fitness would automatically select for the genetic tendency to acquire and transmit it. The next generation would be more likely to learn that instruction. At the same time, instructions which reduced inclusive fitness would be selecting against the genetic basis for acquiring them. Unfortunately, a species is always adapted to its past environment but not necessarily to the present. Thus, some of our formerly adaptive predispositions may now be maladaptive. Regardless of their adaptive status, however, it is necessary to ask: (1) exactly what would a human "behavioral predisposition" look like and (2) in what sense would it "constrain" cultural evolution?

Human behavioral predispositions probably involve ease of learning and activity preference. Hamburg (1963) pointed out some years ago that a species tends to enjoy learning and performing activities which have had survival value in the past. For example, it is not difficult to teach a child to play ball—the task of endlessly improving one's aim with a thrown missile is so frequently an aspect of children's play it may well be a cross-cultural universal, and surely it is germaine to any discussion of the past ecological adaptation of our species. Similarly, Tiger (1969) argues that various types of male-male activities are pleasurable today because they once permitted the cooperation necessary for certain types of hunting (presumably enhancing the fitness of the participants, who thereby became our ancestors). On the other hand, Barash (1977) points out that human beings are harder to toilet train than a dog or cat—this learning task apparently did not have much to do with inclusive fitness during our phylogenesis (if a bit of circularity may here be excused).

Note that missile throwing and male-male bonding represent the indirect means by which the selection pressure for ecological adaptation — hunting success — was mediated. More sociobiological selective pressures can operate in precisely the same indirect, opportunistic fashion. . . .We should be more helpful toward those with whom we share genes than toward others. This inclusive-fitness selection pressure might have generated in us an automatic ability to determine degrees of consanguinity, but there is no evidence that it did and *no theoretical requirement that it should have done so*. The theoretical requirement is the *effect* that we be more helpful toward kin than nonkin, regardless of the particular mechanism through which that result is mediated. There is a certain tendency on the part of the sociobiologists (e.g., Wilson, 1975:119-120) to imagine that the effects they predict are mediated by extremely direct and simple mechanisms.

The mechanism that apparently did evolve, in this case, is one of familiarity and habituation: we tend to be helpful toward those whom we are socialized with, those with whom we grow up or at least have become familiar. In the environment in which we as a species evolved — what Bowlby (1969) termed our "environment of evolutionary adaptedness" — these individuals were likely to have been those with whom we shared genes. Thus, the selective pressure was met. Since our present behavioral predispositions and learning preferences reflect our past rather than our present environment, we still habituate to those with whom we associate, regardless of whether they are kin or not.

If this habituation mechanism is really part of the biogrammar of our species, in what sense can it be said to "constrain" sociocultural evolution? The answer is that it is part of the raw material of human nature upon which sociocultural evolution operates. From it, varying forms of social organization may be generated, forms which may at times separate us from near kin and involve us with distant, but which may never ignore the ease with which we learn to cooperate with those with whom we have long been familiar. Although we may take this trait for granted, it is nevertheless a biological characteristic of the species which once increased inclusive fitness.

Since we are no longer in our environment of evolutionary adaptedness, learning preferences which once maximized fitness may no longer be doing so. Perhaps this fact will result, ultimately, in biological selection away from the predispositions which make particular cultural patterns possible (cf. Durham, 1976c). The extent to which contemporary cultural forms generated in part by our sociobiological biogrammar are or are not helping individuals maximize their inclusive fitness is a fascinating empirical problem. It is a good place for the anthropologist to begin sociobiological research.

But there are other questions, perhaps of greater interest for the cultural (rather than biosocial) anthropologist. Sociocultural evolution, through processes about which we understand embarrassingly little, weaves our complex cultures from social psychological traits evolved in the context of our environment of evolutionary adaptedness. Human social institutions are and can only be patterned expressions of biologically based learning preferences, predispositions and motivations, characteristics which are there because they once, at least, maximized individual inclusive fitness (Barkow, 1973, 1975). Can the cultural anthropologist, armed with knowledge of the kinds of behavioral traits with which our phylogenesis has provided us, finally begin to understand how individuals interacting over time generate and alter their cultures?

Such an attempt would be difficult, at this point, because there has been so little sociobiological analysis of these traits. Social organization, for example, is surely based on more complex traits than mere social habituation! What selective pressures, one wonders, resulted in the evolution of the symbolic ability which permits us to classify a stranger as a kinsman toward whom we have rights and obligations? But rather than wait for the biologists to provide a complete sociobiological analysis of our "capacity for culture," perhaps the social and behavioral scientists will take a hand in the work.

For example, if cultural anthropologists are to formulate theories of sociocultural evolution which take into account the nature of the human animal, we will require from the psychologists an inventory of our learning preferences and behavioral predispositions. So far, psychology has largely used a paradigm in which the existence of "general laws of learning" is axiomatic rather than hypothetical and the question of why a particular stimulus should be "reinforcing" is rarely asked (Lockhard, 1971). Only in recent years have the ethologists and psychologists (e.g., Hinde and Stevenson-Hinde, 1973; Seligman, 1972) begun to examine the problem of which species learns what most easily and why. Psychological anthropologists, with their familiarity with both cross-cultural universals and the varying severity of socialization practices in different societies, are in a good position to survey the relative ease with which human beings learn different types of tasks.

Their findings will *not* involve rigid behaviors tightly linked to genetics. Durham (1976c) rightly criticizes the sociobiologists for often giving the impression that the behavioral traits whose existence they explain must be closely tied to specific genetic substrates. Modern ethological conceptions of human behavior (Barkow, 1973; Bowlby, 1969; Hinde, 1974) recognize that it varies on a stability-lability dimension rather than being either "innate" ("genetic") or "acquired." All behavior requires interaction with the environment, if for no other reason than that each and every gene requires complex interactions and feedbacks with the environment for its expression. The link between genetic substrate and most human behavior is probabilistic rather than deterministic.

We will never find that it is "instinctive" to love those with whom we have been socialized, for example, but only that it is easier to learn to feel loyalty and cooperativeness toward them than toward strangers. Sociobiology will never find that women are innately superior or inferior to men, but it may be that women on the whole are more likely than are men to find some tasks pleasurable and, therefore, to learn them more easily. We will never find a genetic substrate for racial prejudice, but it may well be that we find it easier to learn to like those physically similar to ourselves than those dissimilar.

Empirical research may find that these suggestions, consistent with sociobiological prediction, are accurate. That they conflict with the ideology held by many of us would make us unhappy, but no one ever promised us, as students, that we would always like our research findings. Fortunately, such findings would involve tendencies and not inevitabilities. If our values so dictate, we can utilize socialization experience to cancel out behavioral tendencies which may once have been adaptive for the individual but are no longer so or which are maladaptive for the species as a whole. If it is easier to toilet train a cat than a human being, and if our toddlers may complain of the stress, most of us nevertheless learn to give up our diapers.

Conclusions

A full description of the learning and activity preferences of our species would amount to a theory of human nature. Much of the controversy over sociobiology has stemmed from its claim to have such a theory and to be able to account for such phenomena as parent-offspring conflict, sibling rivalry, sex-role differences, ethnocentrism and race prejudice, nepotism and altruism, incest taboos, reciprocity, and, now, with Kurland's work, the avunculate. These claims are only somewhat exaggerated. What the sociobiologists do have is a powerful and proven conceptual framework which, when properly applied to the evolution and ecology of our species, can indeed yield a theory of human nature. Such a theory, if validated by studies of actual human behavior and if coupled to ethological-psychological study of the mechanisms through which its predictions are mediated (Blurton Jones, 1976), may at last integrate the biological, behavioral, and social sciences.

Anthropology can treat sociobiology as just one more fad, as does Sahlins (1976). We can take advantage of our greater awareness of culture and human diversity to criticize the errors of the biologists when they apply their framework to a species in which we and not they are the experts. We can talk to each other and publish in our journals and ignore the biologists as they create their own biosocial science, selecting only what they consider relevant from our research (a trend already well advanced). Or we can take the time necessary to learn the basic principles of modern evolutionary biology and then join them in studying human behavior.

To what would we apply sociobiology? The first place would be to the rather speculative literature on the evolution of human behavior discussed earlier. Inclusive fitness has two components: (1) adaptation to environment and (2) competition among individuals striving to maximize their respective inclusive fitnesses. External environment is the limiting factor for the latter process, e.g., there is no use being the largest male, as a result of intrasexual selection, if there are periodic famines during which the largest individuals starve to death. Selection always involves compromise among numerous factors, and the sociobiologist will go wrong if he is unaware of some of them — particularly of factors having to do with the ecology. But ignoring considerations of inclusive fitness and concentrating solely on the ecology is also an error. The intrasexual competition discussed by Trivers (1972) probably accounts for more aspects of human aggressivity than does our "hunting" ecology; and perhaps the human trait of "infantilization" or "neoteny" is more explicable in terms of Trivers' (1974) "parent-offspring conflict" than in terms of a long childhood having been necessary for the transmission of cultural information. But sociobiology must be applied not *in vacuo* but to reconstructions of how we evolved, reconstructions of the details of that feedback between biological and cultural evolution which generated our species.

Sociobiology must also be applied to contemporary cultures. A prime empirical question for sociobiology's application to human behavior is the extent to which both our individual learning preferences and our cultural-level practices tend to maximize inclusive fitness. The psychologists and ethologists can concentrate on the individual; only the anthropologist is in a position to relate traditions and institutions to inclusive fitness. Assuming that it is found that some cultural practices do indeed maximize individuals' inclusive fitness and others do not, the question must be, why? What processes of cultural evolution and cultural adaptation to environment generate or fail to generate isomorphism between biological and cultural evolution? Answering this question may make possible a processual theory of culture change and evolution.

But sociobiology must never be applied directly to human behavior without consideration of the role of cultural evolution. "Altruism" is a good case in point. In other species it is explained in terms of "kin selection," in which the organism is altruistic only to the extent to which such behavior maximizes its inclusive fitness. But human altruism is mediated by systems of norms and ethics (Barkow, 1978). Such systems must not be dismissed by the sociobiologist as mere "proximate" causes of little relevance for his task of understanding "ultimate" or evolutionary causes, for *the ultimate causes of animal altruism and human ethics are, in a sense, different*. Animal altruism is produced by biological evolution, human ethics by cultural evolution. The types of evolution are of course linked, as we have seen, and no doubt the evolution of our capacity to internalize systems of ethics can be explained in terms of sociobiology. But the ethics themselves are aspects of a cultural evolution which may or may not be maximizing the inclusive fitness of some or all of its members. Sociobiologists who apply their inclusive fitness theories directly to culturally mediated behavior are engaging in biological reductionism, even when the data are consistent with their expectations (cf. Durham, 1976c).

Anthropologists will never "prove" or "disprove" sociobiology; we will either find it useful or not useful. If we find it useful, we will be utilizing the same paradigm which orders the biological sciences. "Sociobiology" has come to mean not the all-devouring synthesis for which Wilson originally intended it but simply the application of modern evolutionary biology to all species, our own included. To reject sociobiology is to reject modern biological explanation and to fall into a reification of "culture" as an explanatory and causal agent—a cultural reductionism.

There is more to my life, if not yours, thank you, than maximizing inclusive fitness! Culture is an emergent phenomenon and will never be fully reducible to the biological, evolutionary phenomena which make it possible. Ultimately, anthropology will simply assimilate sociobiology, so that its perspectives are taken for granted, and we will go on with our work. . . .

References

Alexander, R. D. (1971) "The Search for an Evolutionary Philosophy of Man." *Proceedings of the Royal Society* (Victoria) 84:99–120.

———. (1974) "The Evolution of Social Behavior." *Annual Review of Ecological Systems* 5:325–383.

———. (1975) "The Search for a General Theory of Behavior." *Behavioral Science* 20:77–100.

Barash, D. P. (1977) *Sociobiology and Behavior.* New York: Elsevier North-Holland.

Barkow, J. H. (1973) "Darwinian Psychological Anthropology: A Biosocial Approach." *Current Anthropology* 14:373–388.

———. (1975) "Prestige and Culture: A Biosocial Interpretation." *Current Anthropology* 16:553–572.

———. (1976) "Attention Structure and Internation Representations," in M. R. Chance and R. R. Larsen (eds.), *The Social Structure of Attention.* London: Wiley, 203–219.

———. (1977a) "Human Ethology and Intra-Individual Systems." *Social Science Information* 16:133–145.

———. (1977b) "Biological Evolution of Culturally Patterned Behavior." manuscript.

———. (1977c) "Conformity to Ethos and Reproductive Success in Two Hausa Communities: An Empirical Evaluation." manuscript.

———. (1978) "Social Norms, the Self and Sociobiology: Building on the Ideas of A. I. Hallowell." *Current Anthropology.* Vol. 19.

Beck, H. (1975) "Ethological Considerations on the Problem of Political Order." *Political Anthropology* 1:109–135.

Bertram, B. C. R. (1976) "Kin Selection in Lions and Evolution," in P. P. G. Bateson and R. A. Hinde (eds.), *Growing Points in Ethology*. Cambridge: Cambridge University Press, 281–301.

Blurton Jones, N. G. (1976) "Growing Points in Human Ethology: Another Link Between Ethology and the Social Sciences?" in P. P. G. Bateson and R. A. Hinde (eds.), *Growing Points in Ethology*. Cambridge: Cambridge University Press, 427–450.

_____ , and R. Sibly (1977) "Testing the Adaptiveness of Culturally Determined Behavior: Do Bushman Women Maximize Their Reproductive Success by Spacing Births Widely and Foraging Seldom?" manuscript.

Bowlby, J. A. (1969) "Attachment and Loss." Vol. 1. *Attachment*. New York: Basic Books.

Cloak, F. T., Jr. (1975) "Is a Cultural Ethology Possible?" *Human Ecology* 3:161–182.

_____ . (1976) "Group Selection to Fixation of an Altruistic Behavior in a Population Divided into Breeding Isolates: A Model." Paper presented at the June Annual Meeting of the Animal Behavior Society. University of Colorado, Boulder.

Clutton-Brock, T. H., and P. H. Harvey. (1976) "Evolutionary Rules and Primate Societies," in P. P. G. Bateson and R. A. Hinde (eds.), *Growing Points in Ethology*. Cambridge: Cambridge University Press, 195–238.

Dawkins, R. (1976) *The Selfish Gene*. New York: Oxford University Press.

Dobzhansky, T. (1963) "Cultural Direction of Human Evolution." *Human Biology* 35:311–316.

Durham, W. H. (1976a) "The Adaptive Significance of Cultural Behavior." *Human Ecology* 4:89–121.

_____ . (1976b) "Resource Competition and Human Aggression, Part 1: A Review of Primitive War." *Quarterly Review of Biology* 51:385–415.

_____ . (1976c) "Towards a Coevolutionary Theory of Human Biology and Culture." Paper presented at the 75th Annual Meeting of the American Anthropological Association, Washington.

Fox, R. (ed.). (1975) *Biosocial Anthropology*. New York: Wiley.

_____ , and U. Fleising. (1976) "Human Ethology," in B. J. Siegel, A. R. Beals, and S. A. Tyler (eds.), *Annual Review of Anthropology*. Palo Alto: Annual Reviews, 265–288.

Geertz, C. (1964) "The Transition to Humanity," in Sol Tax (ed.), *Horizons of Anthropology*. Chicago: Aldine, 37–48.

Hamburg, D. A. (1963) "Emotions in the Perspective of Human Evolution," in Peter Knapp (ed.), *Expression of the Emotions in Man*. New York: International Universities Press, 300–317.

Hamilton, W. D. (1964) "The Genetical Evolution of Social Behavior". *Journal of Theoretical Biology* 7:1–52.

_____ . (1970) "Selfish and Spiteful Behavior in an Evolutionary Model". *Nature* 228:1218–1220.

_____ . (1971) "Selection of Selfish and Altruistic Behavior in Some Extreme Models," in J. F. Eisenberg and W. S. Dillon (eds.), *Man and Beast: Comparative Social Behavior*. Washington: Smithsonian Institution Press, 57–91.

Harnad, S., H. Steklis, and J. Lancaster (eds.). (1977) *Origins and Evolution of Language and Speech*. New York: New York Academy of Sciences.

Hinde, R. A. (1974) *Biological Bases of Social Behavior*. New York: McGraw-Hill.

_____ , and J. Stevenson-Hinde (eds.). (1973) *Constraints on Learning. Limitations and Predispositions*. New York: Academic Press.

Humphrey, N. K. (1976) "The Function of Intellect," in P. P. G. Bateson and R. A. Hinde (eds.), *Growing Points in Ethology*. Cambridge: Cambridge University Press, 303–325.

Irons, W. (1975) "Residence Choice and Biological Fitness." Paper presented at the 74th Annual Meeting of the American Anthropological Association, San Francisco.

_____ . (1976) "Emic and Reproductive Success." Paper presented at the 75th Annual Meeting of the American Anthropological Association, Washington.

_____ . (1977) "Evolutionary Biology and Human Fertility." Paper presented at the 76th Annual Meeting of the American Anthropological Association, Houston.

King, G. E. (1975) "Socioterritorial Units among Carnivores and Early Hominids." *Journal of Anthropological Research* 31:69–87.

Kolata, G. B. (1977) "Sexual Dimorphism and Mating Systems: How Did They Evolve?" *Science* 195:382–383.

Kuhn, T. S. (1962) *The Structure of Scientific Revolutions*. Chicago: University of Chicago Press.

Kurland, J. A. (In press) "Matrilines: The Primate Sisterhood and the Human Avunculate," in Irven DeVore (ed.), *Sociobiology and the Social Sciences*. Chicago: Aldine-Atherton.

Lee, R. B. (1972) "The !Kung Bushmen of Botswana," in M. G. Bicchieri (ed.), *Hunters and Gatherers Today*. New York: Holt, Rinehart and Winston, 326–368.

Lockhard, R. B. (1971) "Reflections on the Fall of Comparative Psychology: Is There a Message for Us All?" *American Psychologist* 26:168–179.

Masters, R. D. (1975) "Politics as a Biological Mechanism." *Social Science Information* 14:7–63.

_____ . (1976a) "Functional Approaches to Analogical Comparisons Between Species," in Mario von Cranach (ed.), *Methods of Inference from Animal to Man*. The Hague: Mouton, 73–102.

_____ . (1976b) "The Impact of Ethology on Political Science," in Albert Somit (ed.), *Biology and Politics*. The Hague: Mouton, 197–233.

Maynard Smith, J. (1972) *On Evolution*. Edinburgh: Edinburgh University Press.

Montagu, M. F. A. (ed.). (1962) *Culture and the Evolution of Man*. New York: Oxford University Press.

Richerson, P. J., and R. Boyd (1977) "A Dual Inheritance Model of the Human Evolutionary Process." *Journal of Theoretical Biology*.

Roe, A. and G. G. Simpson (eds.). (1958) *Behavior and Evolution: A Symposium*. New Haven: Yale University Press.

Sahlins, M. (1976) *The Use and Abuse of Biology: An Anthropological Critique of Sociobiology*. Ann Arbor: University of Michigan Press.

Seligman, M. E. P. (1972) "Phobias and Preparedness," in M. E. P. Seligman and J. K. Hager (eds.), *Biological Boundaries of Learning*. Englewood Cliffs, N.J.: Prentice-Hall.

Simpson, G. G. (1953) *The Major Features of Evolution*. New York: Columbia University Press.

Somit, A. (ed.). (1976) *Biology and Politics*. The Hague: Mouton.

Spuhler, J. N. (ed.). (1959) *The Evolution of Man's Capacity for Culture*. Detroit: Wayne State University Press.

Tax, S. (ed.). (1960) *The Evolution of Man: A Symposium*. Chicago: University of Chicago Press.

Tiger, L. (1969) *Men In Groups*. New York: Random House.

_____ , and R. Fox. (1971) *The Imperial Animal*. New York: Holt, Rinehart and Winston.

Trivers, R. L. (1971) "The Evolution of Reciprocal Altruism." *Quarterly Review of Biology* 46:35–57.

_____ . (1972) "Parental Investment and Sexual Selection," in B. G. Campbell (ed.), *Sexual Selection and the Descent of Man*. Chicago: Aldine, 136–179.

_____ . (1974) "Parent-Offspring Conflict." *American Zoologist* 14:249–264.

_____ , and H. Hare. (1975) "Haplodiploidy and the Evolution of Social Insects." *Science* 191:249–263.

Washburn, S. L. (ed.). (1961) *Social Life of Early Man*. Viking Fund Publications in Anthropology 31.

West-Eberhard, M. J. (1975) "The Evolution of Social Behavior by Kin Selection." *Quarterly Review of Biology* 50:1–34.

Wilhoite, F. H., Jr. (1976) "Primates and Political Authority: A Biobehavioral Perspective." *American Political Science Review* 70:1110–1126.

Williams, G. C. (1966) *Adaptation and Natural Selection*. Princeton: Princeton University Press.

Wilson, E. O. (1975) *Sociobiology: The New Synthesis*. Cambridge, Mass.: Harvard University Press.

_____ . (1977) "Biology and the Social Sciences." *Daedalus*. September.

_____ . (In press) "The Attempt to Suppress Human Behavioral Genetics." *Journal of General Education*.

Wynne-Edwards, V. C. (1962) *Animal Dispersion in Relation to Social Behavior*. New York: Hafner.

6

Toward a Coevolutionary Theory of Human Biology and Culture

William H. Durham

Biological and Cultural Evolution

According to neo-Darwinian evolutionary theory, the genetic traits of a given population of plants or animals track, over generations of time, one or more optimal character states that are specific to the organism and its environment. Changes in phenotype are thought to result most commonly from individual-level natural selection (together with some forms of kin and group selection), which acts to preserve those genotypes that direct the formation of phenotypes best suited to the prevailing conditions. This theory has now proven to be very successful in explaining the genetically coded traits of most organisms.

Particularly in human beings, however, there is an important nongenetic or cultural component of phenotypes. What was apparently selected for during the organic evolution of human beings was *an unusual capability for modifying and extending phenotypes on the basis of learning and experience.* Within limits, culture enables us to alter and build onto aspects of morphology, physiology, and behavior without any corresponding change in genotype. This means, of course, that natural selection by itself is neither adequate nor appropriate for explaining the culturally acquired phenotypic traits of human beings.

Anthropologists realized long ago that nonbiological process or processes were behind the cultural component of human phenotypes, and they have led the search for alternative models or theories for the evolution of this important cultural aspect. A wide variety of theories are explicit and implicit in the anthropological literature (see, e.g., Kaplan and Manners, 1972) and a number

Reprinted by permission of the author from N. A. Chagnon and W. Irons (eds.), *Evolutionary Biology and Human Social Behavior: An Anthropological Perspective* (North Scituate, Mass.: Duxbury Press, 1979), pp. 39–59.

of them have been successful at explaining some within-group and between-group variations in human culture. Curiously, a large number of these models represent a process of selective retention analogous in some sense to natural selection (Campbell, 1965 and 1975; Durham 1976a), although the phenotypes retained in time would be those which best suited a given *cultural* criterion. Unfortunately, there has been little agreement to date regarding the effective criterion or criteria behind any such cultural selection. The list of candidate criteria now includes free energy, satisfaction, profit, population regulation, homeostasis, and even ease of replication of a cultural instruction. Again, each has proven useful for the analysis of cultural characteristics in certain societies, but none has proven adequate for a general theory.

Part of the problem has been that, in the search for theories to explain cultural phenomena, one key factor has been continually overlooked, and that factor has much to do with the relationship between human biology and culture. Many scholars have failed to appreciate that the organic evolution of the *capacity* for culture had, at least at one time, important implications for the actual *process* of cultural evolution. What was presumably genetically selected for in our ancestors was an increasing ability to modify phenotypes through learning and experience, but it was selected for only because those ancestors persistently used that ability to enhance their survival and reproduction. The capacity for culture, one could say, continued to evolve not merely because it *enabled* superior adaptations, but also because it was used to *produce* superior adaptations. Our hominid ancestors must therefore have had ways of keeping culture "on track" of the adaptive optima as those optima varied from place to place and time to time. The conclusion is important: as the capacity for culture evolved, *the developing culture characterizing a group of people, whatever else it was, must have been adaptive for them in terms of survival and reproduction.*

It is important to note that this conclusion does not require that the cultural meaning of things was consciously or unconsciously related to their survival and reproduction consequences. It means only that, however culture changed and evolved, and whatever meaning was given by people to their cultural attributes, the net effect of those attributes was to enhance human survival and reproduction. There is an important deduction from this argument. Although a coevolutionary theory can potentially contribute to an understanding of the adaptive significance of cultural attributes, it is not necessarily the key to understanding the meaning and symbolic significance people may give to those attributes (see also Sahlins, 1976).

Obviously things have changed since the days when the capacity for culture was evolving because it was used by protohominids to produce superior adaptations. It is appropriate to ask whether culture is still used by human beings as a way to enhance their survival and reproduction. Have we lost the ability to keep culture "on track"? Has cultural evolution by some other principle of optimization, for example, more recently run counter to individual survival and reproduction, and has culture therefore lost its original adaptive significance for human existence?

It is, of course, impossible to give a definitive answer at this time, but for a number of reasons I am inclined to think that there is still an important adaptive dimension to human cultural attributes. These reasons can be divided into two parts: those related to the action of cultural selection within groups, and those related to cultural selection between groups.

Cultural Selection Within Groups

For convenience in the description of levels of cultural selection, I will define *social group* to be any subset of a deme or breeding population containing individuals whose survival and reproduction are directly and substantially interdependent because of interactions among them. It can be thought of as a collection of individuals whose behavior creates at least a given arbitrary amount of interdependence so that the collection is bounded by frontiers of far less interdependence. Of course there are a whole variety of forms of interdependence, including ties arising from goods and services exchanged between members, but for most of the arguments that follow, the specific nature of interdependence is not important. It may be helpful here to think of a deme as some entire ethnolinguistic population or "culture" and to think of social groups as smaller, more interdependent camps, bands, or villages within that population.

Basic to any theory of cultural change and adaptation, of course, is the way in which distinct human social groups acquire their cultural attributes. In this section, I propose the hypotheses (1) that the cultural characteristics of human social groups result to a large extent from internal, individual-level selective retention, and more importantly, (2) that this process generally selects for cultural attributes that enhance the ability of their carriers to survive and reproduce.

My reasons are these. First, I believe that there is ample evidence that some process of selective retention continues to operate on the accumulation and modification of cultural attributes within human societies. People remain somehow selective in their receptivity to cultural innovation, for we know that many more innovations are introduced by invention and diffusion that are retained at length within any given society. Second, I believe that this ongoing selective retention is, and always has been, influenced by a number of human biases which tend to keep people from selectively retaining cultural attributes that run counter to their individual survival and reproduction, provided they have a choice. Of these, perhaps the most important are learned biases. Robert LeVine (1973) has argued that the process of socialization teaches children from an early age not only adherence to social norms and traditional patterns of behavior, but also selectivity in the adoption of new forms—a selectivity based on what is held to be adaptive and "for their own good."

Two properties of this bias make it particularly important. First, the development of this selectivity is at least partly in the *combined interest* of the parents, the child, and even the social group as a whole. To some extent, all participants in the process have their own survival and reproduction at stake (this is not to deny some amount of conflict between these interests). Second, it is urgent. Because of the unusual vulnerability of children, the ability or inability to discriminate between positively and negatively adaptive practices in childhood can have direct and immediate consequences in addition to long-term effects.

A second sort of bias might be called the bias of "satisfaction" (see Ruyle, 1973 and 1977). Presumably throughout the organic evolution of hominids there was a persistent, genetic selective advantage for a neurophysiology which rewarded with sensory reinforcements and a feeling of "satisfaction" those acts likely to enhance survival and reproduction, and which produced unpleasant, distressing, or painful feedback in response to potentially dangerous behaviors. When the capacity for culture began evolving, there was already some built-in bias of this kind, biologically programmed in the design of the prehuman nervous system. Eugene Ruyle, among others, has argued that the selective retention of cultural traits has continued to be influenced by the general sense of "satisfaction" that they do or do not bring to their bearer. While we disagree over the definition and relative utility of the concept of satisfaction, I concur with Ruyle that cultural evolution has probably not ignored nor completely overridden the feedback from the neurophysiology that we are born with (cf. Durham, 1977). I agree that "square wheels, crooked spears, and sickly children are unlikely to provide much satisfaction" (Ruyle, 1977:54), but I feel that this is because they are unlikely to do much for survival and reproduction.

There is potentially a third source of bias to be found in the learning structures and functions of the human brain, although I hasten to add that this possibility remains not well documented at present. A knowledge of the structures and functions of the human brain is certainly crucial to understanding the relationship between biology and culture, but I have not been persuaded by hard-core genetic structuralists (e.g., Laughlin and d'Aquili, 1974) that there is a determinism rather than a bias to be found therein. To my knowledge, the best evidence of any learning "canalization" that might affect culture comes from studies by Seligman (1971) showing that some common human phobias are learned with an exposure and rapidity that suggests that these may represent a form of "prepared learning." Other examples of prepared learning have been documented for nonhuman animal species, where they are thought to result from built-in neurophysiological mechanisms of the brain. To the extent that there is a bias on culture imposed by the biochemistry and physiology of the human brain, the organic evolution of that organ would mean a bias in favor of the selective retention of more rather than less adaptive cultural traits.

A fourth kind of bias, which might be called "circumstantial bias," has been suggested recently by Cloak (1977) and Alexander (in press). This kind of bias may occur when the customary organization of child-rearing practices and enculturation in a social group ensure some regularity of learning and reinforcement for culture carriers. Consider the simple example where parents customarily rear and enculturate their own children. "Wherever that is true, a cultural instruction whose behavior helps its human carrier-enactor (or his/her relatives) to acquire more children thereby has more little heads to get copied into." As a result, cultural instructions that enhance survival and reproduction will differentially propagate through social groups as generations go by, "until most extant cultural instructions have that effect" (Cloak, 1977:50).

These four biases (and possibly others unrecognized and undiscovered) taken together represent a reasonably strong probabilistic "force" tending to keep culture on track of the adaptive optima. This force would operate at the level of individual human beings and bias them as culture carriers. As a result, individuals would tend to select and retain from competing variants those cultural practices whose net phenotypic effect best enhances their individual ability to survive and reproduce (Durham, 1976a and b). Hypothetically, this process of cultural selection would result in the spread and maintenance of cultural attributes that are adaptive in the general biological sense of contributing to their bearer's reproductive success. To be more explicit, I hypothesize that cultural features of human phenotypes are commonly *designed to promote the success of an individual human being in his or her natural and sociocultural environment* and, to be consistent with the biological meaning of adaptation, I suggest that *success is best measured by the extent to which the attribute permits individuals to survive and reproduce and thereby contribute genes to later generations of the population of which they are members* (adapted from Williams, 1966:97).

Several implications of this hypothesis deserve elaboration. First, it suggests that successful adaptation be measured by the long-term representation of an individual's genes in a population, a quantity which ecologists and evolutionary biologists often call "individual inclusive fitness" (see, for example, Williams, 1966; Alexander, 1974; West Eberhard, 1975), even though the phenotypic traits in question here need have no special genetic basis whatsoever. This suggestion often leaves both biologists and anthropologists a bit uncomfortable — anthropologists because even cultural ecologists are not accustomed to think in explicit terms of "reproductive success" and "genetic representation" and biologists because they are used to thinking that transmissible reproductive differentials measured between phenotypes are always the result of differences in genotype. Indeed, for rigorous population genetics, fitness is conventionally defined *between genotypes* in a given environment. With culture, however, inter-individual differences in the long-term representation of genes can result from acquired phenotypes that have no special underlying genotype. Put differently, the representation of a wide variety of genotypes may actually benefit (they may or may not benefit equally) from a given cultural phenotypic change. To minimize confusion on this matter I therefore suggest that *individual inclusive fitness* be used to refer to the long-term representation of an individual's genes in a population, and *genotypic inclusive fitness* be used to refer to the differential representation of explicit genotypes. Where differences in phenotypes result from genetic differences between organisms, individual inclusive fitness contributes to the genotypic fitnesses of particular genotypes and there is no problem. However, for humans where phenotypes may be culturally altered, extended, and transmitted, individual inclusive fitness differentials can result from phenotypes with no special genotypic basis. The analysis of the adaptive significance of cultural attributes thus requires a focus on individuals, their phenotypes, and associated differences in reproductive success. With these qualifications in mind, I suggest that relative, individual inclusive fitness (as approximated by the long-term differential reproductive success of an individual and appropriately weighted kin) remains the best measure by which to assess the adaptiveness of a given biological and/or cultural trait.

Second, an important distinction must be made between "the extent and effectiveness of design for survival" and the actual reproduction record of a given individual or sample (cf. Williams, 1966). There may always be chance effects that render a trait in a given case maladaptive or suboptimal. Furthermore, the extent and effectiveness must be judged relative to the particular environment in which the adaptation arose. Third, the analysis of the adaptiveness of a characteristic must always be made in consideration of the alternative phenotypes historically or presently available in a given social context. At any given time, the nature of culture change and the rate of this change will be affected by the availability of alternative forms and the degree of relative advantage and disadvantage among them. Adaptiveness must then be seen as a statement of relative, not absolute, advantage among phenotypes.

To summarize, I hypothesize (1) that human beings are not just passively receptive to cultural innovation but (2) that we have and develop a number of selective biases which result in (3) a tendency to acquire those aspects of phenotype which past experience and some degree of prediction suggest to be most advantageous for personal inclusive fitness. Although the resulting process of cultural selection would normally result in adaptive phenotypic attributes, I should point out that it is actually easier to conceive of cultural influences getting "off track" in the evolution of a phenotype than it is for biological influences. Maladaptive cultural practices *can* be maintained at substantial frequency in a population, particularly when the biases previously mentioned are overridden or prevented from functioning by force, threat, misinformation, or restrictions on alternatives. Maladaptive behaviors can also recur through the conscious or deliberate choice of individuals to behave counter to their reproductive interests, but I am suggesting that this behavior is not likely to become a long-lasting cultural tradition. I am reminded of the "rather extreme example" mentioned in Ruyle (1973:206) of "a religious sect in nineteenth-century Russia whose cultural pool contained a total ban on sexual intercourse. Lacking an adequate alternative method of recruitment, the sect disappeared."

Where circumstances do permit the preceding biases to operate, however, culture would hypothetically evolve to an important extent by the selective retention of nongenetic traits that enhance the ability of human beings to survive and reproduce in their particular habitats (Durham, 1976a and b). In principle, this cultural selection may proceed consciously or unconsciously and it may ironically proceed according to any number of other "proximate" or "cognized" criteria (like free energy yield, homeostasis, etc.) that are closely correlated with the reproductive success of human beings in the environment concerned. In fact, the process may proceed through selective retention not related in any obvious way to reproduction or survival as long as the net effect enhances (or at least does not reduce) the relative fitness of the culture carrier. In this way, cultural characteristics may take on a meaning and value which themselves are not explained by individual inclusive fitness, although their adaptive consequences may be.

Michael Harner (1973:152) implied a way to summarize this hypothesis for cultural selection within groups when he wrote that "culture is learned and transmitted through human effort; therefore it seems unlikely that cultural institutions and traits can be successfully passed on through centuries and millenia without having some regular reinforcement for their maintenance." For the sake of simplicity, let us say that the individual effort involved in culture increases monotonically over the range of a metric phenotypic trait that is culturally variable. Further, let us assume that these "phenotypic costs" to an individual from the effort and/or risk associated with the cultural trait are proportional over the range to any "fitness costs," however slight, of maintaining and perpetuating the practice (see Figure 6.1). What I am suggesting here is that individual-level cultural selection would act in time to increase the frequency of any available phenotype whose resulting net fitness benefits (total benefits minus costs) conferred a differential reproductive advantage relative to other phenotypes. In other words, the reinforcement proposed by Harner is largely to be found in the inclusive fitness benefits of culture. Cultural selec-

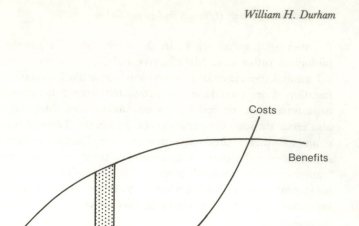

FIGURE 6.1

tion as used here could then be "directional," "stabilizing," or "disruptive" analogous to the modes of natural selection, depending on the shape of the cost and benefit curves. The cost curve figure shows a hypothetical case for stabilizing cultural selection. In an environment where the costs and benefits shown as a function of phenotype persist for some time, the hypothesized process of cultural selection would result in convergence on the intermediate phenotype P_m which effectively maximizes human survival and reproduction in that environment. It should be emphasized that such a trait would spread by individual-level selective retention to all individuals in the given social group for whom these costs and benefits apply. The trait could also spread by diffusion to other groups in the same deme or even other demes. If it continued there to confer individual fitness benefits, this phenotype could spread still further by individual-level selective retention.

One final qualification must be included in this argument. A large number, perhaps even a majority, of the identifiable cultural aspects of human phenotypes involve extremely low fitness costs and/or benefits for their carriers. Cultural traits in some cases may be virtually inconsequential to inclusive fitness and there may be essentially no relative fitness advantage among existing alternative forms. With little basis for fitness discrimination, the hypothesized process of cultural selection would not be effective for these traits. The spread and perpetuation of recognizably low-cost attributes are then likely to be better explained in other ways (like momentary phenotypic reward or arbitrary symbolic value). As I have argued elsewhere (Durham, 1976a), the importance of inclusive fitness to our understanding of human cultural attributes is therefore expected to be conditionally dependent upon the degree to which an attribute taxes the highly variable time, energy, and resource budgets of individuals. My belief is that there are few, if any, cultural practices that are maintained in the absence of force or threat and persist even though individual parents would achieve substantially higher fitness without them or by available alternative practices.

This argument suggests that where cultural evolution proceeds through a process of selective retention within groups, resulting attributes are not likely to require what may be called "fitness altruism" by any individual. Cultural selection, like natural selection, would incessantly oppose any phenotype whose net effect was to assist reproductive competitors in the same population. (Alexander, 1974, makes this point for genetic selection.) This does not mean that cultural selection somehow precludes mutual assistance. On the contrary, cooperative phenotypes would have a cultural selective advantage in any circumstance where joint effort results in mutually enhanced fitness. Nor does this imply that cultural selection within groups necessarily opposes all forms of self-sacrifice. There are now a number of theories showing ways in which genetically based social altruism may actually increase fitness and thereby evolve by natural selection: for example, through reciprocity (Trivers, 1971), mate selection (Blaney, 1976), social rewards (Ghiselin, 1974), and kin selection (Hamilton, 1964). To the extent that cultural evolution is complementary to organic evolution, as I propose, analogous processes may favor cultural forms of social altruism that actually require no net fitness altruism (see also Durham, n.d.).

Cultural Selection Between Groups

Where the spread of some cultural trait within a group or population can be traced to an individual-level process, the preceding arguments may appear plausible. Problems arise, however, when a trait spreads through a deme or between demes because of some group-level process. Where the selective retention of cultural evolution results from group selection, it is not altogether obvious that individual-level fitness costs and benefits are particularly relevant to understanding changes in the distribution of phenotypes.

As with organic evolution, where an individual- versus group-selection debate has been argued for over a decade, the important question concerns not the possibility of cultural selection at group and higher levels, but rather the relative effectiveness and direction of selection at those levels. When the two processes work in the same direction, either for or against a given cultural variant, there is no problem. They are likely to have complementary and reinforcing effects. Two questions arise, however, when individual- and group-level processes run in opposition. (1) Can group-level cultural selection retain cultural traits advantageous to group reproduction (making it less likely that the group will go extinct or more likely that the group will propagate and colonize), even though they decrease individual inclusive fitness and are therefore altruistic? (2) Can individual-level cultural selection maintain traits advantageous to individuals while simultaneously being detrimental to the group?

Again, a definitive answer is difficult at present because of our general ignorance of the processes behind cultural change and because of the paramount importance of situation-specific variables (like rates of innovation, diffusion, group extinction, etc.) to the outcome. However, if we assume that individual-level selection operates continuously and rapidly when choice is available, it is reasonable to hypothesize that the answer to (1) is negative, in general, judging from parallel arguments in organic evolutionary theory (reviewed in Maynard Smith, 1976). The *origin* of an altruistic phenotype by cultural processes would require that groups be small for there to be, through "cultural drift" or some "founder effect," no alternative phenotype more individually beneficial within the groups to be selected. In addition, the *maintenance* of the altruistic trait would then depend on there being low rates of introduction of alternative "selfish" variants to groups of altruists (as through diffusion, migration, and invention) at the same time as rapid extinction of groups where any selfish variant is found. These conditions may well obtain in special circumstances, and there groups of altruists could prevail. In general, though, group selection is not likely to be the mechanism maintaining the frequency of altruistic cultural traits. Where fitness altruism exists, it is more likely a result of incomplete or impeded individual-level selection, and therefore only a characteristic of certain individuals within a group.

When individual selection is not permitted to function as described above, it is hypothetically possible for group selection to aid in the perpetuation of altruistic cultural attributes. Consider a social system in which force or misinformation may be used by some members of a social group to create a degree of altruism in others that is not likely to result from the operation of individual selection under noncoercive conditions. If that altruism is then put to use to lower the probability of group extinction or raise the probability of group reproduction, group selection could favor that social system, which in turn would perpetrate the coercive practices creating real altruism. A few altruists could be especially effective in group selection by intergroup aggression.

My hypothesis would be that the answer to question (2) is also likely to be negative. In most cases, the long-term reproductive success of an individual human being is dependent upon a stable, functioning social group for any number of group benefits (e.g., increased security or efficiency of resource harvest, defense of resources and progeny). Where these benefits are real and apparent, individual-level cultural selection would act to constrain selfishness to a group-preserving form. This argument implies that cultural selection cannot be seen as leading to some sort of universal adaptive optimization, but rather to relatively beneficial compromises required by group living. In order to obtain the benefits of sociality for self and descendants, an individual must behave in ways that at least do not eliminate some net benefit of sociality for others. Where social benefits are real and apparent, the result of cultural selection would likely be norms, rules and cultural controls on excessively selfish individual behaviors in the interest of preserving group integrity.

That individual- and group-level cultural selection are unlikely to be successful in opposing one another in the long run does not mean that group selection is without important consequences for understanding cultural evolution. As a number of authors have now argued, the *acceleration* of changes made possible by group-level extinction and replacement may be the key to understanding the rapid pace of the evolution of *Homo sapiens* (see discussion in Durham, 1976a). Once a trait like P_m gets established by individual-level cultural selection within a social group, that trait may then give its bearers an advantage as a group in competition with other groups. Group selection may then result, reinforcing the spread of the cultural trait within the population. This form of group selection has the interesting property of conserving or even enhancing the original relative fitness value of the trait for the individual culture carriers.

A Coevolutionary Synthesis

In the preceding sections, I have proposed that processes of cultural selection operating within and between human social groups generally result in the selective retention of cultural traits, including behaviors, that past experience and some degree of prediction suggest to be most advantageous to the inclusive fitnesses of individual members. To the extent that this proposition is valid, cultural selection would remain functionally complementary to natural selection, although there need be no genetic basis to the selected aspects of phenotype. Operationally, the process would also be independent of organic evolution — rendering it thus more rapid, better able to track environmental change or stability, and at times even responsive to perceived human need. At the same time, cultural attributes which evolved in this way could have the interesting property of reducing or eliminating organic selection pressures. Similar phenotypic traits acquired by different genotypes may make the genotypes equally or more equally "fit" (Durham, 1976a). As Dobzhansky (1951) once put it, "The transmission of culture short-circuits biological heredity." On the other hand, cultural change has the opposite potential of creating new and different organic selection pressures (cf. Washburn, 1959 and 1960; Geertz, 1973).

The combination of these features gives reason to believe that cultural selection may account for the origin and maintenance of more forms of human social behavior than do mutation and transgenerational changes in the frequency of presumed behavior genes. It will be seen that this theory of cultural evolution shifts the burden of proof for any explicitly biological basis for adaptive human behaviors over to the sociobiologists. Until we have direct and compelling evidence that a given human behavior has a discrete genetic basis, the demonstration that such behavior has adaptive functions does not by any means prove it to be the product of natural selection. Chances are good that it is partly, largely, or even entirely a product of cultural selection. Biologists interested in human adaptations would therefore do well to make explicit allowance for the cultural mechanism for the transmission of traits in a population.

While distinguishable on the basis of their means of transmission, biological and cultural inheritance by the arguments above would be functionally complementary. Indeed, the biological influences molded by natural selection and the cultural influences molded by cultural selection could easily be confounded in human phenotypes. Consequently, I suggest that models for the evolution of human social behaviors should explicitly integrate both the genetic and the cultural inheritance mechanisms.

Simply stated, my hypothesis is that the selective retention in biological *and* cultural evolution generally favors those attributes which increase, or at least do not decrease, the ability of individual human beings to survive and reproduce in their natural and social environments. This perspective has the advantage of explaining both how human biology and culture can often be adaptive in the same sense (cf. Durham, 1976a), and how they may interact in the evolution of human attributes. In addition, a coevolutionary view can explain the adaptive significance of human social behaviors without forcing them into natural selection models — indeed without forcing *any* separation of the confounded influences of genes and culture.

For the analysis of adaptive patterns in human social behavior I therefore suggest that "Selection" (capital S) be used to refer to the selective retention of differentially advantageous phenotypic traits by the fitness criterion regardless of whether the predominant process is a variety of cultural selection or of natural selection.

A coevolutionary perspective implies that for both biological and cultural reasons the interdependence of individual fitnesses among members of a social group can be viewed as the social glue that holds human (and nonhuman) groups together. It further suggests that the *kinds* of fitness interdependence among individuals (e.g., interdependence based on kinship, control of resources, or exchange of goods and services) and the *relative degree* of interdependencies can be used to define "social structure" in a population. Social structure from this point of view reflects the fact that not all individuals in a social group are interdependent in the same way or to the same degree. Indeed, structural asymmetries in dependence relations can give rise to a degree of manipulative control by some over the behavior of others (Durham, n.d.). In extreme cases, these structural constraints on the adaptations of individuals within society can result in behaviors which appear to require altruistic reproductive sacrifice. I should point out, however, that to those in control, manipulated behaviors may accrue handsome survival and reproduction benefits. For those being manipulated, on the other hand, such behavior can actually be seen as another adaptive compromise required by powerful structural constraints. For this reason, social structure defined by fitness relations deserves to be considered an integral part of an individual's environment. Structural influences on the adaptations of individuals may have major effects upon the joint biocultural evolution of social behaviors within a group.

Human intergroup aggression constitutes a particularly suitable form of social behavior for testing the coevolutionary approach and many of the preceding arguments about biology, culture, and levels of selection. Not only is intergroup warfare commonly held to be dysfunctional for the individual participants, but it is also one of the more obvious mechanisms for high frequency group selection in human organic and cultural evolution. Coevolutionary theory suggests the following hypothesis. Human social behaviors, including intergroup aggression, are generally adaptive (i.e., individual fitness-enhancing) for all participants. Where there are exceptions, so that net reproductive sacrifice is demanded of some or all participants, this is either because of some unusual degree of group selection or because of coercive manipulation within a social system. From this, the need arises to analyze how human intergroup aggression is organized and conducted, paying special attention to the distribution of costs and benefits among the participants.

Elsewhere, I have begun an attempt at such an analysis by comparing aspects of intergroup warfare as waged by members of some "primitive" human societies with models for the coevolution of adaptive intergroup aggression in social groups faced with resource competition (Durham, 1976b and n.d.). The models suggest that "individually sacrificial participation in organized group aggression" may have nonobvious fitness benefits in two ways. First, where human groups compete for limited resources, participants in successful group aggression may themselves directly benefit from the fitness value of resources defended or acquired. The requirements for this to be adaptive are only that the spoils must be shared not throughout the deme but within the group or subgroup of aggressors, so that the fitness value of resources gained by each participant exceeds his or her accumulated costs. Second, intergroup aggression may have circuitous benefits such that when the participants do not each derive direct resource benefits from the conflict, their fitness costs are more than compensated by other benefits from within the group. For this to be adaptive, at least one important figure in the group must secure resource benefits from the war, and the benefactors must provide other goods and/or services upon which the other participants' fitnesses depend. What appears to be the self-sacrificing participation of warriors in this case may actually be an imperative for them to continue receiving other benefits from within the group.

These two models for group aggression suggest that knowledge of group structure (i.e., fitness interdependencies among individuals within the group), of the factors or resources constraining the reproductive success of some or all individuals, and of fitness costs likely to be incurred when rival groups clash, allows the prediction or explanation of group-level human behavior. In both cases, this information gives direct means for predicting the characteristics of groups from the behavior of individuals.

The reinterpretation of ethnographic descriptions of primitive warfare in terms of these models reveals that at least some cases of human intergroup aggression can be seen as biocultural adaptation to conditions of competition for limiting resources. The evidence suggests that to an important extent processes of organic and cultural evolution both result in the selective retention of phenotypic traits that enhance the ability of individual human beings to survive and reproduce in a given environment. This finding calls into question the continued practice of analyzing human social behaviors in terms of natural selection models alone, for such analyses consider only one aspect of what may be truly coevolutionary influences on human social behavior.

Summary and Conclusion

Because the capacity for culture allows human beings to modify aspects of phenotype without any concomitant genotypic change, I have argued that it makes no sense to view the evolution of human attributes, including social behavior, solely in terms of the natural selection models of sociobiology. Instead, I have suggested that a process of "cultural selection" functionally complements natural selection by retaining in time those cultural variants whose net effect best enhances the inclusive fitnesses of individuals. Where cultural selection operates in this way, human phenotypes would then evolve *subject to both biological and cultural influences* in the direction of character states that maximize inclusive fitness under prevailing environmental conditions (for additional discussion, see Durham, 1976 a and b).

As I have argued, this coevolutionary perspective has the advantage of explaining both how human biology and culture are often adaptive in the same sense, and how they may interact in the evolution of human attributes. This theory, moreover, contains an important irony. If cultural differences between human societies are largely the result of individual-level cultural selection for more rather than less adaptive traits (possibly reinforced by a process of group selection), then our capacity for culture is a capacity to reduce or even eliminate many of the organic selection pressures that would have favored the refinements of genetic control required by theories which rely solely on the mechanism of natural selection. Put differently, the operation of cultural selection — what some would call only a "proximate" mechanism — may at times replace and preclude the operation of natural selection — which then cannot be considered the "ultimate" mechanism. In short, this theory can explain the biocultural evolution of human attributes without presuming a genetic basis or predisposition for all adaptive forms. To the extent that humans do behave in ways that maximize their individual inclusive fitnesses, this would suggest that it is generally for both cultural and biological reasons.

This coevolutionary view of human biology and culture may be of help to human ecologists and cultural ecologists who have studied human adaptation but have often failed to identify exactly who benefits from a given practice and how in fact they do benefit. It suggests, for example, a renewed emphasis on individuals and their problems of survival and reproduction in society. This may lead to new interpretations of ethnographic studies which have commonly focused on group-level behaviors. It also suggests new directions for future research. Measures of reproductive success may prove useful both as analytic tools for understanding specific social behaviors and as modeling devices for formulating new research questions. This kind of approach should be most helpful where the "costs" of a given practice can be factored out in terms of time, energy, and resources and where it is possible to detect associated differentials in reproductive benefit. Thus I suggest that coevolutionary analysis is most appropriate in studies of medical anthropology, nutrition and food taboos, human intergroup aggression, population regulation and demography, migration, trade and exchange, and other "high-cost" practices. I believe that the theory is also adequate for predicting its own limitations. Considering the abundance of day-to-day cultural practices which involve little time, energy, or resource cost, I reemphasize that this argument does not say that everything we do is best explained in terms of reproductive success.

The approach suggested here bears some resemblance to recent works by Ruyle (1973), Cloak (1975), Campbell (1975), Richerson and Boyd (in press), and Dawkins (1976, Chapter 11). These authors hypothesize, as I do, that the mechanism of cultural evolution can operate independently of the mechanism of natural selection. But they go further than I go to suggest that the differential replication of cultural attributes is independent of the individual fitness criterion as well. Dawkins, for example, proposes the term "meme" to refer to the basic conceptual unit of cultural transmission; he argues in a fashion similar to the other authors that competition among memes results in a selection process (analogous to natural selection) favoring "memes which exploit their cultural environment to *their own advantage*" (p. 213, emphasis added). Like Dawkins, I believe that it is important to ask what gives memes stability and penetrance in their cultural environment, but unlike Dawkins and the others, I argue that the fate of a meme in its pool usually depends upon the meme's fitness costs and benefits to *carriers*. A coevolutionary perspective does not postulate the gradual and cumulative organic evolution of an organ (the brain) that often functions antagonistically to natural selection. It seems to me that other interpretations do.

In conclusion, instead of prolonging once again the debate of biology versus culture, nature versus nurture, and instinct versus learning, I believe real gains in understanding human social behavior can now be made in several ways. First, we must concentrate our efforts on theories which integrate human biology and culture in the study of human adaptation (see also Durham, 1976b). Again, I suggest that "Selection" (capital S) be used to refer to the selective retention of differentially advantageous phenotypic traits by the fitness criterion regardless of whether the predominant process is a variety of cultural selection or of natural selection. Second, we need to examine the specific processes of selective retention in operation so that more may be learned about the mechanisms of cultural selection within and between groups. This endeavor has the interesting prospect of adding a historical dimension to theories of adaptation, allowing practices observed in the "ethnographic present" to be studied in light of their specific paths of coevolution.

Third, we need to develop theories of transition between organizational levels, so that knowlege of behavior on one level can be used to predict behavior on another level. Paradoxically, in all of this, there is a new danger of overemphasizing individuals as independent entities. Gains will be made when individual-level theorists remember that the adaptations of individuals are not independent, nor dependent solely because of shared genes. The effort to understand the characteristics of groups and social systems beginning with a focus on individuals will need a better theory of "interest group" activities, where interest groups are defined by any form of fitness interdependence, including control of access to strategic resources. Related to this is a need for incorporating social structure into coevolutionary models for human social behavior.

Finally, in addition to any understanding of the present gained by a coevolutionary view of the past, the insights from these endeavors should prove useful as tools for contemporary social change.

References

Alexander, R.D. (1974) "The Evolution of Social Behavior." *Annual Review of Ecology and Systematics* 5:325–383.

_____ . (in press) "Evolution, Human Behavior, and Determinism." *Proc. Phil. Sci.*

Blaney, P.H. (1976) Comment on "Genetic Basis of Behavior — Especially of Altruism." *American Psychologist* 31:358.

Blurton Jones, N.G. (1976) "Growing Points in Human Ethology: Another Link Between Ethology and the Social Sciences?" In P.P.G. Bateson and R.A. Hinde (eds.), *Growing Points in Ethology*. Cambridge: Cambridge University Press, 427–450.

Campbell, D.T. (1965) "Variation and Selective Retention in Sociocultural Evolution." In H.R. Barringer, G.I. Blankstein, and R.W. Mack, (eds.), *Social Change in Developing Areas: A Re-interpretation of Evolutionary Theory*. Cambridge, Mass.: Schenckman, 19–49.

_____ . (1975) "On the Conflicts between Biological and Social Evolution and between Psychology and Moral Tradition." *American Psychologist* 30:1103–1126.

Cloak, F.T. Jr. (1975) "Is a Cultural Ethology Possible?" *Human Ecology* 3, no. 3: 161–182.

_____ . (1977) Comment on "The Adaptive Significance of Cultural Behavior." *Human Ecology* 5, no. 1:49–52.

Dawkins, R. (1976) *The Selfish Gene*. Oxford: Oxford University Press.

Dobzhansky, T. (1951) "Human Diversity and Adaptation." *Cold Spring Harbor Symposium on Quantitative Biology* 15 (1950):385–400.

Durham, W.H. (1976a) "The Adaptive Significance of Cultural Behavior." *Human Ecology* 4, no.2:89–121.

_____ . (1976b) "Resource Competition and Human Aggression, Part I: A Review of Primitive War." *Quarterly Review of Biology* 51, no. 3:385–415.

_____ . (1977) Reply to comments on "The Adaptive Significance of Cultural Behavior." *Human Ecology* 5, no. 1:59–68.

_____ . (n.d.) "Resource Competition and Human Aggression, Part II: Dependence and Manipulation." Unpublished manuscript.

Geertz, C. (1973) *The Interpretation of Cultures*. New York: Basic Books.

Ghiselin, M.T. (1974) *The Economy of Nature and the Evolution of Sex*. Berkeley: University of California Press.

Hamilton, W.D. (1964) "The Genetical Evolution of Social Behavior." *Journal of Theoretical Biology* 7:1–52.

Harner, M.J., ed. (1973) *Hallucinogens and Shamanism*. New York: Oxford Press.

Kaplan, D., and R.A. Manners. (1972) *Culture Theory*. Englewood Cliffs, N.J.: Prentice-Hall.

Laughlin, C.D., and E.G. d'Aquili. (1974) *Biogenetic Structuralism*. New York: Columbia University Press.

LeVine, R.A. (1973) *Culture, Behavior, and Personality*. Chicago: Aldine.

Maynard Smith, J. (1976) "Commentary: Group Selection." *Quarterly Review of Biology* 51, no. 2:277–283.

Richerson, P.J., and R. Boyd. (In press) "A Dual Inheritance Model of the Human Evolutionary Process." *Journal of Human and Social Biology.*

Ruyle, E.E. (1973) "Genetic and Cultural Pools: Some Suggestions for a Unified Theory of Biocultural Evolution." *Human Ecology* 1, no. 3:201–215.

————— . (1977) Comment on "The Adaptive Significance of Cultural Behavior." *Human Ecology* 5, no. 1:53–55.

Sahlins, M. (1976) *The Use and Abuse of Biology.* Ann Arbor: University of Michigan Press.

Seligman, M. (1971) "Phobias and Preparedness." *Behavior Therapy* 2:307–320.

Simpson, G.G. (1972) "The Evolutionary Concept of Man," in B. Campbell (ed.), *Sexual Selection and the Descent of Man.* Chicago: Aldine, 17–39.

Trivers, R.L. (1971). "The Evolution of Reciprocal Altruism." *Quarterly Review of Biology* 46:35.

Washburn, S.L. (1959) "Speculations on the Interrelations of Tools and Biological Evolution," in J.M. Spuhler (ed.), *The Evolution of Man's Capacity for Culture.* Detroit: Wayne State University Press, 21–31.

————— . (1960) "Tools and Human Evolution." *Sci. Am.* 203:63–75.

West Eberhard, M. J. (1975) "The Evolution of Social Behavior by Kin Selection." *Quarterly Review of Biology* 50, no. 1:1–33.

Williams, G.C. (1966) *Adaptation and Natural Selection.* Princeton: Princeton University Press.

7

Human Behavior and the Behavior of Other Animals

S. L. Washburn

Over the last few years there has been a great increase of interest in animal behavior. This started with popular books, articles, and television programs. Concern with the environment and ecology played a part. The airplane greatly increased opportunities for travel, both for the individual and the television camera. Popular books came first, well before the popularity of animal-behavior courses became evident on the campus. Robert Ardrey's (1961) *African Genesis* was particularly influential, but it was years later before textbooks on animal behavior were available in quantity. For example, the texts by John Alcock, Jerram Brown, Irenäus Eibl-Eibesfeldt (second edition), and Edward O. Wilson all appeared in 1975. I stress the popular roots because the apparently sudden interest in animal behavior cannot be understood if the academic scene is considered in isolation. Before World War II there was almost no interest in the naturalistic behavior of the nonhuman primates, and the late C. R. Carpenter was deeply disappointed by the reception that his monographs on the behavior of the howler monkey (Carpenter, 1934) and the gibbon (Carpenter, 1940) received.

Many of the popular books—particularly those by Robert Ardrey (1961), Desmond Morris (1967), and Konrad Lorenz (*On Aggression*, 1963)—stressed the importance of animal behavior and evolution in the understanding of human behavior. This emphasis is carried to an extreme in sociobiology and may account both for the great interest in and the resistance to this science. As I see the situation, animal behavior is both fun and science. It is fascinating to learn of the language of the bees, of pheromones, of factors guiding migration in birds and fish, and of the life of the penguin or the world of the herring gull. The emphasis on experiments in recent studies of behavior led to unex-

This article originally appeared in the *American Psychologist*, 33: 5 (May 1978), pp. 405–418. The references have been put into a slightly altered format. Copyright © 1978 by the American Psychological Association. Reprinted by permission.

pected advances, but the studies were fragmented, and there was little emphasis on theory, social behavior, or evolution. Wilson's *Sociobiology* provided a new emphasis, synthesis, and theoretical foundation; it added the excitement of the promise of a new science. If *Ethology* (Eibl-Eibesfeldt, 1975) and *Sociobiology* (Wilson, 1975), both of which appeared in the same year, are contrasted, the new emphasis may be clearly seen.

It might be helpful if a science historian would record these changes in the study of animal behavior while they are still in progress and while the relevant people are alive — the various factors might now be sorted out in a way that will not be possible many years hence. My opinion is that the speed of acceptance of sociobiology shows the need for some such theory, shows that the need is evident in our whole climate of opinion — both popular and scientific, and shows that the controversies of the last two years cannot be understood in terms of the progress of science alone.

Animal behavior is worthy of study in its own right, even if it were never applied to human beings, but the present controversies stem from the use of animal behavior to understand human behavior. The descriptions of the sociobiological controversies in *BioScience* (Sociobiology Study Group of Science for the People, 1976) and *Science* (Wade, 1976) show this to be the case. The accounts in *Time* ("Why You Do What You Do," 1977) and *Psychology Today* (Morris, 1977) indicate a strong popular interest in biological interpretations of human behavior, a thesis with a long history in western European culture.

In the briefest terms, sociobiology is a theory that seeks "to develop general laws of the evolution and biology of social behavior" and to extend such laws to the study of human beings (Wilson 1977b:xiv). It builds on natural selection in its modern form (the synthetic theory, shaped by about 1940), with emphasis on behavior (fully stated by Roe and Simpson, 1958), and adds the theory of kin selection (Hamilton, 1975). Natural selection states that the biology that leaves the most offspring is favored; kin selection shows that altruistic behavior may also be selected for, if it benefits individuals closely related to the altruist. This added element makes possible a much closer fit between evolutionary theory and social behavior — and it is this application to a wide variety of human behaviors that has caused the reaction.

The issues are complex, arising in part from the extreme claims of sociobiology and in part from the long history of biological science that has confused and retarded the development of the social sciences. While sociobiology is new, especially in its enthusiasm and emphasis on social behavior, it also continues a history of scientific error. When applied to human behavior, it renews the mistakes of social Darwinism, early evolutionism, eugenics, and racial interpretations of history. To defend its position sociobiology must (a) attack social science, (b) minimize the difference be-

tween learning and inheritance, and (c) postulate genes for a very odd assort-
ment of behaviors—altruism, cheating, spite, deception, creativity, and
reciprocity, to mention only a few.

Postulating genes for behaviors, the most controversial part of the application of the theory, appears to repeat the mistakes of the eugenicists, who postulated genes for alcoholism, crime, and other behaviors of which they did not ap-
prove. Medawar and Medawar (1977: 38) have described this kind of thinking
as "geneticism," which they define as "the enthusiastic misapplication of not fully
understood genetic principles in situations to which they do not apply."

So sociobiology may be described as new, challenging, and destined to
dominate the future thinking of both biological and social science, or it may be
described as mostly old and given to repeating errors of the past. As shown by
statements in the press and in reviews in magazines and journals, emotions
are deeply involved in this controversy. When this is the case, I think of Paul
MacLean's (1970:337) statement:

> Emotional cerebration appears to have the paradoxical capacity to find equal
> support for opposite sides of any question. It is particularly curious that in scien-
> tific discourse, as in politics, the emotions seem capable of standing on any plat-
> form. Different groups of reputable scientists, for example, often find themselves
> in altercation because of diametrically opposed views of what is true. Although
> seldom commented on, it is equally bewildering that the world order of science is
> able to live comfortably for years, and sometimes centuries, with beliefs that a
> new generation discovers to be false.

In this situation, particularly because of the deep popular interest, there will
be no simple solution to the conflicts. What I hope to do is present a series of
examples that may clarify some issues. In the interest of brevity, the examples
have to be oversimplified, and I hope you will bear with me as I strive for both
accuracy and condensation.

Behavior of the Apes

In the latter part of the 19th century, the behavior of the great apes was the
starting point in many evolutionary sequences. There were scientific controversies over promiscuity, monogamy, and many other issues. A very large
number of papers had been written, and Yerkes and Yerkes (1929) compiled a
major summary (over 500 references) in *The Great Apes*. Yerkes and Yerkes
concluded (p. 590): "As one reflects on the situation it appears first incredible,
then ludicrous, that as professional scientists we should depend on accident instead of intelligently planned and prearranged conditions for the extension of
knowledge and the solution of significant problems." But is it not even more
ludicrous, in retrospect, that the nature of ape behavior and its relation to

human behavior was debated for more than 100 years before there were any reliable data? Robert Yerkes was a major figure in promoting field studies and, though a careful investigator, concluded that the social unit of chimpanzees "is undoubtedly the family" (p. 541), and that gibbons lived in herds of up to 50 animals. C. R. Carpenter and subsequent field-workers have shown that the social unit of gibbons is a male-female pair. Even Yerkes, when he described the situation as "ludicrous," could not believe that the data were as ridiculous as they really were. A comparison of the social behavior of Bigfoot and the Abominable Snowman would be as useful for the study of human evolution!

There are at least three reasons why scientists accepted accounts of the behaviors of the great apes long before there were any reliable data: (1) Animal behavior was considered to be simple and instinctive—therefore anecdotes, stories by local people, and travelers' tales were considered useful. Hunters particularly were credited with knowing a great deal about animals. (2) The theory of evolution so dominated science and popular opinion that the misinformation had to be put in an evolutionary context. The behaviors of highly diversified animals were put in a few simplified stages. (3) There was so much faith in the power of the theory of evolution that it was believed that the theory could compensate for research and careful verification of information. But a theory is only a license for research. Natural selection, a great advance over theories of special creation or evolution by acquired characters, is an advance only because it guides research into more productive channels. There is no way in which the theory of natural selection can substitute for careful research on the behaviors of the animals under consideration.

The beginning of reliable studies on the natural behavior of the great apes may be marked by George Schaller's (1963) study of the gorilla and Jane Goodall's (1968) long-continued investigations of the chimpanzee. The results of these studies are facts of an entirely different order from the anecdotes of the last century. The traditional gorilla was a fearsome beast, but, of course, he was a wounded gorilla facing a brave hunter—a vision the 19th century wanted. It was replaced by the perception of the peaceful gorilla and the friendly chimpanzee, views stemming from the conditions of the early fieldwork and the human desires of the 1960s. Today chimpanzees are seen as aggressive, territorial, dominance-seeking animals; they have been observed in an act involving the killing and eating of an infant chimpanzee from another group (Goodall, 1977). Gorillas fight and on occasion may also kill other gorillas—they too have been observed eating a young gorilla. Audiences who heard talks by Dian Fossey in 1977 were upset by her description of gorilla violence. In her talk at the Leakey Foundation, Galkidas-Brindamour (1977) noted that all old male orangutans have scars and signs of past battles, presumably from struggles with other orangutans. This view of the apes is contrary to the present climate of opinion, and it will be interesting to see how the conflict between behavioral fact and popular desire is mediated.

Goodall and Hamburg (1975) have summarized the evidence for using the chimpanzee as a model for the behavior of early man. The quality and quantity of the information is impressive compared to that in earlier accounts, but the facts still depend on the fieldwork of a very few people in a few localities. It is still uncertain how much additional fieldwork will be necessary before chimpanzee social behavior and ecology are adequately understood. Even less is known about the behaviors of the gorilla and orangutan, so although the data are vastly better than was the case when Yerkes and Yerkes wrote *The Great Apes*, human understanding of these primates is still very much in process. Even with the aid of comparative anatomy, the fossil record, and data from the study of captive animals, major problems remain, and it will be some years before intellectually satisfying comparisons between human behaviors and those of our nearest relatives will be possible.

An example may make the issues clearer. Sociobiologists have revived the old theory that the loss of estrous behaviors in human females is a major factor in giving rise to the human family. The human family has been described as a "pair-bond" whose consistency may be aided by the loss of estrus (Barash, 1977b:293, 295, 297). Ronald Nadler (1977), however, describes the shortest estrus and the greatest limitation of mating behaviors in the gorilla — the most continuously social of the great apes. Orangutans will mate at any time because the males mate whether the females are in estrus or not; yet the orangutans are the most solitary of the great apes. Gibbons form lasting pair-bonds but are the least sexually active of the apes. Further, many monkeys have restricted mating seasons, but the social group continues throughout the year, as in rhesus monkeys (Lindburg, 1977). Maximum fighting among males occurs during the mating season, and many monkeys may be killed (Wilson & Boelkins, 1970).

The idea that sexual attraction is responsible for the existence of the social group in nonhuman primates and for the family in man is appealing. It is simple and easily stated, and in our culture, biological explanations are regarded as more scientific than social ones; but the sexual attraction theory of society does not fit the data — even in the case of our closest relatives. Whether monthly or yearly cycles are considered, social systems continue to function. The importance of sex as *the* binding mechanism is an idea that comes from nineteenth-century European culture, just as the lack-of-estrus–monogamy theory comes from a simplistic view of our culture. Social organization is the most important adaptive mechanism, and sex adds a wide variety of attractive or disruptive behaviors. Adequate data are only now becoming available in 1977, although the subject has been discussed for over 100 years.

As far as the field data go, male-female relations in nonhuman primates may vary from near-promiscuity, to consort relations of varying duration, to lifelong pair-bonds. The interpretation of such relations is complex, and the behavioral classification is only a first step. In the case of gibbons, which do form lasting male-female pairs, the interpretation of the pattern, at a minimum, involves factors of locomotion, territory, diet, teeth, calls, aggression, and the brain (Washburn, Hamburg, & Bishop, 1974). In even this simplest case of a primate social system, adaptation is complex, and a great deal of additional research has to be done before anyone can have much confidence in the interpretation.

Sociobiologists reduce human social behaviors—the extraordinary variety of human male–female customs—to monogamy, or, even worse, pair-bonding, but even the word *monogamy* does not stand for any clearly defined behaviors that could have a genetic base. Monogamy may mean a continuing relationship, a temporary one, or it may be modified by all sorts of extensions and exceptions that have biological consequences (concubines, slaves, mistresses), and these are combined with the widest sort of variation in economic, social, and sexual practices.

The term *polygamy* is open to similar but even greater objections. It may refer to the marriage of one man to more than one woman, or to the marriage of one woman to more than one man. The number of polygamous arrangements in human societies is exceedingly large and must have a variety of genetic consequences. The important point about human monogamy or polygamy is that these terms refer to systems of marriage, not mating. Mating can and does occur outside of marriage in every known society; marriage is a socially recognized arrangement involving rights and duties and encompasses far more than sexual behavior. This fundamental difference between the traditional and reciprocal customs of humans and the mating behaviors of other animals appears to be totally ignored by animal behaviorists. The use of such words by sociobiologists shows a total misunderstanding of social science. Even ape behavior is far too complicated to be analyzed by labels and guessing.

Sociobiologists speak of parental investment as if this were something that could be predicted on the basis of genetics, but, to take but a single illustration, note how different parental investment was in the pastoral Masai culture and in the France of a century ago, where maintaining the small farm was critical. Customs are imbedded in complex social patterns, and it is the patterns that must be compared if the customs are to be understood.

Molecular Taxonomy

One area in which there has been great progress is in the classification of the primates. Recent progress in the study of biochemical evolution (DNA, sequence data, and immunology—reviewed by numerous authors in Goodman & Tashian, 1976) shows that humans, chimpanzees, and gorillas form a very closely related group. Orangutans are considerably less closely related, and Old World monkeys are far less similar. These relationships, futilely debated for many years, are in my opinion now settled, and I believe that a quantitative molecular taxonomy will be a major factor in providing a framework for comparative studies. King and Wilson (1975:108) conclude that "the sequences of human and chimpanzee polypeptides examined to date are, on the average, more than 99% identical."

Polypeptides evolve at different rates, but the rates are relatively constant for each kind of polypeptide. Therefore, it is possible to estimate, from the molecular data, the times at which various lineages separated (Wilson, Carlson, & White, 1977). The procedures are still controversial, but I think it will be possible to estimate divergence times more accurately from the biochemistry than from the fossil record—particularly in the case of groups, such as the primates, for which the fossil record is fragmentary.

Speech

Studies about the communication of many mammals, birds, and insects have revived interest in the old and important problem of the origin of talking. The studies of ape communication have been particularly exciting and have opened a new area for scientific investigation. All of these studies raise fundamental issues on the meaning of words and the nature of comparison and evolution.

Human speech is based on a phonetic code, a system in which short, meaningless sounds (phonemes) are combined into meaningful units (morphemes, words). This system has the characteristic of codes in general—a relatively small number of units may be combined in an almost infinite number of ways. So the human-sound code system of communication is open, and even with the needs of modern science, no limit has been approached.

The behavioral problem has three aspects: (1) to understand the human system, (2) to compare it, and (3) to speculate on its evolution. If we proceed in this manner, the first discovery is that the phonetic code is unique to our species. There is no comparable behavior in any other primate, or any other animal for that matter. Apes cannot be taught to talk in spite of great efforts (Kellogg, 1968). R. Allen and Beatrice Gardner and those who have followed their lead have wisely shifted from communication by sounds to a different anatomical system. Speech, however, is the primary form of human communcation, and if the aim is to understand speech, the phonetic code is the issue—the power to generate new words to meet any need stems from the code.

It should be remembered that the phonetic code is not obvious. Words appear to be the important and meaningful units, and when people started to write, the first form of writing used signs for words. This requires an enormous number of signs, whether in writing or in gesturing. It took some 2,000 years for the people in the Near East to find that a few letters symbolizing sounds could do the job of thousands of hieroglyphs. Millions of man-years have been wasted because the phonetic code was not obvious. The Chinese had to learn more than 10,000 characters instead of two dozen letters. And the spelling of English is a reminder that many still do not understand the phonetic code—every schoolchild wastes countless hours memorizing spellings that should have been discarded long ago.

Some years ago, David Hamburg (1963) made the point that behaviors that have been important in the evolution of a species are easy for the members of that species to learn. That is, selection of the successful behavior led to selection for its biological base, so that, over time, the behavior became both more effective and easier to learn. Languages are easy for humans to learn—but such learning is impossible for other primates. Clearly, evolution has produced a biological base that makes this learning so easy for humans. In both New and Old World monkeys, the characteristic sounds of the species may be elicited by stimulation of the limbic system near the midline (Ploog, 1970; Robinson, 1967, 1976). Extensive removal of cortex does not affect sounds and affects facial expression only slightly (Myers, 1968). The anatomical evidence has been reviewed by Myers (1976), and it has been shown that in humans, the primitive system is still present, but the cortex has become very important in both speech and facial expression and provides the biological basis for learning in both.

In summary, the view briefly presented here is (a) that the phonetic code is the basis for the success of human communication, although supplemented by gestures, postures, and facial expression, (b) that easily learning the code is made possible by the brain, and (c) that some evolution in the articulatory mechanisms is involved. If this brief outline is accepted (at least for the moment), it may be used to illustrate some of the problems of comparing the behavior of human beings and nonhuman primates. There are several points:

1. Comparisons must start with human behavior, or reductionism is almost certain. The only way we know that a phonetic code exists is through studying human beings. If the study begins with monkey communication, for example, it can be observed that monkeys make some two or three dozen sounds (Struhsaker, 1967, 1975), and it can be speculated that more sounds will lead to speech. The monkey system of communication, however, uses both gestures and sounds in combination (Lancaster, 1975). The gestures are almost always more important, and when the sounds are separated and treated as an independent system, the monkey communication system is, in fact, destroyed. It is a very human bias

that sounds should be so important or should constitute a separable mode of communication.

2. There has been an enormous amount of description and speculation, but very few experiments form the base for contrasting the limbic control in monkeys with the cortical control in our species. The critical experiments have not been performed with apes, but judging from learning, the structure of their natural communications will be like that of monkeys. The issue is that there are really two kinds of comparisons. First, sounds may be compared in all sorts of creatures. This has been done by Thorpe (1972) using 16 design features. This is fun—it calls attention to a wide variety of communicative behaviors—but if the purpose is thorough understanding of a particular comparison, it is essential to analyze the biological base experimentally. The weakness in the outline presented above lies in the experiments; there have not been enough comprehensive studies done on enough primates.

3. In the analysis of almost any particular problem, the evolutionary order should be considered last. More is known about human beings than about other animals; if comparisons start with our species, the problems are more likely to be usefully stated. It is almost inconceivable that, starting with the extraordinary diversity of human behavior, the human family would be called a "pair-bond." The fossil record and archeology are essential to give a perspective on time and the diversity of previous forms. But the record is very incomplete, and the study of evolution involves uncertain reconstruction and the evaluation of many different opinions.

4. There is a biological basis for speech. It is the human brain that learns language, but there is no evidence that the brain determines the particular language learned. Any normal human being learns the language of its group, and a second if necessary. This may be the clearest example of the nature of many biosocial problems. The biology is basic—it sets limits, gives probabilities, and quite possibly accounts for some linguistic universals. But the freedom of learning is immense, and constraints are primarily in the learned systems, not in the biology.

In Africa there were hundreds of mutually unintelligible human languages in an area in which baboons used the same system of communication. There were over 100 tribal groups in what is now Tanzania (Bienen, 1970), an area in which there is no evidence for any major behavioral differences in baboons.

The ease with which human languages are learned and the speed with which they change distinguish the behavior of *Homo sapiens* in a way that is characteristic of no other species. In the nonhuman primates there may be minor regional differences in communication, just as there are dialects in birds, but nothing comparable to the diversity of human languages. Language is probably the best example of a common biological base facilitating the learning of an extraordinary variety of behaviors.

Fashions have moved back and forth on the nature-nurture problem. Traditional social scientists stress learning. The sociobiologists attack the distinction, pointing out that both are always present. From a practical point of view, this is not one problem; some behaviors may be largely genetically determined, and for others the environment may be important. Granted basic human biology, there is no evidence for any genetic determination of any particular language.

Language is the behavior that distinguishes human social behavior from the social behavior of the other primates. As the child learns the language of its group, it learns how this system of communication is used in social relations and in economic, political, and religious systems. The social systems of nonhuman primates are based on the biology of the species, observational learning, and interaction. To these the human species adds the social complexity made possible by brain, language, and technical advance. Viewed in this way, biology supports two of the most fundamental assumptions of the social sciences — that human populations, not individuals, have the same behavioral potentials, and that social systems are not determined by the basic human biology. This, then, is the reason sociobiologists and others seeking genetic explanations of human social behavior *must* minimize the difference between learning and inheritance (nurture and nature) and attack the notion that social facts should be explained by other social facts (Wilson, 1977a).

It is language (cognition, speech, articulatory mechanisms) that gives the nature-nurture, genetic-learning controversy a wholly new dimension in human behavior. There is no comparable mechanism, nor any alternative biological system, that allows almost unlimited communication and the development of new symbols when needed.

Social science might be defined as the science that studies the nature, complexity, and effectiveness of linguistically mediated behaviors. Such a definition clearly shows why human social behaviors cannot be reduced to those of other animals, even those of our closest living relatives. Or, alternatively, if one puts the matter positively, it is the evolution of new structures in the human brain that forms the basis for learning language (speech and cognition); so the uniqueness of human behavior may be defined behaviorally or by the biology that makes the behaviors possible. The significance of the biology can only be seen by comparing the behavior of the animals to that of humans. In the primates, the difference is reflected in communication systems that range from one that may be described in a very few pages to one that is only partially described in dictionaries thousands of pages long.

As Alexander (1974:376) has stated, "human social groups represent an almost ideal model for potent selection at the group level." The reason for this is that human groups adapt through knowledge and organization, both of which depend on speech. Knowledge and organization are properties of groups and are transmitted from generation to generation by learning, not genes.

Knowledge and organization, dependent on speech and intelligence, make possible technical progress. The differences between the simplest sort of hut and a modern high-rise building are the result of purposeful human effort, not blind chance. Possibly the greatest difference between biological evolution (changes in gene frequencies over time) and history (human learned behavior over time) is that biological evolution depends on mutations (producing variation that is edited by natural selection), while technical progress is the result of intelligent purpose.

Walking

In discussing the biological basis for speaking, the analysis is limited to comparisons of living creatures. In spite of many ingenious attempts, no way has been found to prove what kind of communication characterized our earliest ancestors. In the case of walking, there is a substantial fossil record, and bipedalism was present more than 3 million years ago. At that time, our ancestors had brains no larger than those of the contemporary apes (Washburn, 1959). The teeth were very human in form, and these early men (genus *Australopithecus*) had probably been using tools extensively for some millions of years, although the earliest stone tools do not appear in the record until 2.5 million years ago (Isaac, Harris, & Crader, 1976). It appears that the evolution of a new pattern of locomotion was the behavioral event that led to the separation of human beings and apes, and this may well have been in a feedback relation with object-using and hunting. The fossil record allows the determination of an order that could not be deduced from the study of the contemporary forms. It is likely that the conclusion of greatest psychological interest is that the large human brain evolved late—millions of years after the separation of man and ape. The human brain is unique because it evolved in response to the selection pressures of the latest phases of human evolution.

However, the fossils alone would give very little indication of the magnitude of the changes correlated with the new locomotor patterns. Not only did the bones change, but there was major reorganization in the muscles, far more than might be inferred from the bones. So interpreting the differences in the locomotion of human beings and apes involves three kinds of comparisons.

First, the behaviors of the contemporary animals show what they actually do. Second, study of the fossils puts a time scale and order into the comparison. Third, analysis of the structure and function of the contemporary forms shows how complex the changes were. Since human locomotion is far better understood than that of any other animal, and because it is in many ways unique, it is useful to start the comparisons with what is now known about human beings, then to shift to comparisons with other animals, and finally to resort to the essential but always incomplete fossil record. The observation of behavior (for example, knuckle walking in the chimpanzee and human bipedal locomotion) gives no information on the very extensive internal anatomical reorganization that makes the behavioral differences possible. To the extent that locomotion is an essential part of human behavior, there cannot be an independent study of behavior, a study independent of major efforts to understand the internal mechanisms that are the basis for the externally viewed behaviors.

Through the process of natural selection, evolution produced a complex structural-anatomical base that makes human bipedal locomotion possible; yet the behavior has to be learned and it takes a child years to walk and run efficiently. Much has been made of the fact that it takes years to learn to speak—but motor learning takes equally long. In both cases the child wants to learn, and, under normal circumstances, learning cannot even be prevented. The basis for walking is common to the whole human species, and although there are minor anatomical variations, all human populations share the structures that make learning to walk, run, etc., possible. It is clear that there is a major, genetically determined biology that separates humans from all other kinds of animals, although nothing is known of the genes involved.

This situation for walking (structural base, propensity to learn, important unique behavior) may be contrasted with that for swimming. Apes cannot swim (Wind, 1976), and most humans never learn to swim. There is a biological base for swimming, but the structure of the arms (primarily the result of the arboreal life) and of the legs (evolved for walking on land) makes human swimming a peculiar, new activity that is not the result of evolution. Granted human intelligence, some humans may learn to use arms and legs in a variety of ways that may lead to swimming. There has not been selection for swimming; no genes different from those involved in other human adaptations are required. The behavior simply uses structures that evolved as parts of different functional-behavioral complexes.

This example shows that even when behaviors are based on well-understood biology, it is not possible to infer that special genes are correlated with the behaviors. Obviously, human hands may learn a very wide variety of behaviors, although the basic biology of bones, joints, and muscles is the same. Further, it should be noted that human beings elaborate on everything. People do not just walk and run; they hop, skip, dance, jump, and race. The same basic biology makes all these behaviors possible. Likewise, people may swim in many different ways, and there is no evidence that the elaborations are based on biological differences. The social sciences assume basic human biology and are concerned with the extraordinary variety of behaviors that may be learned. Human biology is primarily concerned with understanding the common biological base. The biological differences between individuals may be important in medicine and psychiatry or in achievement, but individual biological difference is rarely important to the social sciences.

Evolution

Evolution is a master theory. For a long time it dominated both social and biological science and it became a part of the general climate of opinion. It was influential in rationalizing the nineteenth-century world and proving that its customs were justified by a Darwinism that now seems more like a religion than a theory guiding research. Mayr (1972) has shown that it was difficult for people to accept the theory of evolution because it directly affected custom and belief. Once accepted, however, the theory dominated a very large part of human thought. As noted earlier, the original theory of natural selection was strengthened by the discovery of the genetic mechanisms, clarified as formulated in the synthetic theory, and further strengthened by the addition of kin selection. The theory has been clearly stated recently by numerous authors—Alexander (1974), Barash (1977a, 1977b), Hamilton (1975), and Wilson (1975), to mention only four who have particularly related the theory to the evolution of behavior and sociobiology. Present controversies stem not from the theory but from its applications and, particularly, from its applications to human behavior.

In simplified form, the issue is that the sociobiologists are so confident of the power of evolutionary theory that they think their conclusions must be accepted, or at least accepted with minor modification.

Hamilton (1975:150), a leader in the development of the genetic theory of kin selection, concludes that because benefits to fitness will not go to relatives in large societies, that "civilization probably slowly reduces its altruism of all kinds, including the kinds needed for cultural creativity." The absurd conclusion is a correct deduction from the evolutionary theory. It simply proves that the theory is useless when applied to the interpretation of learned behaviors and recent human history. There is no evidence that civilization reduces altruism—quite the contrary—and there is every evidence that cultural creativity is greatly increased. In his 1975 paper, Hamilton raises the fundamental issues by combining the latest genetic evolutionary theory with an application to human evolution that could have been written 100 years ago. No matter how powerful the theory of evolution, there is no way to go directly from the theory to the interpretation of human behaviors. The theory guides research. It does not provide conclusions.

The problems caused by the overconfidence in evolutionary theory may be illustrated by an example from archeology. The stone tools made by the Neanderthals were ordered by archeologists into several evolutionary stages, but when the assemblages of stone tools were dated by independent methods, some of the supposed states proved to be contemporary. The "stages" may represent different cultural adaptation or, perhaps, only fashions. The reality of earlier traditions (Acheulian) was even more distorted by being arranged in orders from simple to complex without regard to the actual associations and order in the ground. Interest in evolution stimulated interest in archeology, but the science would have progressed far more rapidly if scholars had never heard of the theory of evolution and had been forced to determine the actual sequences of the stone tools rather than placing them in arbitrary evolutionary sequences.

Just as no facts on ape behavior were needed to make the evolutionary reconstructions, so no archeological facts were needed to understand the history of cultures. Even more dramatically and disastrously, the theory of evolution was thought to be so compelling that it gave people confidence to arrange anecdotes, travelers' tales, and trivial information into social sequences that never existed. The evolutionary orders were, in part, the creation of scholars, but they were accepted because they fitted the social and political climate of the nineteenth century. In the order Savagery, Barbarism, Civilization, one can guess where monotheism, monogamy, and European customs will be placed! As noted earlier, the acceptance of conclusions may be a far better guide to intellectual and social reality than the supposed proofs. Theories are necessary guides to research, but an accepted theory (such as the theory of evolution based on natural selection) may be a terrible liability if misapplied. All the prestige of the theory then supports the mistakes.

For example, Wilson (1975:551) gives rules for the reconstruction of phylogenies of behavior from the behavior of contemporary animals. The rules were derived from comparative anatomy, developed before there were many fossils, and they are the very part of comparative anatomy that does not work — or at least works only to a very limited extent. These are the rules that were used to create the missing links, but none of the reconstructed links looked like the fossils that were actually found. When people, both laymen and scientists, wanted missing links, they made them. As regards human behavioral evolution, there are fossils and a rich archeological record, but no way that the actual historical past can be deduced from the present. At one time it was believed that the brain evolved early and led in human evolution, but the record shows that bipedal locomotion evolved some millions of years before large human brains. While the evidence is less clear, it is probable that tool-using and hunting also preceded large brains by many hundreds of thousands of years. It is more useful to regard our brains as products of human evolution rather than as causes. Obviously, the brain and behavior were in a feedback relation.

To suggest that the evolution of human behavior should be reconstructed from the behavior of contemporary peoples is particularly unfortunate for two reasons. First, this is precisely what was done in the nineteenth century, and this is what created the mistaken sequences. We have lived through those mistakes. Second, in addition to written history, there is now a great deal of archeology that carries the direct evidences for human behavior back many thousands of years.

When people anatomically like ourselves (*Homo sapiens*) appear in the fossil record, history accelerated to a remarkable degree. Geographically, people crossed water and arrived in Australia. They conquered the Arctic and arrived in the New World. The development of boats, harpoons, fishing, bow and arrow, and many other behaviors are reflected in the record. Lenski and Lenski (1974, especially on p. 131) give a very useful review of the technical advances. The end of this era is marked by the domestication of the dog, one of the many indications of the cultural similarity of all the late populations of *Homo sapiens*.

In contrast to the earlier changes, measured in times of hundreds of thousands of years, these late changes do not seem to correlate with biological evolution, or at least not in any simple way. It appears from the record that, granted the basic biology of our species, learning was the dominant factor in determining behavior, even 30,000–40,000 years ago. Putting the matter somewhat differently, human cognitive abilities, speech, and social systems — that is, human nature as we know it today — had fully evolved before 30,000 years ago.

If this point of view is accepted, then the background to Cohen's (1977) major reappraisal of the origins of agriculture is the basic biology of *Homo sapiens* and the cultural consequences of this kind of biological organization.

With agriculture, a series of changes follow that affect the application of the theory of natural selection to human behavior. The more people there are, the more mobility, the more knowledge, and the more technology; and the shorter the time span, the less will genetic factors be important in determining human behaviors. With agriculture, human populations expanded *at least* 200 times, and history is full of documentation of trade with distant places, migrations, and wars. Sociobiologists clearly recognize that their view of the evolution of society depends on acts benefiting relatives (Hamilton, 1975) and that this becomes increasingly improbable as the conditions of the world changed after the agricultural revolution.

Ethology has been so important in the development of studies of animal behavior that a brief mention is essential, even though its distinctive characteristics are disappearing and it is merging into a much more general study of animal behavior (Bateson & Hinde, 1976). The genius of ethology was not the study of natural behavior; it was the design of imaginative experiments analyzing the behavior. Ethologists devised methods for determining what the animal was responding to, and this led to a science far from the early anthropomorphic studies of animal behavior. Unfortunately, these behavioral experiments led to postulating physiological mechanisms rather than to further experimentation. Interestingly, Barash (1977b:6) severely criticizes their methods, but later (p. 277) he praises human ethologists for using precisely the same methods! Surely the concepts that are inadequate for animals with relatively simple nervous systems will be even worse when applied to speaking, culture-bearing human beings.

Human ethology, a growing and enthusiastically supported branch of the field, is based on the direct observation of behavior, free of experimental intervention. *Human ethology might be defined as the science that pretends humans cannot speak.* Even infants respond to sounds long before they can talk, and mothers live in cultures where the customs, including how to take care of children, are transmitted in large part by speaking. A long history shows that the problems of human behavior that can be effectively studied by observation alone are very limited. Clearly, this is an extreme case of the study of human behavior being limited by the drawing up of the rules on the basis of the behavior of other animals. As noted before, a rich study of *human behavior must start off with human beings*; otherwise, critical behaviors are lost. Human ethology is an extreme example of a science not adjusting to uniquely human problems.

The human cortex is far more important in controlling human facial expression than is the case in monkeys. A minimum of experimental and clinical information suggests that human expressions are not reducible to a small number of biologically controlled, universal kinds. The ethological emphasis on classification rather than on internal biological structure precludes the possibility of usefully comparing human facial expressions with those of the nonhuman primates.

Ethologists often compare the behavior of highly diversified animals to that of human beings, often to the behavior of a single tribe. This mode of comparison (aggression in insects, fish, birds, lions, wolves, apes) is interesting. It raises questions. I like Michael Chance's expression that the comparison *alerts* us to possibilities. But it is not proof.

Lorenz (1963) concluded, after reviewing aggressive behaviors in a number of animals, that "the main function of sport today lies in the cathartic discharge of aggressive urge" (p. 280). The conclusion is based on mistaken physiology, and Lorenz has been criticized for his conclusions in *On Aggression*. The point is that the problem is *the method*, not the particular book. Animal behavior is extraordinarily diversified, and almost any thesis may be defended if an author is free to select the behavior of any animal that supports the contention of the moment.

Students of animal behavior feel free to use the behaviors of nonhuman species when making points about human behavior. For example, in a recent book, the chapter on human behavior cites the behaviors of many non-primates to make important points. The possibility of atavistic behaviors in human beings is illustrated by a picture of a musk-ox in a defensive position. To show how peculiar this habit of proof really is, consider what the reaction would be if I sent to a zoological journal a paper on the musk-ox with defensive positions illustrated by the British squares at the Battle of Waterloo! The editor would be surprised, to put it mildly, and yet this is an accepted mode of thought when animal behavior is compared to that of man.

Ethology has a very strong bias toward equating behavior with easily visible external behaviors (Blurton-Jones, 1975). Careful observation is essential, and visible behaviors may be organized in a scientific manner. As far as human behavior is concerned, Hinde's (1974) *Biological Bases of Human Social Behavior* is the most useful statement reflecting this point of view. But most of the examples of behavior are not of human behavior, but of birds and monkeys. The brain is not mentioned, speech is minimized, and the book contains little biology. A contrasting view of the nature of behavior is given in Altman's (1966) *Organic Foundations of Animal Behavior*, in which the emphasis is on understanding the internal mechanisms of behavior. The external view and the internal view supplement each other up to a point — but I believe that progress in understanding the human behavior and its relations to the behaviors of other animals will come through analysis and understanding of physiological and anatomical factors, primarily the brain. From this point of view, fieldwork and observation of behavior are necessary in setting the problems, but such science will remain superficial unless supported by the much more complicated analysis of the internal mechanisms. It should be stressed that the external and internal points of view are, in theory, supplementary. Unfortunately, in practice, they frequently are not.

Genetics

The theory of natural selection is a genetic theory. As such, it will be useful in guiding genetic research. If long time spans are involved, it will be helpful in guiding evolutionary research. As noted earlier, it is a great improvement over such theories as creation or the one that hypothesizes that new characters may be acquired through use or disuse. If the issues are behavioral and anatomical changes over very long periods of time, natural selection must be an important guiding theory. The present controversies stem from differing opinions on the importance of the theory for interpreting short-term changes.

The fundamental calculus in sociobiology is based on the genetic resemblance between relatives. It is included in almost every statement on sociobiology but is particularly clearly stated by Barash (1977b:85–89). Parents share one half of their genes with an offspring, full siblings share one half, and there is less sharing with more distant relatives. It should be noted that the genetic sharing decreases very rapidly — far more rapidly than social obligations in any human social system. Sahlins (1976) has shown that actual kinship behaviors in human societies do not follow the genetic calculus, but his book, so far, seems to have had little influence.

This whole calculus upon which sociobiology is based is grossly misleading. A parent does not share one half of the genes with its offspring; the offspring shares one half of the genes in which the parents differ. If the parents are homozygous for a gene, obviously all offspring will inherit that gene. The issue then becomes, How many shared genes are there within a species such as *Homo sapiens*? King and Wilson (1975) estimate that man and chimpanzee share 99% of their genetic material; they also estimate that the races of man are 50 times closer than are man and chimpanzee. Individuals whom sociobiologists consider unrelated share, in fact, more than 99% of their genes. It would be easy to make a model in which the structure and physiology important in behavior are based on the shared 99% and in which behaviorally unimportant differences, such as hair form, are determined by the 1%. The point is that genetics actually supports the beliefs of the social sciences, not the calculations of the sociobiologists. The genetic basis for the behaviorally important common biology of the species (in evolutionary order — bipedal walking, hand skills, intelligence) lies in the 99% and is undoubtedly modified by genes in the 1%.

The unity of mankind is in the genetic material, in the biology it determines, and in the basic human behaviors based on the biology. The sociobiological calculus is necessarily racist because geographical distance was a major factor in determining the formation of races (Barash, 1977b:311). In general, the further that two populations were apart at the time races were forming, the greater the genetic difference; hence, the less ethical responsibility people should have for members of the other group. The contrary argument is that most genes are shared and that gene frequencies in which races differ are behaviorally unimportant (with some exceptions such as sickle cell disease).

As I stated at the beginning of this article, I am not concerned with proving that the position I am taking is correct, but rather with showing that the application of the genetic theory of natural selection requires research. The form of the study might be (1) evolutionary theory, (2) major research effort — where the time and energy must go, and (3) tentative conclusions. In applying evolutionary theory to human behaviors, sociobiologists make practically no effort to understand human behavior and they perform no research to validate their claims as far as human behavior is concerned. The personal opinions of the authors are presented as facts — or at least as serious contributions.

Postulating genes to account for behaviors is a major feature of the application of sociobiology to the interpretation of human behaviors. For example, in the last chapter of *Sociobiology* (Wilson, 1975), genes are postulated to account for more than 25 behavioral situations. There are conformer genes, genes for flexibility, genes predisposing to cultural differences, and many others. No evidence is given for any of these. Even the altruistic genes that are central to the whole concept of kin selection are not demonstrated for human beings. The logic is that there must be altruistic genes to account for altruistic acts — just as we learned many years ago that if there are criminal acts there must be criminal genes. There is, obviously, no need to postulate genes for altruism. It would be much more adaptive to have genes for intelligence, enabling one to be altruistic or selfish according to the needs of the moment.

Postulating genes to account for human behaviors allows sociobiologists to minimize the difference between the genetically determined biological base and what is learned. They are not worried by their repetition of the errors of the eugenicists, social Darwinists, or racists.

On the matter of homosexual behavior, Wilson states that it could be understood either by postulating selection of heterozygotes, or, following Trivers, by homosexuals helping relatives and thus their own genes (kin selection). This assumes that the actions described as homosexual in our culture are general. It illustrates the repeated mistake of regarding our culture as synonymous with human nature. Consider highland New Guinea, where boys and men lived in men's houses and all males had homosexual relations. The women lived with the younger children and pigs, and husbands and wives had intercourse in the daytime by the gardens. Just as in the cases of polygamy mentioned earlier, the whole pattern of life was different from ours — and it is the patterns that must be compared. It is futile to take an American word and guess about possible genetic influences.

Just as the power of the theory of evolution in its nineteenth-century form gave people the confidence to arrange stone tools, animal behavior, or human customs into supposedly chronological sequences, so the power of the genetic theory of natural selection gives sociobiologists the confidence to provide genetic explanations for social customs without producing careful analyses or supporting facts.

Sociobiologists revel in the hope that genes will be found to account for the behaviors that social scientists think have already been explained by social facts. Fortunately, it is possible to accept the theory of evolution and the importance of genetics without ignoring the known historical record, social science, or the psychology of the individual.

Summary

Recently there has been a great increase in interest in animal behaviors. It has been claimed by both popular writers and scientists that knowledge gained by the study of other animals may be directly applied to the interpretation of problems of human social behaviors. The proponents of this point of view minimize the difference between genetics and learning, attack Durkheim and the notion of social facts, and postulate genes as important in a very wide variety of human behaviors.

Surely the full understanding of the behaviors of any species must include biology. Biology is the basis for the differences between species. But the more learning is involved, the less there will be any simple relation between basic biology and behavior. Because of intelligence, speech, and recent history, human beings provide the extreme example in which highly diversified behaviors may be learned and executed by the same fundamental biology. Biology determines the need for food, but it does not determine the almost infinite number of ways in which this need may be met.

The desire, both popular and scientific, to apply biological evolutionary thinking to the interpretation of human behaviors has been, and is, so strong that conclusions came long before facts in social evolution, racism, and eugenics. Even the archeological record was misinterpreted by the belief that all that needed to be done was to arrange the stone tools in the order of simple to complex. History was even more distorted by arranging cultures into supposed evolutionary stages.

Sociobiologists are now repeating many of the errors of the past. *The laws of genetics are not the laws of learning*, and as long as sociobiologists confuse these radically different mechanisms, sociobiology will only obstruct the understanding of human social behaviors.

Positively, the increase of interest in animal behavior and the enthusiasm that has come with sociobiology will lead to the development of a biologically and socially based behavioral science. Such a science will be interdisciplinary, but will, in my opinion, contain a large element of social science and will be very different from the science suggested by Wilson (1975) in *Sociobiology*.

Negatively, as far as the interpretation of human behavior is concerned, if the application of biological thinking amounts to ignoring history, sociology, and comparative studies, and to postulating genes to account for all sorts of behaviors, it will amount to no more than a repetition of the errors of the past.

References

Alcock, J. (1975) *Animal Behavior: An Evolutionary Approach*. Sunderland, Mass.: Sinauer Associates.

Alexander, R. D. (1974) "The Evolution of Social Behavior." *Annual Review of Ecology and Systematics* 5:325–383.

Altman, J. (1966) *Organic Foundations of Animal Behavior*. New York: Holt, Rinehart and Winston.

Ardrey, R. (1961) *African Genesis*. New York: Atheneum Press.

Barash, D. P. (1977a) "The New Synthesis". *The Wilson Quarterly* 1:108–120.

———. (1977b) *Sociobiology and Behavior*. New York: Elsevier North-Holland.

Bateson, P. P. G., and R. A. Hinde. (1976) *Growing Points in Ethology*. Cambridge: Cambridge University Press.

Bienen, H. (1970) *Tanzania*. Princeton: Princeton University Press.

Blurton-Jones, N. (1975) "Ethology, Anthropology, and Childhood," in R. Fox (ed.), *Biosocial Anthropology*. London: Malaby Press.

Brown, J. (1975) *The Evolution of Behavior*. New York: Norton.

Carpenter, C. R. (1934) "A Field Study of the Behavior and Social Relations of the Howling Monkeys (*Alouatta palliata*)." *Comparative Psychology Monographs* 10, 1–168.

———. (1940) "A Field Study in Siam of the Behavior and Social Relations of the Gibbon (*Hylobates lar*)." *Comparative Psychology Monographs* 16, 1–212.

Cohen, M. N. (1977) *The Food Crisis in Prehistory: Overpopulation and the Origins of Agriculture*. New Haven: Yale University Press.

Eibl-Eibesfeldt, I. (1975) *Ethology: The Biology of Behavior*. 2nd ed. New York: Holt, Rinehart and Winston.

Galkidas-Brindamour, B. (1977) "New Insights About the Behavior of Indonesian Orangutans." *L.S.B. Leakey Foundation News*. Spring/Summer, p. 4.

Goodall, J. (1968) "The Behavior of Free-living Chimpanzees in the Gombe Stream Reserve." *Animal Behavior Monographs* 1, 161–311.

———. (1977) "Watching, Watching, Watching." *The New York Times*. September 15, p. 27.

Goodall, J., and D. A. Hamburg. (1975) "Chimpanzee Behavior as a Model for the Behavior of Early Man: New Evidence on Possible Origins of Human Behavior." *American Handbook of Psychiatry*. 2nd ed. New York: Basic Books.

Goodman, M., and R. Tashian. (1976) *Molecular Anthropology*. New York: Plenum Press.

Hamburg, D. A. (1963) "Emotions in the Perspective of Human Evolution," in P. Knapp (ed.), *Expression of the Emotions in Man*. New York: International Universities Press.

Hamilton, W. D. (1975) "Innate Social Aptitudes of Man: An Approach from Evolutionary Genetics," in R. Fox (ed.), *Biosocial Anthropology*. London: Malaby Press.

Hinde. R. A. (1974) *Biological Bases of Human Social Behavior*. New York: McGraw-Hill.

Isaac, G. L., J. W. K. Harris, and D. Crader. (1976) "Archeological Evidence from the Koobi Fora Formation," in Y. Coppens, F. C. Howell, G. L. Isaac, and R. E. F. Leakey (eds.), *Earliest Man and Environments in the Lake Rudolf Basin*. Chicago: University of Chicago Press.

Kellogg, W. N. (1968) "Communication and Language in the Home-raised Chimpanzee." *Science* 162, 423–427.

King, M. C., and A. C. Wilson. (1975) "Evolution at Two Levels in Humans and Chimpanzees." *Science* 188, 107–116.

Lancaster, J. B. (1975) *Primate Behavior and the Emergence of Human Culture* (Basic Anthropology Unit Series). New York: Holt, Rinehart and Winston.

Lenski, G., and J. Lenski. (1974) *Human Societies: An Introduction to Macrosociology*. 2nd ed. New York: McGraw-Hill.

Lindburg, D. G. (1977) "Feeding Behavior and Diet of Rhesus Monkeys (*Macaca mulatta*) in a Siwalik Forest in North India," in T. H. Clutton-Brock (ed.), *Primate Ecology*. New York: Academic Press.

Lorenz, K. (1963) *On Aggression*. New York: Harcourt, Brace and World.

MacLean, P. (1970) "The Triune Brain, Emotion, and Scientific Bias," in F. O. Schmitt (ed.), *The Neurosciences: Second Study Program*. New York: Rockefeller University Press.

Mayr, E. (1972) "The Nature of the Darwinian Revolution." *Science* 176, 981–989.

Medawar, P. B., and J. S. Medawar. (1977) *The Life Science — Current Ideas of Biology*. New York: Harper and Row.

Morris, D. (1967) *The Naked Ape: A Zoologist's Study of the Human Animal*. New York: McGraw-Hill.

Morris, S. (1977) "The New Science of Genetic Self-interest." *Psychology Today*. February, pp. 42–51; 84–88.

Myers, R. E. (1968) "Neurology of Social Communication in Primates," in H. Hofer (ed.), *Neurology, Physiology, and Infectious Diseases. Proceedings of the Second International Congress of Primatology*. Vol. 3. Basel, Switzerland: Karger.

_____ . (1976) "Comparative Neurology of Vocalization and Speech: Proof of a Dichotomy," in S. R. Harnad, H. D. Steklis, and J. Lancaster (eds.), *Origins and Evolution of Language and Speech. Annals of the New York Academy of Sciences*.

Nadler, R. (1977) "Sexual Behavior of the Chimpanzee in Relation to the Gorilla and Orang-utan," in G. H. Bourne (ed.), *Progress in Ape Research*. New York: Academic Press.

Ploog, D. (1970) "Social Communication Among Animals," in F. O. Schmitt (ed.), *The Neurosciences: Second Study Program*. New York: Rockefeller University Press.

Robinson, B. W. (1967) "Vocalization Evoked from Forebrain in *Macaca mulatta*." *Physiological Behavior* 2, 345–354.

_____ . (1976) "Limbic Influences on Human Speech," in S. R. Harnad, H. D. Steklis, and J. Lancaster (eds.), *Origins and Evolution of Language and Speech. Annals of the New York Academy of Sciences*.

Roe, A., and G. G. Simpson.(1958) *Behavior and Evolution*. New Haven: Yale University Press.

Sahlins, M. (1976) *The Use and Abuse of Biology*. Ann Arbor: University of Michigan Press.

Schaller, G. B. (1963) *The Mountain Gorilla: Ecology and Behavior*. Chicago: University of Chicago Press.

Sociobiology Study Group of Science for the People. (1976) "Dialogue (the critique): Sociobiology — Another Biological Determinism." *BioScience*.March 26, 182–190.

Struhsaker, T. T. (1967) "Auditory Communication Among Vervet Monkeys," in S. A. Altmann (ed.), *Social Communication Among Primates*. Chicago: University of Chicago Press.

_____ . (1975) *The Red Colobus Monkey*. Chicago: University of Chicago Press.

Thorpe, W. H. (1972) "The Comparison of Vocal Communication in Animals and Man," in R. A. Hinde (ed.), *Non-Verbal Communication*. Cambridge: Cambridge University Press.

Wade, N. (1976) "Sociobiology: Troubled Birth for New Discipline." *Science* 191, 1151–1155.

Washburn, S. L. (1959) "Speculations on the Interrelations of the History of Tools and Biological Evolution," in J. N. Spuhler (ed.), *The Evolution of Man's Capacity for Culture*. Detroit: Wayne State University Press.

Washburn, S. L., D. A. Hamburg, and N. H. Bishop. (1974) "Social Adaptation in Nonhuman Primates," in G. V. Coelho, D. A. Hamburg, and J. E. Adams (eds.), *Coping and Adaptation*. New York: Basic Books.

"Why You Do What You Do; Sociobiology: A New Theory of Behavior." (1977) *Time*. August, pp. 54–63.

Wilson, A., and R. C. Boelkins. (1970) "Evidence for Seasonal Variation in Aggressive Behavior by *Macaca mulatta*." *Animal Behaviour* 18, 719–724.

Wilson, A. C., S. Carlson, and T. J. White (1977) "Biochemical Evolution." *Annual Review of Biochemistry* 46, 573–639.

Wilson, E. O. (1975) *Sociobiology: The New Synthesis*. Cambridge, Mass.: Harvard University Press.

————. (1977a) "Biology and the Social Sciences." *Daedalus* 11, 127–140.

————. (1977b) "Preface," in D. P. Barash (ed.), *Sociobiology and Behavior*. New York: Elsevier North-Holland.

Wind, J. (1976) "Human Drowning: Phylogenetic Origin." *Journal of Human Evolution* 5, 349–363.

Yerkes, R. M. and A. W. Yerkes (1929) *The Great Apes*. New Haven: Yale University Press.

8

Anthropology and the Nature of Things

Napoleon A. Chagnon

Anthropologists familiar with the history and tradition of the discipline might properly ask, . . . what is so distinctive about considering human behavior in terms of evolutionary biology, viewing man and his behavior as a product of natural selection? After all, our craft began with the purpose of explaining both man's natural and cultural variations and has always held both social and biological questions as within its legitimate domain. Anthropology has always been, and will continue to be, what anthropologists do; and it is a prescient, if not presumptuous, soul who could hazard an accurate definition of what the future scope of the field will be.

One of my former teachers, Leslie A. White, was clearly aware of this. He whimsically advised his classes on the history of the discipline that "Anthropology is the study of anything that has to do with any primate at any point in time." On occasion White was dismayed by this prodigious scope, but he shared the vision of many of our academic forebears that anthropology by necessity incorporated and depended upon knowledge that other disciplines generated about the nature history, and evolution of man. One of our distinguished intellectual ancestors, Edward B. Tylor, was more pointed and ebullient: he argued, with admirable confidence, that anthropology had a mission that entailed assembling all the knowledge about man and making it intelligible. In this enterprise, many of the other sciences, as Tylor (1910:109) expressly argued, served subordinate roles: "Various other sciences . . . must be regarded as subsidiary to anthropology, which yet hold their own independent places in the field of knowledge." Among these, Tylor explicitly included anatomy and physiology, psychology, philology, ethics, sociology, archaeology and geology. Tylor's boldly articulated vision presumably came unwelcomed to other scholars of his day, whose already mature disciplines were making notable advances in knowledge and shedding considerable light on the track of man. All the more, since anthropology was then a nascent discipline, just taking form and substance, yet rendering unto itself the supreme responsibility, if not privilege, of assuming the role of queen of the sciences.

All of this should remind us that anthropology has always concerned itself with the study of human behavior in a biological as well as a cultural sense, has always depended on the knowledge accumulated by other sciences to achieve this end, and has always represented itself as the most holistic of disciplines, destined to be supreme in a hierarchy of knowledge. Yet, one cannot help being amused by the fact that, despite Tylor's confident vision, there still exist as independent and vigorous disciplines all the "subsidiary" sciences he iden- tified. Many of our colleagues seem to fear that evolutionary biology will aspire to the role that Tylor envisioned for anthropology. I am confident that their concerns are exaggerated. This is not because I share Tylor's view about the supremacy of anthropology but because . . . man is at once a product of culture and nature and a comprehensive understanding of his behavior re- quires both a biology and an anthropology.

Claude Lévi-Strauss, who characteristically focuses his attention on enigmatic themes and who, for that reason, often determines major trends in anthropological inquiry, has always puzzled over a fundamental dichotomy characteristic of the intellectual concerns of most of the human species: the Nature/Culture opposition. The myths of peoples all over the globe reflect, elaborate upon, and attempt to reconcile the contradictions of an almost unac- ceptable Truth: that Man is at once part of Nature but yet, as distinct from other animals, independent of it because he has Culture — fire, tools, souls, language and immortality. Thus, in the *tristes tropiques* of Amazonas, Jaguar can successfully hunt and devour men unarmed and uncultured, but we deny this to him in our stories about him: in myth, he is a fool and invariably duped by Men. In a curious and amusing sense, the ideology of cultural an- thropology is very much like the ambivalence of myth regarding Jaguar's nature: Yes, we say early in our textbooks, humans are primates and behave according to the laws of nature, but because humans can learn and have culture they are, in later sections of the textbook, almost immune to these laws and apart from nature. So prevalent is this attitude that Alexander (1979) con- cludes that two of the major obstacles to accepting general notions of evolution as applicable to humans are organized religion on the one hand, and cultural anthropology on the other!

This remarkable outgrowth of our philosophical tradition stems in part from a zealous and uncritical adherence to Durkheim's general admonition that the proper explanation of social facts had necessarily to be sociology in its narrowest form, a perspective that Leslie White himself elaborated in his compelling works on the science of culture. Their views, in their most exclusivist expressions, were challenged and modified by the cultural-ecological works of the 1960s and 1970s, when the "environment" was painfully admitted into the functional scheme of things. The deterministic dimension emerging in the harder side of social anthropology could hardly be incompatible with arguments that humans, like all other organisms, had to subsist to survive, and that their subsistence regimes reflected ecological realities which necessarily had to be considered in explanations of both human behavior and cultural adaptations (although the latter were the primary focus of attention).

But the conspicuous opposition of social anthropologists to biological models of human behavior is, in another sense, a consequence of the history of anthropology itself. Social and cultural anthropology set off on a specialized course nearly one hundred years ago while physical anthropology and human biology went a different way—and few of the respective practitioners had much awareness of what the others were doing. The fiction of a holistic anthropology was largely maintained through introductory textbooks and by the fact that all "good" departments had to include both physical and cultural anthropologists. Thus, much of the lack of understanding, or even the suspicion, that characterizes the relationships between biologically oriented and culturally oriented anthropologists is built into the discipline itself, a product of increasing specialization and narrower and narrower focuses on smaller and smaller problems—coupled with stronger and stronger convictions about the symbolic nature of kinship, marriage, and even reproduction itself. Today it is commonplace for social and cultural anthropologists to scorn the very suggestion that kinship has biological attributes and functions, and that kinship behavior might make sense in terms of predictions from evolutionary biology. If in some quarters the significance of the "environment" has won a grudging acceptance, the possible significance of the "biogram" still incurs an apprehensive aversion.

Curiously, the reservations many of us in social anthropology have about the utility of biological models reflect in an uncanny way the theme that pervades the myths of tribesmen: Men are part of Culture and apart from Nature. Why is it so difficult, even repugnant, for humans to admit that they are as much a part of Nature as they are a part of Culture? We so willingly admit, both in scientific ideology and in myth, that humans and animals are one with each other and for many purposes interchangeable. We even permit them in fiction to beget each other, if not in enchanting stories of creation, then in evolutionary sequences. But in both instances we ultimately insist on a sharp break, a great divide, an insuperable gulf separating ourselves from the rest of the creatures. One is almost compelled to suggest that an idea so firmly entrenched in the minds of men has some adaptive function or meaning. Would admitting our "naturalness" reduce our capacity to effectively adapt to our surroundings? Does the optimistic conviction that Nature is subordinate to Culture confer any advantage in dealing with — struggling with — the external world, in the past or in the present?

. . . We can imagine nothing more exciting or scientifically profound than the possibility that much of human behavior conforms to predictions from evolutionary biology — and nothing more legitimate as a field of anthropological inquiry. But we also know that premature conclusions are not good science — they are not science at all. The recent impact of evolutionary biology on anthropological studies has come at a time when biological theory itself has gained new, powerful, and far-reaching insights into the nature of all behavior. The number of critical concepts or new ideas is small — inclusive fitness, nepotism, reciprocal altruism, kin selection, mating strategies, parental investment — but their implications for many kinds of characteristically human behavior are great. And behavior is the key word, particularly as it is relatable to strategies of reproduction and differences in reproductive success. The sexual asymmetries in reproductive physiology widespread in nature are likewise characteristic of our species, and in that simple truth a great many profound questions about human nature must necessarily lie. Anthropologists have been studying human kinship and marriage for over one hundred years, and yet we are hardly able to claim more than Morgan did in 1870: systems of consanguinity and affinity in the human family vary. But how does reproduction within them vary, individual by individual, sex by sex?

It should be obvious by now that definitive answers to the key questions will require new and highly detailed information. Lamentably, anthropology, in its traditional concerns, stands in the twilight of a rapidly disappearing era, for the kinds of societies in which new work can be done — or previous work extended — are vanishing, and many of those remaining societies are inaccessible for political reasons. While the now-limited ethnographic cosmos may hinder us, it does not preclude new studies altogether. Indeed, valuable work in this vein can be done in any society, for the variations of which we speak lie not only in the exotic hinterlands of remote places and anywhere therein, but everywhere. We believe that new studies of human behavior from the vantage of both evolutionary biology and traditional anthropology should be initiated on a broad scale with tests of natural selection hypotheses in mind, not only because such inquiries have always been within the traditional scope of our science, but also because they are scientifically important. We may enter blind alleys on some or make new discoveries on others, for such is the fate of those who take new paths and fresh ideas into unknown domains. Almost no explicitly sociobiological fieldwork in human societies has yet been accomplished. But, . . . some existing data give us reason to believe that the return for such efforts will be great. To make this step, future field researchers must set aside the cliché of Nature-opposed-to-Culture, hold in abeyance some of the preconceptions and prejudices that mark our profession's recent parochial history, and responsibly reflect on the kinds of questions that aroused an earlier generation of students of man. It is entirely fitting . . . to capture some of the caution and optimism that marked the measured words of Tylor:

> None will deny that, as each man knows by the evidence of his own consciousness, definite and natural cause does, to a great extent, determine human action. Then, keeping aside from considerations of extra-natural interference and causeless spontaneity, let us take this admitted existence of natural cause and effect as our standing-ground, and travel on it so far as it will bear us [1958(1871):3.]

While Tylor had in mind the distinction between science and supernaturalism, which need not concern us here, his dismissal of causeless spontaneity surely applies to the question of the independence of man's behavior from his evolutionary and biological character. To deny any relationship or oppose any inquiry is to ignore the great aphorism of Lucretius: that nothing yet from nothing ever came.

References

Alexander, R.D. (1979) "Evolution and Culture," in N. A. Chagnon and W. Irons (eds.) *Evolutionary Biology and Human Social Behavior: An Anthropological Perspective.* Belmont, Mass.: Wadsworth, pp. 59–78.

Tylor, E.B. (1910) "Anthropology." *Encyclopaedia Britannica*, 11th ed., vol. 2.

_____. (1958) *The Origins of Culture, Pt. I* (originally published as chapters 1–10 of *Primitive Culture*, 1871). New York: Harper and Bros.

Part 4
Economics

Introduction to Part 4

Economics appears to have a somewhat different relationship to biology than that of the other social sciences. What seems to be emerging is a mutually rewarding synthesis; the nature and possible intellectual outcome of this two-way relationship is discussed in this section by Kenneth E. Boulding and Jack Hirshleifer. Both authors see advantages as well as potential pitfalls in the connection.

Although Boulding begins negatively, his views change as he develops his analysis. He writes that "the relation of economics to the biological sciences can be described as that of 'second cousins twice removed' in the extended family of the sciences." Boulding proceeds, however, to point out that "in spite of this remoteness of genetic connection, . . . there are some quite surprising family resemblances and, as the communication between them is limited, an extension of that communication might be quite fruitful."

Boulding provides a broad overview of some classical economic interests in biology. He indicates that human beings are not the only organisms that economize or make choices. "An amoeba," he states, "faced with a piece of food on the one hand or a piece of dirt on the other, will ingest the food and reject the dirt. This implies that even the amoeba has a value function and, in a sense, makes choices."

It is at the more general level of analysis, however, that Boulding feels most comfortable. He sees conceptual relationships between the biosphere and the price system, between a production function and aspects of the biosphere, between evolution and economic development, and between biological regeneration and social replacement. All of these ideas are discussed in some detail.

Boulding is skeptical of the development of a fruitful relationship between biology and economics, yet he remains open to and intrigued by such a prospect. He concludes by returning to a geneological analogy. "These second-cousin relationships between economics and, indeed, the social sciences generally, and the biological sciences may not be any more than suggestive of some future possibilities." He goes on to assert, "nevertheless, they are tantalizingly suggestive, and one hopes that a few family reunions might set in motion conversations and learning processes which would lead to mutual enrichment."

Boulding's broad sweep is brought under close examination in the selection by Hirshleifer. The latter's *tour de force* explores numerous macro and micro dimensions of a biological perspective in economics. Hirshleifer expresses an appreciation for what he calls the "special link" between sociobiology and economics. Indeed, he argues, "the fundamental organizing concepts of the dominant analytical structures employed in economics and in sociobiology are strikingly parallel." This appears to be the case because the subject matter of biology can be viewed as "Nature's economy."

Before proceeding to a detailed discussion of how economics could be regarded as a biological phenomenon, Hirshleifer explores some mutual influences between the two disciplines. His is an unusual review in the sense that, as this volume demonstrates, most of the borrowing of explanatory concepts has been unidirectional, essentially *from* biology *by* the social sciences. However, biologists such as Darwin, Ghiselin, Wallace, Gadgil and Bossert, Trivers, Cody, and E. O. Wilson have adapted economic theories, findings, and methodological techniques to their own studies. In spite of this, Hirshleifer explains, the stronger intellectual influences have been in the reverse direction.

With the preliminaries aside, Hirshleifer proceeds to examine numerous economic concepts from a biological — for the most part sociobiological — vantage point. He explores biological models of the business firm with references to fitness, adaptation, genetics, evolution, and niche theory. He also discusses some biological bases for economic tastes and preferences before moving on to an insightful section on selfishness. Other economic concepts explored include monetary interest, organized markets, competition, specialization, division of labor, size, and diminishing returns.

Again emphasizing a possible flow of knowledge in the "opposite" direction, Hirshleifer observes that biologists have focused on the elements of change in the natural world at the expense of a sensitivity to equilibrium. Here he points out that economic models of equilibrium have much to offer biological researchers.

The conclusion of this section raises some especially interesting, but challenging, questions for both biologists and social scientists, questions that must be answered if scholars are going to move on to a more precise and empirical intermingling of the two intellectual cultures. At this point, says Hirshleifer, "it is [perhaps] sufficient to say that the sociobiological approach holds out great hope for breaking down not only the 'vertical' discontinuity between the sciences of human behavior and more fundamental studies of life, but also the 'horizontal' barriers among the various social studies themselves."

T.C.W.

9

Economics As a Not Very Biological Science

Kenneth E. Boulding

The relation of economics to the biological sciences can be described as that of "second cousins, twice removed" in the extended family of the sciences. In spite of this remoteness of genetic connection, however, there are some quite surprising family resemblances and, as the communication between them is limited, an extension of that communication might be quite fruitful.

The historical connections could not be described as extensive. Adam Smith, who might properly be regarded as the founder of scientific economics, was a contemporary of Linnaeus, although Smith's economics was much more Newtonian than Linnaean. His concern was for the perception of nature's diversity and speciation. This tradition has continued to the present day. The mainstream tradition in economics, and even in its Marxian underground, has been, on the whole, an attempt to find a "celestial mechanics" of prices and commodities, incomes and classes. In 1870, W. S. Jevons (1911), one of the founders of the marginal utility school, described economics as the "mechanics of utility and self-interest." Whatever taxonomy has been done in economics has been done by casual empiricism and intellectual model building. The "factors of production" of classical economics—land, labor, and capital—are heterogeneous and dimensionally confused categories. The Marxist categories of class, means, and relations of production are also heterogeneous and diffuse categories. Among the social sciences, anthropology is the only one which has had much interest in careful taxonomy. The great tradition of biological taxonomics simply passed economics by.

Nevertheless, the penchant of economists for system building was not without its impact on the biological sciences. Darwin acknowledged his debt to Malthus as the originator, or at least the popularizer, of the idea of an equilibrium population of the species, that in which birth and death rates were equal, each of them being functions of the size of the population and the nature of the environment. The basic ideas of an equilibrium population are already implicit in Adam Smith's *The Wealth of Nations,* although Malthus certainly deserves the credit for bringing the idea clearly out into the open. Implied in Malthusian theory is also a theory of ecological equilibrium which, in turn, is an essential component of the theory of evolution. The movement of the biological sciences from taxonomy into dynamic systems, therefore, has a second-cousin relationship to Malthusian economics.

A good many economists have been uneasy with the mechanical and Newtonian character of economic theory. Alfred Marshall (1961), a great English economist of the end of the nineteenth century, had at least a slightly bad conscience about the essentially mechanical substructure of his economic theory and made general libations in the direction of linking economics more closely with biology although, it must be admitted, he did not really do very much about it. Thorstein Veblen (1919), perhaps the most singular, dramatic, and stimulating figure in American social science, wrote a penetrating article on "Why is economics not an evolutionary science?" He did not do very much himself to make it so. One of the most serious attempts to link economics with the biological sciences, at least with physiology, was that of Reinhold Noyes, whose extraordinary work, *Economic Man* (1948), was an attempt to reduce economic behavior to its physiological substrata. However, the book remained largely unread and made virtually no impact on economists. In my own work, I have tried to link certain ideas in regard to biological growth to social and economic organizations, for instance, in *The Organizational Revolution* (1953). I have also been interested in the application of evolutionary theory to social and economic systems, for instance, in *A Primer on Social Dynamics* (1970). These exercises, I suspect, have been regarded by the economics profession as an amiable eccentricity rather than a major contribution.

In spite of this not very encouraging history, I am still confident that economics has a great deal to learn from the biological sciences, and perhaps, the biological sciences have something to learn from economics. Insofar, indeed, as there are parallels or homologies between economic systems and biological systems, we would expect to find fruitful interactions. There are three major areas where these parallels may be found: One is the theory of the organism and its behavior; the second is the theory of the ecosystem, that is, the interaction of populations of different organisms; and the third is in the theory of evolution or the succession of ecosystems through time. In each of these three areas, each science, I believe, has something to learn from the other.

In economics the theory of the organism, or economic behavior, has two major divisions: the theory of the firm and the theory of the household. The taxonomic poverty of economics is reflected very clearly in this division. The variety of economic organizations is certainly not as enormous as that of biological species, but, nevertheless, simple categorization into households and firms is wholly inadequate. Economics has had very little to say, for instance, about foundations, semigovernmental enterprises, port or valley authorities, hybrids like Comsat or Amtrak, and all the rich variety of organizations that is found in what Etzioni has called "the third sector." Economics still, perhaps, has to find its Linnaeus who will carefully observe and classify the structure, genetics, growth, and behavior of social species. Nevertheless, the narrow taxonomy of economics has some advantages in the development of systematic formal theory and the identification of common patterns which might easily be lost in a wider perspective.

The key to the theory of economic behavior is the concept of *optimization* through choice. The organism is perceived as examining the set of images of possible futures, ordering these on a value scale — that is, a scale of better or worse — and then selecting that one which is "best," that is, first in the value order. The theory is almost formally tautological, for, almost by definition, an alternative which is actually chosen by the decision-maker must have been, in his own mind, the best at the time of the choice. If somebody chooses what he says is the worse of two alternatives, one suspects either that he is lying or that, in the language of his value system, what he calls the worse is in fact the better.

On these rather slender assumptions and on some further assumptions about what might be called the "plausible topology of value orderings," economics has built an elegant general theory of behavior under conditions of choice, from which, in spite of its formality, certain conclusions emerge. Thus, it can be deduced that, in an exchange relationship, a worsening of the "terms of trade" (the ratio of what we get per unit to what we give up) is almost certain to result in a diminution in the amount offered, and the amount of this diminution is related closely to the substitutability of the two goods being exchanged.

The theory of the firm and the theory of the household are in fact formally identical. The only difference is that, in the case of the firm, we suppose as a first approximation a simple relationship between profits and preferability, in the sense that the firm will always prefer larger profits to smaller, though even this assumption is by no means true and can easily be modified. What emerges for economics first of all is a formal theory of choice which could be applicable to all organizations. In its broadest form, the theory becomes a kind of "game tree" in which the organization comes to one decision point after another, a decision point being a point at which it perceives alternative futures. At each decision point, it selects one of these which it pursues until another decision point is reached. A theory as general as this, of course, has very little content; a richer theory is derived from its application to some rather specific cases, in which the alternative futures can be specified in terms of what is called a "possibility boundary" in the variable space of the organization. The possibility boundary, as the name suggests, divides possible combinations of variables from impossibile ones. It is, thus, a reflection and a definition of "scarcity," in the broad sense of implying that not all things are possible. It frequently, however, applies to scarcity in a more restricted sense. Usually the possibility boundary has the character that an increase of one variable could only be obtained by the sacrifice of another. Along with the possibility boundary, we then postulate a preference function in the field which tells us which of any two elements in a certain field is preferred.

These concepts are illustrated in two variables in Figure 9.1. Here we suppose two variables, A and B; each point in the field represents a combination of the two. The possibility boundary, HKLM divides the field into a possible area and an impossible one. As drawn, the line has two sections, HK and LM, in which it has a negative slope, indicating that from any point on the line we

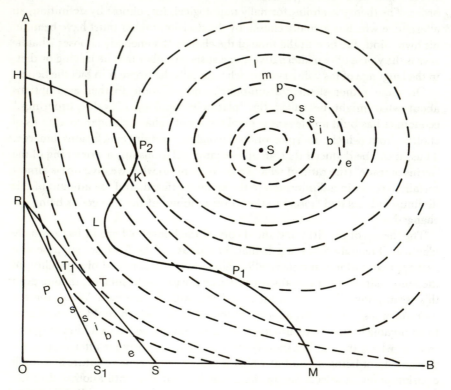

FIGURE 9.1
(Explanation in text.)

cannot move to any position where there is more of both A and B, but we can move to a position where there is more of one and less of the other. This is scarcity in the narrower sense. Between K and L the line has a positive slope. Here it is possible to go from a position on the possibility boundary to another where there is more of both A and B. In an economic system, this would be regarded as a very peculiar case.

We then postulate a utility or value function, which can be thought of as a surface in the third dimension, the height of which measures the "preferredness" of each point of the field. The dotted lines are contours of this surface and are known as "indifference curves." They join all those points on the field which represent combinations of A and B that have the same value, towards which, therefore, the decision maker is indifferent. In the diagram we have supposed that the value function in the vertical is a dimension "mountain," where the summit at S represents satiety. The indifference curves will be roughly circular around S. The "value mountain" will have four quadrants; south and west of S, both A and B are "goods," that is, an increase in either of them is preferred; north and east of S, both of them are "bads," that is, an increase in them is not preferred. North and west of S, B is a good and A is a bad; south and east of S, A is a good and B is a bad.

An optimum in the small is where the indifference curve touches the possibility boundary, as at P_1 or P_2. From each of these points any small movement, either along the possibility boundary or within it, leads to lower indifference curves representing lower levels of preference. It will be noted that in the large P_2 will be preferred to P_1, although, in order to get from P_1 to P_2, the organization would have to pass through regions of lower preference than P_1. If, now, in a more restricted case, A and B are commodities which can be exchanged at a fixed exchange ratio, and the decision-maker starts with an amount of A equal to OR; the possibility boundary is a straight line RS, the slope of which is equal to the ratio of exchange, that is, the number of units of B that can be gotten for one unit of A. Under these circumstances, the optimum position is T, where RS is touched by an indifference curve. A worsening in the terms of trade will be reflected in a shift in this line, say, to RS', and a shift in the optimum point to T'. The results of the change here depend on the nature of the indifference curves, that is, of the value function.

I am not sure whether this kind of analysis has the slightest value to biologists. Man, however, is not the only animal who economizes or who makes choices. An amoeba, faced with a piece of food on the one hand or a piece of dirt on the other, will ingest food and reject the dirt. This implies that even the amoeba has a value function and, in a sense, makes choices. As we go up the scale of complexity, the role of choice and, therefore, of evaluation in the behavior of living organisms becomes more and more important. In the less complicated forms, of course, the value system is largely genetic in origin and, hence, not much subject to change during the life of the organism. With increase in complexity, however, learned values become more and more important. Even in the birds we find the phenomenon of imprinting, as in the famous goose who thought Konrad Lorenz was his mother. In the mammals there is a good deal of learning of values in infancy, and in man, of course, almost all values are learned even though they are built on a genetic substructure.

In regard to the growth, success, or failure of the organization or organism, it would not surprise me if economics has more to learn from biology than biology from economics, even though this learning process may not be much more than a hope for the future. The particularly important contribution of biology here is the concept of "allotropy," as Bertalanffy calls it, or the principles which give any particular form of organization, whether living organism or social organization, an optimum size or, at least, an optimum range of sizes. I recall being enormously influenced as an economist by Julian Huxley's famous little essay "On Being the Right Size." The proposition, that the surface is increased as the square of the length and volume of the cube as we increase the linear dimensions of a particular structure, has very far-reaching implications in both biology and the social sciences. It explains the small size of the one-celled organism, the moderate dimensions of the exoskeletal insect, the general size range of the reptiles and mammals, and even why the whale has to live in the ocean. It explains, also, how increased size has to be compensated for by change of structure and particularly in terms of endoskeletons and convolutions of lungs, bowels, and brain in order to increase the surface area relative to the volume. Nothing can happen that is not superficial; that is, all transactions or interactions take place on surfaces. Hence, the proportion of surface to volume is one of the most important parameters of any organization. This is one of the most universal of principles. It applies, for instance, to architecture where, as long as buildings had an exoskeleton like an insect, they could not be much bigger than, shall we say, the Palace of Versailles, but once the endoskeleton, that is, the steel frame, had developed, they could be as large as the Empire State Building and even larger. Similarly, artificial lighting, plumbing, and ventilation permit the development of much larger structures than would be possible where all the inputs and outputs had to come in directly through the exterior walls.

There are similar principles in regard to social organizations, although they are harder to detect. Communications follow a linear pattern. Inputs from and outputs to the external world take place on the "surface" of organizations. It is the sales clerk who meets the customer, the infantryman who meets the enemy, the priest who meets the congregation, and the teaching assistant who meets students. The upper members of any hierarchy have to derive their information indirectly through channels of communication, and the longer these are, the more likely they are to be corrupted. What I call the "organizational revolution" came about as a result of a change mainly in the techniques of communication, such as the telephone, the telegraph, the typewriter, the mimeograph, and, perhaps, the vice president or the staff organization. All this took place around 1870 and permitted an enormous expansion of the scale of organizations, giving rise to such monsters as General Motors, the United States Department of Defense, and the Soviet Union, all of which would have been inconceivable before 1870. In economics the phenomenon is known as "decreasing returns to scale." Some economists have doubted whether this exists, using the argument that if we could change all inputs in exactly the same proportions, there seems no reason to suppose why the outputs should not be increased in the same proportion. Perhaps, if they had known a little more biology, they might have been spared this fallacy, though we can perhaps get around it formally by supposing that what "returns to scale" really means is that it is impossible to increase all inputs in the same proportion—if only because of the laws of squares and cubes.

Another phenomenon, where a little interaction between economics and biology might be helpful, is in the study of growth. This is a phenomenon which is common to all the sciences and the possibility of a general theory of growth which cuts across the disciplines is extraordinarily tempting. The growth of a baby from the fertilized egg in the womb of its mother is a process which is not wholly unlike the growth of an automobile in the womb of its factory. In both cases, there is a blueprint—the genetic code in biology or the factory plan in the case of the automobile. In both cases, there is assembly of different parts. In the biological case, the parts and the whole grow together in a way that they do not in the case of the automobile. All these processes imply some sort of destabilizing feedback. I doubt if an embryologist would learn much from studying the growth of the automobile in the factory, but I cannot help wondering whether the concept of the "payoff" might be useful in biology as it is in social sciences.

Moving now from the individual organism or organization to the larger environment or ecosystem in which it finds itself, we find striking parallels between biological and socioeconomic systems, so that the sciences again might have something to learn from each other. It could be an interesting exercise to compare the work of Walras, who developed a set of equations for the general equilibrium of the price system, with the work of Volterra, who developed a model of the dynamic interaction of populations. Walras is a little weak on the dynamics of the system and, perhaps, Volterra in what an economist would call "comparative statics," that is, what difference in the position of the final equilibrium would be created by a given change in the parameters of the system. The similarity between the two systems, however, is highly significant. Both depend essentially on the simple proposition that in any system of N variables, if each variable has an equilibrium value which depends on the position of all the others, we can immediately derive a system of N equations with N unknowns, for we have one equation for each of the N variables. If this system of equations has a solution, which usually has to fulfill some limiting conditions such as that all the equilibrium values should be positive, then, at least, there is specified what might be called a "conditional equilibrium" of the whole system in the sense that a certain set of values of the variables can be specified in which the value of each variable is consistent with the value of all the others. This conditional or general equilibrium does not necessarily have to be stable, that is, the dynamics of the system could pull it away from the equilibrium rather than pulling it towards it. As Samuelson (1947) has pointed out, we have to know the dynamics of the system before we can specify the stability of any equilibrium.

The mathematical problems become increasingly difficult as we increase the number of variables. The general principle, however, is a relatively simple one that applies to biological, as well as to social, ecosystems. I have learned to think of society, indeed, as a "great pond," a pool of social species which consists of types of organizations and artifacts as well as occupations and persons. Seventh Day Adventists, corner gas stations, automobiles, international corporations, foundations, and national states all jostle each other in the environment provided by the biosphere, the geosphere, the atmosphere, and the hydrosphere, and something like an ecological equilibrium can be perceived, at least in part of the system for short periods of time. Thus, a relative price structure may persist even through large inflations. If a pound of butter is worth ten pounds of bread before an inflation, this ratio is likely to be not very different after it. Even such things as geographical price structures have astonishing persistence. Commodities have complementary, competitive, or predatory relationships, much like biological organisms. There are food chains in economics just as there are in biology — a tractor eats gasoline, wheat eats fertilizer, flour eats wheat, bread eats flour, and people eat bread.

Biological ecosystems tend to be more cyclical than social ecosystems. In biology, nitrogen goes round and round, financing protein on the way. Economic processes are much more linear, going from mines and wells to commodities, garbage, and dumps. Nevertheless, if the doomsayers are right, nemesis is only just around the corner, and at some time or other, mankind has to come to terms with circularity and establish a "spaceship earth," in which most materials which are transformed into commodities are recycled back into the source from which they came. The dumps, in other words, have to become mines. A system of this sort needs inputs of energy to drive it, otherwise the second law of thermodynamics takes over very rapidly. This is as true of the biosphere as it is of the "sociosphere."

A very interesting question, to which I have never been able to give a satisfactory answer, is what, if anything, in the biosphere corresponds to the concept of a price system, and especially to an equilibrium price system, in economics. Prices have a parallel in the biosphere in the concept of metabolic rates or input-output ratios. The animal "exchanges" oxygen for CO_2, and must have an approximately "perfect market" for this exchange, that is, if the proportion of oxygen or even of CO_2 in the environmental air changes substantially as he breathes, the organism very soon gets into trouble. Evolution has proceeded for a very long time on the assumption that a lung full of air contains approximately the same amount of oxygen no matter when or where it is inhaled.

The economic concept of production, or a production function, also has counterparts in the biosphere. Every organism has inputs and outputs, and the relations of these to one another provide essential parameters for the ecosystem. If we have not yet developed a general theory of the ecosystem applicable to both biological and social systems, it is perhaps because biological systems have had to come to terms with circularity before this necessity has imposed itself on social systems.

Some of the complexities of these relationships can be illustrated even in the simple case of a two-population ecosystem. This is illustrated in the parts of Figure 9.2. Here we measure the size of one population (A) vertically and the other (B) horizontally. In Figure 9.2a we suppose two mutually competing populations such as lions and tigers; they are, let us say, competing for the same food. We can postulate a partial equilibrium "lion curve," LL', showing the equilibrium number of lions for each number of tigers. With no tigers, there will be OL lions, and with OL' tigers, there will be no lions at all. The curve TT' is the corresponding "tiger curve." These curves intersect at E, which is a position of equilibrium. The dynamics of the system can be represented by the dynamic path lines that are shown with arrows. From each point, we can suppose that in the next time period, each population will move towards its equilibrium level, and it will move towards its own particular equilibrium curve. Thus, from point P, we can suppose that in the next time period, the number of tigers will decrease by PP_t, the number of lions by PP_1, the next point being P', the result of these two movements. In the limiting case, these paths become the dynamic functions of Volterra. In Figure 9.2a we see that all the dynamic paths converge on the equilibrium point E, and the equilibrium is clearly stable. If, however, we reverse the position of the two curves, as in Figure 9.2b, we again may have a position of equilibrium E, but it is unstable. On the upper left-hand side of the dotted line through E, the system moves to the point T, at which the lion becomes extinct and there are OT tigers. Downward and to the right of this line, all the dynamic lines move towards L', with OL' lions and no tigers.

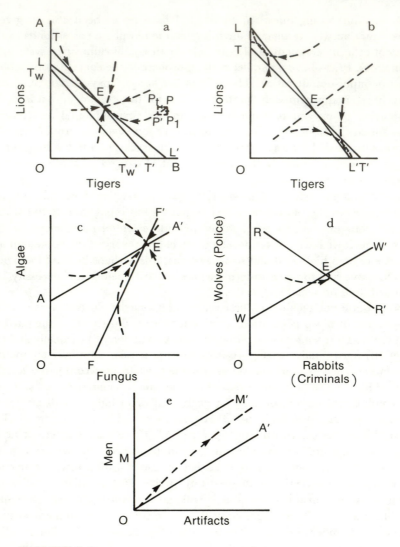

FIGURE 9.2
(Explanation in text.)

Figure 9.2c shows the corresponding case for two mutually cooperative or complementary species, such as the algae and the fungus which together constitute a lichen. Here, again, there may be an equilibrium point at E which, in this case, is stable. There are unstable cases that could easily be formulated. Figure 9.2d is a very familiar case of predation or parasitism; in this case, we suppose populations of wolves and rabbits. We have a wolf equilibrium line, WW', suggesting that, with no rabbits, there will be some wolves (OW), but that after that point the more rabbits, the more wolves. The rabbit line, RR', is downward sloping, indicating that the more wolves, the fewer rabbits. Here, again, there is an equilibrium point at E which is usually stable. Under some circumstances, there might be a circular equilibrium producing a constant cycle. Under other circumstances, there might be a converging cycle, or even an explosive or divergent cycle which might destroy the equilibrium.

One very interesting problem here is the sensitivity of the system; by this we mean what happens to the equilibrium position when the parameters of the equations change. When the partial equilibrium lines have the same general slope, as in Figures 9.2a, 9.2b, and 9.2c, the system is highly sensitive. Thus, if in Figure 9.2a, there is a slight worsening of the comparative position of the tigers, through the shift in the partial equilibrium line TT' to $T_wT'_w$, tigers will become extinct and the lions will triumph. In Figure 9.2d, the equilibrium is much less sensitive, and it will take very large shifts in the parameters to lead to the extermination of either of the populations. This perhaps explains why the predation-parasite relationship is so popular.

Any of the above cases could be applied to social systems. Figure 9.2a for instance, could be automobiles and horses or better, perhaps, two makes of automobiles. Figure 9.2b could be automobiles and stagecoaches; Figure 9.2c could be automobiles and gas stations; Figure 9.2d, criminals and police — the more criminals, the more police; the more police, the fewer criminals. Figure 9.2e is a suggested explanation for the extraordinary explosion of the human population. Man and his artifacts are mutually cooperative. The partial equilibrium line for man is MM'. There will be some men even without artifacts; thereafter, the more artifacts, the more men. The partial equilibrium line for artifacts is OA'. With no men, there would be no artifacts, but the more men, the more artifacts. If these two lines are parallel, the population of both men and artifacts will expand indefinitely. One point which is not noted in the diagrams is that, for biological populations, there is some size of the population below which reproduction is virtually impossible. A biological population with sexual reproduction cannot come down to one member, or even to a population consisting all of one sex, without dying out very rapidly. For such populations, therefore, we can postulate a band of survival roughly paralleling the other axis.

A third area where biological and social systems have a great deal in common is in evolution. Within biology, evolution is regarded as ecological succession produced by mutations in the genetic codes. The dynamics of the system is, of course, appallingly complicated. It would be nice if we could assume that at any time and place the ecological equations of interacting populations would work themselves out towards an equilibrium. A genetic mutation would then change the parameters and move the system towards a new equilibrium with perhaps some of the old species failing to survive and a new species surviving in the new ecosystem. Unfortunately, things are not this simple. Genetic mutations and environmental changes go on all the time, so that ecosystems rarely have time to achieve definite equilibrium. The dynamic paths of Figure 9.2 are continually being changed by genetic mutations which also change the partial equilibrium curves and the equilibrium position of the system. If these paths dip below the critical survival numbers of the species, then that species will become extinct. The unique elements of its genetic code, which distinguish it from other species, will disappear from the gene pool, and its extinction will change the equilibrium positions of the ecosystem and, therefore, the chances of other species for survival. Nevertheless, the principle that it is ecosystems rather than species that are selected is a significant one, even though it may be hard to pin it down to particular equilibrium cases. The great Darwinian vision of evolution as a process with genetic mutation and recombination, and phenotypic selection, nevertheless, holds up as a poetic vision even though it is extraordinarily hard to formulate in explicit models. Evolution is a theory without adequate mathematical models and with virtually no predictive power; nevertheless, it is one of the most profound illuminations to ever hit the human consciousness.

The mutation-selection pattern is just as characteristic of human history—that is, of the dynamics of the social system—as it is of the biosphere, but in social systems, it is harder to distinguish the genotype from the phenotype. It is tempting to regard the "noosphere," to use Teilhard de Chardin's term, that is, the sphere of all human knowledge as it is embodied in human nervous systems spread around the globe, as the social genotype. Out of this knowledge comes artifacts on the one hand, and organizations on the other. Human artifacts, indeed—automobiles, machines, airplanes, organizations, and so on—are social species, the genetic base of which is human knowledge imposing itself on the material and social world. There is a parallel here to the way in which the genetic code, which can also be regarded as knowledge—or at least, "know-how"—imposes its organizing potential on the material world in the creation of the phenotype. Organizations, likewise, require "know-whom," as well as "know-how," and a complex of images and values which can be regarded as the genotype of the organization.

The parallel between biological and social evolution, however, must not be carried too far, for at some crucial points, it breaks down. The survival of human knowledge depends only loosely on the survival of the phenotypes which it creates, for it is embodied, not in artifacts or in organizations, but in human nervous systems, and it is transmitted from one human being to another by communication and learning, which again are only loosely related to the organizations within which they may take place. Nevertheless, there is some relationship between the survival of the phenotype and the survival of the genotype in social systems in the sense that if there is a general collapse of the organization of the transmission of knowledge, knowledge will simply come to an end. A good example of this was the collapse of the Mayan civilization within which the organization, whatever it was that transmitted the elaborate astronomical and technical knowledge of the Mayans, collapsed, and the knowledge itself disappeared as a result.

Another fundamental difference between biological and social evolution is that, in the biosphere, the genotype of a particular individual comes usually from two parents of opposite sexes, except in the case of asexual reproduction, whereas in social systems and in the transmission of knowledge, there are innumerable "sexes." The knowledge stock of one person is derived, not from his parents alone, but from all the people and, indeed, all the experiences with which he has had contact. The transmission of language and culture within the family have something of a genetic quality about them in the sense that languages perpetuate themselves by children growing up with parents who both speak the language, but here, again, the parallel is not close, and the analogy must not be pushed too far. Culture traits may be propagated by something that looks almost like asexual reproduction, that is, by simple imitation. The same is true of technology. Thus, the Japanese discovered Western technology after 1868 and adopted a great deal of it by sending their young men to Europe to learn the new science and the new technology, and when they returned to Japan, as most of them did, this became part of the Japanese knowledge stock. We are now witnessing a great diffusion of culture traits as a result of increased transportation and communication which have resulted from the scientific revolution. Some of these are so universally recognized to be valuable, such as the periodic table and nuclear physics, that they are almost universally adopted. Other traits are more specific to the subcultures in which they are perpetuated, so each society represents a combination of almost universal traits together with highly particular traits of particular subcultures, such as language, art, ideology, religion, nationalism, class, and so on.

In economics, evolution becomes "development," which is almost the same word. The main emphasis is on the total output of the system, at least in terms of economic goods, and especially in terms of per capita output of these goods. A number of economic models of growth have been developed, especially in the last thirty years. These models have not, as far as I know, found much application in biology. Perhaps a good reason is that the total output, or throughput, of the biosphere is not of particularly salient quantity although it is by no means devoid of interest as at least a possible quantitative measure of the evolutionary process itself.

Today, there is a sudden realization by economists that the growth process cannot go on forever and that mankind is expanding into a biological niche, the niche in this case being the whole earth. The quasi-religious manifestos of the Club of Rome may be received with some skepticism in the economics profession. Nevertheless, the problem cannot be brushed aside, and the concept of the "carrying capacity" of the earth, in terms of the human population, has suddenly become of first importance. Up to this century, man has conceived himself as expanding on a virtually infinite plane. Now, suddenly, the plane has become a sphere, and he has become acutely aware of the limitations of the tiny "spaceship earth" to which he is confined and on which he must travel towards some unknown destination. It is at this moment of truth that economics suddenly becomes ecology.

Even on the spaceship earth, however, we must beware of an overemphasis on equilibrium. The earth has not been in equilibrium, certainly as far as the biosphere is concerned, for three or four billion years, and it is certainly not going to reach equilibrium now. What we are facing is what we have always had — an evolutionary process within the limits of the terrestrial environment. The evolutionary process itself has had its moments of disaster. Each geological age, indeed, is separated from its successor by a disaster, and it is still a moot question as to the significance of these evolutionary disasters in the general evolutionary process. It can be argued that they have been necessary for evolution, for otherwise the earth would have reached an equilibrium long ago, and evolution would have come to an end. We may be coming to another evolutionary disaster as a result of the uncontrolled expansion of human population and throughput. If this is not fatal, however, it may again set the stage for a new phase of evolutionary development, although this may not be a particularly cheerful thought for mankind if we are a species that is not included in the next development.

The role of catastrophe in evolution is somewhat related to the problem of the role of dialectical processes in human history. Dialectical processes are those which involve systems-conflict, that is, the struggle of one fairly well defined system against another, leading to the overflow of one and its replacement by the challenger or, of course, possibly leading to the failure of the challenger and the continued existence of the challenged. This reflects itself in human history in such processes as the succession of empires, the conflict of states and classes, and revolutions. I argue that evolution is an essentially nondialectical process in the sense that it operates, not by the conflict of systems, but by the succession of ecosystems as a result of almost continuous small changes in the parameters, either through genetic mutation or through irreversible changes in environment. Nevertheless, the role of catastrophic changes, which destroy a previously established equilibrium and hence permit a new surge of evolutionary development, is by no means to be ruled out.

The real difficulty is that neither in biological evolution nor in social evolution do we understand very much about the generation of evolutionary potential. Why was it that the vertebrates developed organized intelligence rather than the octopus? Why did it, then, develop through the simians rather than the felines? Both evolutionists and historians tend to assume too easily that what happened had to happen. Both evolution and human history are the result of a mixture of random and nonrandom processes. The nonrandom element is suggested by the fact, for instance, that the marsupials of Australia, or even the birds in the oceanic islands, evolved to fill the mammalian niches. This suggests that there is a potential niche structure which provides a significant nonrandom element in the evolutionary process. Similarly in social systems, Japan, in relative isolation, developed many of the institutions in a somewhat different form than Europe developed under feudalism. Classical Japan could almost be described as a marsupial society. Nevertheless, the random elements are also there and cannot be denied. The survival of the early examples of any major mutation has a strong random element in it. We see this very clearly in human history, especially in the foundation of the great "phyla" of religion, ideology, and culture. It is hard to believe that this is not true also in biological evolution, and I suspect biologists have paid too little attention to this problem.

There is one final area in which striking parallels exist between biological and social processes and in which, also, there seems to be very little interaction between the two sciences. This is in the phenomenon of regeneration, whether at the level of the phenotype or that of the ecosystem. Many lower organisms can regenerate a limb that is cut off. Part of the price of complexity seems to be a certain loss of regenerative power, although even man's body can heal a cut and reorganize a brain. Ecosystems, likewise, regenerate. After a forest fire, a whole succession of stages takes place until the original forest is regenerated. The necessity for regeneration may also change that which is regenerated—thus, a forest which is not subject to forest fire may end up as a very different kind of forest to one that is.

Social systems exhibit similar properties. A role occupant of an organization, if he quits, retires, or dies, is usually replaced by another. If a college loses its whole football team in an airplane accident, in a couple of years it will have another one. A country, like Germany, which loses territory in a war may do much better economically on its restricted territory rather than on its original territory. An industry may be destroyed by law, as the liquor industry in the United States was destroyed by prohibition. It may reestablish itself surreptitiously or, if the law is removed, it will grow back again just like the leg on a salamander. This "pattern persistence" phenomenon, as it might be called, is a characteristic of virtually all complex systems. As far as I know, there is very little general theory of this phenomenon. In social systems, the payoff structure is a very important element in this process. In the economic model, the "price-profit mechanism," as it is called, is an important explanatory factor explaining both the distribution of economic activity and also its regeneration. Crime will expand roughly to the point and not much beyond the point where it pays the going average wage. The liquor industry was smaller under prohibition because of the legal costs and penalties involved. Once these had been removed, it grew again to approximately its previous size, again to the point where the economic returns in it were approximately normal. It is a fascinating speculation as to whether there are any processes corresponding to this in the biosphere. In an ecosystem, each species expands up to the point where it no longer "pays" — at least in terms of birth and death rates — to expand any further. It is harder to perceive processes of this kind in the body and hard, perhaps, to conceive of a process of "payoffs" for individual cells. But the line of thought at least seems worth pursuing.

These second-cousin relationships between economics and, indeed, the social sciences generally, and the biological sciences may not be any more than suggestive of some future possibilities. Nevertheless, they are tantalizingly suggestive, and one hopes that a few family reunions might set in motion conversations and learning processes which would lead to mutual enrichment.

References

Boulding, K. E. (1953) *The Organizational Revolution*. New York: Harper and Row.

———. (1970) *A Primer on Social Dynamics*. New York: Free Press.

Jevons, W. S. (1911) *The Theory of Political Economy*. 4th ed. London: Macmillan and Co.

Marshall, A. (1961) *Principles of Economics*. C. W. Guillebaud (ed.), 9th ed. New York: Macmillan.

Noyes, C. R. (1948) *Economic Man*. New York: Columbia University Press.

Samuelson, P. A. (1947) *Foundations of Economic Analysis*. Cambridge, Mass.: Harvard University Press.

Veblen, T. (1919) *The Place of Science in Modern Civilisation*. New York: B. W. Huebsch.

10

Economics from a Biological Viewpoint

Jack Hirshleifer

I. Economics and Biology

The field variously called population biology, sociobiology, or ecology is concerned to explain the observed interrelations among the various forms of life—organisms, species, and broader groupings and communities—and between forms of life and their external environments. The subject includes both material aspects of these interrelations (the geographical distributions of species in relation to one another, their respective numbers, physical properties like size differences between the sexes) and behavioral aspects (why some species are territorial while others flock, why some are monogamous and others polygamous, why some are aggressive and others shy).

From one point of view, the various social sciences devoted to the study of mankind, taken together, constitute but a subdivision of the all-encompassing field of sociobiology (Wilson, 1975). The ultimately biological subject matter of economics in particular has been recognized by some of our leading thinkers. There is however a special link between economics and sociobiology over and above the mere fact that economics studies a subset of the social behavior of one of the higher mammals. *The fundamental organizing concepts of the dominant analytical structures employed in economics and in sociobiology are strikingly parallel* (see also Rapport and Turner, 1977). What biologists study can be regarded as "Nature's economy" (Ghiselin, 1974). Oswald Spengler perceived (and regarded it as a serious criticism) that Darwin's contribution represented "the application of economics to biology" (Himmelfarb, 1959). Fundamental concepts like scarcity, competition, equilibrium, and specialization play similar roles in both spheres of inquiry. And terminological pairs such as species/industry, mutation/innovation, evolution/progress, mutualism/exchange have more or less analogous denotations.

Reprinted from the *Journal of Law and Economics,* vol. 20, pp. 1–52, April 1977, by permission of the University of Chicago Press. © 1977 by the University of Chicago Press. The article has been slightly condensed, the citations have been reorganized, and footnotes have been eliminated.

Regarded more systematically, the isomorphism between economics and sociobiology involves the intertwining of two levels of analysis. On the first level, acting units or entities choose strategies or develop techniques that promote success in the struggle or *competition* for advantage in given environments. The economist usually calls this process "optimizing," the biologist, "adapting." The formalizations involved are equations of constrained maximization. The second, higher level of analysis examines the social or aggregate resultant of the interaction of the striving units or agents. The formalizations here take the form of equations of equilibrium. (In more general versions, the static solutions may be embedded in "dynamic" equations showing the time paths of approach to solution states.) The solutions on the two levels are of course interdependent. The pursuit of advantage on the part of acting units takes place subject to opportunities and constraints that emerge from the social context, while the resulting social configuration (constituting at least part of the environment for each separate agent) depends in turn upon the strategies employed by the advantage-seeking entities.

Among the methodological issues that might arise at this point are two with somewhat opposed thrusts: (1) Given the validity of a sociobiological outlook on human behavior, are we not claiming too much for economics? What role is there left for the other social sciences if economics can be regarded as essentially coextensive with the sociobiology of human behavior? (2) But alternatively, are we not claiming too little for economics (and a fortiori for the other social sciences) in adopting the reductive interpretation of human behavior implicit in the sociobiological approach? May it not be the case that the cultural evolution of the human species has carried it into a realm where biological laws are determinative of only a minor fraction of behavioral phenomena? (Or perhaps economics is the discipline that regards mankind as merely sociobiological in nature, while the other social sciences treat of the higher aspects of human culture?)

Consideration of the second group of questions will be reserved for the concluding sections of this paper. With regard to the first — a seeming claim that the domain of economics is coextensive with the total sphere of all the social sciences together — a unified social-science viewpoint is adopted here, in which economics and other social studies are regarded as interpenetrating rather than compartmentalized. The traditional core area of compartmentalized economics is characterized by models that: (a) postulate rational self-interested behavior on the part of individuals with given references for material goods and services, and (b) attempt to explain those interactions among such individuals that take the form of market exchanges, under a fixed legal system of property and free contract. That only a very limited portion of human behavioral association could be adequately represented under such self-imposed analytical constraints has often been pointed out to economists by other social scientists. In recent years economics has begun to break through these self-imposed barriers, to take as subject matter all human activity that can be interpreted as goal-directed behavior constrained by and yet, in the aggregate, determinative of resultant social configurations. Significant innovative instances of the application of techniques of economic analysis to broader social issues include Schelling (1960) and Boulding's (1962) works on conflict and warfare, Downs (1957) and Buchanan and Tullock (1962) on political choice, and Becker (1968, 1973) on crime and marriage. And each of these efforts has been followed by a growing literature, in which both economists and other social scientists have participated. The upshot is that (at least in their properly scientific aspect) the social sciences generally can be regarded as in the process of coalescing. As economics "imperialistically" employs its tools of analysis over a wider range of social issues, it will *become* sociology and anthropology and political science. But correspondingly, as these other disciplines grow increasingly rigorous, they will not merely resemble but will *be* economics. It is in this sense that "economics" is taken here as broadly synonymous with "social science."

One of the obvious divergences between economics and sociobiology, it might appear, is that men can consciously optimize — or so we often like to think — whereas, for all but a few higher animals, the concepts of "choice" or "strategy" are only metaphorical. What happens in the biological realm is that, given a sufficiently long run, *natural selection* allows survival only of entities that have developed successful strategies in their respective environments. So the result is sometimes (though not always, as we shall see) *as if* conscious optimization were taking place. The idea that selective pressure of the environment can do the work of conscious optimizing (thus freeing us of any need to postulate a "rational" economic agent) has also received some controversial discussion in the economics literature. This topic will be reviewed in Section III.

After these preliminaries, the central portions of the paper will survey some of the main parallels and divergences in economic and sociobiological reasoning. Since this is written by an economist with only an amateur interest in the biological sciences, attention will be devoted to "what message sociobiology has for economics" rather than to "how we can set the biologists straight."

II. Some Mutual Influences

The most famous example of the influence of an economist upon biological thought is of course the impact of Malthus upon Darwin and Wallace. The codiscoverers of evolution each reported that Malthus' picture of the unremitting pressure of human population upon subsistence provided the key element leading to the idea of evolution by natural selection in the struggle for life.

Malthusian ideas of compounded growth also play a role in modern biological theory. The "Malthusian parameter," as defined by biologists, represents the exponential rate at which a population will grow as limited by its genetic capabilities and constrained by the environment.

In the very recent period a number of biologists have come to make significant use of tools and approaches of economics. Michael T. Ghiselin (1974) has urged fellow biologists to adopt the "methodological individualism" of economics in preference to the open or disguised "teleologism" of assuming optimizing behavior on the part of higher-level groupings and species. A few instances of recent biological optimization studies that seem to be consciously modelled upon economic analytical techniques can be cited: (1) Rapport (1971) showed that the extent of "predator switching" from one prey species to another in response to changes in relative abundance could be expressed in terms of shapes of the predator's indifference curves and opportunity frontier; (2) Gadgil and Bossert (1970) interpreted various characteristics of organisms' life histories — such as the timing and scale of reproductive effort and the determination of survival probabilities at various ages — as the resultant of a balance between "profit" (that is, gain) and "cost" (that is, foregone gain or opportunity cost) in choosing strategies to maximize the Malthusian parameter of population growth; (3) Trivers (1972) demonstrated that several aspects of parental behavior, in particular the differing extent in various species of male versus female "investment" in care of offspring, could be explained in terms of differences in the selectional return on investment to the male and female parents (that is, in terms of the comparative propagation of their respective genetic endowments); (4) Cody (1974) examined the conditions determining the relative competitive advantages of "generalist" versus "specialist" strategies in the exploitation of a mixed-resource environment; (5) E. O. Wilson (1975) employed linear programming models to determine the optimal number and proportion of castes in the division of labor among social insects; (6) Charnov (1976) developed an optimality theorem for foraging animals, in which the forager terminates exploitation of a given food patch when the marginal energy intake falls to equality with the average return from the habitat.

But the more significant intellectual influence has been in the other direction, from biology to social science. The success of theories of evolution and natural selection in the biological realm led quickly to the body of thought called "Social Darwinism" — the most characteristic figures being the philosopher Herbert Spencer in England and the economist William Graham Sumner in America. On the scientific level Social Darwinism represented an attempt to explain patterns of social stratification as the consequence of the selection of superior human types and forms of organization through social competition. To a considerable extent, its exponents went on to draw the inference that such existing stratification was therefore ethically *justified*. The political unpalatability of this conclusion has led to an exceptionally bad press for Social Darwinism — at the hands of other social scientists, jurists, and philosophers, as economists after Sumner have scarcely discussed the question. The Social Darwinists, or some of them at least, did confuse descriptive with moral categories so as to attribute excessive beneficence to natural selection on the human level. In the real world, we know, success *may* sometimes be the reward of socially functional behavior, but also sometimes of valueless or disruptive activities like monopolization, crime, or most of what is carried on under the heading of politics.

It would be incorrect to assume that Darwinism is necessarily conservative in its social implications. The implications would seem to be radical or conservative according as emphasis is placed upon the necessity and importance of mutability and change *(evolution)* or upon final states of harmonious adaptation as a result of selection *(equilibrium)*. Similarly, racist and imperialist theories, on the one hand, and pacifist and universalist theories, on the other hand, could both be founded on Darwinian ideas. The first would emphasize the role of ongoing struggle, and the latter the role of social instinct and mutual aid, in promoting selection of human types. And even among those for whom the key lesson of Darwinism is the competitive struggle for survival, there are a variety of interpretations, ranging from individualistic versions of Spencer and Sumner to a number of collectivist versions: the idea of superior or fitter social classes (Karl Marx), or systems of law and government (Bagehot, 1948), or of course racial groups.

> In the spectrum of opinion that went under the name of social Darwinism almost every variety of belief was included. In Germany, it was represented chiefly by democrats and socialists; in England by conservatives. It was appealed to by nationalists as an argument for a strong state, and by the proponents of laissez-faire as an argument for a weak state. It was condemned by some as an aristocratic doctrine designed to glorify power and greatness, and by others, like Nietzsche, as a middle-class doctrine appealing to the mediocre and submissive. Some socialists saw in it the scientific validation of their doctrine; others the negation of their moral and spiritual hopes. Militarists found in it the sanction of war and conquest, while pacifists saw the power of physical force transmuted into the power of intellectual and moral persuasion (Himmelfarb, 1959:407).

But the too-total rejection of Social Darwinism has meant a lack of appreciation of its valid core of scientific insights: (1) that individuals, groups, races, and even social arrangements (democracy versus dictatorship, capitalism versus socialism, small states versus large) are in never-ending competition with one another, and while the results of this competition have no necessary correlation with moral desert, the competition itself is a fact with explanatory power for social phenomena; (2) that the behavior of mankind is strongly influenced by the biological heritage of the species, and that the forces tending toward either cooperation or conflict among men are in large part identical with phenomena observable in the biological realm.

The sweeping rejection of biological categories for the explanation of human phenomena, on the part of social scientists, is strikingly evidenced by the concluding paragraph of Hofstadter's (1955:204) influential and penetrating study:

> Whatever the course of social philosophy in the future, however, a few conclusions are now accepted by most humanists: that such biological ideas as the "survival of the fittest," whatever their doubtful value in natural science, are utterly useless in attempting to understand society; that the life of man in society, while it is incidentally a biological fact, has characteristics that are not reducible to biology and must be explained in the distinctive terms of a cultural analysis; that the physical well-being of men is a result of their social organization and not vice versa; that social improvement is a product of advances in technology and social organization, not of breeding or selective elimination; that judgements as to the value of competition between men or enterprises or nations must be based upon social and not allegedly biological consequences; and, finally, that there is nothing in nature or a naturalistic philosophy of life to make impossible the acceptance of moral sanctions that can be employed for the common good.

This statement is on solid ground in rejecting attempts to draw moral claims from biological premises. But it promotes confusion in confounding these claims with — and therefore rejecting out of hand — the entirely scientific contention that man's biological endowment has significant implications for his social behavior.

Following Nicholson, Darwinian evolution involves four main factors: the occurrence of *variations,* some mechanism of *inheritance* to preserve variations, the Malthusian tendency to *multiplication* (leading sooner or later to *competition* among organisms), and finally environmental *selection.* From this broad point of view it is clear that there may be cultural evolution even apart from any biological change. Hofstadter seems to regard the forms of human association and the patterns of human social and cultural change as almost entirely free of biological determinants — apart, presumably, from permanent human characteristics like degree of intelligence which determine and constrain the *possibilities* of cultural advance. In contrast, the sociobiological point of view is that cultural and biological change cannot be so totally dichotomized; cultural tracking of environmental change is a group-behavioral form of adaptation, which interacts in a variety of ways with genetic and population responses (Wilson, 1975:145). There is cultural evolution even in the nonhuman sphere, as animals discover successful patterns of behavior which then spread by learning and imitation. Apart from the direct implications for population composition (those individuals who succeed in learning more efficient behavior survive in greater numbers), there may be genetic consequences in that the behavioral changes may modify the conditions of selection among genetic mutations and recombinations.

Along this line, the anthropologist Alland (1967) emphasizes that culture itself should be regarded as a kind of biological adaptation. And there is a long tradition among biologists which encourages attention to the implications of human biological origins for social behavior and institutions. Among the important recent instances are J. Huxley, Fisher, Dobzhansky, Lorenz, Tiger and Fox, and of course E. O. Wilson. On the more popular level are such works as Ardrey (1961 and 1970) and Morris (1967). But these ideas have won relatively little acceptance among social scientists.

Turning now to economics, the relevance of quasi-biological (selectional) models has been the topic of controversial discussion since Alchian's paper in 1950. Alchian argued that environmental selection ("adoption") could replace the traditional analysis premised upon rational profit-maximizing behavior ("adaptation") as a source of verifiable predictions about visible characteristics of business firms. This discussion, which has interesting parallels within biology proper, will be reviewed next.

III. Biological Models of the Firm: Optimization Versus Selection

Alchian contended that optimization on the part of the business firm (profit maximization in the traditional formulation) was an unnecessary and even unhelpful idea for purposes of scientific explanation and prediction. While profit is undoubtedly the firm's goal, the substantive content of profit *maximization* as a guiding rule erodes away when it is realized that any actual choice situation always involves profit as a probability distribution rather than as a deterministic variable. And even if firms never attempted to *maximize profit* but behaved purely randomly, the environment would nevertheless select ("adopt") relatively correct decisions in the sense of meeting the *positive realized profit* condition of survival. Without assuming profit maximization, therefore, the economist can nevertheless predict that relatively correct (viable) adaptations or decisions will tend to be the ones observed — for example, the employment of low-skilled workers becomes less viable a practice after the imposition of a minimum-wage law.

Enke (1951) expanded on Alchian's discussion, with a significant shift in point of view. He suggested that, *given sufficient intensity of competition*, all policies save the optimum would in time fail the survival test. As firms pursuing successful policies expand and multiply, absorbing a larger fraction of the market, a higher and higher standard of behavior becomes the minimum criterion for competitive survival. *In the long run, viability dictates optimality.* Consequently, for long-run predictive purposes (under conditions of intense competition), the analyst is entitled to assume that firms behave "as if" optimizing.

"As if" optimization is of course what the biologist ordinarily has in mind in postulating that organisms (or, sometimes, genes or populations) "choose" strategies leading to evolutionary success. Two levels of the optimization metaphor in biology may be distinguished. First, there are axes along which the organism can be regarded as having a degree of actual choice (what size of territory to defend, how much effort to devote to the struggle for a mate, what intensity of parental care to confer upon offspring). Here we speak only of "as if" optimizing because we do not credit the animal with the intelligence necessary for true (nonmetaphorical) optimization. Secondly, there are axes along which the organism cannot exercise choice in any meaningful sense at all (whether or not to be an unpalatable insect, whether or not to be a male or a female). Nevertheless, such is the power of selection that the optimization metaphor often seems workable for "choice" of biological characters even on this second level.

There is, however, a serious problem here not yet adequately treated in either economics or biology. If, as applies in almost all interesting cases, the strategic choice is *among probability distributions,* what is the "optimum?" According to what criterion does natural selection select when strategies have uncertain outcomes?

In evolutionary theory, the "as if" criterion of success (the maximand) is generally postulated to be *fitness:* the ratio of offspring numbers to parent numbers at corresponding points in the generational life cycle. In a deterministic situation, no doubt it is better adaptive strategy to choose higher fitness over lower. (Or, translating from metaphorical to literal language, in the long run the environment will be filled by those types of organisms who have developed and passed on to descendants traits permitting higher multiplication ratios.) But what if the situation is not deterministic, so that some or all of the strategies available generate probability distributions rather than definite deterministic numbers for the fitness ratio? In such circumstances the strategy that is optimal in terms of *mean* fitness—that yields the highest mathematical expectation of offspring per parent—might be quite different from the strategy that rates highest in terms of viability (that minimizes the probability of extinction). Where such a conflict arises, some biologists have suggested that viability considerations dominate over mean fitness.

No solution to this general problem in evolution theory will be offered here. The point to be underlined is that Enke envisaged a situation where the outcome of each alternative policy option for the firm is *objectively* deterministic, although *subjectively* uncertain from the point of view of the firm's decision maker (acting under limited information). Under these conditions there really does exist an objectively optimum course of action leading to maximum profit, which intense competition (even in the absence of knowledge) ultimately enforces—in Enke's view—upon all surviving firms. Alchian (1950:212) sometimes seems to have the same idea. In saying that *maximum* realized profits is meaningful while *maximizing* profit is not, he means that one cannot "maximize" a probability distribution representing subjective uncertainty about profit, but there is nevertheless a deterministic or objective "maximum" of profit that could be attained if the knowledge were available. Usually, however, Alchian seems to have in mind the quite different case in which the outcomes are intrinsically or *objectively* probabilistic, rather than merely subjectively uncertain because of imperfect knowledge. Here there does not exist any unequivocal optimum, and Enke's argument does not apply. For Alchian, it is in such an environment that viability (positive realized profit) becomes the relevant success criterion.

Independent of Alchian's introduction of the viability argument, but parallel in its implications, was Herbert A. Simon's (1955) contention that firms are better regarded as "satisficing" than as optimizing. Starting from a psychological rather than evolutionary orientation, Simon contended that decision makers are conservative about modifying established routines yielding satisfactory results—unless forced to do so by exogenous changes that threaten unacceptable outcomes. The reason given was informational: the decision maker who recognizes the inadequacy of his knowledge, or the costs of performing the computations necessary for determining optimality even if he had all the relevant data, does not find that it pays even to attempt to optimize. Simon did allow for a long-run approach toward optimization under stationary conditions in the form of a gradual shift of the decision maker's "aspiration level" toward the best outcome attainable. But, he emphasized, business decisions take place in a context of ever-recurring change; the process of gradual approximation of optimality can never progress very far before being confounded by events. Thus, for Simon as for Alchian, the environment primarily plays a selective role in rewarding choice of *viable* strategies. Simon, in contrast with Alchian, chooses to emphasize how this process has in effect been internalized into the psychology of decision makers.

A closely related aspect of the optimizing-selection process is the question of "perfection." It is possible in evolutionary models alternatively to emphasize the *achieved state of adaptation,* or the *process of adaptive change* toward that state. In the biological realm a high state of perfection on the organismic level has been attained: " . . . organisms in general are, in fact, marvellously and intricately adapted, both in their internal mechanisms, and in their relations to external nature (Fisher, 1958:44). The high degree of perfection is evidenced by the fact that the vast majority of mutations, which follow a random law, are harmful to the organism rather than beneficial. An important and less obvious consequence of the high degree of perfection is that the environment, as it changes under a variety of random influences, is always (from the organism's viewpoint) tending to deteriorate. So even relatively well adapted organisms, or particularly such organisms, require the ability to track environmental changes. In the economic sphere, in contrast, we do not—though perhaps we should—think in terms of a very high degree of perfection in the adaptations of individuals or firms. The argument in terms of perfection has been at the heart of much of the critical discussion of the biological model in economics.

Penrose (1952) criticized Alchian by contending, in effect, that the achieved state of economic adaptation is generally *too perfect* to be accounted for by merely random behavior on the part of businessmen. Although high states of adaptation are indeed attained in the biological sphere even without rational optimizing, that is due, she argued, to the extreme intensity of competition forced by organisms' innate urge to multiply—the Malthusian principle. This urge being lacking in the economic sphere, and competition therefore less intense, the businessman's purposive drive to make money is required to supply the analogous driving force.

Of course, the *desire* to make money is not enough. The key point of the Penrose criticism is that this desire must, for the most part, be realized. Businessmen must expect to be successful if they are to enter the competitive arena. And any such expectation would be too regularly refuted to persist if actual outcomes realized were no better than would ensue from random action. So the Penrose image is one of a changing environment (else there would not be much in the way of profit opportunities) very effectively tracked by rationally optimizing businessmen.

The selectional process of nature, driven by random variation and Malthusian competition, are profligately wasteful of life and energy. An implication of the Penrose thesis is that the wastage cost of economic selection should be considerably less than that of biological selection. Quantitative estimates of the selectional wastage cost (bankruptcies, abandonments, etc.) would be of interest, therefore, in providing some measure of the prevalence and success of rational optimization.

While Penrose argued that the observed degree of adaptation in the economy is *too perfect* to be accounted for by blind environmental selection, Winter's (1964) critique is based on the opposite contention—that the state of adaptation is *too imperfect* to be accounted for by a process that leads to the same outcomes "as if" firms actually optimized. His argument is therefore directed against Enke's extension of the selectional model, against the idea that in the long run viability requires optimality, rather than against Alchian's original version. The main evidence of imperfection cited by Winter is the prevalence in business practice of conventional rules of thumb (for example, a pricing policy of fixed percentage markups) even where seemingly in conflict with profit-maximizing behavior.

Winter contributed interesting suggestions about the nature of *inheritance* and *variation* in economic selectional models. For Alchian, the inherited aspect of the firm was described as "fixed internal conditions"—in effect, simple inertia due to the fact that the firm is more or less the same from one day to the next. Variation was attributed to imitation of successful firms, or simply to trial-and-error exploration. For Winter the inherited element, analogous to the biological genotype, is represented by certain more permanent aspects of the firm (its "decision rule"). This is to be distinguished from the specific decision made in a given context, which is analogous to the biological phenotype. What the environment selects is the correct action, even though it be the chance result of a rather inferior decision rule. In natural selection as well, well-adapted and less well-adapted genotypes might be represented at a given moment by the same phenotype. But, over a number of generations, natural selection working together with the Mendelian laws of inheritance will tend to fix the superior genotype in the population. The economic mechanism of repeated trials is somewhat different, as no genetic recombination is involved. But surely we can expect that, as a variety of selectional tests are imposed over time, those firms providing a merely lucky action-response to a particular environmental configuration will tend to be selected against as compared with those following a more correct decision rule.

In his first article Winter employed the term "organization form" for what his later papers call "decision rule" or "rule of action." While the intended referent is the same, and is indeed better described by the words "decision rule" or "rule of action," the initial term had interesting implications that might well have been pursued. "Organization form" would ordinarily be understood to mean something like corporation or partnership, large firm or small, etc. This is a more visible and operational concept than "decision rule." Since even the best decision rule (in the usual sense of that term) might not make possible survival of a firm with an ill-adapted organization form, we should really think of three levels of selection—action, decision rule, and organization form.

The broadly similar views of Alchian and Winter represent, it might be noted, a Lamarckian evolutionary model. Lamarck believed (as did Darwin) that acquired characters can be inherited, and also that variations tend to appear when needed. Failure-stimulated search for new rules of action (Winter), taking in particular the form of imitation of observed success (Alchian), is—if the results are assumed to be heritable—certainly in the spirit of Lamarck. The Lamarckian model is inapplicable to inheritance and variation (whether somatic or behavioral) mediated by the *genetic* mechanism, but it seems to be broadly descriptive of *cultural* evolution in general, and of economic responses in particular.

Perhaps Winter's most important contribution in this area is his actual modelling of possible *selectional equilibrium* situations. Space does not permit adequate exposition or review of these formulations here, but the following summary may be suggestive:

> Those organization forms which have the lowest zero growth price are viable, others are not. Or, to put the matter another way, price will tend to the lowest value at which some firm's organization form still yields non-negative growth. Firms whose organization forms result in decline at that price will approach zero scale as time goes on, leaving the firms which have the minimum zero growth price to share the market. (Winter, 1964:253)

This language suggests the "long run zero-profit equilibrium" of the competitive industry, reinterpreted in terms of the biologists' population equilibrium condition of zero growth. But Winter is at pains to show that even a firm with the lowest possible zero-growth price (lowest minimum of Average Total Cost curves) might—as a result of using an inappropriate decision rule—not actually be a survivor in selectional equilibrium. So the traditional competitive equilibrium might not be generated, or, once generated, might not respond in the standard way to changes in exogenous determinants. One reason for this divergence from the traditional result, however, is that Winter's model is limited to the single adjustment mechanism of *firm growth*. Among the factors not considered, *entry pressure* on the part of new firms and (a more surprising omission in view of the previous emphasis) *failure-stimulated search* on the part of unsuccessful existing firms would tend to force a progressively higher state of adaptation upon survivors.

In his 1971 article Winter indicates that in order to achieve the optimality properties of the standard competitive model an "innovating remnant" is needed. This category consists of firms that are, for unexplained reasons, inveterate searchers who will ultimately hit upon any as-yet-undiscovered superior decision rules. But new entrants, upon whom standard theory relies to discipline firms already in the industry, can also serve this exploratory role. A fruitful approach, consistent with biological observation, would be to recognize that one of the many possible survival strategies adopted by organisms (firms) is a tendency to search—and at any moment of time there will be a balance between organisms searching for new niches and organisms adapting to existing ones. (This point will come up again when competitive strategies are discussed below.)

It is a rather odd accident that biological models entered into economic thought in connection with the theory of the *business firm*—a highly specialized and consciously contrived "cultural" grouping. To some extent, as just seen, evolution theory is applicable to firms: inheritance, variation, competition, selection, adaptation — all play roles in explaining the observed patterns of survivorship and activity. Still, if biological models were being explored afresh for possible relevance to economic behavior, one's first target for consideration would naturally be the *individual* together with the *family* — entities of direct biological significance. Without any preconceived limitation of attention to the business firm, several aspects of economic theorizing will now be examined from a biological orientation: the nature and provenance of preferences; the evolution of patterns of competition, cooperation, and conflict; and resulting tendencies toward equilibrium, cycles, and progressive change.

IV. Elements of Economic Theorizing: A Biological Interpretation

The contention here is that the social processes studied by economics, or rather by the social sciences collectively, are not mere analogs but are rather *instances* of sociobiological mechanisms — in the same sense in which chemical reactions have been shown to be a special class of processes following the laws of physics. For this to be in any way a useful idea, it remains to be shown that a more general sociobiological outlook can in fact provide social scientists with a deeper and more satisfactory explanation of already-known results, or better still can generate new ones.

A. Utility, Fitness, and the Provenance of Preferences —
Especially, Altruism

Modern neoclassical economics has forsworn any attempt to study the source and content of preferences, that is, the goals that motivate men's actions. It has regarded itself as the logic of choice under conditions of "given tastes." But many of the great and small social changes in history have stemmed from *shifts* in people's goals for living. The very terminology used by the economist — preferences, wants, tastes — tends not only to trivialize these fundamental aims and values, but implies that they are arbitrary or inexplicable *(de gustibus non est disputandum)*. Nor have the other social sciences, to whom the economists have unilaterally delegated the task of studying preferences, made much progress in that regard. The healthy aggrandizing tendency of modern economics requires us, therefore, to overstep this boundary like so many others.

No doubt there is a large arbitrary element in the determination of wants. Individuals are idiosyncratic, and even socially influenced preferences may reflect chance accidents in the histories of particular societies. But it is equally clear that not all preferences for commodities represent "mere taste." When we learn that Alabamans like cooling drinks more than Alaskans do, it is not hard to decipher the underlying physiological explanation for such differences in "tastes." Unfortunately, the refusal of modern economics to examine the biological functions of preferences has meant that the bridge between human physiology and social expressions of desires has been studied by no one (except, perhaps, by practitioners of empirical "human engineering").

On a very abstract level, the concept of *homeostatis* has been put forward as the foundation of wants: the individual is postulated as acting to maintain vital internal variables within certain limits necessary for optimum functioning, or at least for survival. But homeostatis is too limited a goal to describe more than very short-run human adaptations. And in any case, the internal "production function" connecting these internal variables with external social behavior has somehow fallen outside the domain of any established field of research.

Of more critical importance to social science than tastes for ordinary commodities are preferences taking the form of attitudes toward other humans. Anger and envy are evidently antisocial sentiments, while benevolence and group identification promote socialization. Socially relevant attitudes differ from culture to culture: in some societies hierarchical dominance is a prime motive for action, in others not; marital partners value fidelity highly, in others promiscuity is regarded as normal; in some cultures people cluster closely together, in others they avoid personal contact. The programmatic contention here is that such preference patterns, despite seemingly arbitrary elements, have survived because they are mainly adaptive to environmental conditions. (No strong emphasis will be placed upon the issue of whether such adaptations are cultural or genetic in origin, in line with the argument above that the ability to evolve cultural traits is itself a kind of genetic adaptation.) This contention will surely not be always found to hold; in the biology of plants and animals as well, it is often unclear whether a particular morphological or behavioral trait is truly adaptive or merely an accidental variation. Nature is unceasingly fertile in producing random modifications. But if a trait has survived, as a working hypothesis the biologist looks for an adaptive function.

As a nice example, in a famous passage in *The Descent of Man* Darwin asserted that for hive bees the instinct of maternal hatred rather than maternal love serves an adaptive function. He went on to generalize that, for animals in general (and not excluding mankind), "sentiments" or social attitudes are but a mechanism of adaptation (Ghiselin, 1974:218–219). The anthropologist Ronald Cohen (1972) has similarly pointed to variations among cultures in degrees of "affect" (that is, of interpersonal emotional attachment) as adaptive responses to environmental circumstances.

The biological approach to preferences, to what economists call the utility function, postulates that all such motives or drives or tastes represent proximate aspects of a single underlying goal—fitness. Preferences are governed by the all-encompassing *drive for reproductive survival*. This might seem at first absurd. That all humans do not solely and totally regard themselves as children-making machines seems evidenced by phenomena such as birth control, abortion, and homosexuality. Or, if these be considered aberrations, by the large fractions of income and effort devoted to human aims that compete with child rearing—among them entertainment, health care beyond the childbearing age, personal intellectual advancement, etc. Yet, all these phenomena might still be indirectly instrumental to fitness. Birth control may be a device leading *on net balance* to more descendants rather than fewer; health care beyond the childbearing age may more effectively promote the survival and vigor of children or grandchildren. And, as we shall see shortly, even a childlessness strategy *may* be explicable in fitness terms!

In any attempt to broaden the application of economic reasoning, to make it a general social science, a key issue is the problem of altruism (the "taste" for helping others): its extent, provenance, and determinants. Old-fashioned, narrow economics was often criticized for employing the model of economic man—a selfish, calculating, and essentially nonsocial being. Of course, it was impossible to postulate such a man in dealing with that essential social grouping, *the family*. Neoclassical economics avoided the difficulty by abandoning attempts to explain intrafamily interactions! Some economists formalized this evasion by taking the household rather than the individual as the fundamental *unit* of economic activity; in effect, they postulated total altruism within and total selfishness outside the family.

Modern economic "imperialists" have been dissatisfied both with the excessively restrictive postulate of individual selfishness and with the exclusion of intrafamily behavior from the realm of economic analysis. The modern view postulates a generalized preference or utility function in which selfishness is only the midpoint of a spectrum ranging from benevolence at one extreme to malevolence at the other. But, standing alone, this is really an empty generalization. Where an individual happens to lie on the benevolence-malevolence scale with regard to other individuals still remains a merely arbitrary "taste." And yet we all know that patterns of altruism are not merely arbitrary. That a parent is more benevolent to his own child than to a stranger's is surely capable of explanation.

From the evolutionary point of view the great analytical problem of altruism is that, in order to survive the selectional process, altruistic behavior must be profitable in fitness terms. It must somehow be the case that being generous (at least sometimes, to some beneficiaries) is selectively more advantageous than being selfish!

A possible semantic confusion arises here. If altruism were defined simply as accepting injury to self in order to help others, without countervailing benefit of any kind, then indeed natural selection would quickly eliminate altruist behavior. When biologists speak of altruism they do mean to rule out offsetting or redeeming mechanisms making unselfish behavior profitable in some sense; indeed, their analysis requires that such exist.

The redeeming mechanisms identified by biologists seem to fall into two main categories. In the first, altruistic behavior survives because, despite initial appearances, a fuller analysis shows that *the preponderance of benefit or advantage is really conferred on the self*. We may, though paradoxically, call such behavior "selfish altruism"; being ultimately selfish, such altruism does not require compensation or reciprocity to be viable. In the second class of redeeming mechanism compensation does take place; Trivers (1971) has termed such behavior "reciprocal altruism." Reciprocal altruism, apart from motivation, approaches what economists would of course call *exchange*. It will be discussed, in connection with that topic, in Section B following.

The clearest cases of selfish altruism, of behavior only seemingly unselfish, stem from the fact that *in the biological realm there are two levels of self*. On one level is the morphological and physiological constitution of the organism (the phenotype); on the other level the organism's genetic endowment (the genotype). The genetic constitution may contain recessive genes that are not expressed in the phenotype; perhaps even more important, the phenotype is subjected to and modified by environmental influences that leave the genotype unaffected. "Unselfish" action defined as behavior that injures the organism's phenotypical well-being may yet tend to propagate the organism's genotype. Indeed, since all living beings eventually die, ultimately the only way to achieve a payoff in fitness terms is to help certain other organisms — most notably, of course, one's offspring — carry one's genetic endowment beyond the death barrier . . . .

Altruistic behavior may prove to be viable in selectional terms even in the absence of any reciprocation. Over the course of human and prehuman evolutionary development, drives or instincts promoting such behavior have evolved and ultimately taken the form that the economist so inadequately calls preferences. And what is true for the specific "taste for altruism" holds in considerable degree for preferences in general — that these are not arbitrary or accidental, but rather the resultants of systematic evolutionary processes. This does not mean that such attitudes are now immutable. On the contrary, the inbuilt drives themselves contain the capability of expressing themselves in diverse ways depending upon environmental circumstances, which will in turn be modified by cultural evolution. The main lesson to be drawn, therefore, is not that preferences are biologically determined in any complete way — but rather, that they are scientifically analyzable and even in principle predictable in terms of the inheritance of past genetic and cultural adaptations together with the new adjustments called for by current environmental circumstances.

B. *Exchange and Other Competitive Strategies*

Exchange, the sole form of social interaction traditionally studied by economists, is a particular competitive strategy in the great game of life—one involving a mutually beneficial relation among two or more organisms. It fits into the more general category called "mutualism" by biologists, of which there are both interspecific and intraspecific examples. Among the former are the symbiosis of alga and fungus that constitutes a lichen, the pollination-nectar exchange between bees and flowers, the presence of nitrogen-fixing bacteria on the roots of leguminous plants, and the resident protozoa in the gut of the termite that facilitate digestion of cellulose. Particularly interesting are the complementary associations among somewhat higher animals, which can be regarded as involving a degree of consciousness and discretionary choice. Here mutualism approaches the economic concept of change.

In the absence of legal enforcement of compensation for acts conferring advantages on others, such patterns of mutual aid in the biological realm may represent instances of altruism on the part of one or more of the participants. A nice example of what Trivers (1971) called reciprocal altruism is the interaction wherein certain fish species feed by grooming other, larger species—who in return refrain from eating their cleaners.

The key question for the selectional advantage of such reciprocal aid (in economic terms, for the viability of a pattern of exchange or "market") is control of cheating. As Trivers points out, this is a Prisoner's Dilemma—a special case of the more general public-good situation. However great the advantage jointly to the trading pair of establishing a reciprocal relationship, it pays each member to cheat if he can. The big fish, once having been properly groomed, would seem to be in a position to profit by snapping up his helper. (The little cleaner fish often does his work actually within the mouth of his client.) On the other side of the transaction, mimics have evolved that imitate the characteristic markings of the true cleaners. Upon being permitted to approach the big fish, the mimic takes a quick bite and then escapes!

The problem here is essentially the same as the cheating, sale of "lemons," or "moral hazard" that arises in a number of market contexts. While these phenomena threaten market viability, given the mutual advantage of trade the market can tolerate *some* slippage through cheating, provided it is kept within bounds. A number of devices have evolved, in both market and biological contexts, to limit the degree of slippage. The market cheater may be punished by law, the mimic cleaner fish by being (with some probability) caught and eaten. Noncheaters in markets establish personal reputations and brand names, while cleaner fish develop (so it is claimed) a regular clientele of satisfied customers.

Mutually advantageous exchange is facilitated by altruistic motivations: the emotions of affection and sympathy have evolved, Trivers contends, because they provide a better guarantee of reciprocity than any mere calculated advantage of doing so. Put another way, altruism economizes on costs of policing and enforcing agreements.

Becker (1976) has contended that sympathetic motivation may be required *only on one side* of reciprocal-altruism interactions. The other party can be quite selfish in his aims, yet may still find cooperative behavior advantageous. Consider a selfish beneficiary of a parent's benevolence: a "rotten kid." The key proposition is that the rotten kid may still act benevolently toward the parent, simply in order to maximize the latter's capacity to bestow benefits upon him. And, in these circumstances, the mutual advantage of cooperative behavior may be such that even the "unselfish" parent ends up *selfishly* better off than he would if he were not altruistic! Consequently, in biological terms, no loss of fitness on either side is involved. This altruistic "contagiousness" — unselfish motivation on one side breeding cooperative behavior on the other side — would seem to promote the evolution of mutual aid patterns. Let one party be so motivated, for whatever reason (for example, altruism on the part of the parent could evolve simply from kin selection), and we will tend to observe reciprocity and mutual aid.

More generally, Trivers argues that human evolution has developed a balance between the abilities to engage in and to detect and suppress subtle cheating while participating in reciprocal interactions. The sense of justice, what Trivers calls "moralistic aggression," is an emotion that involves third parties as additional enforcers to punish cheaters. Finally, the selectional advantage of these emotions has led to evolution of the ability to simulate or mimic them — to hypocrisy. Note once again how these emotional qualities, absent from the makeup of "economic man," turn out to have an important place in the biological economy of human relationships. Economics can, as the economic imperialists allege, deal with the whole human being, and indeed *must* do so even to explain the phenomena in its traditional domain of market behavior.

The chief biological example of *intraspecific* exchange is of course mating interaction. Here vying for trading partners, sexual competition, not only has market parallels but is of course an important economic phenomenon in its own right. In some human societies marriage partners are explicitly sold, but more generally the marriage relationship constitutes a form of "social exchange." The competition for mates in the biological realm displays many familiar and some unexpected parallels with market phenomena.

Health and vigor in sexual partners are obviously desirable qualities, correlated with the probability of generating and rearing viable offspring. As a means of demonstrating these qualities (that is of advertising), sexual displays, combats, and rituals have developed. There is a nice analogy here with recent economic theories of "competitive signalling." Some characteristics may be acquired by economic agents not because they *confer* competitive superiority, but only because they *demonstrate* a preexisting superiority (in potential for mutually advantageous exchange). Just as success in display or combat, even in cases where biologically useless in itself, may signal sexual vigor — so educational attainment, even where of itself useless in contributing to productivity, may yet be a signal of useful qualities like intelligence.

Another desirable quality in a mate is possession of territory, generally by the male. This is advertised in birds by the call. Presumably it is not the artistic excellence of the male's call that attracts the female, but the mere announcement effect — since the quality of the product (of the territory) is evident on inspection. But for goods whose quality can be determined only by experience, the main message conveyed by advertising is simply that the product is worth the effort of advertising! Sexual displays seem to fall in this category.

Sexual competition also provides parallels with what is sometimes called "excessive" or "destructive" competition for trade. Cheating is once again a factor, as it pays males to mimic vigor by convincing displays even if they do not actually possess it. (The "coyness" of the female is said to have evolved to prevent premature commitment of her limited reproductive capacity to males with only a superficially attractive line.) Sexual combats may go beyond mere demonstration and actually harm the vanquished party, or sometimes the victor as well. Biologists have devoted considerable attention to cases like the peacock, where the extreme development of sexual ornaments appears to be disfunctional to the species or even to the individual. The explanation seems to be that positive *sexual selection* can to a degree overcome a disadvantage in terms of *natural selection* — the peacock with a splendid tail does not survive so well or so long but is more likely to find a mate. Such a development requires that male ornamentation and female preference evolve in parallel, which when carried to an extreme degree may represent a rather unstable equilibrium.

In economic exchange, another mechanism of competition is *entry and exit* — variation of numbers to equalize on the margin the net advantages of the various types of activity. This also operates in sexual competition; the sex ratio varies to equalize the advantage of being a male or female! Other things equal the equilibrium male/female sex ratio is 1/1. Taking any offspring generation exactly half its genetic endowment is provided by male parents and half by female parents. Hence, if one sex were scarcer than the other in the parent generation at mating age, its *per capita* representation in the offspring generation's genes (genetic fitness) would be greater. If the disproportion persisted, it would pay in fitness terms to have offspring of the scarcer sex, and an adaptive response in this direction would correct the disparity. Even such practices as disproportionate infanticide of females will not affect the equilibrium 1/1 ratio. (This outcome displays the power of individual as opposed to group selection, since a 1/1 ratio is not the most "efficient" from the point of view of species growth. In terms of group selection it would generally be much more desirable to have a larger proportion of females.)

One factor that does distort the equilibrium sex ratio has been described by

Trivers and Willard (1973). It is nearly universal among mammals that male parents have a higher *variance* in number of offspring than female parents. (A single male can father hundreds or even thousands of offspring, but the female's reproductive capacity is much more severely limited.) Also, healthy, vigorous parents tend to have healthy, vigorous offspring and physically weak parents, weak offspring. Taken together, these two considerations imply that it pays stronger parents to have *male* offspring; strong male children will tend to engender a relatively larger number of descendants. Conversely, it pays weaker parents to have *female* offspring, to minimize exposure to this variance. Thus an explanation is provided for the otherwise mysterious tendency of the human male/female sex ratio to rise with socioeconomic status (since status tends to be correlated with health and vigor). More generally, the normally higher early male mortality is explained. Prenatal and postnatal mechanisms discriminating against males permit stronger parents (who will suffer relatively less early mortality among their offspring) to end up with relatively more male children and weaker parents with relatively more female children.

Even *interest,* Trivers (1971) suggests, ultimately has a biological origin. *Reproductive value* (the average number of offspring an organism will engender in the future) declines with age in the childbearing life phase. A loan today involves a cost to the lender in fitness terms; since his reproductive value upon repayment will be less, the repayment would have to be proportionately greater to make up the difference.

So exchange in a variety of forms, and with many familiar implications, exists in the biological realm. But what does seem to be a specifically human invention is the *organized* market, a form of exchange involving "middlemen" specialized to trading activity. This must have been what Adam Smith really had in mind in his otherwise too-sweeping assertion that "the propensity to truck, barter, and exchange" is specifically associated with the human species. Sexual competition and cleaning symbioses provide sufficient evidence to the contrary. And associations such as pack membership also undoubtedly involve "social exchange."

But competition for trading partners remains only one very special type of biological competition. The more general concept used by biologists is illustrated in Figure 10.1 (see Boulding, 1962). Let N_G and N_H signify numbers of two populations G and H. Then if N_G, the time-derivative of N_G, is a negative function of N_H, and N_H of N_G, the two populations are called competitors. In the diagram we can draw for population G what the economist would call a "reaction curve" showing the population levels for which N_G = zero, and similarly for population H. Since the populations are competitors, the reaction curves have negative slope. Their intersection will be a state of equilibrium. (Whether the equilibrium is stable or unstable depends upon the relative slopes at the point of intersection—as will be explored further in the

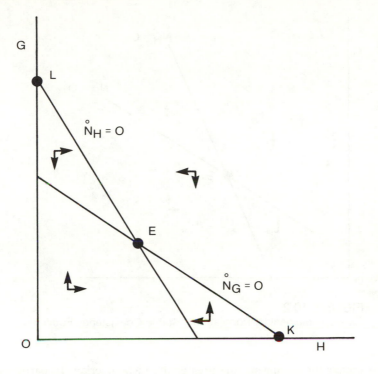

FIGURE 10.1
Two Competitive Populations, Stable Coexistence Equilibrium

next section.) If the reaction curves are *positively* sloped as in Figure 10.2, the two populations are complementary rather than competitive. (Again, depending upon the relative slopes, the intersection point may be stable or unstable.) Finally, there is a mixed case, typified by predator-prey interactions, where the reaction curve of the predator has N_G as an increasing function of the prey population N_H, while N_H is a falling function of N_G. (Again the equilibrium at the intersection may or may not be stable.)

Competition in the general sense exists because some resource of relevance for two or more organisms is in scarce supply. The consequent *universality of competition* (the "struggle for existence") was of course the main message Darwin drew from Malthus. The ecologists speak of an organism's "fundamental niche" as the volume of abstract resource space in which it can exist—and of the "realized niche" as the volume which it actually occupies. Where niches overlap, there is competition. These considerations have one very essential implication: *the competition is generally more severe the more similar the organisms.* The

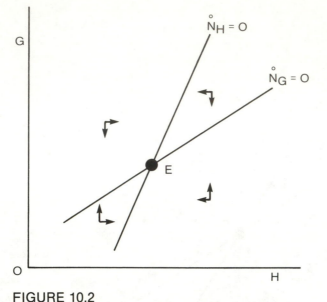

FIGURE 10.2
Two Complementary Populations, Stable Coexistence Equilibrium

more similar the organisms, the greater the niche overlap. In particular, *in-traspecies* competition tends to be more intense than *interspecies* competition. For example, territorial birds exclude conspecifics but to a greater or lesser extent tolerate birds of other species. And, we have seen, competition tends to be particularly severe within families and especially among littermates; the high correlation of genetic endowments and of positions in the generational life cycle, plus physical proximity, make for near identity of resource requirements (niches).

There are two opposing forces which together constitute what might be called the "dilemma of sociality." On the one hand, altruistic preferences or motivations stem mainly from degree of relationship (from correlation of genetic endowments), not only among close kin but extending to more distant relatives. And even, perhaps, to a degree over the entire species. (Other things equal, a man's genes would tell him to favor his fellowman fighting with a bear.) This is the main socializing force. On the hand, competition, which opposes socialization, tends to be most intense precisely where degree of relationship is closest. (The other man will often be a closer competitor than the bear.) In consequence, as organisms strike some balance between cooperative and competitive strategies, there is an element of instability in the outcome. The degree of conflict or of social cooperation is not a simple function of closeness of relationship, but depends upon the specific details of kinship as related to the environmental situation.

Competition-limiting strategies range over a spectrum, from minimal patterns of "holding back" to full cooperation. "Holding back" means that the economic unit or biological organism merely competes somewhat less intensely for resources than short-run selfish interest would dictate. An obvious economic example is cartelization, but more praiseworthy forms of holding back — for example, refraining from blowing up your competitor's premises — also fall into this category. In human societies the institutions of government and law provide reinforcers for what might otherwise be the too-frail force of altruism in limiting the extent of destructive forms of competition. Unfortunately, as evidenced most strikingly by the phenomenon of war, human genetic and cultural evolution have not progressed as far in this direction as might be desired.

Limits on competition have also evolved in the biological realm. In what is called "exploitation competition" organisms scramble to utilize resources but ignore competitors, whereas, in "interference competition," they gain resources precisely by hampering competitors. Interference may take the milder form, as in territoriality, of fighting only as necessary to deny a limited zone of resource access to others. But more aggressive versions also exist, of direct attack upon conspecifics — even of cannibalism, where the competitor himself is converted into a resource. This is relatively rare, however. Presumably, extreme forms of interference strategies have mainly proved disfunctional to the groups or species evolving them, and have therefore been selected against. (*Group* selection need not be involved here, as there is a fitness loss to the individual to the extent that his own descendants are inclined to eat one another up.) Biologists have observed that interference competition is more likely to evolve when resource limitations are particularly severe. In economic affairs as well, "cut-throat competition" is a product of hard times. When organisms are occupying unfilled environments, on the other hand, or firms are interacting in a growing market, competition takes place mainly through the externality of resource depletion (in economic terms, bidding up prices of inputs or driving down prices of products).

Another important means of limiting competition is *specialization*. It is useful to distinguish the specialization that results from competitive pressure, on the one hand, from the kind of cooperative specialization more properly called *the division of labor*. Unfortunately, there has been some confusion on this score. The valuable pioneering study on biology and economics by Houthakker (1956) confounds the two categories. The very important analysis by the biologist Ghiselin (1974: 233–240), on the other hand, distinguishes what he calls the *competitive* division of labor (represented by the subdivision of ecological niches in the biological sphere, corresponding to product or locational differentiation in the economy) from the *cooperative* division of labor. In the former case (which, preferably, ought to be termed simply competitive specialization) there is no mutual dependence or complementarity among the entities. Each would be better off if the others were to vanish. The latter type of differentiation, the division of labor proper, is associated with true alliance—to achieve a common end, or at least for mutual benefit where a degree of complementarity exists.

In competitive specialization in the biological realm, each of the contending species is forced away from the zone of resource overlap—not only in locational terms, but in the form of divergent evolution of characters. This process of character displacement, resulting in an equilibrium *separation distance* between the species, is completely parallel to the economic mechanisms described in our textbooks under the heading of product differentiation competition and locational competition ("monopolistic competition"). But on the other hand, the biologists emphasize, such specialization is constrained by the possibility that a generalist of intermediate character might outcompete the set of specialist types. Relative abundance and certainty of resources favor specialists; relative scarcity and unpredictability favor generalists.

Biologists, having developed a more subtle and elaborate approach to this question of specialization/generalization strategies than economists, recognize a variety of different dimensions of "generalist" competition against specialists. Individuals of a species might tend to a common intermediate character, able to make tolerably good use of a range of resources. Or the *individuals* might be specialized, yet the *species* show enough inter-individual variety to generalize its command over resources. Still another form of generalization is *plasticity*, whereby the species is enabled to change its character in response to environmental shifts. Such plasticity might be genetically determined if the population maintains a reserve of variety in the form of a largely heterozygotic genetic composition. Or failing this, it may have evolved a high mutation rate as a way of tracking the environment. Finally, even with a fixed genetic constitution the capability for learning and *behavioral* adaptation may exist to a greater or lesser extent. The human species, of course, has concentrated upon becoming a generalist of this last type.

Turning now to cooperation in the true sense, we arrive at what is properly called the division of labor. Since competition is most intense when organisms are all attempting to do the *same* thing (to occupy the same niche, to use the same resources), one way out is for individuals or groups to cooperate by doing *different* things. For the group, or rather for each member thereof, command over resources is thereby extended.

The division of labor in Nature penetrates profoundly into the deepest aspects of the differentiation of living matter. In multicelled organisms the parts unselfishly cooperate to serve the whole, which is of course warranted by the fact that all the cells of an individual organism are genetically identical (save the germ cells, of course). Sexual differentiation also represents an evident instance of the cooperative division of labor in the interests of reproductive survival. Here altruism is less perfect, in that each member of the parental team is altruistic toward the other only to the extent necessary for promoting the reproductive survival of his or her own genetic endowment. Nevertheless, the mechanism works well enough to have won out, for the most part, over asexual reproduction. Going beyond this most elemental social unit—the male-female pair—the *family* involves a related type of role differentiation: that associated with the generational life cycle. This provides a temporal division of labor; each generation plays its role, in due course, in promoting the reproductive survival of the parent-offspring chain. While altruism between generations is by no means unlimited, as seen above, the differentiation of tasks ties together the interests of the family group.

For larger cooperative associations, necessarily among more remotely related organisms, specialization through the division of labor with its concomitant of social exchange must, to be viable, become compensatingly productive as the force of altruism is diluted. Traditional economics, epitomized by Adam Smith, demonstrated the economic advantage of the division of labor even for a group of entirely selfish individuals. The sociologist Durkheim (1933), in contrast, claimed that the division of labor generates a kind of superorganismic "solidarity." He argued that the economic benefits of the division of labor are picayune compared to this solidarity, a union not only of interests but of sentiments (as in the case of friends or mates). As so often occurs in social analysis, however, Durkheim fails to distinguish properly between desires (preferences) and opportunities. If there is any superorganismic tie among individuals, it can only be (according to the hypothesis accepted here) their sharing of genetic endowments. Yet in many important instances of the division of labor (for example, bees and flowers) there is no genetic association at all. The cooperative division of labor in such cases is no more than an alliance for mutual benefit. With genetic sharing it is no doubt easier for cooperation to evolve, but superorganismic ties are not sufficient causes and certainly not necessary consequences of the division of labor.

The human species, of course, has carried the divison of labor to extraordinary lengths. The extent to which this represents genetic versus cultural evolution is not a simple matter to resolve. The regulation of cheating, necessary to make exchange and therefore the division of labor possible, has, as we have seen, been achieved in Nature to some degree. Even emotional supports for exchange, like the sense of justice ("moralistic aggression") may represent genetically evolved characters. On the other hand, human culture has evolved institutional supports for exchange and the division of labor—property, law, and government.

Analysis on the part of economists of the determinants of the division of labor has gone little beyond Smith's (1776) famous proposition: ". . . That the division of labour is limited by the extent of the market." Houthakker (1956), taking the standpoint of the individual, views him as the potential beneficiary of a number of activities some or all of which may however be disharmonious if undertaken together. The choice to be made is for individuals either to act as nonspecialists and incur costs of internal coordination, or else to separate and distribute the activities via a division of labor that entails costs of external coordination. Here Smith's "extent of the market" is taken as the inverse of inter-individual transaction costs, the absence of which would facilitate specialization with external coordination. Stigler's (1951) analysis is fundamentally similar, though concentrating on firms as decision units rather than individuals. Again there are a number of activities, all desirable or even essential in the production of output, but diverging mainly in offering economies or diseconomies of *scale*. The firms would do better to divest themselves of at least the increasing-returns activities, if a specialized external supplier were available. As the *industry* expands, such specialized suppliers become economically viable entities. Thus, for Stigler, "extent of the market" signifies *aggregate* scale of output.

The discussion by the biologist Ghiselin (1974: 233–247) provides many apt illustrations: for example, that an insect colony must reach a certain size before it pays to have a specialized soldier caste. But Ghiselin is inclined to stress that there are important advantages of nonspecialization, such as the existence of complementarities among certain activities (for example, teaching and research). In addition, there may be sequential rather than individual specialization, as when members of an ant colony all progress through a common series of different productive roles in the course of the life cycle.

Following up a suggestion by Ghiselin, it might really be better to think in terms of "combination of labor" rather than "division of labor." Division is the first step; it is the combination (external coordination) that produces the result. Apart from the division of labor as a form of *complementary combination* of individuals undertaking different specialized tasks, there is also the possibility of *supplementary combination* whereby individuals reinforce one another in performing the *same* task. A simple example would be men tugging on a rope to move a load; such "threshold phenomena" are quite important and widespread. Wherever scale economies for a given activity dictate a minimum efficient size greater than the full output of a single individual, we would expect to see a mixture of complementation and supplementation, of specialization and multiplication of numbers, in the general process of cooperation through the combination of labor.

A number of other dimensions of choice have been explored by biologists. One such is between "K-strategies" and "r-strategies." K symbolizes the carrying capacity of the environment, that is, the species number N^* at which the time-rate of change N = zero. The symbol r signifies the maximum rate of Malthusian growth, which obtains under conditions where the environment is not constraining. The *r*-strategists are opportunist species, who pioneer and settle new unfilled environments. The *K*-strategists are solider citizens, who compete by superior effectiveness in utilizing the resources of relatively saturated environments. The *r*-strategists thus make their living from the recurrence of disequilibrium situations (entrepreneurial types, we would say). But their success can only be transient; ultimately they will be displaced by the more efficient *K*-strategist species. The *r*-strategists tend to be characterized by high early mortality, as they must continually disperse and take long chances finding new unsaturated habitats. A high birth rate is therefore a necessity. Among other tendencies are rapid maturity, small body size, early reproduction, and short life. *K*-strategists, in contrast, tend to develop more slowly, have larger body size, and longer life. Their inclination is to produce a smaller number of more carefully optimized offspring.

Analogs in the world of business exist for a number of these strategies. In the high-fashion industry we observe high birth rates and death rates of firms, in public utilities the reverse. In general, pioneering strategies tend to be more suitable for small firms—which survive better in highly changeable environments.

But as applied to *firms,* as emphasized previously, biological reasoning is only a metaphor. In particular, firms do not follow the reproductive laws of biology: small firms do not give birth to other small firms, and firms of one "species" (industry) may transfer to another. By way of contrast, human individuals, families, races, etc. *are* biological entities which may be regarded as choosing competitive strategies. Martial races may concentrate on success through politics, conflict, or violence ("interference strategy"); others may have proliferated and extended their sway through high birth rates; others through lower birth rates but superior efficiency in utilizing resources ("exploitation strategy"). The *r*-strategist pioneering human type was presumably selected for in the early period of American history—a period long enough for genetic evolution, though cultural adaptation may have been more important. This type was not entirely antisocial; altruist "pioneer" virtues such as mutual defense and sharing in adversity can emerge under *r*-selection. In the present more crowded conditions the preferred forms of altruism represent "urban" virtues of a negative rather than a positive sort: tolerance, nonaggressiveness, and reproductive restraint (Wilson, 1975:107–108). Even today it seems likely that a suitable comparison of populations in environments like Alaska on the one hand and New York City on the other would reveal differential genetic (over and beyond merely cultural) adaptations.

C. *The Results of Social Interaction—Equilibrium Versus Change*

Equilibrium in biology has one striking feature with no close counterpart in economics: a dualism between processes taking place simultaneously on the level of *organisms* and on the level of *genes*.

In dealing with the interactions of *organisms* the biologist generally uses a partial-equilibrium model, taking genetic compositions as fixed. He then asks such questions as: (1) For a given species G, what will be the limiting population number in a particular environment (the "carrying capacity" of the environment for that species)? (2) Or, with two or more interacting populations, G and H, what will be their respective equilibrium numbers N_G and N_H? And, in particular, will one drive the other to extinction, or might they even *both* become extinct? (The last possibility may seem surprising. Yet a predator might conceivably be so efficient as ultimately to wipe out its prey, in which case its own extinction may follow.) (3) Where new species may enter an environment by migration, thus offsetting loss of species from extinction, what is the equilibrium number of distinct species, and how do the species partition the total biomass?

To take up the second of these three questions, it was remarked above that the intersection of the two reaction curves of Figure 10.1 (two competitive populations) might be a stable or an unstable equilibrium point. It will be evident, by consideration of the nature of the interaction (as illustrated by the arrows showing the directions of change of the two populations from any N_G, N_H point in the positive quadrant), that the intersection equilibrium as shown is stable. Thus, we have here a coexistence solution at point E. If the labels on the reaction curves were reversed, however, it may be verified (by making appropriate changes in the arrows showing the directions of change) that the coexistence of equilibrium would be unstable. Depending upon the initial situation, population H would drive G to extinction at point K, or population G would drive H to extinction at point L.

A similar analysis of the complementary populations in Figure 10.2 will show that the coexistence equilibrium at point E is again stable. But if the labels on the reaction curves were reversed, the populations would jointly (depending upon the starting point) either decay toward zero or explode toward infinity. (Of course, in the latter case another branch of at least one of the reaction curves would eventually be encountered, beyond which the rate of change of population would again become negative.)

The arrows of directional change in the predator-prey diagram of Figure 10.3 show that a kind of spiral or cobweb exists around the intersection point E. Depending upon the slopes of the curves, the cobweb could: a) repeat itself indefinitely, b) converge to the coexistence equilibrium at E, or c) oscillate explosively. In the latter case the result may be extinction of the predator (if the spiral first hits the prey axis, since the prey can continue to survive without the predator), or the extinction of both (if the spiral first hits the predator axis, in the case where the predator cannot continue to survive without prey). The theoretical tendency of predator-prey interactions toward cycles in population numbers has in fact been confirmed in empirical observations.

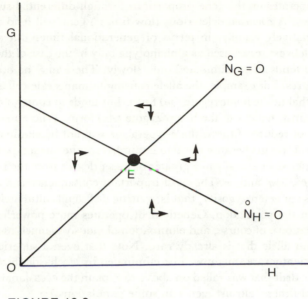

FIGURE 10.3
Predator-Prey Interaction

These models have rather direct analogies with a number of processes in the realm of the human sciences. The reaction-curve format closely parallels Lewis F. Richardson's (1948) models of arms races and Lanchester's (1916) equations of combat. Economists will of course recognize the duopoly solutions associated with Cournot.

Biological models of equilibrium on the *genetic* level are again of a partial-equilibrium nature, since they typically involve only processes within a single population. The simplest version of such models is known as the Hardy-Weinberg Law. If at a particular gene locus two alleles *A* and *a* exist, under sexual reproduction there are three possible genotypes: *AA, Aa,* and *aa.* With random mating, if selective and other pressures determine the proportions p and q (where $p + q = 1$) for the prevalence of alleles *A* and *a* respectively, then the equilibrium proportions for the genotypes will be p^2 for *AA, 2pq* for *Aa,* and q^2 for *aa.* This equilibrium is reached extremely rapidly, in fact — apart from random fluctuations — in the first filial generation.

The proportions p and q will not in general remain stable, however. They are affected by mutation (*A* may change into *a*, and vice versa), by gene flow due to migration, by random fluctuation ("genetic drift"), and most importantly by natural and sexual selection associated with differing fitnesses of the three genotypes.

Selection operates on the gene proportions through differential survival of the phenotypes. A *dominant* deleterious (low-fitness) gene will tend to be extinguished relatively rapidly, in terms of generational time. But a *recessive* deleterious allele expresses itself as a phenotype only in the case of the *aa* gentoype, and so tends to be eliminated only slowly. There may be other complicating features. For example, the allele causing human sickle-cell anemia is a recessive lethal in the homozygote *(aa)* form, but tends to confer a degree of immunity against malaria in the heterozygote *(Aa)* form. Where malaria is a serious cause of reduced fitness, the *a*-type allele will not be eliminated.

"Genetic drift" occurs because the actual numbers of the phenotypes *AA, Aa,* and *aa* will differ stochastically to a greater or lesser degree from the respective mean values p^2, *2pq*, and q^2. The most important consequence is a tendency toward the loss of heterozygosity, that is, genetic drift tends ultimately to fix a single allele in the population. Genetic drift operates more powerfully upon smaller populations, of course, and elimination obviously is much more likely to occur for an allele that is already rare. Note that even a superior-fitness allele, if sufficiently rare, might well be eliminated by stochastic fluctuations. (It was genetic drift that was called on above to explain the occasional fixing of low-individual-fitness "altruist" genes in some populations.)

Somewhat tenuous analogies exist between genes and ideas, between mutation and invention, etc. A human population might increase fitness by "mutations" like a new form of social organization or the invention of a new tool or weapon. And ideas, like genes, are subject to the selectional test of competition. But the laws of the generation and propagation of ideas are so different from those of genes that the comparison does not really seem fruitful.

Some broader parallels might still be of interest, however. Sexual reproduction may be interpreted as a device that (among other things) provides populations with a *reserve of variability of characters*. Heterozygosity makes a range of different phenotypes available for selection in each generation, thus permitting the tracking of environmental shifts while delaying the loss of potential characters that might turn out to be useful in the future. Asexual organisms, lacking this reserve of variability, are more vulnerable to environmental shifts. In effect, sexual reproduction provides species with "memory," though at the cost of some loss of efficiency. In each generation, as was seen above, each of the combinations *AA, Aa,* and *aa* will generally be "recalled" and tried again — so long as zero $< p < 1$. And in actuality, more than two alleles are often "stored" at a given locus, and in addition there may exist other, more complex forms of genetic recombination or recall. The widened opportunities provided by sexual reproduction are related to the issue of satisficing versus optimizing discussed at several points previously. In the absence of "memory" of alternative possibilities, a biological entity could not successfully stray very far from any current combination that leads to even minimally satisfactory outcomes — since it cannot remember anything old, it can scarcely afford to learn something new. The mental development of the human species, culminating in speech and writing, has permitted the vast development of *cultural* memory independent of genetic storage of variability, thus widening the ability to explore alternatives and approach closer to true optimization.

Another feature that operates to store variety in the economic system is *the law of diminishing returns,* in its various forms. Rising marginal cost tends to lead to interior or coexistence solutions; entities or forms of organization that are favored by environmental changes tend to increase in prevalence, but not ordinarily so totally as to drive out all others. Thus, a capacity for rapid response to change tends to be preserved. The concept corresponding to diminishing returns in biology is called "density dependence," though biologists tend to call upon this mainly to explain why single populations do not increase without limit. With respect to competing populations the biologists have a proposition that seems to run counter to diminishing returns in economics — Gause's Exclusion Principle. The idea is that no two species that fill the same ecological niche can permanently coexist. Here, at least, it would seem that the biologists can learn from us. Because of diminishing returns to any form of expansion (density-dependent effects), coexistence equilibria in the same niche should be perfectly possible. Ultimately, the same forces preventing a single *organism* from monopolizing a niche against conspecifics also tends to control the expansion of the species as a whole against its competitors.

Biologists, as compared with economists, seem to devote relatively more effort to the description of processes of ongoing *change* as opposed to processes leading to *equilibrium* in the sense of stationary states. This is historically understandable, in that modern biology was faced at the outset with the great polemical problem of winning public acceptability for the fact of evolutionary change. In consequence, perhaps, biologists do not seem to have developed (or at any rate do not pay much attention to) concepts of *general* equilibrium. They do not seem, to cite one example, to have felt the need for integrating the two partial-equilibrium developments described above — one on the level of population numbers, the second on the level of genetic composition. On the other hand, they have developed models showing the working of a rich variety of mechanisms of change — mutation and recombination, selection and migration, learning, genetic drift, etc. — as well as useful generalizations concerning the extent and prevalence of certain patterned responses to change such as mimicry, convergence, character release, speciation, and the like.

Related to the intellectual problem of the relative importance of equilibrium versus change is an issue that has concerned both disciplines — the question that biologists call teleology. In Panglossian terms, is this the best of all possible worlds? Or, if not the best just yet, does our world at least progress toward such a desirable goal?

In biology, the teleological theme seems to underlie the concluding sentence of *The Origin of Species:*

> Thus, from the war of nature, from famine and death, the most exalted object which we are capable of conceiving, namely, the production of the higher animals, directly follows. There is grandeur in this view of life, with its several powers having been originally breathed by the Creator into a few forms or into one; and that, whilst this planet has gone cycling on according to the fixed law of gravity, from so simple a beginning endless forms most beautiful and most wonderful have been, and are being evolved (Darwin, 1859).

Darwin's language suggests, though it does not quite say, that evolution is directed by some higher force and that its results represent in some sense progress. Herbert Spencer and others went further to develop an evolutionist ethics — moral conduct is *defined* as that which contributes to better adaptation and progress toward higher forms. T. H. Huxley, Darwin's great supporter, declared: "The absolute justice of the system of things is as clear to me as any scientific fact."

The alternative mechanistic view, that evolution is an entirely undirected process, is almost universally and emphatically postulated by modern biologists. Ghiselin (1974) contends further that hidden teleology lurks wherever adaptation is explained in such terms as "the good of the species" or "the good of the community." But this accusation does not seem warranted. The scientific question is simply whether the mechanistic processes of evolution can lead to the emergence of characters benefiting larger groups although harming the individual bearer. That this is at least possible, as in the devotion of parents to offspring, can scarcely be denied. More generally, the genetic-relationship argument for altruism (kin selection) shades gradually in diluted form to groups up to the level of the species, and possibly beyond. Since Nature does select simultaneously on both the organism and the gene level — and on higher population and community levels as well — and since groups of genes or groups of individuals may become coadapted in a variety of ways and so coselected, it would seem that some of Nature's productions could validly be interpreted as responding to "the good of the group" rather than solely of the organism (or the gene).

Yet, it is evident, the argument of "perfection" does not hold with any force above the organism level. The many forms of destructive competition in Nature — from sexual combats within species to predation between species — preclude any inference of a universal harmonious adaptation to the nonliving environment. Still, it seems that there may be at least some slow long-run pressure in this direction.

A related question is the degree to which *cultural* evolution, which necessarily concerns group rather than individual traits, is adaptive. Again, one can hardly make any strong arguments for perfection of cultural adaptation. And yet, selection processes are certainly at work which tend to destroy societies that have somehow evolved seriously maladapted cultures.

The main classical tradition in economics has similarly been subjected to criticism on grounds of teleology. Adam Smith's (1776) view, that under laissez-faire an "invisible hand" leads to a kind of *harmony* of private interests, has been attacked as apologetics for the capitalist system — as a tendentious attempt to prove that what exists is indeed the best of all possible worlds. Setting questions of motivation aside, it is indeed true that much of the intellectual effort of modern theorizing has gone into proving social optimality — in the very special sense of *Pareto-optimality* — of idealized versions of the laissez-faire capitalist economy. (Or, in some cases, of the welfare-state or even the socialist economy!) More specifically, what has been shown is that the equilibrium outcome under an unregulated economy with fully defined property rights is a social optimum in the sense that it would not be possible to improve the situation of any individual (in his own eyes) without harming one or several individuals (in their own eyes).

However, these results might equally well be interpreted as antiapologetics. For, the idealized conditions necessary to make them valid evidently do not fully apply to any actual capitalist (or welfare state or socialist) economy. And in fact, economists have devoted major energy to examination of forces leading to failures of Pareto-optimality — natural monopoly, oligopoly, externalities, and public goods being leading examples.

The lack of the institution of *property* — founded, in turn, upon the larger institutions of *law* and *government* — in the economy of Nature is an important element explaining the "imperfection" of social adaptations in the biological realm. Some observers have regarded animal *territoriality* as closely analogous to property, but this is incorrect. Territory in Nature is held only so long as it is continuously and effectively defended by the force of its possessor. Property does sometimes need to be defended by force, but what makes it property is the availability of impersonal enforcement through the law of the community. To the extent that the property system is effective, a degree of progressive cultural adaptation tends to take place over time. Individuals need not expend energy in combat or other contests for possession, but are instead motivated to search out mutually advantageous ways of employing property so as to achieve a more complete division of labor. In particular, they are motivated to find ways around the failures of Pareto-optimality mentioned above.

Yet, lest this seem too unguardedly hopeful, it must be pointed out that the institutions of law and government are powerful mechanisms that may be employed to achieve many private or group ends quite apart from Pareto-optimality. Law and government may destroy some individuals for the benefit of others, may penalize rather than promote the division of labor, may undermine rather than support the institution of property. Nor can we say on scientific grounds that law and government "ought not" do so. But to the extent that they do not, the progress of adaptation to the environment will be hampered or even reversed.

V. Points of Comparison — A Tabular View

Tables 10.1 and 10.2 have been designed as a way of pulling together, without undue repetition, the strands of the preceding discussions. The first table is an attempt to systematize, in a comparative way, the entities or units of action as viewed by biologists and by economists. The second table is intended to display, again in a comparative way, the *processes* of action and interaction involving these entities.

For the economist the fundamental acting unit or agent is of course the *individual*. Individuals organize into many types of composite units for purposes of joint action — these are the "Cooperative Groups" in Table 10.1. A useful though somewhat rough distinction can be made between "unselfish" groupings, whose dominant feature is the existence of altruistic preference functions connecting the goals of the members, and "selfish" aggregations where

Table 10.1

	ECONOMIC SYSTEM	BIOLOGICAL SYSTEM A	BIOLOGICAL SYSTEM B
AGENTS	Individuals	Organisms	Genes
COOPERATIVE GROUPS			
"Unselfish"	Families, "brotherhoods"	Reproductive associations	(None)
"Selfish"	Firms, parties and other political associations, gangs, exchange associations	Packs, mutualists	Organisms, chromosomes and other gene linkages
COMPETITIVE CLUSTERS	Industries, crafts and professions, other contending sets (of gangs, parties, nations, etc.)	Sexes, species, set of niche competitors	Set of alleles, of genotypes
UNIVERSAL GROUP	Society	Biota	Gene pool

cooperative action is motivated only by mutual anticipation of selfish gain.

The family is of course the standard example of a supposedly "unselfish" grouping. As explained at length above, some or all participating family members may actually be motivated to a greater or lesser degree by considerations of personal advantage rather than by other-regarding love and concern. But for the most part, family associations respond to supraindividual goals (kin selection). A variety of other communal associations ("brother-hoods")—social, religious, and the like—also exist, at least purportedly, to unite the members thereof in unselfish fellowship.

Economics, in contrast with other social sciences, has concentrated attention upon the "selfish" associations in the next line of the Table. These include *alliances* of all sorts: the firm in the realm of economics, the gang for criminal

Table 10.2

	ECONOMIC SYSTEM	BIOLOGICAL SYSTEM
OBJECTIVE FUNCTION	Subjective preferences ("tastes")	Reproductive survival ("fitness")
PRINCIPLE OF ACTION	Optimization (alternatively, "satisficing")	"As if" optimization
OPPORTUNITIES	Production Exchange via market Crime, war Family formation	Exploitation of resources Mutualism Predation, war Reproduction
PRINCIPLE OF COMPETITIVE SELECTION	Economic efficiency	Superior "fitness"
PRINCIPLES OF EQUILIBRIUM a) Short-run b) Long-run c) Very long-run	 Markets cleared Zero-profit Stationary state	 ? Reproductive ratio = 1 Saturated environment
"PROGRESS"	Accumulation, techno-logical advance	Evolution: improved adaptation via mutation, recombination, migration, drift, and behavioral adjustment
SOCIAL OPTIMALITY CONCEPTS	Pareto-optimality	None (?)

activity, political parties and other associations for achieving or exercising power. "Exchange associations" are links in the division of labor. Just as the "unselfish" associations are in fact not completely so, similarly the "selfish" combinations typically have and may indeed require a certain social cement in the form of feelings of fraternity and community (altruism). This cement is perhaps least binding in the case of exchange associations, but even there at least a simulation of uncalculated fellowship between the parties may be essential for good business. While the state or polity falls into the "selfish" grouping, its survival in the face of military competition probably requires a high degree of unselfish patriotic sentiment.

The next major heading represents "Competitive Clusters." The term, for lack of a better, is intended to represent aggregations of units that are mainly *striving against* rather than *cooperating with* one another. Here there may be no sense of actual association on the part of the participants, the cluster being merely a discrete *classification* as viewed by an observer. Such an aggregate of closely competing firms we call an industry, of competing workers a craft or profession, etc. We lack accepted single words for clusters of competing gangs, of competing parties and political associations, of competing nations, etc. (Sometimes we refer to them as the players in the political game, the diplomatic game, and so forth.) The members of cooperating groups may do *different* things, so as to complement one another; or they do the same thing, where scale economies make supplementation a more advantageous cooperation technique than complementation. But members of competitive clusters are trying to do the same thing in a rivalrous sense, in a context where the success of one entity to some extent precludes that of others.

Here again, the distinction is not always so sharp. Contending groups or individuals generally have some mutual interest in limiting at least the degree of competition. They are better able to find this opportunity for mutual gain if an element of "brotherhood" is thought to exist among the competitors. Trade unions (often actually called "brotherhoods") call on class sentiment to limit the competition among workers.

Finally, at the bottom line we have the "Universal Group" — society itself. Society as an entirety is a complex structure of cooperating and competing elements.

In the biological realm, as was indicated earlier, there are two interwoven *systems* of thinking — here simply denoted A and B. In A the organism is the fundamental unit, in B it is the gene. In system A the egg serves to reproduce the chicken, in system B the chicken is the means of reproducing the egg (that is, the gene). Genes are chemical units that have somehow evolved ways of reproducing themselves. (Not that they "want" to do so, of course, but rather that once self-reproduction somehow came about it tended to be selected by Nature for survival.) In system A there are "unselfish" (kin-selected) cooperative groupings like the family, here more abstractly called reproductive associations. But in system B there are no "unselfish" genes!

Now consider the "selfish" cooperative groupings of individual organisms in system A—packs or other alliances (within or between species) whose members gain by mutual association in feeding or defense or reproduction. The leading analog in system B is the *organism* itself. That is, the individual organism represents a kind of alliance of the various genes making up its genetic endowment! As a rather less important point, study of the details of the process of genetic reproduction reveals that the genes are themselves not isolated but are organized into chromosomes and other linkages whose prospects for reproduction are connected in various ways.

The most obvious instance of the "Competitive Cluster" category in system A is the species itself—regarded as the aggregate of its competing individual members. While competition is severest within a species, interspecific competition also occurs where the potential niches of different species overlap. Each *sex* also represents a competitive cluster (that is, all males compete against one another, as do all females) within a sexually reproducing species. In system B the set of competing alleles at a given locus, and the set of alternative genotypes, are instances of competitive clusters. Finally, the "Universal Group" is the entire biota in system A. In system B the gene pool represents the universe in which various forms of cooperation and competition may take place.

In Table 10.2 the chief point of interpretation to be emphasized is that the biological processes and mechanisms represent more general classes into which the economic ones fall as particular instances. Where standard economics takes the satisfaction of preferences as the primitive objective or "utility function" of the acting individuals, biological theory suggests that what seems like mere preference or taste evolves out of the objective dictates or reproductive survival. As to the principle of action or behavior, the process of calculated optimization postulated in standard economics can be regarded as a special instance of the uncalculated "as if" optimization dictated by the selective forces of Nature. The thrust of the "satisficing" controversy in descriptive economics is that, even in the economic sphere, explicit optimization cannot always serve as the principle of action.

The *opportunities* available to organisms in the biological realm can be categorized in ways that seem familiar to the economist. Exploitation of resources is akin to production; mutualism corresponds to exchange; predation and war have obvious analogs in human society. Biology's emphasis on reproduction corresponds to the range of choices involved in family formation in the social context.

In terms of selective processes at work, the biological environment chooses for superior fitness, the analog being superior economic efficiency in the processes studied by standard economics. However, since economic efficiency is not propagated by mechanisms closely analogous to inheritance in biology, the processes of competition in the two areas are not closely comparable.

Economics distinguishes three levels of equilibrium: (1) short-run exchange equilibrium (market-clearing); (2) long-run entry/exit equilibrium, in which there is no longer any net advantage from redirection of resources (zero-profit condition); and (3) a hypothetical very long-run stationary state where there is no longer any advantage to the formation of new resources (by accumulation). There seems to be no close analog in biology to the short-run concept. The equivalent of the long-run equilibrium condition of economics can be taken to be the biological situation where each type of population (on the organism level) or each type of allele (on the genetic level) has a reproductive ratio ("fitness") equal to unity. And one can also imagine a hypothetical very-long-run equilibrium condition in which the environment is so totally saturated as to leave no niche for the formation of new life entities.

"Progress" takes place in the economy in two main ways: accumulation of resources by saving and technological advance. In biology the analogous process is of course *evolution,* the improvement of adaptation to environment by a variety of processes.

Finally, we have the question of social optimality. In biology, the standard mechanistic view seems to leave no room for such a concept. In economics we have the one rather debatable, and in any case highly limited, criterion of Pareto-optimality. While Pareto-optimality is usually regarded as a normative concept, it does have positive content in one respect—that there is at least a weak tendency in the competitive economy to move toward Pareto-optimal outcomes. Despite the "teleological" ring of the argument, it is conceivable that a similar tendency, toward solving the Prisoners' Dilemma by arriving at cooperative rather than conflictual outcomes, may be operating, however weakly, in the biological realm.

VI. Economy, Biology, and Society

I have tried here to trace some of the implications of Alfred Marshall's view that economics is a branch of biology. Or, in more sweeping terms, of the contention that the social sciences generally can fruitfully be regarded as the sociobiology of the human species. Yet, at the same time, it was suggested, we might well claim that certain laws of the economizing process—optimization on the individual level, and equilibrium on the societal level—apply to biology as well. Viewed this way, economics can be regarded as the general field, whose two great subdivisions consist of the natural economy studied by the biologists and the political economy studied by economists proper. Considerable light has been shed, I believe, upon many of the questions and results of the social sciences. These involve broad issues like the provenance of tastes (including, what is particularly essential for social processes, individuals' "taste" for *altruism*), the balance between optimization and selection in governing social outcomes, the forces favoring cooperation versus conflict as competitive strategies in social interaction, and the determinants of specialization in human productive activities. And some specific phenomena as well: the correlation of the male/female sex ratio with socioeconomic status, the recent tendency to have smaller numbers of "higher-quality" children, the predominance of small firms in transient economic environments, positive interest or time preference, and minimum separation distances in locational or product-differentiation situations.

It was not very debatable, perhaps, that the sociobiological approach does have *some* utility for social science purposes. But how much? The central question is whether or not the human species has entered a new domain of experience where general biological laws will have only negligible relevance or have even been abolished by the unique developmental advances achieved by mankind. Among such might be included: (1) the transcending importance of cultural as opposed to genetic change; (2) the degree of intelligence and awareness, suggesting that man can henceforth regulate and control the evolutionary process by deliberate cultural and even genetic modifications of the human material itself—quite apart from operations on the environment; (3) the invention of weapons of intraspecies competition that threaten the survival of all mankind; and (4) what might hopefully be a countervailing factor, man's possession of moral, spiritual, and ethical values.

At this point it is possible only to pose the question, not to answer it. In terms of the proximate goal of research strategy, perhaps it is sufficient to say that the sociobiological approach holds out great hope for breaking down not only the "vertical" discontinuity between the sciences of human behavior and more fundamental studies of life but also the "horizontal" barriers among the various social studies themselves.

References

Alchian, A.A. (1950) "Uncertainty, Evolution, and Economic Theory." *Journal of Political Economy* 58:211.

Alland, A. (1967) *Evolution and Human Behavior.*

Ardrey, R. (1961) *African Genesis.*

_____. (1970) *The Social Contract.*

Bagehot, W. (1948) *Physics and Politics.*

Becker, G.S. (1976) "Altruism, Egoism, and Genetic Fitness: Economics and Sociobiology." *Journal of Economic Literature* 14:817.

_____. (1968) "Crime and Punishment: An Economic Approach." *Journal of Political Economy* 76:169.

_____. (1973) "A Theory of Marriage: Part I." *Journal of Political Economy* 81:813.

Boulding, K.E. (1962) *Conflict and Defense.*

Buchanan, J.M. and G. Tullock. (1962) *The Calculus of Consent.*

Charnov, E.L. (1976) "Optimal Foraging: The Marginal Value Theorem." *Theoretical Population Biology* 9:129.

Cody, M.L. (1974) "Optimization in Ecology." *Science* 183:1176.

Cohen R. (1972) "Altruism: Human, Cultural or What." *Journal of Social Issues* 2:3.

Darwin, C. (1859) *The Origin of Species.*

Downs, A. (1957) *An Economic Theory of Democracy.*

Durkheim, E. (1933) *On the Division of Labor in Society.*

Enke, S. (1951) "On Maximizing Profits: A Distinction between Chamberlin and Robinson." *American Economic Review* 41:566.

Fisher, R.A. (1958) *The Genetic Theory of Natural Selection.*

Gadgil, M. and W.H. Bossert. (1970) "Life-Historical Consequences of Natural Selection." *American Naturalist* 104:1.

Ghiselin, M. (1974) *The Economy of Nature and the Evolution of Sex.*

Himmelfarb, G. (1959) *Darwin and the Darwinian Revolution.*

Hofstadter, R. (1955) *Social Darwinism in American Thought.* New York: Braziller.

Houthakker, H.S. (1956) "Economics and Biology: Specialization and Speciation." *Kyklos* 9:181.

Lanchester, F.W. (1916) *Aircraft in Warfare.*

Morris, D. (1967) *The Naked Ape.*

Penrose, E.T. (1952) "Biological Analogies in the Theory of the Firm." *American Economic Review* 42:804.

Rapport, D.J. (1971) "An Optimization Model of Food Selection." *American Naturalist* 105:575.

———. and J.E. Turner. (1977) "Economic Models in Ecology." *Science* 195:367.

Richardson, L.F. (1948) "Variation of the Frequency of Fatal Quarrels with Magnitude." *Journal of the American Statistical Association* 43:523.

Schelling, T.C. (1960) *The Strategy of Conflict.*

Simon, H.A. (1955) "A Behavioral Model of Rational Choice." *Quarterly Journal of Economics* 69:99.

Smith, A. (1776) *The Wealth of Nations.*

Stigler, G.J. (1951) "The Division of Labor Is Limited by the Extent of the Market." *Journal of Political Economy* 59:185.

Trivers, R.L. (1971) "The Evolution of Reciprocal Altruism." *Quarterly Review of Biology* 46:35.

———. (1972) "Parental Investment and Sexual Selection," in B. Campbell (ed.), *Sexual Selection and the Descent of Man, 1871-1971.*

———. and D.E. Willard. (1973) "Natural Selection of Parental Ability to Vary the Sex Ratio of Offspring." *Science* 179:90.

Wilson, E.O. (1975) *Sociobiology: The New Synthesis.* Cambridge, Mass.: Harvard University Press.

Winter, S.G. (1964) "Economic 'Natural Selection' and the Theory of the Firm." *Yale Economic Essays* 4:225.

Part 5
Political Science

Introduction to Part 5

The relationship between political science and the biological sciences is somewhat different than that between the other social sciences and biology. First, political scientists appear to have developed a contemporary sensitivity to the life sciences a bit earlier than economics, sociology, and to some extent current anthropology. Second, political scientists seem to have engaged in a very broad "crossing over" into the natural sciences. This has included borrowing not only from sociobiology and ethology but also from psychophysiology, neurobiology, and medicine. Third, as will be seen, political scientists have been especially sensitive to the public policy aspects of a range of biologically based issues.

Describing the discipline of political science as pre-behavioral, John Wahlke's words take on a special significance in view of the fact that they formed a major portion of his 1978 presidential address to the American Political Science Association. Though Wahlke applauds the technical and methodological expertise that is apparent in most political-behavior studies, he is critical of this work for not being anchored in an identifiable macro-level political theory. Further, he says, such research is dependent on "an inadequate and erroneous model of the functioning individual human organism." These two flaws are the major causes of what he sees as a prebehavioral posture in political science.

These deficiencies can only be overcome by developing a good deal of knowledge about the biobehavioral sciences and incorporating that knowledge into what we already know about human political behavior. Wahlke surveys two examples of applications of biobehavioral knowledge to political science, focusing on ethology and aspects of psychophysiology. He asserts that a biobehavioral approach will provide "the only justifiable baseline for comparing variations in the behavior of various human groups." In addition, a sensitivity to the biobehavioral sciences will force political analysts to explore behavioral uniformities that are shared by all human beings.

The emphasis in the selection by Roger D. Masters is on the relationship between contemporary developments in biology and the study of traditional political philosophy. "The time has come," he comments, "to reconsider the conventional assumptions underlying twentieth-century social and political theory." Masters suggests that political behavior can be looked upon as a biological phenomenon leading scholars to abandon the "simplistic dichotomy" between nature and culture that has influenced Western thought since the seventeenth century.

As a prelude to discussing politics, Masters outlines a general theory of human life as a biological phenomenon by discussing genes, culture, and learning. He develops an elaborate graphic presentation linking biological considerations with human society, culture, and language. From this general perspective he proceeds to a more precisely focused discussion of politics that he defines as "behavior which simultaneously partakes of the attributes of dominance and submission (which the human primate shares with many other mammals) and those of legal or customary regulation of social life (characteristic of human groups endowed with language)." If this is an accurate definition of politics, then "political science has a peculiar status, for it lies at the intersection of ethology and anthropology — or more broadly, at the point where the social and natural sciences meet."

The concluding section of Masters' article explores the impact of modern evolutionary biology on the roots of political philosophy. Here he looks at Hobbes, Rousseau, Hegel, and Marx through the glasses of Darwinian evolution. Masters concludes by observing that the writings of Plato and Aristotle demonstrate that these two giants of classical political philosophy shared a conceptualization of the relationship between nature and nurture that was quite similar to that of contemporary biologists.

Glendon Schubert displays a broad familiarity with the critical dimensions of political theory and methodology as well as the emergence of biologically based public policy issues. He asserts that political scientists must begin to study political life at the level at which it is lived; and this requires a reorientation from the study of political behavior to the study of biopolitical behavior. Schubert's critique strikes at the very heart of analyses of human political behavior: "Virtually all of political science knowledge about political motivation is based upon only two types of evidence: i.e., either (a) that of a subject individual's own verbal articulations about how he feels, or why he wants to do something; or else (b) upon other person's observations of and inferences from his behavior (including his speech behavior, upon which type (a) data depend)." For Schubert, this knowledge base is at best inadequate and at worst false. He exhorts political scientists to become sensitive to the facts of biological life including the life history of *Homo sapiens* as a species. This will require a redefinition of the roots of political behavior, ultimately resulting in a redefinition of the discipline itself.

In examining the broad outlines of biobehavioralism, Schubert explores three sets of variables that he utilizes to construct a "life science paradigm" of political behavior. These variable sets relate to basic human needs, environmental sustenance, and biofeedback. The final section of the Schubert selection lays out the traditional social science paradigm of political behavior which, the author asserts, conceptualizes human beings as akin to gods. This paradigm is contrasted to a biological paradigm of animal behavior. The social science and biological paradigms are then combined in a powerful conceptualization that Schubert feels is more appropriate to the study of the "political animal."

This group of essays concludes with a selection by the editor of this volume, who attempts to look ahead to the future development of a biobehavioral orientation within political science. This chapter cautions political analysts to not accept blindly a biological perspective that does not account for human purposive activities, and to be cautious about cross-species comparisons. Beyond this, however, the chapter points out some elementary needs of a very fundamental and concrete character that must be addressed if real interdisciplinary progress is to be made. The needs that are discussed include a healthier orientation toward basic research, a more comprehensive knowledge of natural science research methods, the development of interdisciplinary teams of researchers, innovative curricula for training new scholars, a more intensive focus on policy-related issues, and, perhaps most important, a willingness to take intellectual risks. The chapter concludes with a brief reflection on whether biopolitically oriented researchers remain within the humanistic tradition of scholarship.

T.C.W.

11

Overcoming Pre-Behavioralism in Political Science

John C. Wahlke

. . . In spite of the technical and methodological expertise found in individual projects of political behavior research, collectively they exhibit two serious conceptual shortcomings which severely hamper their capacity to obtain theoretically (or practically) significant results. First, they are not anchored in macro-level political theory. That is, research on political behavior is not oriented by an awareness of fundamental questions about the polity or its citizens, nor does it link up findings about individual behavior to any such concerns, whatever the original motivation for the research. Second, they rely on a deficient general behavioral theory, on what earlier political philosophers would call a flawed conception of human nature and modern biobehavioral scientists would call an inadequate and erroneous model of the functioning individual human organism. In both respects, although in different senses, the condition of political behavior research can be accurately described as "pre-behavioral."

I

Remedying these deficiencies calls for more than a little additional random borrowing of a few more terms and ideas from a few more behavioral sciences besides social psychology. It requires surmounting our "biobehavioral illiteracy."[1] That is, it calls for learning in some detail the knowledge about human behavior offered by the "hard science" behavioral disciplines as well as that offered by the "softer" brands of psychology. It is worth emphasizing that what these disciplines have to offer is *knowledge* about human behavior, find-

This article appeared originally under the title "Pre-Behavioralism in Political Science," in *The American Political Science Review,* Vol. 73, no. 1, March 1979, pp. 9–31. Reprinted by permission of the author and the publisher. Sections I and II have been deleted except for the summary, and remaining sections have been renumbered.

ings about how the human organism works as valid and reliable as other natural science knowledge about other phenomena. Political scientists ignore that knowledge at their peril; they rest their work on flimsier, less scientific and untestable pseudo-theories and models of human behavior at the risk of talking utter nonsense about political behavior. The people whom political scientists study are, after all, no more exempt from the laws of behavioral dynamics than from the laws of gravity.

The desired relationship between political science and the biobehavioral sciences is analogous to the relationship between astronomy on the one hand and physics and chemistry on the other. Astronomers know that all the relevant laws of physics and chemistry apply to all celestial phenomena just as they do to other physical phenomena. Astronomers do not look to the more basic sciences for suggestive analogies or novel conceptions to titillate their imaginations into creating novel, ad hoc hypotheses and theories uniquely applicable to planets, stars, and galaxies. They look for established principles about the behavior of all matter from which they can logically deduce hypotheses about heavenly bodies in particular. And they also take care in their work to see that none of their assumptions, postulates, or hypotheses, from wherever derived, contradict such basic principles. In the same way, the biobehavioral sciences must be recognized as "basic" to the study of political behavior, and what they tell us about the mechanisms and principles governing human behavior must guide our hypothesizing and theorizing about political behavior.

We cannot spell out here how political scientists might go about applying basic biobehavioral knowledge in their research. But we may get some rough ideas by glancing at some of the tentative steps already being taken in this direction. One is what is commonly called "biopolitics"; the other is the application of psychophysiological and psychophysical concepts and methods to the study of political attitudes now going on primarily in the Laboratory for Behavioral Research in the Department of Political Science at Stony Brook.

Insofar as the term "biopolitics" connotes a special, esoteric subfield of study, it is an unfortunate misnomer. "Biopolitics" is better seen as providing a perspective applicable to the entire field, attempting to view human social and political affairs in the light of Darwinian evolutionary biology. Most writers on "biopolitical" subjects, however, draw more heavily on modern ethology than on evolutionary biology per se.[2]

Although *Homo sapiens* is one of the animal species least studied by ethologists, what they have learned about other species applies to human beings also. Especially important is the principle stated by Konrad Lorenz (1965) in a discussion of Darwin's work:

> Darwin was fully aware of a fact which, though simple in itself, is so fundamental to biological behavior study that its rediscovery . . . is rightly considered the

starting point of ethology.

This fact, which is still ignored by many psychologists, is quite simply that *behavior patterns are just as conservatively and reliably characteristic of species as are the forms of* bones, teeth, or any other bodily *structures.* . . . That *behavior patterns have an evolution exactly like that of organs* is a fact which entails the recognition of another: that they also have the same sort of heredity (pp. xii–xiii, emphasis added).

Most of us are aware of many examples of the kind of species-characteristic, "pre-programmed" behavior patterns which the ethologists have in mind: the stylized nest-building of Baltimore orioles, the courtship dances of bower birds, the ritualized mate-seeking and domicile-building of beavers, submissive groveling and baring of the throat by dogs or wolves toward their more dominant conspecifics, to name but a few.

Social scientists, however, except for those few identified with "biopolitics," shy away from this principle, refusing to admit its applicability to human behavior. As Niko Tinbergen, the Nobel Prize-winning ethologist observed, criticizing "the almost universal misconception that the causes of man's behavior are qualitatively different from the causes of animal behavior,"

somehow it is [falsely] assumed that only the lowest building-stones of behavior, such as impulse flow in peripheral nerves, or simple reflexes, can be studied with neurophysiological or, in general, objective methods, while behavior as an integrated expression of man as a whole is the subject matter of psychology. Somehow it is assumed that when, in investigating behavior, one climbs higher and higher in the hierarchical structure, ascending from reflexes or automatisms to locomotion, from there to the higher level of consummatory acts, and to still higher levels, one will meet a kind of barrier bearing the sign, "Not open to objective study; for psychologists only" (Tinbergen, 1969, p. 205).

The reason most commonly offered by social scientists for rejecting this important principle is that the human being is a cultural and not an "instinctual" animal. But this argument dodges the main issue. In the words of Rene DuBos (1968, pp. 40, 68):

Culture is an expression of man's response to the physical and human environment. These responses take the form of behavioral patterns and emotional relationships as well as the development of utilitarian objects . . .

Considered broadly, evolution always involves learning from experience. The learning may take place by storage of genetic information by chromosomes, by accumulation of knowledge and skills in the individual organism, or by transmission of practices and wisdom in institutions or in society as a whole.

Political scientists need not argue dogmatically about which patterns of human behavior are uniquely "genetic" and which are uniquely "cultural."

They need simply to recognize the inseparable interdependence of both, and to distinguish those cases where people are behaving in ways characteristic of all human organisms acting in similar circumstances from cases in which their behavior is better described as distinctively individual responses, i.e., behavior different from what might be observed or expected of other individuals responding to similar stimuli in similar circumstances. Instead of arguing about learning or inheritance, nature or nurture, genetics or culture, political scientists can more profitably observe political phenomena carefully, identify and describe accurately whatever widespread patterns of behavior they detect, and ask to what extent those patterns embody the kind of species-characteristic, pre-programmed behavior studied by ethologists. In other words, the investigator of political behavior should apply ethological principles first as working hypotheses about fundamental behavioral mechanics, as directives for future research. Ethology is a source of *questions* to be asked, not answers to questions political scientists have not yet formulated, let alone asked. To demand to know, "What great and illuminating truth about mankind follow[s] from our realization of his having evolved?" is, as Sir Peter Medawar (1976) has said, to put the question wrongly:

> It is, indeed, not a grand ethological revelation that the scientist should seek from his awareness of the evolutionary process, but rather an enlargement of the understanding made possible by a new or wider angle of vision, a clue here and an apt analogy there, and a general sense of the evolutionary depth in contexts in which it might otherwise be lacking (pp. 497–98).

As illustration, consider one of the most striking but least examined sets of political behavior phenomena which does suggest the working of the pre-programmed behaviors studied by ethologists: the ubiquity of warfare in human history. First, from an ethological perspective, one must conclude that war is statistically "normal," in that at any given time there is either the actuality or probability of war somewhere in the world. Second, very little of the lethal and violent behavior manifested by those participating in the complex social and political-action pattern we call war is explainable as the result of some "instinct of aggression" peculiar to the individual war-makers, or even of some aggressive urge "pre-programmed" into all people. On the contrary, the evidence is overwhelming that

> the human attributes that underlie organized group violence probably have very little to do with the capacity to get angry at someone. Instead, paradoxically, war depends on the *cooperative, group-bonding, authority-accepting* aspect of human nature. Consequently it is likely that group aggression has very different motivational bases than individual-versus-individual fighting, although the two may overlap in some situations (Alcock, 1978, pp. 24–25).

Several more directly political working hypotheses are suggested by this capsule account. One concerns the nature of the groups at war. To over-simplify, apparently the phenomenon we call war is by definition distinguished from all other forms of violent intergroup human conflict by being a contest between "polities," or "political communities." Such communities (which resemble what some ethologists have called "pseudo-societies," in that they tend to become semi-discrete breeding populations) are distinguished in terms of differences between members' conflict behavior. Within polities, ultimate violence between persons or groups is suppressed or severely inhibited. Against "outsiders," however, not only is it tolerated; during inter-polity conflicts it is encouraged, rewarded, and often required. Inconsistent as this may appear ethically or rationally, it appears to be utterly consistent biologically.

Moreover, organization of human life through division into such political communities has apparently always been the universal rule. Although much fruitful research could be done on the relationship of political bonding to other ties, such as individual ties to family, party, and work-groups, political bonding seems in some respects fundamental and central to all the others. Although individuals can subsist outside a family, a club, or any limited human group, a single person subsisting normally outside of any polity is almost unknown. This bears out the earliest known ethological working hypothesis expressed in classic form by Aristotle: "Man is a political animal."[3]

Just as the pre-programmed behaviors which constitute membership in *some* polity underlie war, they also underlie government, and in particular the relationship of the polity's members to the persons and symbols which constitute their government. Political order within the community rests not on the members' pre-programmed membership alone, however, but on similarly pre-programmed "authority-accepting behaviors" as well (Alcock, 1978, pp. 24–25). This is to say, as indeed Fred Willhoite (1972) has well said, that

> man's biological nature incorporates propensities to establish and sustain dominance-deference hierarchies within his social groupings, that is, that stratification of political authority. . . .

Systematic social science offers no better evidence of the enormous power of these pre-programmed "authority-accepting behaviors" to shape individual action in everyday life than the behavior of subjects in Milgram's study of obedience cited earlier. Varied though the mode of their compliance may have been, *all* of Milgram's subjects manifested authority-accepting behavior, clearly justifying the working hypothesis that their behavior was shaped and determined to an important degree by some sort of "pre-programming."

Though this excursion into the implications of evolutionary biology and ethology has been sketchy, it should show that the utility of these biobehavioral sciences lies first in their forcefully directing the attention of political researchers back to broad and fundamental problems, most of which have been central concerns of traditional political philosophy and of political science in earlier times. The biobehavioral perspective views political phenomena from the standpoint of the entire human species, in the context of its evolutionary history. It thus provides the only justifiable baseline for comparing variations in the behavior of various human groups. Second, it clearly forces us to reexamine our two-dimensional, oversimplified, supercognitive, social-psychological model of the acting human individual. It makes us take into account important uniformities in all human behavior so far ignored by political behavior research.

But application of these particular biobehavioral sciences alone is not enough. *Variations* in political behavior require explanation at least as urgently as basic uniformities. Ethology and evolutionary biology tell us little about the internal mechanisms underlying both the uniformities and the variations. Ethologists, for example, speak of "key stimuli" which can "trigger" "innate releasing mechanisms," which in turn effect complex patterns of pre-programmed behavior. And, to be sure, ethological research provides numerous well-documented generalizations about observed sequences of key stimuli and resulting behaviors. Unfortunately, such concepts as "innate releasing mechanisms" are identified with no identifiable physiological processes or anatomical structures within the organism. They are concepts no less insubstantial and ghostly than the social psychologists' attitudes, despite having a material-sounding name and an explicitly non-*mental* definition.

II

How other biobehavioral sciences come into play can be illustrated by further examination of the problems of maintaining the polity and obedience to political authorities. The problems have, of course, been dealt with by political science in various ways. There is a respectable body of literature on political obligation, but most of it concerns ethical problems of compliance or resistance. It sheds little light on the relationship of observed compliance behavior to proposed ethical guidelines. In political philosophy and in the general field of comparative politics there are some discussions of "legitimacy," both as a normative and as an empirical concept, but there is little systematic research on it.

Most empirical research literature, virtually all of it considered "behavioral," concerns "political support." This literature displays virtually all the conceptual and theoretical characteristics we have been describing. Resting on an almost exclusively "attitudinal" conception of human behavior,

all the key variables, such as political trust, political alienation, political ef-
ficacy, and so on, are invariably conceived as broad mental images which can
be verbalized. Data are collected by surveys and attitudes are measured by
usually simple instruments and scales constructed from questions of the
familiar survey type:

(Do you agree or disagree), I don't think public officials care much what people
like me think.
Do you think that people in the government waste a lot of the money we pay in
taxes, waste some of it, or don't waste very much of it?
Do you think that quite a few of the people running the government are a little
crooked, not very many are, or do you think hardly any of them are crooked at
all?

And so on.

Not only the key variables defining political support, but also those investigated as dependent upon it are often attitudinal in character. "Attraction
to radical rightist policies and programs," "negativism toward all things
political," alleged to be the most common consequences of declining political
support (Wright, 1976, pp. 77–87), are clearly such. Other dependent
variables which appear at first glance to be direct behavioral reflections of
these, such as abandonment of democratic procedures ("taking to the streets")
or voting for rightist candidates, are almost always measured by self-reports
about willingness to engage in or past engagement in such action, as are such
variables as participating in riots or violent and aggressive behavior against
police and others. The only behavioral correlate of the relevant attitudes indexed by reference to actual behavior instead of self-report is the decline in
voting participation among those found to be politically alienated, but even
that is just as commonly indexed by survey responses as by genuine behavioral
data (Wright, 1976, pp. 251 ff.).

It seems clear that, unless there is some link between the basic political support attitudes in question and the genuine behavior variables of real interest to
political science, research on the subject is likely to be uninteresting or trivial.
The most extensive review of that research to date, finding no such link,
seriously questions its value (Wright, 1976). The conclusion to be drawn with
respect to further research is not that we have found out little because we have
been examining the wrong attitudes, and that we should therefore look for
others which will more reliably explain riots, rebellions, etc., but that we
should abandon the notion that verbal self-reports about attitude items are
isomorphic surrogates for supportive or non-supportive attitudes, and that all
"overt behavior" is "caused" by such conscious attitudes, and should stop using
verbal self-reports as dependent variables. To understand obedience to or

rebellion against political authority requires taking a more realistic look at such behavior.

The Milgram (1974) experiments again offer a suggestive clue for doing this. In those experiments, researchers gathered not only question-and-answer data before, during, and after the experiment, but also some less systematic data about verbal and nonverbal behavior exhibited by subjects while complying with commands to "increase the shock level" they thought they were administering—exclamations, gasps, groans, intense perspiration, nervous or hysterical laughter, tensing, writhing, and so on. These data suggest as much about the internal state of the subject as verbal answers to questions. For verbal behavior *is* essentially *overt* behavior, and should be so studied. The fact that words can be used to express ideas does not exempt the physiology of speech mechanisms from responding to unconscious impulses. Whether a speaker is talking sense, nonsense, or turkey, physiological evidence of internal reactions, as measured by psychophysiological recording techniques, is often a better indicator of attitudes or emotional state than the overt meaning of words, and therefore, in an important sense, of the "meaning" of situations and stimuli. Viewing Milgram's subjects in this light makes it clear why it is necessary, as a leading psychophysiologist has recently urged,

> that we conceive of the human organism engaged in [the complex regulation of multiple psychophysiological processes] as being a symphony of biological organs that are orchestrated and conducted by the brain (Schwartz, 1978, p. xii).

Reactions to stimuli (such as Milgram's experimental commands), thoughts, feelings, verbalizations about the situation, memories of other situations, habitual responses to certain cues—all are embedded in a manifold of continually ongoing neural, hormonal, and other physiological activity. Human beings do not live and move simply and solely by motor responses to orders from the central nervous system, issued in response to cognitive and affective ideation. Simultaneous with any such activity there is always occurring integrally related activity of the autonomic nervous system and the glandular, hormonal, and other systems innervated by it. Much of the organism's emotional state and its physical readiness to do or not do certain acts (e.g., "fight or flight"), are the direct expression of the state of this neurophysiological system. Although the functioning of this system is not accessible to conscious introspective examination, save in its grossest aspects, the evidence of its working is observable in such psychophysiological activity as sweating of the palms, release of adrenalin into the blood stream, rise or fall in heart rate, increase or decrease in blood pressure, slower or more rapid respiration, and many others.

By observing psychophysiological responses in different situations and to different stimuli, and by observing other behavior of the individual at the same time, including verbal behavior in interview situations, psycho-physiologists can tell us much more about the internal state of a person than answers to the usual survey-type questions can tell us. Research being done by Milton Lodge, Bernard Tursky, Josephy Tanenhaus and others at Stony Brook moves in this direction. In one study, for example, using classical conditioning techniques familiar in behavioral psychology, they conditioned half the subjects to react to stimuli connoting "white race" to them and half to react to stimuli connoting "black race." They then measured various physiological responses (heart rate, galvanic skin response, etc.) to ambiguous verbal and visual stimuli conceived of as political stimuli, judging from the subjects' response (or lack of it) the extent to which each perceived the stimulus as a racial one. Such studies promise to reveal more about the various political "meanings" of such symbols than the subjects' reports of their thoughts about them. For example, the overt (though internal) physiological response to the stimulus word "busing" by a subject who has been conditioned to respond to any stimulus perceived as having a racial connotation tells us more about probable overt motor behavior in a race riot than merely verbal answers to questions (Tursky et al., 1976; Wahlke and Lodge, 1972).

Stony Brook political scientists are also producing psychophysical tools, which, on technical and statistical grounds, will give us far more reliable data about the verbal behavior of interview respondents and therefore a more sophisticated grasp of the possible mental-process correlates of verbal behavior. Put simply, the psychophysical scales produced by multi-modal methods (i.e., methods using other modalities of response besides verbal, such as sound production, magnitude estimation, or line production) have the statistical properties not of simple categoric (nominal) or ordinal-level scales which is all that prevailing techniques permit, but of interval and ratio scales which will eventually permit cross-individual and cross-cultural comparisons of measurements made by them (Lodge et al., 1975, 1976).

Psychophysiological and psychophysical research is thus beginning to explain some variations in individual behavior and enhance our understanding of the nature and function of verbal behavior, both in actual politics and in survey research. This work may seem far removed from the concerns of ethologists and evolutionary biologists; however, these two kinds of work and the different biobehavioral sciences on which they draw are not alternative approaches. They are equally valid, mutually supporting elements in a body of science which is producing a growing and interrelated body of general propositions about human behavior.

III

I will conclude not by attempting to summarize the already compressed discussion but by restating an important point: I have not been proclaiming new knowledge about political behavior but urging renewed attention to the task of acquiring some. I do not call for establishing a new discipline or converting political scientists to new faiths, but I do wish to call attention to a mounting set of facts of life established in a wide range of biobehavioral sciences, facts which have been not merely neglected in all but recklessly contradicted in some political behavior research.

Although I have been critical of political behavioralists, I would emphasize that I think the basic premises and objectives of political behavioralism are correct. Indeed, I think the only way to move political research beyond its current prebehavioral state is to make it much more genuinely behavioral. This is not to say that political science must become "sociobiology," or that "biopolitics" is the embodiment of truth about political behavior. On the contrary, only genuine behavioral political scientists will be able eventually to answer the questions which are the real concern of political science.

But being a genuinely behavioral political scientist requires substantial mastery of at least the rudiments of a formidable array of biobehavioral disciplines. Moreover, in addition to being biobehaviorally literate, political scientists must also have the wisdom, insight and imagination of the best traditional political scientists plus the methodological skills of the best political behavioralists. Biobehavioral science may help political science move out of its prebehavioral stage, but it does not make being a competent political scientist easier.

Notes

1. The term is paraphrased from Albert Somit's comments on several occasions lamenting our "biological illiteracy."

2. The first political science usage of the term was in the title of an article by Lynton K. Caldwell (1964), but the word became familiar only after publication of Thomas Landon Thorson's book of that title (1970). As W. J. M. Mackenzie has noted, the word was actually coined earlier by Morley Roberts (1938), in an organic corporate analogy of the body politic to a biological organism, and then "independently reinvented" later (Mackenzie, 1975, p. 297n). A bibliography of the literature of biopolitics is provided by Peterson (1976) and Somit (1976, pp. 279–330).

3. The fact that Aristotle considered the *polis* the "natural" form of human polity in a teleological sense, and that a great deal of his writing is devoted to normative implications of an ethical premise, should not obscure the fact that he recognized that other forms of polity besides the *polis* also did occur "naturally" in the empirical sense of the word. Aristotle was thus not only the first political scientist, but, indeed, the first *bio*political scientist.

References

Alcock, John (1978) "Evolution and Human Violence." In L. L. Farrar, Jr. (ed.), *War: A Historical, Political and Social Study*. Santa Barbara: ABC-Clio Press, pp. 21–27.

Caldwell, Lynton K. (1964) "Biopolitics." *Yale Review* 54:1–16.

Lodge, Milton, David Cross, Bernard Tursky, Joseph Tanenhaus and Richard Reeder (1976) "The Psychophysical Scaling of Political Support in the 'Real World.'" *Political Methodology* 3:159–82.

Lodge, Milton, David V. Cross, Bernard Tursky, and Joseph Tanenhaus (1975) "The Psychophysical Scaling and Validation of a Political Support Scale." *American Journal of Political Science* 19:611–46.

Lorenz, Konrad (1965) "Preface" to Charles R. Darwin, *The Expression of the Emotions in Man and Animals*. Chicago: University of Chicago Press.

Mackenzie, W. J. M. (1975) "Political Apathy." *Political Studies* 23:297–394.

Medawar, Peter B. (1976) "Does Ethology Throw Any Light on Human Behavior?" In P. G. Bateson and R. A. Hinde (eds.), *Growing Points in Ethology*. Cambridge: Cambridge University Press, 496–507.

Milgram, Stanley (1974) *Obedience to Authority*. New York: Academic Press.

Peterson, Steven A. (1976) "Biopolitics: A Bibliographical Essay." In Albert Somit (ed.), *Biology and Politics*. The Hague: Mouton.

Roberts, Morley (1938) *Bio-Politics: An Essay in the Physiology, Pathology, and Politics of the Social and Somatic Organism*. London: Dent.

Schwartz, Gary E. (1978) "Preface" to James Hassett, *A Primer of Psychophysiology*. San Francisco: Freeman.

Somit, Albert, ed. (1976) *Biology and Politics*. The Hague: Mouton.

Tinbergen, Nikolas (1969) *The Study of Instinct*. New York: Oxford University Press.

Tursky, Bernard, Milton Lodge, Mary Ann Foley, Richard Reeder, and Hugh Foley (1976) "Evaluation of the Cognitive Component of Political Issues by the Use of Classical Conditioning." *Journal of Personality and Social Psychology* 34:865–73.

Wahlke, John C. (1976) "Biopolitics and Political Science: In Search of a Dependent Variable." Paper prepared for the Tenth World Congress of the International Political Science Association, Edinburgh.

Wahlke, John C. and Milton Lodge (1972) "Psychophysiological Measures of Political Attitudes and Behavior." *Midwest Journal of Political Science* 16:505–37.

Willhoite, Fred R., Jr. (1971) "Ethology and the Tradition of Political Thought." *Journal of Politics* 23:615–41.

Wright, James D. (1976) *The Dissent of the Governed: Alienation and Democracy in America*. New York: Academic Press.

12

Politics as a
Biological Phenomenon

Roger D. Masters

. . . The time has come . . . to reconsider the conventional assumptions
underlying twentieth century social and political theory. The biological
sciences are an appropriate ground for such an endeavor, for human life
is — by definition — a manifestation, albeit unique in many respects, of living
matter. In so doing, I will argue that a comprehensive approach to human
behavior, bridging the existing gaps between the various social sciences and
linking them to the natural sciences, is not only necessary but possible. More
specifically, I will suggest that political behavior can most fruitfully be
understood as a biological phenomenon, precisely because in so doing we are
led to abandon the simplistic dichotomy between "nature" and "culture" which
has dominated the last three centuries of Western science and thought. . . .

1. Human Behavior as a Biological Phenomenon

A. *Five Implications of Biology for the Social Sciences*

Contemporary biology indicates the untenability of a sharp dichotomy between nature and culture. Although the actions of humans contribute to
changes in their physical surroundings, their phenotypes, and their species'
gene pool, the physical and biological characteristics of *Homo sapiens* interact
with the natural environment throughout individual development and social
history. Simplistic assertions that "man makes himself" or "man's innate com-
pulsions are genetic and ineradicable" do not reflect an understanding of the
myriad processes involved in human behavior when viewed as a biological
phenomenon.

Originally published in *Social Science Information*, vol. 14 (2), pp. 7–63 (1975). Reprinted by permission of the author and publisher. Footnotes have been eliminated, sections 1 and 2 deleted,
and remaining sections renumbered.

Five implications of this perspective should be emphasized. *First*, different aspects of human life must be analyzed with care, without *a priori* assumptions concerning the presumably "cultural" or "natural" status of the causal processes and functional regularities involved. Phenomena that vary from one human population to another are not thereby totally "cultural," as is evident from the example of cross-cultural differences in the age of puberty (Johnston, Malina and Galbraith, 1971). Similarly, many "natural" characteristics of normal human beings presuppose individual learning and social tradition; such elemental actions as copulation, defecation, and eating are simultaneously biological and cultural.

Second, it is imperative to distinguish carefully between individuals, groups, and the entire species (Masters, 1973A, 1973B). Causal processes or functional consequences of individual behavior cannot be simply generalized to populations, nor can phenomena discovered in groups or populations be simply equated with the species *Homo sapiens* as a whole. Much sloppy thought and writing—particularly using the collective noun "man" to gloss over unwarranted generalizations—must be reconsidered with care. From a biological point of view, our species can be viewed as a gene pool which reproduces itself through time as populations of phenotypes successfully adapt to various environments.

This suggests a *third* implication of great importance. In the evolutionary process, the phenotype serves primarily as the carrier of the genes, not vice versa. If . . . "the chicken is the egg's way of making another egg," our tendency to attribute primacy to the material and sensual universe of human experience—the realm of the human phenotype—may be an illusion. The significance of many human events may lie not in the realm of perceived physical consequences on individuals or societies, but in their selective effects on our gene pool. While the impact of modern medicine is obvious in this regard, a wide range of cultural and individual practices may have great functional implications for the evolution of the species.

A *fourth* conclusion follows: we must constantly beware of an all-too-human tendency to overestimate the importance of our own conscious intentions, plans, and rationalizations. One is almost tempted to propose, as a general rule, that the latent functions of human behavior are *always* more important than the manifest or intended consequences (cf. Merton, 1949; Levy, 1952). Without going this far, it should be clear that the expression of purpose or motivation does not constitute a comprehensive explanation of human phenomena, since from a biological perspective one must explain the existence of human intentions as well as the selective consequences of the means of fulfilling them.

Fifth, and finally, biology reminds us of the crucial importance of time. Evolution represents a sequence of events that is generally irreversible, as is the individual life cycle. Neither cell differentiation in ontogeny nor species differentiation in phylogeny can be entirely reduced to "the physical principles of repeatability, predictability, and parity of prediction and explanation" (Simpson, 1969:9-10). Biology — like the social sciences — thus deals with problems of historical development as well as collective processes that cannot be reduced to the sum of their individual components.

These five conclusions suggest the desirability of using the biological sciences — rather than physics or the philosophy of science — as a paradigm for the social sciences (Thorson, 1970; Masters, 1970). Unlike physics, the biological sciences deal with open systems of great complexity, in which time plays an essential role in both individual development and the evolution of populations. Whatever its status in physics (cf. Gal-Or, 1972), the traditional understanding of the Second Law of Thermodynamics does not adequately explain life. Living systems can decrease entropy through time by evolving a more complex organization of matter and energy — and on this crucial point, social systems are comparable to biological ones, not to the phenomena studied by classical physics (compare, however, Bohr, 1958: 13-22).

If we take such a perspective, the common ground between the biological and social sciences would seem to be the capacity of populations to reproduce themselves through a process capable of evolutionary change. In other words, human life, like that of any other species, represents negative entropy or infor-mation — i.e., a nonrandom distribution of matter and energy (Morin, 1973). The individual's genotype and the species' gene pool cannot be fully understood in terms of their chemical composition, for it is the sequence of the nucleotide bases on the DNA chain — and not the simple percentage of each nucleotide base in the cell nucleus — which encodes the information specifying the amino-acid sequences which can be manufactured by each living cell.

To put this same proposition another way, complex structures cannot be ex-plained solely in terms of the combinations and permutations of the simpler elements of which they are composed (Anderson, 1972). At each higher level of complexity, new structures emerge which are best understood as a non-random organization of information — and structural properties at a higher level of complexity cannot be simply "reduced" to a manifestation of their com-ponents. This characteristic, which has been particularly notable not only in modern genetics but in the analysis of the physiology of perception (Ohloff, 1971; Stent, 1972), has also been examined in human cultures by what is generally known as the "structuralist" school (Lévi-Strauss, 1962 and other writings; Derrida, 1967; Piaget, 1970).

Although the convergence of structural analysis in the biological and social sciences deserves further examination, suffice it to say that any general theory of human life as a biological phenomenon seems to rest on the properties of complex systems that are capable of encoding, transmitting, and processing information (Pattee, 1973). The general model presented in the following pages can thus claim to overcome the obsolete dichotomy between nature and culture without thereby running the risk of a naive reductionism. And, as I will argue, the resulting theoretical approach should make possible not only a more coherent relationship between the social and natural sciences, but a better understanding of human politics.

B. Genes, Culture, and Learning

Since each phenotype must fall within the reaction range of its genotype, the gene pool of a species can fruitfully be conceptualized as a system of information storage, processing and transmission. Cultural roles or norms establish, in an analogous fashion, the reaction range within which individual personalities fall, depending on the specific experience of each human being; culture or tradition, like genetic inheritance, is a means of storing, processing, and transmitting information concerning adaptive responses to varied contingencies (Willey, 1960:111; Spuhler, 1959:12). Finally, the learning and memory of the individual establishes his or her probable range of reaction to all future environmental conditions and stimuli, both natural and cultural.

It is obvious that the informational systems of the human gene pool, a human culture, and a human individual do not exist in a vacuum; rather each is an analytically separable component of a concrete physical system — the species *Homo sapiens* on the planet earth, a human population adapted to a particular environment and ecological niche, and a human phenotype with its unique life history. Even more important, these three levels of information, each corresponding to a different level of physical system, are hardly independent. Rather, they form a nested series: each human population forms part of the species, just as each individual is part of a population. Similarly, the three information coding systems form a nested set: cultural norms must lie within the potentialities of the human gene pool, just as individual learning must lie within the potentialities of the individual's culture and genotype. Yet neither cultural norms nor individual learning can be simply reduced to the information coded in the human chromosomes, for both a verbal language and the central nervous system can function within limits as an autonomous, open information system.

To clarify the relationship between these three levels and types of information systems, the basic model is set forth as a flow chart in Figure 12.1. In this chart the species as a whole, an interacting population or society, and an individual each are represented by a pair of related systems: a physical or material system in its environment, and an information coding, processing, and transmission system present in the physical system. Each of the less inclusive physical systems must lie within the reaction ranges determined by the higher level, although feedback mechanisms produce evolutionary changes at all levels of both physical and informational systems. Hence solid lines repre-

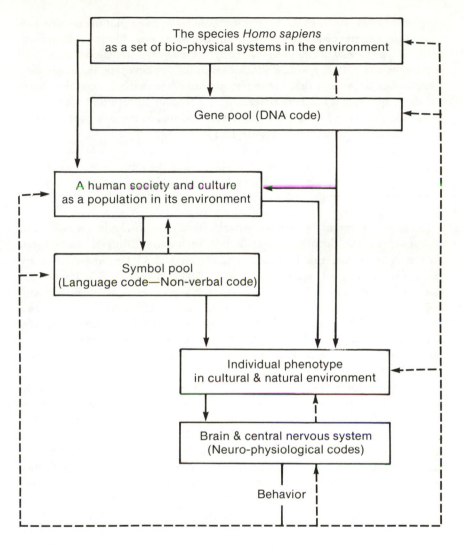

FIGURE 12.1
Human Behavior as a Biological Phenomenon

sent direct causation, dotted lines represent feedback, and the boxes represent analytically separable systems which evolve through time.

There will presumably be little disagreement with the notion that the gene pool represents an information acquisition, storage, and transmission system which simultaneously governs the living processes of human organisms and transmits genetic reaction ranges to subsequent generations (Lorenz, 1965,

chap. 3; Marais, 1969, chap. 3). But it should be stressed that the resulting effects of the genetic code are complex: human genes not only provide instructions to each cell in the human body, setting the reaction range and
developmental patterns within which each human phenotype develops; they
also produce organisms that live in populations whose social interactions form
a distinct systemic level, here described as a human culture and society.

René Dubos, as a biologist reflecting human life, has stressed part of the interrelated model presented in Figure 12.1:

> Each person's constitution is therefore made up of the evolutionary past em-
> bodied in the genetic apparatus and of the experiential past incorporated in the
> various forms of mental and biological memory (1968:100).

While it is perhaps understandable that the biologist would thus
underestimate the distinctive contribution of human cultures, many social
scientists have shown that human societies survive and adapt in ways that are
analogous to animal species (Steward, 1955; Gerard, Kluckholn and
Rapoport, 1956; Tax, ed., 1960; Sahlins and Service, eds., 1960; Braidwood,
1960; Willey, 1960; Alland, 1967; Spielman, et al., 1974; Katz et al., 1974).
One must, therefore, add the distinct dimension of human culture, especially
since—as Edward T. Hall (1969:24) emphasizes—"people from different
cultures not only speak different languages but, what is possibly more important, *inhabit different sensory worlds.*"

While the individual's phenotype is a direct expression of genotypical potentiality in the environments encountered through ontogeny, it is also an expression of the cultural and social reality in which each human being lives. For
example, the color of human hair is a phenotypical trait, reflecting the interaction of genotype and environment, whereas the length and style of hair is a
cultural phenomenon (and one that, of late, has even had political significance
in some societies). Since human cultures and societies encode, process, and
transmit information through a system that is neither entirely in the gene pool
nor entirely in any one individual's brain and central nervous system—namely
human verbal language and the related set of non-verbal symbols—each of the
three levels has a degree of autonomy, and can be viewed as an open system.

The complex model sketched in Figure 12.1 clarifies the difference between
Homo sapiens and other living species by pointing to the unique role of human
language as an information coding system that can evolve independently
(Masters, 1970). At the same time, the model situates human behavior as a
biological phenomenon: the capacity to understand and produce verbal speech
must fall within the inherited reaction ranges of individual human
phenotypes, who can thus acquire and process cultural as well as genetic information (Lenneberg, 1964).

The structural, functional, and evolutionary analogies between the genetic code and a human language have been elaborated in detail (Masters, 1970). Without repeating that analysis here, suffice it to say that no other living species has developed a non-genetic information coding system whose capacity and evolutionary potential is so directly analogous—in the precise biological sense of the term "analogy" (Simpson, 1967; Rensch, 1966; Lorenz, 1974)—to genetic material. This point deserves particular emphasis, because it helps explain why the differentiation and evolution of human cultures is so distinctly parallel to the differentiation and evolution of animal species.

As a result, the model in Figure 12.1 serves as the basis for a pragmatic distinction between the social and biological sciences (since social evolution is, within limits, not reducible to physiological causes). At the same time, the model avoids the common misconception that the existence of social or individual adaptation and learning supercedes biological causal processes and functions within the human phenotype. And above all, the schema reminds us of the awesome complexity of our own species as an evolving system which cannot be entirely reduced to the sum of its constituent populations and individuals.

Human behavior is thus the product of an integration, within the brain and central nervous system of each human individual, of phylogenetically selected information transmitted by the genes, historically selected information transmitted by language and cultural symbols, and individually learned information acquired during the life cycle. Individuals and societies can and do evolve new patterns of behavior, just as every species including our own evolves new physical and behavioral traits, but in all cases these changes (represented by the feedback arrows in Figure 12.1) must be encoded in a relevant information system in order to influence future behavior.

Since variations or modifications in any of the physical systems in Figure 12.1 must be encoded in one of the informational systems if they are to influence future behavior, there are two general requisites for evolutionary change. First, the modification or variation—i.e., the new structure or behavior— must be accessible to the previously existing physical system; just as no single genetic mutation could give rise to wings on the human body, so a primitive human tribe could not invent the airplane. Second, once the modification or variation occurs (whether by accident or design) it must be encoded in the information processing system, where its transmission to future generations either by cultural or genetic means will depend on the operation of selective mechanisms (Campbell, 1960, 1965A).

The second criterion for adaptive change is particularly relevant to politics. Just as Leonardo Da Vinci's conceptualization of human flight with artificial wings was not effectively realized until long after the Italian Renaissance, so political ideals or inventions are often subjected to a negative selection pressure if they conflict too sharply with the opinions of the time. In the United States, the "Townsend Plan" and Huey Long's "Share-the-Wealth" program, viewed as "crackpot" in the 1930's (Morison, 1965:973–975), became respectable political proposals a generation later when rebaptised "Guaranteed Annual Income" (Stoffaës, 1973).

As this example reminds us, the various systems sketched in Figure 12.1 do not change at a constant, harmonious rate. Individuals may learn to solve problems before their society is ready to adopt their solution, as in the case of Leonardo. Conversely, of course, individuals may lag behind social change, refusing to abandon ideals or judgments which arose in earlier epochs. Hence contradictions between the expectations and behaviors of different individuals or groups are — as observers of *Homo sapiens* have long recognized — frequent in almost every human society. For this reason, if no other, politics is a characteristic feature of human life.

C. Homo sapiens *as the Political Animal*

The model presented above gives full weight to both the similarities and the differences between humans and other animal species. In particular, it focuses attention on the unparalleled extent to which *Homo sapiens* fulfills biological functions through cultural traditions and individual learning, and relates this specifically human adaptation to the development of verbal speech made possible by the complex neurological system of the human brain. As a result, this approach treats human beings as biological forms without denying the unique attributes of their social and cultural evolution.

To express the extent to which natural selection has produced, in *Homo sapiens*, a species which cannot survive without culture and individual learning, some have spoken of "man as a cultural animal" (Geertz, 1965; Montagu, 1968). Others have used the phrase "the imperial animal" (Tiger and Fox, 1971) or the "human animal" (Hass, 1970) to express the duality of our species' nature. Perhaps, however, it is more fitting to use Aristotle's term, and describe human beings as "the political animal."

The approach suggested in Figure 12.1 emphasizes the information coding systems which enable living populations and individuals to survive and reproduce. That the gene pool serves such a function is evident, particularly as biologists gain increasing knowledge of the grammar as well as the biological mechanisms of the genetic code. Since every cell in the human body contains the same information in its nucleus, the chromosomes can appropriately be viewed as a set of programs or rules instructing various cells to produce different proteins under given intra- or extra-cellular conditions. Both cell functioning and cell differentiation or growth can thus be explained in terms of the portion of the chromosome whose message is disinhibited or activated, so that RNA templates produce the appropriate amino-acid sequence and assemble the resulting components into a specific protein molecule (Beadle and Beadle, 1965).

Although it may be less evident, the behavior of the individual phenotype also represents an information processing system. As recent research shows, sensory stimulation can best be understood as a physiological code, in which sense receptors respond to preprogrammed features of the environment (Stent, 1972); the sense of smell, for example, depends decisively on the geometric shape of molecules in contact with the sensory apparatus, and not merely on their chemical composition (Ohloff, 1971). In like manner, it appears that all sensory stimulation is communicated to the brain through preprogrammed neurological pathways, such that activation of a given neuronal sequence is coded as a specific message for the central nervous system (Moyer, 1968). Recent work on the action of hormones stresses their role as "messengers" conveying precise information to specified organs in the body (Vallotton, 1970), and some have proposed a molecular/RNA code as the basis of memory (Ungar, 1972).

In much the same way, cultures can be viewed as information systems based on a series of interrelated codes. As Edward T. Hall (1959, 1969) so emphatically put it, "culture is communication." To be sure, human cultures and societies elaborate complex systems of material artifacts, both in the form of tools that serve to manipulate the environment and as symbolic objects or works of art. As Hass emphasizes (1970), such artifacts can be understood as "artificial organs" or structural extensions of the human body which are not transmitted through the gene pool. But such artifacts become extinct if humans cannot communicate the mode of producing, using, or understanding them; hence, without speech, variability is limited to those actions that can be visibly imitated, such as techniques of using pre-existing objects or moving through the environment. While some species *use* tools, humans have an unequalled capacity to *make* them—in all probability because only humans can communicate verbal instructions to program the production of tools (K.R.L. Hall, 1967; Oakley, 1959; Bounak, 1958).

Like genetic material, speech is an information coding system that permits the preservation of previously successful modes of adaptation. The analogy of computer programming is useful: while the physical "hardware" of a computer makes possible a range of programs, actual use of the computer depends on prior mastery of the relevant computer language—or rather, of that part of the computer language needed for the task at hand. Once developed and stored in the computer, moreover, a program permits subsequent users to solve a problem without having to reproduce the entire sequence needed to write the original program. At the same time, of course, continued computer use can lead to further evolution of the basic program as modifications solve new needs and problems.

The analogy between a human society and a cybernetic system has been developed in great detail by Deutsch (1963). The shortcoming of Deutsch's original presentation was his failure to stress the analogies between man-made cybernetic information nets, such as the computer, and the information systems occurring in nature, like the gene pool or a human language. As a result, he limits the possible analogies between human society and biological systems to the paradigm of the organism (1963:30–34 and 77–78), despite increasing awareness that it is always a population that is the basic unit of evolution (Mayr, 1963). Nonetheless, Deutsch's model points to the advantage of relating political systems to the process by which information is transmitted and communicated within human groups.

Just as there is a hierarchy of programs in a computer, so the information which programs or renders predictable human behavior has a structure. For example, the computer program establishing the procedure for user validation has a temporal and logical priority over user-initiated programs, since access to the computer presupposes satisfactory user validation. In much the same way, among the informational programs or rules that establish the probable range of individual human behaviors, some determine access to resources and relative status in cases of competing claims to them. These rules, whether codified as written law or simply cultural practices and traditions, constitute what is often called the "regime" (Easton, 1965B, chap. 12) or "political system."

Because the genetic reaction range of *Homo sapiens* is so broad that humans must utilize culturally transmitted and individually learned information in order to survive and reproduce, the probability of contradictions between individuals or groups is exceptionally high. Moreover, the larger a human population and the more rapid its rate of social change, the greater the variation in the information communicated to different members, and in the experiences or environments which condition individual learning. Humans therefore often develop patterns of behavior which are not entirely congruent with the cultural and political norms of the society as a whole, or of other individuals and groups with whom they interact.

Since the three pairs of systems in Figure 12.1 are virtually never in complete equilibrium, the regime or political system of a society has the central function of determining the priority of potentially conflicting messages and rules of action. Because this function can be satisfied without the existence of a "state" — i.e., a social institution specialized in the establishment and enforcement of the "rules of the game" — politics is present in all human populations; even primitive tribes without rulers or the present international system are in this precise sense of the term, political systems (Masters, 1964). In particular, law functions as a program, whose primary function is to channel the behavior of individual members of a society. Though laws also establish procedures for resolving conflicts, use of these mechanisms is — in a technical sense — a secondary function which reflects ambiguity or conflict in the interpretation of social rules by different individuals (Barkun, 1968).

2. A Biological Definition of Politics

The distinctive characteristic of *Homo sapiens*, related to the evolutionary emergence of the large brain, language, and cultural diversification, would thus seem to be the sheer complexity of the factors contributing to human behavior. Morin (1973) has spoken of "hypercomplexity," arguing that the wide range of human adaptability necessarily implies an equally high risk of irrationality, insanity, and conflict; he speaks of our species as the "crisis animal," and suggests that its appropriate scientific designation should be *"Homo sapiens/demens."*

Such an understanding of human nature provides added rationale for the Aristotelian conception of the *zoon politikon*, the political animal. From a biological perspective, conflicts between the behavioral programs encoded in genes, in language, or in individual learning must be regulated (though not necessarily "resolved") if the species is to survive. Just as a computer can be rendered inoperable by certain contradictory programs, an organism can be seriously disturbed if not killed when genetic and learned behavioral programs are in radical contradiction. For example, when primates are deprived of normal maternal care, the failure to learn behaviors congruent with innate propensities leads to severe abnormalities similar to human psychoses — and, in extreme cases, inability to copulate or rear young (Harlow and Harlow, 1963; Harlow, 1971).

Given the extraordinary complexity of the information which must be integrated by the human central nervous system, it should hardly be surprising that discontinuities between genetic, cultural, and individually learned behavioral programs constantly produce deviance and social conflict. The biological function of politics, then, would seem to arise from the insufficiency of other modes of regulating social interaction. Laws — whether customary or written — do not suffice in all situations, for as common experience has long indicated they are all too easily broken. Hence the political process, by which laws are changed, enforced, and challenged, would seem to be an inevitable counterpart of the "hypercomplexity" represented above in Figure 12.1.

In the common usage of the term, "politics" is a form of rivalry to determine which humans will have the status permitting them to transmit "authoritative" messages or commands to the rest of the society. In this sense, high status and political office are, in themselves, symbolic messages; just as the dominance hierarchy of many animal populations is communicated by gestures or personal recognition of each individual's status, so human groups represent social and political status by verbal and non-verbal symbols which regularize social interactions (Maclay and Knipe, 1972).

In a secondary sense, however, politics is also rivalry concerning the *content* of "authoritative" messages in a human population (Edelman, 1964). While this is obvious to the extent that political conflict is directed to changes in laws or customs, behavior can be said to have a "political" element even when it is not ostensibly directed to legal or institutional change, hence, for example, novels or popular songs can be crucial political messages, particularly in regimes where other channels of communication are closed to significant sectors of the population (Holland, 1968; Green and Walzer, 1969).

One can therefore define politics more precisely as behavior which simultaneously partakes of the attributes of dominance and submission (which the human primate shares with many other mammals) and those of legal or customary regulation of social life (characteristic of human groups endowed with language). Politics is not merely what ethologists have called "agonistic" behavior (Altmann, 1967): competitive rivalry for dominance exists in sports, on school playgrounds, and in business without thereby deserving the name "politics." Nor is all behavior governed by legal norms in itself politics: as cultural anthropology teaches us, legal or customary rules govern childhood, marriage, and the entire range of human social life.

Political behavior, properly so called, would seem to be those actions in which the rivalry for the perpetuation of social dominance impinges on the legal or customary rules governing a group. As such, political science has a peculiar status, for it lies at the intersection of ethology and anthropology — or, more broadly, at the point where the social and natural sciences meet. Indeed, this definition of politics may help explain why political theorists, at least before the middle of the nineteenth century, were almost always concerned with the definition of human nature and the relationship between nature and society.

It follows from the above definition that politics becomes more salient whenever social change increases the probability of conflict between genetic, cultural, and individually learned behavioral programs. Hence this definition of political behavior immediately suggests an explanation for the most massive — and least understood — characteristic of politics in the twentieth century, namely its increasing pervasiveness; totalitarianism, "cultural revolution," and the decline of *laissez-faire* liberalism (which today can only be approximated by continual state intervention in the economy) all reflect the essential role of politics as a regulatory mechanism.

While the biological approach suggested here is generally compatible with much recent work in political science, it permits the inclusion of dimensions that are frequently ignored. There is no reason to limit the analysis of biological variables in politics to the remark that human nature is "essentially uniform" or that "biological traits" are part of the "environment" of the political system (Deutsch, 1963:12, 29; Easton, 1965A:72). In fact, on each of the three levels of analysis distinguished above (the species, societies, and the individual), a biological definition of politics points to phenomena which have not traditionally been studied by political scientists.

For example, the evolution of our species is obviously not liberated from natural constraints merely because of the tremendous extension of human technology (Meadows, et al., 1972), yet the "Limits to growth" pose specifically *political* problems (Ophuls, 1973; Sprout and Sprout, 1971). Can one find, in biological evolution, criteria that would permit a better understanding of these new issues, if not guidelines for policy (Corning, 1971, 1972)? Do political movements evolve in ways that are analogous, in the biological sense of that term, to species (Locker, 1973)?

At the level of modern societies, much has been said of the decline in power of legislatures and the rising influence of individual leaders. To what extent is this development — and the related increase in the phenomenon of charismatic leadership — linked to rapid social and cultural change? Can charisma be more fully understood in the context of ethological studies of dominance and submission (Hummel, 1973; Larsen, 1973)? Do increased population densities, which produce behavioral disturbances in other species, tend to rigidify dominance hierarchies as well as to increase the frequency of "pathological" or aggressive behaviors (Galle, Cove, and McPherson, 1972; Booth and Welch, 1973)?

Although the political behavior of individuals, whether leaders or followers, has traditionally been interpreted in terms of attitudes and interests, recent events often seem irrational by these criteria. Current biological research shows the possible role of genetic abnormalities in deviance (Hook, 1973), of physiological variables in crisis decision making (Wiegele, 1973), and of hormonal correlates of dominance behavior (Corning and Corning, 1972). Is there an innate sexual dimorphism which helps explain the different political behaviors of males and females (Tiger, 1969; Dearden, 1974)? Are the physiological correlates of drug use relevant to political departicipation among the poor or powerless (Stauffer, 1971)?

Even if the above questions were viewed as irrelevant to political analysis, they suggest areas in which policy makers will necessarily make decisions of biological as well as political importance. What are the specifically political implications of biomedical technologies which could drastically modify the human gene pool (Taylor, 1968)? To what extent do proposals for Zero Population Growth or genetic screening have political consequences (Attah, 1973; Hemphill, 1973)? What are the consequences of psychosurgical or psychopharmacological technologies as an alternative to the penal system, regulating deviant behavior without formal legal processes (Somit, 1968; Corover, 1973)? Should leaders be treated with drugs in order to limit their aggressive behaviors, thereby diminishing the risk of global warfare (Clark, 1971)?

It is hardly conceivable that these issues — and many others like them — can be understood without reference to the biological sciences. Although it has been traditional to distinguish "nature" and "culture," the resulting dichotomy between the natural and social sciences is contradicted not only by scientific findings, but by the dilemmas facing contemporary governments.

Lest political science continue its isolation from the rapid developments in contemporary biology, it is important to treat political behavior as a biological phenomenon on both causal and functional levels. Since the human central nervous system makes possible a highly complex integration of genetic, cultural, and individually learned information, physiological states or appetites are combined with culturally determined symbols and personal idiosyncracies in all actions we call political. And even if a careful study of political behavior reveals the absence of inherited causal mechanisms, human societies — and especially their political systems — cannot be fully understood without reference to the biological functions they fulfill.

In suggesting a biological definition of politics, it must be reemphasized that human behavior is not thereby "reduced" to animal instinct or evolutionary necessity. Each of the three levels of systems distinguished in Figure 12.1 is "open": naive reductionism, characteristic of nineteenth century Social Darwinism and eighteenth century mechanism, is incompatible with the notion of complex systems in terms of information or negative entropy (Anderson, 1972; Gal-Or, 1972; Morin, 1973). Thus, even though the conception of politics as a biological phenomenon need not contradict many findings of contemporary political science, it does put them in a new theoretical perspective.

3. Evolutionary Biology and Political Theory

The full development of a synthetic theory of human life, like that proposed above, still lies in the future. The application of a biological perspective to politics and cultural evolution is extremely complex, and requires further research before it can produce empirically testable hypotheses that would markedly differ from those now used by political scientists. While existing theories will almost certainly have to be modified once the interrelationships and analogies between organic and sociocultural evolution have been more fully established, it will therefore be useful to conclude by showing the relevance of this perspective to a less empirical part of political science.

The history of political theory continues to be an important part of the study of politics. Such questions as the bases of political legitimacy, the influence of history on politics, and the functions of legal institutions are all too often approached solely in terms of the ideology or world view of a particular time and place. By reading the works of great political philosophers, we confront these perennial issues as seen in other social contexts and thus can gain a deeper understanding of the nature and limits of political life. And since most political scientists have studied such works as the *Republic* or the *Social Contract,* the great theorists of the Western tradition continue to influence modern political science — if only indirectly. It may be useful, therefore, to show briefly the extent to which recent biology forces us to reconsider the tradition of modern political philosophy.

The "social contract" is one of the more important concepts in Western political thought. In modern times, this notion was developed by a series of major writers who thereby treated political society as the result of an agreement or convention between previously free individuals. Hence, for example, Hobbes (*Leviathan,* chap. 13 [1960:82–83]) and Rousseau (*Second Discourse,* Part 1 [1964:126]) presented evidence that nature "dissociates" men or "little prepared their sociability." In the light of recent scientific research, Hobbes' assertion of man's antisociality, as well as Rousseau's assumption that he is naturally isolated, must be reconsidered.

It is conceivable that the political life of some primitive societies can best be understood in terms of the contractual or quasi-contractual bonds within the group (Lévi-Strauss, 1967). But evidence from ethology and paleontology casts doubt on the accounts of the state of nature and origin of society in both Hobbes and Rousseau. No living primate species studied by ethologists is asocial; as Köhler said, "it is hardly an exaggeration to say that a chimpanzee kept in solitude is not a real chimpanzee at all" (1959:251). Although fossils of early man and his australopithecine ancestors include little evidence of behavior as such, there are many indications of social life. As far as specialists are concerned, there is no question that man has always been a social animal; debate centers, rather on the kind of group that was characteristic at various periods of hominid evolution (Reynolds, 1966; Fox, 1967; Spuhler, 1959; DeVore and Washburn, 1967; Washburn and Howell, 1960; Morin, 1973).

This is not to say that the theories of Hobbes and Rousseau were absurd, as is sometimes hastily concluded. Each merely emphasized a supposedly natural aspect of human behavior without full knowledge of primate behavior and the evolution of our own species. For example, Hobbes was quite right to point to aggression within the human species as a decisive problem underlying all political life. The difficulty is that aggressive behavior is an indication of sociality, not antisociality. Hence, in many primate species, intraspecific social rivalry functions to establish hierarchies of social dominance, regulate group behavior or defend territory (Southwick, 1963; DeVore, 1965; Altmann, 1967).

Similarly, Rousseau also had good reason to argue — against Hobbes — that intraspecific aggression could not have been a life-and-death problem in man's primitive state, for it does not prevent the survival of other animals. Ethologists now show, however, that conflict is usually not lethal in many other species: "ritualized" movements or signs of submission by the weaker animal may lead the stronger to desist, or dominant individuals may end an aggressive encounter by threatening the participants.

The confrontation of past political theories with the data of modern biology, anthropology, and ethology can thus lead not only to a reconsideration of the thought of well-known political philosophers, but also to substantive insights of value. Recently, as throughout the Western tradition, theorists have tried to show that human nature is *either* intrinsically aggressive *or* altruistic (cf. Campbell, 1965B and 1972). Contemporary ethology suggests that *both* traits have similar evolutionary status: "both aggressive and altruistic behavior are preprogrammed by phylogenetic adaptations . . . man's aggressive impulses are counter-balanced by his equally deep-rooted social tendencies" (Eibl-Eibesfeldt, 1971:5).

To be sure, innate rituals that inhibit intraspecific killing in many species seem to be weak if not absent in humans (Lorenz, 1966; Goustard, 1965). Since cultural information fulfills biological functions that are satisfied by genetically programmed behavior in other animals, aggressive moods are not restrained by inherited ritualization in humans, and can be released by learned, socially variable symbols. But this suggests that human violence can best be explained by the *addition* of cultural symbols to genetic material as a means of transmitting adaptive behavior—and not by a simple *substitution* of culture for instinct (Corning and Corning, 1972).

Submissiveness to a leader—an element of cooperation within the group—often triggers hostility and violence toward outsiders. In general, human warfare simultaneously reflects the altruism of sacrifice for one's own society and intraspecific aggression. Since both cooperation and competition are partly innate and partly learned (Eibl-Eibesfeldt, 1971), the distinction between natural instinct and cultural acquisition is less interesting than the complex processes by which humans organize and coordinate both aspects in their behavior.

The concept of a social contract at the origin of society is not misleading insofar as it points to the element of convention in every human culture. But since culture is the product of an evolutionary process, and has become necessary in all human populations due to such biological characteristics as lengthy infancy, cortical control of sexual behavior, and increased brain size (Spuhler, 1959), it is impossible to accept a radical dichotomy between nature and culture (Washburn and Howell, 1960; Geertz, 1965). The ability and willingness of men to kill each other may indicate the fragility of political institutions; it does not prove that society in some form is not a natural need in our species. On the contrary, a comparison between the efficacity of animal ritualization and the imperfection of cultural restraints on human violence suggests that the greater plasticity of human behavior is not without its biological costs. Sociocultural evolution is a process of trial-and-error adaptation which is subject to many of the same natural constraints and imperfections as organic evolution.

A satisfactory empirical theory of human behavior cannot, therefore, totally exclude the biological functions and causal processes found in other animals. Moreover, the traditional concern of political philosophy — the definition of the "good" or healthy human society (Strauss, 1953) — would seem to have a legitimate and indeed necessary place in political science. The definition of "natural right" or "natural law," which had once been at the center of serious thought about politics would be vindicated by the return to a biological perspective in the social sciences.

Although this conclusion might be drawn, theoretically, from the biological definition of politics sketched above, it is also reinforced by current work in the biological sciences. Ethologists have found that apparently conventional and variable norms of human cultures satisfy biological functions — and can indeed be judged in terms of their adaptiveness (e.g., Bischoff, 1972; Wickler, 1972). Other biologists have been led to speculate on the political and social effects of human evolution in terms reminiscent of traditional political philosophy (e.g., Stent, 1969; Dubos, 1968; Simpson, 1969; Monod, 1970). And even where this is not the case, the increasing awareness of the consequences of modern biomedical technologies has produced a renewed interest in the forms of political society which are not merely consistent with human survival, but "good" in the classical sense of being in harmony with human nature (Morin, 1973).

This return to the traditional concerns of political philosophy does not mean that, from the perspective of modern biology, the understanding of all past theorists is equally sound. The fundamental deficiency of the modern social contract theories derived from Hobbes and Rousseau has already been mentioned; given the Darwinian conception of evolution, it would appear that *Homo sapiens* is a naturally social species whose behavior is the product of historical development. If so, the judgment of many European (though not American) thinkers who assume that Hegel and Marx are the most profound of the modern philosophers would be supported. Moreover, if it is correct to interpret life in terms of information structures (as outlined in Section 1 above), among the moderns, Hegel would seem to have developed the most satisfactory political and social theory.

Lest this conclusion seem absurd, it should be added at once that the Hegelian view of history as progress toward the "Absolute Idea of Freedom" does not correspond with the contemporary view of evolution as a nondirected process of trial and error. Even if Hegelian idealism can be defended as consistent with the relationship between the genotype and phenotype—or more broadly, the relationship between information (negentropy) and physical structures—the optimism of Hegel's conception of history seems to contradict not only the experience of the twentieth century, but the tenets of modern biology.

In the last analysis, we are led to recognize the superiority of what is usually called classical political philosophy over that of the epochs succeeding the fall of Rome. As has been pointed out, the Greeks invented the concept of nature on which our science rests. Yet the greatest of the classical political philosophers—both Plato and Aristotle—did not conclude that the gap between nature and culture was as profound as the pre-Socratics had claimed. Whereas the Ionian philosophers and the Sophists were led to a social contract theory not totally unlike that of Hobbes and many modern thinkers, both Plato and Aristotle shared an understanding of the relationship between nature and human culture not unlike that of contemporary biology (cf. Masters, in press).

These brief comments do not, of course, suffice as an examination of the philosophical issues posed by the reconsideration of politics as a biological phenomenon. Many will not find them of interest; others will see them as too sketchy to be of value. But it is perhaps necessary to conclude by indicating that the relevance of contemporary biology to political science transcends the analysis of behavior, and can clarify the philosophical questions that have traditionally arisen from the study of politics. It is no accident, then, that Aristotle's definition of our species has been suggested as the appropriate basis for contemporary political science: from a philosophical as well as an empirical point of view, man is a political animal.

References

Alland, Alexander. (1967) *Evolution and Human Behavior*. Garden City, N.Y.: Natural History Press.

Altmann, Stuart A. (ed.). (1967) *Social Communication Among Primates*. Chicago: University of Chicago Press.

Anderson, P.W. (1972) "More is Different." *Science* 177:393-96.

Attah, E.B. (1973) "Racial Aspects of Zero Population Growth." *Science* 180:1143.

Barkun, Michael. (1968) *Law Without Sanctions*. New Haven: Yale University Press.

Beadle, George, and Muriel Beadle. (1965) *The Language of Life*. Garden City, N.Y.: Doubleday.

Bischoff, N. (1972) "Biological Foundations of the Incest Taboo." *Social Science Information* II, 6:7-36.

Bohr, Niels. (1958) *Atomic Physics and Human Knowledge*. New York: Science Editions.

Booth, A., and S. Welch. (1973) "Crowding as a Factor in Political Aggression: Theoretical Aspects and an Analysis of Some Cross-National Data." *Social Science Information* 13:151–162.

Bounak, V. V. (1958) "Origine du Langage," in *Les Processus de l'Hominisation.* Paris: CNRS.

Braidwood, Robert J. (1960) "Levels in Prehistory: A Model for the Consideration of the Evidence," in Tax (ed.), *The Evolution of Man.* Chicago: University of Chicago Press.

Campbell, Donald T. (1960) "Blind Variation and Selective Retention in Creative Thought as in Other Knowledge Processes." *Psychology Review* 67:380–400.

——— . (1965A) "Variation and Selective Retention in Socio-Cultural Evolution," in H. Barringer, G. Blanksten, and R. Mack (eds.), *Social Change in Developing Areas.* Cambridge, Mass.: Schenckman.

——— . (1965B) "Ethnocentric and other Altruistic Motives," in D. Levine (ed.), *Nebraska Symposium on Motivation.* Lincoln: University of Nebraska Press.

——— . (1972) "On the Genetics of Altruism and the Counterhedonic Components in Human Culture." *Journal of Social Issues* 28:21–37.

Clark, Kenneth B. (1971) "The Pathos of Power." Presidential Address, American Psychological Association Convention, Washington, D.C.

Corning, Peter A. (1971) "Evolutionary Indicators." Boulder: University of Colorado, Institute of Behavior Genetics (Mimeo).

——— . (1972) "Evolutionary Functionalism." Colloquium Paper, Stanford University (Mimeo).

——— , and Constance H. Corning. (1972) "Toward a General Theory of Violent Aggression." *Social Science Information* II:7–35.

Corover, Stephen. (1973) "Big Brother and Psychotechnology." *Psychology Today* (October).

DeVore, Irven, and Sherwood Washburn. (1967) "Baboon Ecology and Human Evolution," in Korn and Thompson (eds.), *Human Evolution.* New York: Holt, Rinehart and Winston.

DeVore, Irven (ed.). (1965) *Primate Behavior.* New York: Holt, Rinehart and Winston.

Dearden, John. (1974) "Sex-Linked Differences of Political Behavior." *Social Science Information* 13:19–45.

Derrida, Jacques. (1967) *De La Grammatologie.* Paris: Editions de Minuit.

Deutsch, Karl W. (1963) *The Nerves of Government.* New York: Free Press.

Dubos, Rene. (1968) *So Human an Animal.* New York: Scribner's.

Easton, David. (1965A) *A Framework for Political Analysis.* Englewood Cliffs, N.J.: Prentice Hall.

——— . (1965B) *A Systems Analysis of Political Life.* New York: Wiley.

Edelman, Murray. (1964) *Symbolic Uses of Politics.* Urbana: University of Illinois Press.

Eibl-Eibesfeldt, Irenaus. (1971) *Love and Hate.* New York: Holt, Rinehart and Winston.

Fox, Robin. (1967) "In the Beginning: Aspects of Hominid Behavioral Evolution." *Man* 2:415–33.

Gal-Or, Benjamin. (1972) "The Crisis About the Origin of Irreversibility and Time Anistropy." *Science* 176:11–17.

Galle, Omer, Walter Cove, and J. Miller McPherson. (1972) "Population Density and Pathology: What are the Relations for Man?" *Science* 176:23–30.

Geertz, Clifford. (1965) "The Impact of the Concept of Culture on the Concept of Man," in John Platt (ed.), *New Views of the Nature of Man*. Chicago: University of Chicago Press.

Gerard, Ralph, Clyde Kluckhohn, and Anatol Rapoport. (1956) "Biological and Cultural Evolution: Some Analogies and Exploration." *Behavioral Science* 1:6–34.

Goustard, M. (1965) "Adaptation et Aggressivité en Bio-Ethologie Comparée," in R. Kourilsky, A. Soulairac, and P. Grapin (eds.), *Adaptation et Aggressivité*. Paris: Presses Universitaires.

Green, Philip, and Michael Walzer (eds.). (1969) *The Political Imagination in Literature*. New York: Free Press.

Hall, Edward T. (1959) *The Silent Language*. Greenwich, Conn.: Fawcett.

———. (1969) *The Hidden Dimension*. Garden City, N.Y.: Doubleday Anchor.

Hall, K.R.L. (1967) "Tool Using Performances as Indicators of Behavioral Adaptability," in Korn and Thompson (eds.), *Human Evolution*. New York: Holt, Rinehart and Winston.

Harlow, Harry F. (1958) "The Evolution of Learning," in Anne Roe and George Simpson (eds.), *Behavior and Evolution*. New Haven: Yale University Press.

———. (1971) *Learning to Love*. New York: Ballantine.

———, and Margaret Harlow. (1963) "A Study of Animal Affection," in Charles Southwick (ed.), *Primate Social Behavior*. Princeton: Van Nostrand.

Hass, Hans. (1970) *The Human Animal*. London: Hodder and Stoughton.

Hemphill, Michael. (1973) "Pretesting for Huntington's Disease." *Hastings Center Report* 3:12–13.

Hobbes, Thomas. (1960) [1651] *Leviathan* (ed. Oakeshott). Oxford: Blackwell.

Holland, Henry M., Jr. (ed.). (1968) *Politics Through Literature*. Englewood Cliffs, N.J.: Prentice Hall.

Hook, Ernest B. (1973) "Behavioral Implications of the Human XYY Genotype." *Science* 179:139–52.

Hummel, Ralph P. (1973) "A Psychology of Charisma." Paper presented to the 9th Congress of the International Political Science Association, Montreal.

Johnston, Francis, Robert Malina, and Martha Gailbraith. (1971) "Height, Weight and Age at Menarche and the 'Critical Weight' Hypothesis." *Science* 174: 1148.

Katz, S., M. Hediger, and L. Valleroy. (1974) "Traditional Maize Processing Techniques in the New World." *Science* 184:765–73.

Kohler, Wolfgang. (1959) *The Mentality of Apes*. New York: Vintage.

Larsen, R.R. (1973) "Leaders and Non-Leaders: Speculation on Charisma." Paper presented to the 45th meeting of the Southern Political Science Association, Atlanta.

Lenneberg, Eric H. (1964) "A Biological Perspective of Language," in E.H. Lenneberg (ed.), *New Directions in the Study of Language*. Cambridge, Mass.: MIT Press.

Lévi-Strauss, Claude. (1962) *La Pensée Sauvage*. Paris: Plon.

———. (1967) [1944] "The Social and Psychological Aspects of Chieftanship in a Primitive Tribe," in R. Cohen and J. Middleton (eds.), *Comparative Political Systems*. Garden City, N.Y.: Natural History Press.

Levy, Marion J., Jr. (1952) *The Structure of Society*. Princeton: Princeton University Press.

tical Movements." Paper presented to the 9th Congress of the International Political Science Association, Montreal.

Lorenz, Konrad Z. (1965) [1961] *Evolution and Modification of Behavior*. Chicago: University of Chicago Press.

_____ . (1966) [1963] *On Aggression*. New York: Harcourt, Brace and World.

_____ . (1974) "Analogy as a Source of Knowledge." *Science* 185:229–34.

Maclay, George, and Humphry Knipe. (1972) *The Dominant Man*. New York: Delacorte.

Marais, Eugene. (1969) *The Soul of the Ape*. New York: Atheneum.

Masters, Roger D. (1964) "World Politics as a Primitive Political System." *World Politics* 16:595–619.

_____ . (1970) "Genes, Language and Evolution." *Semiotica* 2:295–320.

_____ . (1973A) "Functional Approaches to Analogical Comparison Between Species." *Social Science Information* XII:7–28.

_____ . (1973B) "On Comparing Humans — and Human Politics — With Animal Behavior." Paper presented to the 9th Congress of the International Political Science Asssociation, Montreal.

_____ . (in press) "Human Nature, Nature, and Political Thought," in J. Pennock and J. Chapman (eds.), *Human Nature and Politics*. (NOMOS 18). New York: Atherton.

Mayr, Ernst. (1963) *Animal Species and Evolution*. Cambridge, Mass.: Harvard University Press.

Meadows, Denis, et al. (1972) *The Limits to Growth*. New York: Potomac.

Merton, Robert K. (1949) *Social Theory and Social Structure*. Glencoe, Ill.: Free Press.

Monod, Jacques. (1970) *Le Hasard et la Necessité*. Paris: Le Seuil.

Montagu, Ashley (ed.). (1968) *Man and Aggression*. New York: Oxford.

Morin, Edgar. (1973) *Le Paradigme Perdu*. Paris: Le Seuil.

Morison, Samuel. (1965) *Oxford History of the American People*. New York: Oxford.

Moyer, K.E. (1968) "Kinds of Aggression and their Physiological Basis." *Behavioral Biology* 2:65–87.

Oakley, Kenneth P. (1959) *Man the Tool-Maker*. Chicago: University of Chicago Press.

Ohloff, Gunther. (1971) "L'Odorat et la Forme des Molecules." *La Recherche* 2:1068–70.

Ophuls, William. (1973) "Locke's Paradigm Lost." Paper presented at the meeting of the American Political Science Association, New Orleans.

Pattee, Howard H. (ed.). (1973) *Hierarchy Theory*. New York: Braziller.

Piaget, Jean. (1970) *Le Structuralisme* (4th ed.). Paris: Presses Universitaires.

Rensch, Berhard. (1966) *Evolution Above the Species Level*. New York: Wiley.

Reynolds, Vernon. (1966) "Open Groups in Hominid Evolution." *Man* I:441–52.

Rousseau, Jean-Jacques (1964) [1755] *First and Second Discourses* (ed. Masters). New York: St. Martin's.

Sahlins, Marshall, and Elman Service (eds.). (1960) *Evolution and Culture*. Ann Arbor: University of Michigan Press.

Simpson, George. (1967) *The Meaning of Evolution* (rev. ed.). New Haven: Yale University Press.

_____ . (1969) *Biology and Man*. New York: Harcourt, Brace, Jovanovich.

Somit, Albert. (1968) "Toward a More Biologically-Oriented Political Science." *Midwest Journal of Political Science* 12:550–67.

Southwick, Charles H. (ed.). (1963) *Primate Social Behavior*. Princeton: Van Nostrand.

Spielman, R., E. Migliazza, and J. Neel. (1974) "Regional Linguistic and Genetic Differences Among Yanomama Indians." *Science* 184:637–44.

Sprout, Margaret, and Harold Sprout. (1971) "Ecology and Politics in America." New York: *General Learning Press Module 3018*.

Spuhler, J.N. (ed.). (1959) *The Evolution of Man's Capacity for Culture*. Detroit: Wayne State University Press.

Stauffer, Robert B. (1971) "The Role of Drugs in Political Change." New York: *General Learning Press Module 3016*.

Stent, Gunther S. (1963) *The Coming of the Golden Age*. New York: Natural History Press.

————. (1972) "Cellular Communication." *Scientific American* 227:49–51.

Steward, Julian. (1955) *Theory of Culture Change*. Urbana: University of Illinois Press.

Stoffaës, Christian. (1973) "De l'Impot Negatif sur le Revenue." *Contrepoint* 11:31–50.

Strauss, Leo (1953) *Natural Right and History*. Chicago: University of Chicago Press.

Tax, Sol (ed.). (1960) *The Evolution of Man*. Chicago: University of Chicago Press.

Taylor, Gordon. (1968) *The Biological Time-Bomb*. New York: Mentor.

Thorson, Thomas L. (1970) *Biopolitics*. New York: Holt, Rinehart and Winston.

Tiger, Lionel. (1968) *Men in Groups*. New York: Random House.

————, and Robin Fox. (1971) *The Imperial Animal*. New York: Holt, Rinehart and Winston.

Ungar, Georges (1972) "Le Code Moléculaire de la Mémorie." *La Recherche* 3:19–27.

Valloton, M.B. (1970) "Operational Definition of the Hormone." *Helvetica Medica Acta* 35:459–78.

Washburn, S., and F. Howell. (1960) "Human Evolution and Culture," in Tax (ed.) *The Evolution of Man*. Chicago: University of Chicago Press.

Wickler, Wolfgang. (1972) *The Sexual Code*. Garden City, N.Y.: Doubleday.

Wiegele, Thomas C. (1973) "Decision-Making in an International Crisis: Some Biological Factors." *International Studies Quarterly* (September).

Willey, Gordon. (1960) "Historical Patterns and Evolution in Native New World Cultures," in S. Tax (ed.), *The Evolution of Man*. Chicago: University of Chicago Press.

13

Politics as a Life Science:
How and Why the Impact of Modern
Biology Will Revolutionize the
Study of Political Behavior

Glendon Schubert

. . . Whether as a virus, a werewolf, or a living organism in its own right, traditional political science certainly continues to be an integral part of our publication, our teaching, and our thinking as a profession; and it remains the only emphasis in the discipline that journalists understand, and hence to which they pay any attention. By traditional I mean those political scientists who look to law, history, and philosophy for their models and inspiration, as indicated graphically by Figure 13.1. The original figure from which Figure 13.1 is adapted relates specifically to a particular subfield of political science; but its implications are perfectly general, as I thought at the time when I first proposed it almost a decade ago. It is notable that the professional discipline of biology marks the core of political behavioralism, and that biology flanked by anthropology on the one side and psychology on the other, with sociology, political science, and economics positioned at successively greater distances from the biological core of behavioralism. . . .

The implications of biological theory, for the perpetuation of much of traditional political science, are much more revolutionary than those of political behavioralism as it has been understood heretofore. Our Scopes trial as a profession has yet to play out its drama, as the merest glance at where we begin our study of politics makes evident. Biological theory implies the rejection of the presumption that our political theory as a species began 2,500 years ago in Athens, or (alternatively) as described in "naturalistic" fables (whether optimistic like that of Rousseau or pessimistic like that of Hobbes), or according

Reprinted with permission from Albert Somit (ed.), *Biology and Politics* (The Hague: Mouton, 1976), pp. 163–180. Most footnotes have been eliminated and references have been recast.

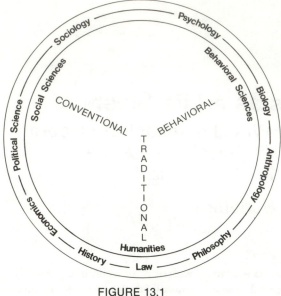

FIGURE 13.1
Academic Ideologies

to the authoritative allocation of values in the even more popular fable of Genesis. The roots of political behavior go back not thousands but millions of years (Edey, 1972; Fried, 1967; Pilbeam, 1972; Tiger and Fox, 1971) and political man did not spring (garbed in full civic regalia, and uttering a partisan war-cry) from the forehead of Socrates—as our teaching of the well-springs of political philosophy might lead innocents to infer. The implications of contemporary research in physical anthropology, archeology, paleontology, and related sciences are going to jack political philosophy off its classical assumptions—once political scientists become better educated in, and start facing up to the facts of, biological life, including their own life history as a species.

It seems altogether likely that the apparent things about political behavior, that could be learned through direct observation of one human by another, already have been learned during the course of the past half million years. It is also entirely possible that the Greeks of Periclean Athens (and for a century thereafter) had a particularly felicitous way of stating such observations, which can provide us with at least a benchmark against which to measure what we may have learned since then as a species. But we would not wish to rely upon either Hippocrates' or Aristotle's knowledge of human anatomy or medicine. It is at the level of folk wisdom (disregarding questions of general knowledge base, cultural dissonance, language, etc.) that Socrates excelled;

and one can appreciate the attractive simplicity of confining political analysis to this level of understanding: it is indeed basic. But there are other things about human behavior that could not have become observed until the development of appropriate technologies: photography in general is one example, and high-speed photography of human facial changes is a more particular example (Tomkins, 1962; Leventhal and Sharp, 1965). Behavioral science has not hesitated to take advantage of what additionally could be learned about human behavior by adopting technologies that enhance the capacity to observe organisms in action. What remains to be learned will be primarily the previously *unobservable,* and this will consist mostly of events that take place within the human body, or of human organismic behavior in the context of environments that previously were inaccessible to observation (like the long political past that antedates the invention of writing, or that parallels the absence of documentary evidence about it).

1. Biobehavioralism

Peter Corning has pointed out that a fundamental challenge to political scientists was levied in "Christian Bay's assertion that a satisfactory political theory must be derived from an adequate understanding of the 'basic human needs,' as well as from man's overt and often variable preferences" (Corning, 1971). Bay was anticipated, in at least this respect, by James C. Davies in his *Human Nature in Politics* (1963)—a book that borrows its title from Graham Wallas and its substantive approach from Abraham Maslow's theory of human needs (with credits going also to Freud and David Krech). Davies' book is a creative attempt to tease out of social psychology the "satisfactory political theory" that Bay has called for; but in precise accord with my own thesis in the present paper, events have demonstrated that social psychology—the guts of what has been perceived to be the political behavioral approach—is not enough.

Whatever their respective merits and styles as professional writing and contributions to political theory, it is now a matter of history that it was Bay's radical critique of political behaviorism rather than Davies' focus on basic human needs that sparked the protest movement within the profession that led to the organization of the Caucus and the professional confrontations of the late sixties. The approach fostered by the Caucus itself featured well-meant shooting from the hip by ertswhile political engineers, both within and without the profession, which may not do too much harm but is also likely to do little good except by chance: our expectation of the probable payoff for any therapy based on substantial ignorance of underlying causes (to say nothing of both direct and indirect effects) ought to be something close to zero improvement. The situation is not really that favorable, however; with only distressingly finite time and resources available for whatever constructive endeavors may yet be made to cope with some of the more pressing policy problems that face us, the waste of professional time and resources (in retreats to phenomenology, parapsychology, yoga, and transcendental meditation, to say nothing of encounter groups and the other standard bill of fare featured in *Psychology Today*) has to be reckoned as downright harmful *socially,* whatever its private psychological benefits to the individuals who become so involved.

An alternative approach to an adequate understanding of basic human needs is to study the way in which those needs are understood by the research scholars who know most about them, at a level of causation more fundamental than what can be inferred from observations of either what human organisms do, or what they can articulate about their internal states of being. This does not mean that we need to disregard either of the latter types of behavioral information; quite the contrary. But it does mean that other types of information, relating to independent observations of the operations of the neural, hormonal, and motor systems (among other internal ones) of humans must be taken into consideration if we are to become more realistic in our studies, of such phenomena as political action. At the very least we need to understand — and to deal with in our own theories of political behavior — how the satisfaction of basic human needs affects the possibility and the modes of acting politically.

Before considering in the following section of this paper a paradigm that will attempt to explicate what these interrelationships are between our conventional analysis of political behavior, and biological analysis of human behavior, it is necessary to discuss the relevant sets of variables that will be used in constructing that paradigm. This section of the paper will examine first basic human needs from a biological point of view, followed by environmental sustenance, then some indicators of human development that figure in both social and biological theory, and it concludes with a discussion of biofeedback.

A. Basic Human Needs

From a biological point of view, the most basic need of any animal is to survive long enough to reproduce. It is the gene pool (to use the language of population genetics) and not the individual phenotype that natural selection operates, ceteris paribus, to preserve; but that can be done only through the successful adaptation of some minimally large population of phenotypes that do reproduce successfully and rear their young to the stage of self-sufficiency. To survive that long an individual human animal must continuously satisfy certain physical/chemical requirements which have long been crudely understood: air, body temperature maintenance, sleep, water, and food. Aristotle was quite aware of the need for air, but he could not have known that it is specifically oxygen that is needed, nor why and how it enters into metabolism. He was aware also of both sleep and dreams; but more recent observations of brain-wave fluctuations are suggestive of support for a structural typology of sleep and a theory of its function for decisional purposes that became possible only with the development of the technology of the electroencephalogram (McAlpine, 1970). Relatively sophisticated technical knowledge concerning most of these needs (adequate nutrition, potable water, and oxygen energetics) is indispensable for an understanding of what many biologists, and at least some political scientists, consider to be the most crucial problems of public policy confronting political science today; and these involve the ecologies of land, sea, and air.

A fifth type of physical/chemical need is that for sensory stimulation. It is through the senses (tactile, visual, auditory, olfactory, gustatory) that an animal maintains contact with its environment, and such contact on a continuing basis is essential to survival. The evolution of internal homeostatic limits for animals presumes that appropriate stimulation will be forthcoming; hence the "vacuum activity" to which ethologists have directed attention, referring to extreme lowering of threshold for a behavior; and hence the probability that humans, like other animals, require a certain minimal continuing stimulation of at least several of their senses, quite apart from the question of the use of those receptors to provide environmental information needed by the animal for other purposes.

A sixth type of physical/chemical need is that of infants to be held, touched, and otherwise stimulated. Such care, which until very recent times was part of the human maternal role, appears to be necessary to the survival of infants up to about two years of age; and it appears also to be essential (although not directly to survival) to learning, growth, and security for older human children as well as for other primate juveniles.

There is a problem about sex. As Davies points out, Maslow classified "sex" (evidently signifying sexual intercourse) as a physical need; but that seems to reflect his having to categorize it in relation to the even greater unsuitability of the other alternatives in the Maslowian typology, and it results in the blurring of one of the unique characteristics peculiar to the human species. Here is an instance where reference to zoology results in a much more humanistic judgment than one based upon the softer side of psychology. In animals other than primates it is not usually necessary (or possible) to distinguish between sexual interaction and sexual reproduction; but in primates these two functions can readily be separated, and especially is this true of humans (because of the loss of estrusity in human females), and the policy issue today is to what extent and for whom they should be completely separated.

It seems to be consensual, among social scientists and biologists, that sexual interaction is a human *social* need, which is important to good health (both mental and physical) but not otherwise or directly essential to survival of the interacting individuals. Much more controversial is the question of whether and how to limit sexual reproduction, with the primary objective of attaining zero or negative population growth on a worldwide basis, and eventually (i.e., in some future century) working toward a reduction in the absolute global level of the species population. Because neither voluntary nor democratic decision making is considered feasible as a means to attaining global ZPG, the issue will be a difficult one for political scientists to help resolve — and they have as yet barely begun to take cognizance of the existence of the problem.

Other social needs, confirmed by both sociological and primatological research, include group association with and orientation to conspecifics. This means that humans need to touch, see, talk with, and otherwise to interact with other humans — for direct sensory gratification, for information about the environment in addition to what an individual can derive directly from his own sensory contacts, and for the security in relation to the environment that the individual finds in association with other humans. During infancy such needs are critical to the point of survival; subsequently they are necessary if humans are to become sufficiently skilled and involved in social transactions to be able to act politically.

Maslow's typology specified certain psychological needs, of self-esteem and self-actualization; but if an operationalized theory of psychological needs is to be developed, evidence to test it is at least as likely to come from social psychology as from physiological psychology or biology. It is entirely possible that the satisfaction of such psychological needs, before a person is competent to act politically, is just as critical as is the prior satisfaction of the social needs described above. But only the physical/chemical needs are literally and directly prerequisite to the survival of individual adult humans.

B. *Environmental Sustenance*

There are two principal respects in which the environment makes possible both the satisfaction of basic human needs, and the practice of politics. The first and most fundamental is ecological, and involves energetics; the global distribution and other aspects of the species population; and the niches occupied by various subpopulations of humans in relation to other species with whom we share the biosphere. Less basic (in long-run terms of *species* survival) but at the same time more obvious in its impingement upon political behavior, and also more immediately critical for the survival of any particular individual, is the social environment, which educates him into a particular culture. To a greater or lesser extent the social environment facilitates the manipulation of an individual's psychophysical systems so as to attempt to influence that person's behavior (including political behavior).

Energetics is so painfully obvious as a critical dimension of public policy for all countries today that little argument seems necessary in support of the proposition that political science is likely to remain preoccupied, during any future that now seems imaginable, with problems of energy types, quality, production and distribution costs, dissipation (pollution), consumption priorities, and conservation. . . .

Evidently the distribution of human population in relation to the availability of resources for the satisfaction of basic needs, and in relation to different cultures, is likely to continue to be of concern to political scientists, in the future as now and as in the past. Other aspects of population dynamics, such as density differentials and differences in both the absolute sizes and growth rates of human populations, seem at least equally viable for political analysis. Except for growth rate, these have long been the stock in trade of traditional studies of international politics; but it is likely that a more technical level of knowledge, reflecting the escalating growth of demography as a specialized field, will characterize future political analysis of population policy.

The biological niche of *Homo sapiens* is a much less obvious matter of concern for most social scientists, and largely because they seem capable of indulging in the almost incredible smugness of feeling that they can take the niche of humanity for granted. Such humanistic conceit is credible only on an hypothesis of sheer and utter ignorance of the manner in which the biosphere has operated historically, works at present, and seems most likely to evolve in the future.

The success of humans in the competitive exclusion of other living species (of both flora and fauna), particularly during the most recent ten to twelve thousand years since we began in a serious way to scarify the natural land surface with our agriculture, has by no means necessarily been adaptive for our species except from a point of view with as short a range as that. Our increasing capacity and tendency to eliminate, more often unwittingly or accidently than by design, other living species upon whom we previously had relied for sustenance — and now also each other, as usual but with the aid of the improved and more complex technologies of the latter half of the twentieth century — is an index of the extent to which our trophic niche, defined as the *functional* status of an organism in its community, is being redetermined as much by the indirect as by the direct effects of our predatory activities; and the fossil record is replete with evidence of extinct species whose predation was so successful that they themselves starved to death. The issue goes far beyond the restoration of token vegetation to, and the elimination of domestic pets from, urban areas; or even the apparent trends in the direction of human conspecific predation ranging from licensed hunting in season (under circumstances such that other hunters present more frequent targets of opportunity than the crops of ruminants or rodents available for harvesting) to the ubiquitous predations now characteristic of all large urban areas in the United States (where only humans can be and are hunted by each other, and at least in part because all other prey have been extermined).

Mankind cannot destroy the biological community of which he has been a part, without his degradation of that biological community returning as feedback to threaten the human political community; and I should like to give two examples which are textbook material for undergraduate zoology courses (Clapham, 1973):

a. "The most obvious example of an ecosystem that has been altered by man is . . . agricultural fields. Essentially, one species of organism is allowed to exist while other species are removed by tremendous expenditures of energy, herbicides, and pesticides, and the abiotic environment is controlled by extensive use of irrigation, fertilization, and tilling. . . . [T]he successful exploitation of natural ecosystems in order to increase the production of human food has led in most cases to a dramatic lowering of the fitness of the exploited ecosystems. Technology can allow these ecosystems to remain viable and productive, but only at considerable cost. There are clearly limits to which technology can overcome the tendency of ecosystems to revert to natural equilibrium, and the instability and uncertainty of the system's capacity to produce products useful to man increase greatly as these limits are approached."

b. "Current agricultural economics dictates that livestock should be fattened in feedlots rather than on the range. On the range, the urine and feces from the animals fertilize the land naturally to replace much of the nutrients removed by herbivory. In feedlots, however, the nutrients contained in the feed are removed from fields in their entirety, causing a reduction in soil fertility which must be made up with massive fertilization, and the excreta of the livestock are too concentrated to be utilized by plants in the feedlot area, and so are washed into nearby waterways, where they become pollution problems. This is a classic example in which the disruption of a normal biogeochemical cycle has led to the deficiency of materials in one ecosystem and a surplus in another, reducing the fitness of both."

In the past political science has assumed the complete beneficence of both the fattening of livestock for market, and the raising of grain with which to do it. Perhaps that complacency has been unwarranted, and has skewed our assumptions about the political economics of food policy, at both the national and international levels of public policy making.

The effects of social environment tend to be much better recognized as pertinent to political science, as a sampling of the recent literature in political behavior (above) and in biopolitics (below) demonstrates. Political socialization, and particularly as it relates to the modes and quality of political learning among schoolchildren, has emerged as a distinctive subfield of the discipline of both political science and social psychology — in political science since the beginning of the sixties, and somewhat earlier than that in social psychology. This work is well known, and what is most necessary to note here is that political scientists to date have paid precious little attention to the developmental psychobiology of political learning. I presume that as our interests in the subject deepen and broaden, both we and our sociologist cohorts are going to have to take into consideration the biological aspects of the learning process just as psychologists already are doing. Moreover, we shall sooner or later have to broaden our focus in another respect: learning is accelerated during, but not monopolized by, childhood; and in any case questions of the reinforcement and loss of learning are also part of the relevant subject (Jaros, 1972). So both political learning among adults, and the eventual loss in both the quality and quantity of political knowledge and ability to accept new political learning among the elderly (Cutler and Bengtson, 1974) (or "desocialization," as it is increasingly being described) are a part of the study of normal political education.

There is a marked shift in both emphasis and interest, when we turn to the experimental manipulation of psychophysical systems, as a means of influencing political learning. One very common method of so doing is through the customary activities of the medical profession: the dispensation of either drugs or surgery is designed to change the ways in which certain of an individual's bodily systems are operating; and the execution of that experiment often entails uncontrolled (or uncontrollable) side-effects for the person's political behavior (as by affecting his attitudes, mobility, appearance, or personality). We have recently been passing through a period during which many persons have experimented with their own minds and bodies, by ingestion of drugs subject to little control of either quality or quantity; typically the effects of such experiments have been to lessen political participation: "Tune in, turn on, and drop out!" Other experiments have been conducted on a social scale by public health programs, and in this form they have been a part of political science as long as there has been such a subject; the leading Supreme Court decision in regard to compulsory vaccination or sterilization go back half a century or more. The fluoridation of water supplies—though still controversial in some outback regions, such as Hawaii—is now generally countenanced like chlorination, although it must be admitted that the latter has been in innocence of serendipitious discoveries such as the recent detection of carcinogens as a by-product of the chemical interaction between chlorination and pollutants in the metropolitan drinking water supplies of New Orleans and Indianapolis. It is hardly comforting to think so, but this may prove within another decade or so to have become a major factor in the reduction of population densities in urban centers—and especially those with modern water purification systems—throughout the world. Other novel subjects, such as sickle-cell anemia, present perplexing political issues (Frankel, 1974) and the range of such questions is going to expand, with demands for positive preventative medicine emanating from crowded populations who are becoming aware that they are experiencing a plethora of biogenic pathologies, as fallout from the urban physical/chemical environment (Chase, 1971).

Quite another form of experimental manipulation is operant conditioning. It happens that the chief proponent, an unsuccessful and presumably frustrated writer of fiction during his younger years, thinks of himself as a political philosopher. So it is not surprising that B. F. Skinner's ideas have finally begun to attract some serious critique by political scientists, as we shall note presently. What is relevant here is that both his technical research and his popular writings have direct implications for political science, and their thrust is in the direction of proliferating relatively simple (though generally, laboratory) techniques for controlling human behavior. The practice of Skinnerism on human subjects to date seems to have been largely confined to his own prototypical daughter and a few hundred other infants raised in Skinner boxes, a few dozen patients in veterans hospitals, and sundry other captive and relatively helpless institutionalized populations. But the potentiality for expansion is tremendous, particularly if political decisions during the next generation are supportive of future life styles (viz., cities afloat, or completely underground, or in space stations) that tend to further reduce some of the analogical differences that now seem still to distinguish humans from pigeons and rats.

C. Biosocial Indicators

There are difficult *biological* problems in regard to many key "social" variables (which are imputed categories for classifying individuals). Among the indicators of human development that are central to political behavior are race, age, sex, and intelligence; but political scientists study them strictly on a sociological level because that is the (limited) degree of sophistication to which our data (and presumably, therefore, our understanding) extend. Race no longer is a viable concept for use in biology, except in discussion of human evolution and in regard to the distribution ranges of certain genetically determined aspects of blood chemistry that are important to public health and nutrition; but it remains of critical importance to the social and cultural identifications of most persons throughout the world, and political scientists work with a research literature that reflects overwhelmingly the presumption of a generation ago: that half a dozen nominally distinguished categories provide an adequate basis for policy and analysis alike in regard to human subpopulation genetic variations. The possible impact on political science of the alternative premise supported by modern biology, that the relevant gene pool with which public policy should be concerned is that of species, is staggering to contemplate.

Similarly with sex: the ongoing drive for redefinition of sex roles goes far beyond an increase in political participation by females (or in their practice of political science), which is a level at which sex still is dealt with as a natural dichotomy and its chief problem is defined as equalizing (in so far as possible) cultural values to be associated with the two halves of the split variable. Modern biology is concerned with a proliferation of policy spinoffs from human reproduction, ranging from qualitative changes in populations, to biological engineering; and developmental psychobiology studies specific sexual differences (including those relating to the central nervous system) that may affect both political attitudes and political behavior; but none of these matters (except for population growth) is involved in the usual treatment of sex in contemporary political science literature.

The work in political socialization is from a methodological point of view straightforward survey research, but it does treat age as a developmental construct (and not simply as an index to constitutional eligibility for voting, public office holding, and trial in the regular criminal courts). There are, however, other (and possibly more important) implications of aging, for the quality of political attitudes and participation, as a direct consequence of biophysical and biochemical changes — all deleterious from the point of view of optimality of function — that are products of aging and that bear directly upon perception, memory, judgment, and other behavioral subcomponents of political decision-making. In any society (like the United States and other industrialized countries) whose age/sex population "pyramid" has become virtually a parallelogram (i.e., with as many persons over fifty as under twenty, and with more older females than males) and with prospects for even greater top-heaviness in the closing decades of this century, it might seem important to study political desocialization (viz., loss of learning, decrease in participation) both quantitatively and qualitatively, and in regard to both affective and effective qualities. The political problem is there, whether we choose to study it or not.

Political scientists seem to have managed pretty well to have avoided becoming involved very much in the Jensen-Shockley heresy, which concerns a direct attack at the genetic level of argumentation upon the possibility of establishing racial equality. Of course the question of intelligence does enter into the socialization studies of children; and there is one recent book — not by a political scientist and not yet (at least) reviewed in the *A.P.S.R.* so as to have showed up in the sample that I shall discuss below — which does deal with the question of the extent to which genetic variation in IQ (if not in intelligence) affects social and political status. We should be reminded, I suppose, that Harold Lasswell always has stressed the intelligence function as a key value in his grammar of professional obligation in policy research (Lasswell, 1963); but political scientists seem to have regarded a concern for (to say nothing of the practice of) intelligence as undemocratic. In American academia the measurement of intelligence (like the measurement of performance) is not in vogue. Nevertheless, substantial differences in human learning ability and creativity obtain and remain relevant to political attitudes, participation, and decision-making, although we have no choice but to continue to treat intelligence as a constant (rather than a variable) unless and until we attempt to acquire a better understanding of how it does affect political behavior.

Health, likewise, remains unexamined in any systematic way, notwithstanding its evident importance to the performance of certain political roles (of which those of President of the United States, and Supreme Court Justice, are only among the most conspicuous). But health may also be directly relevant to mass political attitudes as well as to participation, as several recent papers suggest. One of these is a research design on the effects of John Kennedy's chronic illnesses upon his foreign policy decisions as president (Bernstein and Schwartz, 1973). A second is a study of a large sample of high school students, relating their health (and body image) to their political knowledge, attitudes, and participation; while a third study analyzes the relation between the physical fitness of college students and their attitudes towards international politics (Schwartz, Garrison and Alouf, 1973A; Wiegele, Plowman and Carey, 1973). Other research indicates the importance of health as a condition prerequisite to effective mass political participation (Stauffer, 1969), which thereby serves to limit the possibility of either political democracy or political revolution throughout much of the nonindustrialized world today—just as failing health is functioning also as a reinforcing constraint upon the participatory behavior of those persons in industrialized societies who are enjoying the "golden years" that increasingly are becoming characterized as a time of "poverty, fear, and malnutrition."

D. Biofeedback

Biofeedback refers, in this discussion, to observations of an individual's ongoing bodily processes, processes which may be operating either at the level of biophysical-chemical systems, or at the level of biophysical-chemical systems interacting with cognitive systems. Such observations may, in the latter case, be made by the individual of himself; or the observations can be made, in either case, by other persons' monitoring of the individual's physiological systems. It is also possible for other persons to make observations of his behavior, from which they, in turn, make cognitive inferences concerning what is (or has been) ongoing in the physiological system and/or cognitive systems of the subject individual. Virtually all of political science knowledge about political motivation is based upon only two of these types of evidence: i.e., either *a)* that of a subject individual's own verbal articulations about how he feels, or why he wants to do something; or else *b)* upon other persons' observations of and inferences from his behavior (including his speech behavior, upon which type *a* data depend). A major part of the work in political behavior—indeed, one is tempted to say "most"—has been respondent testimony about self-motivation, or inferences about motivation based upon observed actions. Evidently, independent observations of the variations in operation of the psychophysical systems of subjects of political analysis, and particularly when such data relate directly to theories of motivation grounded in biological (rather than social) events, ought to be extremely important in helping to appraise the degree of confidence warranted by much of our present knowledge base about political behavior.

The validation of political motivational theory at the level of biological theory has one great advantage, deriving from the circumstance that the biological theory is based almost entirely on comparative research, whether ethological or laboratory in method; whereas sociopsychological (and derived political) motivational research is both confined to a single species and then confounded by a babel of cross-cultural dissonance resulting in a focus upon a very limited set of variables out of which to attempt to construct a viable theory of political motivation. However well (or poorly) such a theory might correspond to our present understanding of political culture, at least we should expect that it will be consistent with what otherwise is known to be true of the motivation of animals generally, mammals in particular, and especially of primates. (To the extent that unresolved inconsistencies might become apparent, the task then would become to guide inquiry at the biological level, to ascertain the particular events in human evolution that account for the deviation(s) in human morphology that make human motivational processes, in this respect, different [from all other primates, or mammals, or animals, or whatever]; conversely, it would become incumbent to focus inquiry at the social science level upon aspects of human motivation that seem to be peculiarly human.)

An example of what presently appears to be a morphological idiosyncrasy of our species is found in the theory of aggression. In most other animals there is noncognitive, psychophysical-level (probably neural and biochemical, in almost all instances) inhibition of the *killing* of adult conspecifics. Humans (even unlike other primates) have lost, and apparently completely, any inhibition response to signals of appeasement and submission. Some evidence, from cultural anthropological work on surviving remnants of neolithic cultures in New Guinea, suggests that a *possible* explanation of how the inhibitory loss may have been species-adaptive is that the loss was a useful device in maintaining population control among small bands of humans, where competitive exclusion (for niche space at the *habitat* level) kept the overall level of local populations of the species within existing levels of variation of supporting resources. In any case existing restraints upon the killing by humans of each other are completely cultural rather than biological; and the cultural inhibitors do not operate very reliably. Conceivably this unreliability reflects contradiction among the norms more than (or rather than) ineffective learning: in virtually all societies of which we have historical evidence, the "Thou shalt not kill"s are balanced by an equal and opposing array of "Kill"s, depending upon the social circumstances. At all levels of governance, or the lack thereof, violence is of sufficient political concern today that the question may soon be raised of the possibility of a technical solution (i.e., at the level of biological engineering: estrogens as well as carcinogens in public water supplies?) to what is clearly a social, and political, problem.

A complicating biological factor in our efforts to cope with social, including political, violence may well prove to be that we are using a single word to describe the output of what may be both causally and operationally a variety of *different* biogenic systems of aggression. It has been proposed, for instance, that animal aggression generally *a*) includes several types which, although individually distinct, can coexist in complex relationships of mutual inhibition and reinforcement; *b*) involves typally distinct stimuli (or "releasers," in the more quaint terminology derived from continental ethology); and *c*) operates through typally *independent* neural substrates and hormonal systems. At this level the theory may find considerable support notwithstanding many species-specific differences in the details of repertoires of both stimuli stereotypy and behavioral action sequences. The presumption certainly must be that humans are (like other animal species) only a special case, and that disinhibition of intraspecific killing among humans is an empirical detail which in no way contradicts the general theory.

We are not likely to make much progress with either world peace or criminal justice reforms (to take two subfields of the discipline that remain fashionable) if we limit ourselves in our understanding of human aggression to either what political historians tell us about the careers of a relative handful of leading personages, or what social psychologists tell us about the frustrations of our pent-up storages of hydraulically engineered reserves of aggressive energy. Moyer's (1971) physiological model of aggression proffers what is probably a better fit to even our present empirical data than the rationalistic models of game (econometric) theory on the one hand or the irrationalistic models of Neo-Freudian social theory on the other, the two stools between which falls our contemporary understanding of the theory and practice of both war and crime. There is a not inconsiderable amount of support in zoological research, for example, for the proposition that sexual and aggressive behaviors are both physiologically and genetically interdependent in primates, which raises the question of possible interactive effects between political policies designed to promote world peace (Larsen, 1973:77–104) and those intended to reduce population levels.

Similarly, we can consider that the study of biofeedback can function as a means for the articulation of biological with political theories of behavior in many other ways, not only in regard to motivation theory but in diverse other respects as well. A continuing and important effort in this direction, that began in work by John Wahlke and Milton Lodge at the State University of Iowa during the sixties (1972), and is now being carried out by Lodge and his associates in the Laboratory for Behavioral Research at the State University of New York at Stony Brook, is an investigation into the correlation, between conventional verbal or ordinal responses to sociopsychological stimuli (slogans, pictures with *prima facie* political content), and psychophysical measures of arousal (galvanic skin potential, pulse, heart rate, and blood pressure). The measured relationships between the cognized and the autonomic responses are so close that more recent work as focused on the methodological problem of the development of scales, designed to measure the cognitive response, that are anchored in autonomic systemic bench marks; and because the latter *are* measurable on interval (and often, ratio) scales which parallel those long in common use in behavioral survey research, those scales of political behavior now can be given an interval-level interpretation. This is a methodological improvement that adds tremendously to the power (in the sense of statistical efficiency) of work done along these lines. It seems fair to add that the results of the initial efforts that have been published thus far barely scratch the surface of what may be possible to do, both from the point of view of the technology of the observation of psychophysical responses, and the articulation of those responses with the social science theory of political behavior.

Two developments in recent biopolitical research should be mentioned: studies of body image, and of posture. The work on body image hypothesizes that there is an important relationship between the qualitative appraisal that an individual makes of his own self as a discrete, phenotypic human organism; and his attitudes toward and (therefore) participation in the political process (Schwartz, Garrison and Alouf, 1973B; Shubs, 1973). Preliminary findings are suggestive of a correlation sufficient to be mutually supportive with other research (on health and nutritional minima as prerequisites to effective political behavior), and indicate that personal body images tend to be projected onto the body politic. Evidently, body image requires self-perception, and is therefore to be associated (like self-perceptions of arousal, emotion, and motivation) with that category in our typology of biofeedback. The other recent development lies (like laboratory monitoring of psychophysical systems) in the other category, of analyst observation of biofeedback, and it concerns bodily posture as an indicator of psychophysical states and changes (Schwartz and Zill, 1972). The possibility of using body language in a serious way for the observation and analysis of political behavior ought to be of considerable interest to political scientists because of the widespread potential that it offers for field (as distinguished from laboratory) investigations.

2. A Paradigm of Biopolitical Behavior

Let us turn now to a consideration of how it is possible and useful to interrelate the conventional paradigm of political behavior with a radically different but nevertheless complementary paradigm of biological behavior.

The political behavioral paradigm is shown in Figure 13.2. Political actors are classified, for purposes of data observation and aggregation, according to a set of indicators of their attributes that are deemed relevant for analysis (party, age, sex, socioeconomic status, etc.); these inputs of the system of political action have themselves been determined by the social environment. Political behaviors are classified in terms of a set of equally conventional action modes (policy choice, vote, role performance, speech, etc.); these are the outputs of the system. Intervening between social attributes and political action are the cognitions of the individual actors (beliefs, attitudes, decisions, preferences, etc.); by making conscious choices among competing alternatives political actors determine what their behavior will be (Schubert, 1968:415).

As I have pointed out elsewhere, such a paradigm postulates a (social)

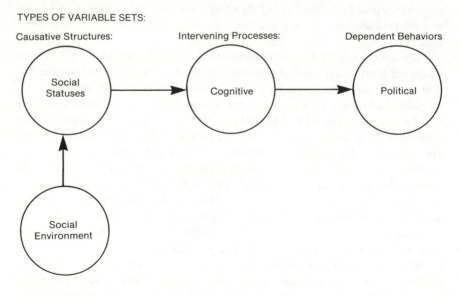

FIGURE 13.2
The Social Science Paradigm of Political Behavior

psychological model of decision-making; and this lies modally between the more strictly *logical* model of traditional political science, and the *nonlogical* models that are suggested by clinical psychology (on the one hand) and comparative psychology (and biology) on the other hand. (Schubert, 1968:417). The social indicators are (admittedly crude) indices to learning and experience, and the indicators function as surrogates for the total life history and socialization of the individual. According to this psychological model (and the paradigm of political behavioralism), differences in political behavior are explained by differences in conscious choices as to how to behave, which in turn are explained by differences in the life experiences of the actors.

The biological paradigm of behavior is sketched in Figure 13.3. It directs attention to the nonlogical influences — at least, from the point of view of the logic of political behavior — upon all behavior, and to the hierarchy of survival requirements, the satisfaction of which is preconditional to indulgence in political behavior. According to the biological paradigm, human needs have to be satisfied through sensory and appetitive interaction with an environment that is both partly natural and partly social; and different kinds of needs find sustenance in differing parts of the environment. Such biological charac-

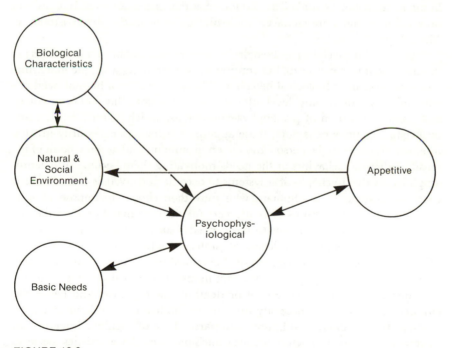

FIGURE 13.3
The Biological Paradigm of Animal Behavior

teristics as age and sex are reciprocally engaged in interactions with both the natural and the social environment: how either sector of that environment will affect individuals differs according to their stage and type of development, and how they will respond to that environment is partially determined by such aspects of their development. Similarly, an animal's pschophysical systems are directly affected by age, sex, health, and the other biological characteristics. Appetitive behavior involves searching of either the natural or the social environment (or both) and hence the feedback link indicated in Figure 13.3; while the satisfaction of physical-chemical needs necessarily entails feedback through psychophysical systems to the organic causes of those needs. So the biological paradigm states that needs autonomically activate psychophysical systems which introduce appetitive behavior, the consequence of which is to cause the animal to probe its environment, which in turn provides further stimulation for the animal.

Figure 13.2 puts humans more in the stance of gods than of animals, and hence is incomplete and inadequate precisely to the extent that humans *are* animals. Figure 13.3 describes human behavior as animal behavior, and it is incomplete and inadequate precisely to the extent that humans *are* different from other animals. So Figure 13.4 attempts to put them together, so that humans can better be studied as and for what they are—not gods, but also the only animals that were characterized—and quite properly—by Aristotle, as "the *political* animal."

Figure 13.4 depicts the psychological system of political behavioralism as (as in one sense it is) superior to, but continuously interacting with, the more fundamental system of biological behavior. The statement of a human need occurs initially not at any level of conscious thought, but rather involves autonomic invocation of psychophysical systems, which in turn activate appropriate appetitive behaviors; those appetitive behaviors necessarily involve interactions between the person and the environment, and at some point of intensity either the behaviors or the needs motivating them become sufficiently amplified by the psychophysical systems to become perceived as *bio*feedback to cognitive systems of the human, who may then choose to impose various (perhaps cultural) restraints or reinforcers (as the case may be) upon the appetitive behaviors. In relation to basic needs, such restraints never can be more than a temporary reordering of preferences because the feasible time scale for postponement of basic physical-chemical satisfactions is strictly determined by the operating limits of interacting psychophysical systems, which if exceeded result in the disablement or death of the organism and hence the elimination of both the necessity and the possibility for any kind of choice making. In addition to that limited and partial kind of cognitive intervention in appetitive behavior, cognition affects one's biosocial characteristics, because (for example) sex identification and attitudes toward age and aging are impor-

TYPES OF VARIABLE SETS:

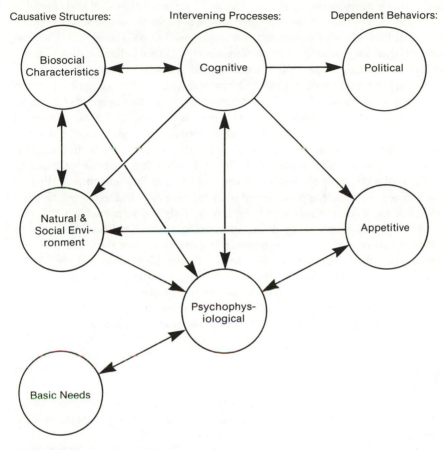

FIGURE 13.4
A Life Science Paradigm of Political Behavior

tant feedback to the further development of these facets of a human organism. Moreover, cognitions about the environment can lead to choosing behaviors that will affect the environment as feedback to it.

The set of characteristics that are designated as "social" in Figure 13.2 and as "biological" in Figure 13.3, are redesignated as *biosocial* in Figure 13.4 because those with which we are concerned here (age, sex, race, intelligence, and health) belong clearly in both realms of discourse: all have a clear and direct biological significance which is determinative of the social statuses that are derived from them. The environmental variables provide an indirect link between basic needs and biosocial characteristics; and consciously perceived *bio*feedback serves as one important link between psychophysical and cognitive systems, although direct two-way interaction between these two sets of systems (without biofeedback through self-conscious awareness) is much more important to behavior generally, and possibly also to political behavior. Biofeedback refers here strictly to perceived physiological systemic effects upon cognitive systems; the reverse link, postulated by humanistic psychology (with cognition affecting or "controlling" physiological systems) lacks the degree of consensual support among physiological psychologists, zoologists, and other biologists that does undergird the other relationships denoted in Figure 13.4. No direct link is shown between political and appetitive behavior, which constitute discrete and alternative modes of action. (Of course it is possible for a dinner at the White House or a Washington cocktail party to function empirically and simultaneously as *both* appetitive and political behavior; but to suggest this is a semantic quibble, and raises no question of analytical importance.)

What clearly needs to be done, in moving beyond political behavior to biopolitical behavior, is to design research that will explore the vertical as well as the horizontal relationships depicted in Figure 13.4. That will necessitate consideration of the interfaces between the biological and the social sciences, and will point political science in the direction of a study of political behavior which, for the first time, can deal with political life at the level it is lived and not as an exercise in puns, rhetoric, or intellectual dilettantism.

References

Bernstein, P., and D.C. Schwartz. (1973) "A Note on the Impact of Health on Presidential Decision Making." Paper presented to the 9th Congress of the International Political Science Association, Montreal.

Chase, A. (1971) *The Biological Imperatives: Health, Politics, and Human Survival.* New York: Holt, Rinehart and Winston.

Clapham, W.B. Jr. (1973) *Natural Ecosystems.* New York: Macmillan.

Corning, P.A. (1971) "The Biological Bases of Behavior and Some Implications for Political Science." *World Politics* 23:321–70.

Cutler, N.E., and V.L. Bengtson. (1974) "Age and Political Alienation: Maturation, Generation and Period Effects." *Annals of the American Academy of Political and Social Science* 415:160–75.

Davies, James. (1963) *Human Nature in Politics.* New York: Wiley.

Edey, M.A. (ed.). (1972) *The Missing Link.* New York: Time-Life Books.

Frankel, M.S. (1974) "Political Responses to Controversial Issues in the Development of Biomedical Technologies." Paper presented at the 70th Annual Meeting of the American Political Science Association, Chicago.

Fried, M.H. (1967) *The Evolution of Political Society.* New York: Random House.

Jaros, D. (1972) "Biochemical Desocialization: Depressants and Political Behavior." *Midwest Journal of Political Science* 16:1–28.

Larsen, K. (1973) "Aggression and Social Cost." *Peace Research Reviews* 5,1:1–104.

Lasswell, H. (1963) *The Future of Political Science.* New York: Atherton.

Leventhal, H., and E. Sharp (1965) "Facial Expressions as Indicators of Distress," in S.S. Tomkins and C.E. Izard (eds.), *Affect, Cognition, and Personality: Empirical Studies.* New York: Springer.

McAlpine, W.E. (1970) "Information Reduction Processes and Politics." Paper presented to the 8th Congress of the International Political Science Association, Munich.

Moyer, K.E. (1971) *The Physiology of Hostility.* Chicago: Markham.

Pilbeam, D. (1972) *The Ascent of Man.* New York: Macmillan.

Schubert, Glendon. (1968) "Behavioral Jurisprudence." *Law and Society Review* 2:407–428.

Schwartz, D.C., J. Garrison, and J. Alouf. (1973A) "Health and Body Image Correlates of Political Attitudes and Behaviors." Paper presented to the 9th Congress of the International Political Science Association, Montreal.

———. (1973B) "Health Processes and Body Images as Predictors of Political Attitudes and Behaviors: A Study in Political Socialization." Paper presented to the 9th Congress of the International Political Science Association, Montreal.

Schwartz, D.C., and N. Zill. (1972) "Psychophysiological Arousal as a Predictor of Political Participation." (Mimeo.)

Shubs, P. (1973) "Political Correlates of Self-Body Image." Paper presented to the 9th Congress of the International Political Science Association, Montreal.

Stauffer, R. (1969) "The Biopolitics of Underdevelopment." *Comparative Political Studies* 2:361–87.

Tiger, L., and R. Fox. (1971) *The Imperial Animal.* New York: Holt, Rinehart and Winston.

Tomkins, S.S. (1962) "The Primary Site of the Affects: The Face," in S.S. Tomkins, *Affect Imagery Consciousness: The Positive Affects.* New York: Springer.

Wahlke, J. and M.G. Lodge. (1972) "Psychophysiological Measures of Political Attitudes and Behavior." *Midwest Journal of Political Science* 6:505–37.

Wiegele, T.C., S. Plowman, and R. Carey. (1973) "International Crisis, Cardiorespiratory Health, and Political Attitudes: A Literature Review and a Pilot Study." Paper presented to the 9th Congress of the International Political Science Association, Montreal.

14

The Future of Biopolitics

Thomas C. Wiegele

A major thesis of this chapter is that political beings are not ethereal essences floating around in an intellectual construct called a political system. Because human nature is rational, psychological, *and* physical, analysts of political behavior must begin to conceive of the subjects of their investigations as biological beings with intellective capacities. At the present state in the development of the discipline, we can characterize ourselves as having ignored an enormous amount of information about humanity and its real nature, that is its nature *as it is lived*. Because our vision has often been narrowly focused down safe, well traveled tunnels, we have been insufficiently attentive to the powerful findings of the twentieth-century life science.

When the potential exists to enhance explanations of political phenomena with variables from the life sciences, we should not fail to realize that potential. When we find evidence that human political behavior is shaped or influenced by biological considerations, we cannot, in the spirit of intellectual honesty, ignore that information. Thus, it is incumbent upon us to add a biological perspective to our work; in doing so we need not engage in a blind acceptance of a biological determinism that pays no heed to human purposive activities.

We must adopt a more comprehensive definition of human nature, one that includes in an operational way the biological as well as the rational and psychological. If we do so, we will have to pay the price of making our discipline increasingly more complex. At the same time, however, the findings generated will be more realistic and—we hope—more accurate. Such a broadened definition of human nature will force us to adopt a much more basic orientation in our research efforts.

Strategies for Pursuing a Biopolitics of Human Life

. . . Researchers who have worked in the area now known as biopolitics

Reprinted with permission from *Biopolitics: Search for a More Human Political Science*, Boulder, CO.: Westview Press, 1979, pp. 145–156.

have been interested in several aspects of the life sciences. The most prominent among these are ethology, evolutionary studies including population biology, and what might very loosely be referred to as physiology.

All of these areas will have an increasing relevance to political inquiry. Ethology has given us many useful organizing concepts including territoriality, bonding, imprinting, dominance, and ritualized behavior. Ethology has the powerful advantage that many of its insights have grown out of a comparative perspective on animal social behavior. Some work is beginning to link data from animals with human data, leading to the emerging field of human ethology (see Eibl-Eibesfeldt, 1970).

Population biology has proved to be a rich source of information on evolution, and at least one political scientist (Peter Corning) has focused almost exclusively on the evolutionary perspective in his work. Animal studies have also contributed a good deal of knowledge in this area.

Physiologically oriented work has adopted perspectives from subspecialties that have focused, for example, on nutrition, health, neurology, psychophysiology, and medicine. This research is different from that of ethology and evolution in that it has concentrated, for the most part, on the individual human being or on specific groups of humans rather than on the species as a whole.

Yet several problems remain with these orientations. For example, the body of ethological literature poses some methodological and epistemological difficulties when an attempt is made to extend it to human behavior. Peterson (1977), a political scientist, has strongly cautioned his colleagues on what he calls the "hazards of cross-species comparison," particularly in extending primate investigations to the study of human behavior. Comparisons have followed a fairly typical methodological approach that, according to Peterson (1977:3), consists of the following schedule of tasks: "(1) a search of the primate literature to detect patterns which may have human political analogues; (2) pointing out human behavior which seems similar to the primate pattern(s); and (3) the consequent positing of common biological explanations for this similarity (e.g., similarity because of congruent selection pressure or descent from the same ancestor)." (See also Sahlins, 1976.)

What is the nature of a criterion for similarity? At what point can we say that dissimilarity exists? If we are examining human political analogues, precise definitions of "humanness" usually are not offered. Furthermore, there are numerous cultural differences among human beings that influence behavior patterns.

Because human beings have the capacity for symbolic communication of a very high order, it can be argued that *Homo sapiens* is a fundamentally different creature from those found in the animal world. Indeed, speech transmits not only information but also meaning, and this implies that human culture is strongly conditioned by communication. Such culture might not be as genetically influenced as that of, say, nonhuman primates.

While other examples of difficulties in moving across species lines can be offered, the several cited above should suffice to make the point that a political scientist, whose interests focus on the human being, will necessarily embroil himself in arguments relating to the validity of cross-species comparisons by adopting a rigorously ethological perspective. Not only have some American scientists recently brought a lawsuit against popularizers of ethological knowledge, but scientists in the United Kingdom have formed the British Society for Social Responsibility in Science with a working group on sociobiology to examine distortions of ethological work as they have been applied to human behavior. These problems, however, should not deter imaginative political scientists from a careful use of ethological information in their research work.

Perhaps the most productive avenues for the political scientist to exploit in developing a more operationally comprehensive definition of human nature lie in the life sciences that are devoted exclusively to the study of man. The bodies of knowledge that have dealt with the human organism directly and empirically include medicine, psychopharmacology, neuroanatomy, biochemistry, epidemiology, human biology, psychosomatic medicine, psychophysiology, human physiology, human endocrinology and behavioral ecology. Each of these is a significant discipline in its own right; each has focused on the human species; each has the potentiality of adding to our understanding of political society. Much of the work relating to the study of elites, conflict and aggression, and even the general political system, has grown out of these life sciences. However, it is this empirically useful knowledge that is the most difficult to acquire for a political scientist. One important reason why progress linking the "harder" life sciences with political science has been slow is that political scientists who want to utilize these disciplines must undertake serious retraining in the form of heavy immersion in the literature of another field and, if possible, the establishment of a mentor relationship with a colleague in the appropriate life science discipline. Such arrangements often are satisfactory for establishing credentials to *begin* interdisciplinary work. However, as work develops, the substantive and methodological issues associated with further progress become increasingly complex. However, there is one development that most assuredly should not take place.

When interdisciplinary work becomes complex, there is a danger that biologically oriented political researchers may "give up" because the knowledge required is highly technical and progress is slow. This could result in a situation in which the nontechnical literature of the life sciences — since it is the literature that we can read with comfort — becomes the only biological information relevant to our inquiries. This would be unfortunate because it would create a situation in which biopolitics would remain in the realm of speculative thought. That is not to say that such thought does not have an important contribution to make to the study of biopolitics; but without a heavy emphasis on the empirical findings of the life sciences, biopolitics will be little more than a "literary" area devoid of any basic knowledge about real political behavior.

In sum, the danger with the ethological thrust is that researchers might treat *Homo sapiens* as little more than another animal species; the danger with what we have called the "physiological" thrust is that work might become overly complicated and "payoffs" so distant that researchers will decline the challenge. Fortunately, biopolitical scholars have shown a remarkable awareness of these potential problems and it is unlikely that either will come to pass.

Some Elementary Needs

Several important future requirements are necessary for biopolitics to establish itself firmly as an innovative orientation in the discipline. First, we need a healthier and more optimistic orientation to *basic* research. There are two implications of this need. While the "so what?" question should be asked of all scholarship at all times, this question should be one of honest inquiry and anticipation, not disdain. Scholars using human biological variables in their work are finding significant associations between those variables and political behavior. And that is really quite enough at this point in our attempts to utilize a more comprehensive definition of political humanity. To require that all research have immediately identifiable applications to the political system or to public policy is to effectively close off the development of basic research questions and studies. Applications are not always readily apparent in basic research work, as we all know, but an expanded knowledge of associations — citing the natural sciences again as an example — will ultimately lead to causal inference and to practical applications.

An additional implication of the development of a more healthy attitude toward basic research is that we must, as Wahlke (1976:258) has suggested, employ experimental methods in our work. Experimental orientations must guide our inquiries in both laboratory and real-world environments. Indeed, we might quite intentionally design studies that would incorporate both settings. An experimental orientation may lead us into new research methods that many will initially find awkward. But we should not be fearful of the unfamiliar nor should we shrink from reporting negative results. It will be important for journals to publish negative as well as positive findings and our attitudes toward all reports will need to be positive and open.

The new approach to basic research will also lead quite naturally to the need for a more comprehensive knowledge of biopolitical research methods. Until such methods are further developed, collated in texts, and widely known, it will be difficult to intensify our work in the years ahead. The methodology of ethological research could exercise a profound influence on a broad spectrum of political questions. So too, the methodology of physiology, especially psychophysiology, should provide new dimensions in the methodological training of professional political scientists.

A third need concerns the necessity of developing interdisciplinary teams of researchers. Properly constructed, these teams can overcome many of the problems that result when individuals attempt to blend knowledge from another discipline into their own disciplinary stores of information. However, meaningful interdisciplinary cooperation, normally praised in the abstract, is not easy to develop. Joint studies must be conceived in ways that are professionally productive to each discipline represented in the effort if they are to expand the limits of methodological tools, approaches, and substantive insights available to the single scholar. Because of the complexities involved, this kind of collaboration is frequently difficult to arrange on a long-term basis. One effective way to address this problem would be to encourage academic departments to offer regular appointments to relevant professionals from outside their own disciplines. But the likelihood of such a development taking place on any meaningful scale is negligible.

Given this situation, a fourth need becomes obvious. If biopolitics is to establish itself as a continuing orientation within the discipline of political science, interdisciplinary curricula for the training of new scholars will have to be created (see Caldwell, 1979, Corning, 1978; and Kort and Maxson, 1978). But as we have seen in this book, biopolitics is more than an "orientation"; rather, biopolitics speaks to a fundamental reordering of the substantive knowledge needed to understand political life. Such a reordering is required across all the subfields of the discipline. Somit (1968) saw this situation clearly over a decade ago when he suggested that political scientists acquire at least a minimum of biological expertise to allow them to utilize the literature of the life sciences.

Further, we are not dealing here with a momentary aberration or a fad that will wither away in due time. The twentieth-century impact of the life sciences on the understanding of social behavior across all species has been awesome. The effects of these are being felt in sociology, economics, history, and psychology. In short, the necessity to incorporate biological considerations into our understanding of social man will not disappear. It is imperative that at least a few political science departments launch pilot programs to train students to work at the disciplinary juncture of the life and social sciences.

Fifth, and related to curricular considerations, is the need for some students of biopolitics to become interested in the political policy relevance of certain aspects of the life sciences. . . . Only a few scholars have been interested in pursuing such an orientation, most notably in technology and genetic engineering. However, the "applications" side of biopolitics should expand in the immediate future because of its strong vocational prospects. But a word of caution is in order. Given the preliminary state of much of our work in biopolitics, we cannot afford to lessen our basic research efforts. Because interdisciplinary progress is often slow, a much more intensive devotion to basic research is not only desirable but also the *sine qua non* of a meaningful expansion of biopolitical knowledge.

The willingness to make a long-term intellectual commitment toward pursuing a research question of biopolitical interest is a sixth important need. Because progress in the uncharted areas of any discipline is frequently difficult, researchers could easily become discouraged. Wise colleagues can offer support and encouragement, especially to their junior partners, over the course of a long-term research effort. Demands for immediate and numerous publications should not be allowed to distort the inquiry process.

Seventh, we need to rid ourselves of the fear of taking intellectual risks. By and large, political science has been a conservative discipline. However, scholarly tradition is built, not just guarded and maintained. At the intersection of the social and biological sciences can be found many enticing research questions holding the prospect of producing stunning insights and knowledge that could enhance and expand traditional wisdom. But to address these questions requires rather high risk research efforts; that is, after a significant investment of time the findings might be negative. If we are going to make intellectual breakthroughs, however, we are going to have to take these risks. I am confident that it will be worth the investment and that substantial intellectual payoffs will result.

As an interim measure, those who aspire to pursue a biopolitical orientation can become familiar with natural science journals that deal with behavioral aspects of human nature. Several of these journals are:

Journal of Human Stress
Journal of Psychosomatic Medicine
Journal of Health and Social Behavior
Journal of Social Biology
Journal of Medical Psychology
Journal of Applied Physiology
Journal of Medical Ethics
Journal of Biological Psychology
Biology and Human Affairs
Developmental Psychobiology
Environmental Biology & Medicine

Journal of Social and Biological Structures
Physiology and Behavior
Journal of Medicine and Philosophy
Psychophysiology
Behavioral Neuropsychiatry
International Journal of Social Psychiatry
Neuroscience and Behavioral Physiology
Human Ecology
Journal of Environmental Health
Urban Ecology
Bioethics Digest
Environmental Health
Culture, Medicine and Psychiatry
The Behavioral and Brain Sciences
Brain and Language
Medical Anthropology
Behavioral Engineering
Environment and Behavior
Journal of Genetic Psychology
Journal of Biosocial Science
Journal of Ecology
Ecological Studies
Behavioral Ecology and Sociobiology
Biobehavioral Reviews
International Journal of Psychobiology
Progress in Psychobiology and Physiological Psychology
Ethology and Sociobiology

Another publication that has grown out of the humanities and often deals with natural science topics is the *Journal of Interdisciplinary History*. This partial listing of journals is offered as evidence that scholars in the human life sciences *are now generating and will continue to generate* a good deal of behaviorally oriented information about the human species. We cannot afford to ignore this work.

Finally, it will be important for us to develop professional affiliations with appropriate organizations of colleagues in related fields such as human ethology, animal behavior, primatology, psychophysiology, and social ecology.

Conclusions

In our efforts to develop a more human operational definition of *Homo sapiens,* we should always remember that we are political scientists whose inquiries should begin with a professional desire to understand *political* problems, issues, and behavior. After identifying the subject area of our research, we should ask ourselves how the human life sciences might contribute to a more complete understanding of the political phenomena under investigation. In those instances where the life sciences contribute nothing, we should not bend to employ them. Moreover, we should be cautious about encouraging a biological reductionism that leaves little room for rational judgments and the mediating effects of social situations.

As research progresses in the vein suggested, . . . we probably should resist the temptation to build grand theory. Our most productive work will, in all likelihood, be in developing islands of biopolitical knowledge from which general theory will emerge at a later time. Once we feel comfortable with the inclusion of biological variables in our work, the real "post-behavioral revolution" will have been accomplished. At that point a much more basic research-oriented political science will have been established. At that point too, the "Great Academic Wall" separating the disciplines that concerned Glendon Schubert (1976) should be in the process of breaking down. Perhaps by that time we will have developed curricular programs based upon a more comprehensive definition of human nature that will train students to carry out biopolitically based research with ease.

Some critics have implied that political researchers who incorporate human biological variables into their work in an attempt to understand political phenomena and behaviors are somehow guilty of adopting an antihumanist posture toward political life. . . . I have argued that our discipline has functioned, for the most part, with an incomplete operational definition of human nature. To the extent that our views of humanity have been distorted we have been antihumanist for we have failed to appreciate the true complexity of human nature. Likewise, to the extent that we blend human biological variables into what we already know about human rational behavior, we will become increasingly humanistic. And that seems to me to be a worthy objective.

It is no longer a question of *whether* we should incorporate human life science data into our studies of human social behavior: that is already being done by the life scientists, and the journals listed above ought to be a minimal testament to this activity. The more crucial questions are: who is best equipped to study human social behavior, the life scientist or the social scientist, and who will have a deeper appreciation of humanistic values, the life scientist or the social scientist?

References

Caldwell, L. K. (1979) "Implications of Biopolitics: Reflections on a Politics of Survival." Paper presented to the annual convention of the International Society for Political Psychology, Washington, D.C., May.

Corning, P. A. (1978) "Biopolitics: Toward a New Political Science." Paper presented to the annual convention of the American Political Science Association, New York, August 31–September 3.

Eibl-Eibesfeldt, I. (1970) *Ethology: The Biology of Behavior.* New York: Holt, Rinehart and Winston.

Kort, F., and S. C. Maxson. (1978) "The Study of Politics in a Biobehavioral Perspective: A Report on a Course Based on a New Paradigm." Paper presented to the annual meeting of the American Society of Criminology, Dallas, November.

Peterson, S. A. (1977) "On the Hazards of Cross-Species Comparison: Primates and Human Politics." Paper presented to the Research and Planning Committee for Biology and Politics of the International Political Science Association, Bellagio, Italy, November.

Sahlins, M. (1976) *The Use and Abuse of Biology.* Ann Arbor: University of Michigan Press.

Schubert, G. (1976) "Politics as a Life Science: How and Why the Impact of Modern Biology Will Revolutionize the Study of Political Behavior," in A. Somit, (ed.), *Biology and Politics.* The Hague: Mouton.

Somit, A. (1968) "Toward a More Biologically-Oriented Political Science: Ethology and Psychopharmacology." *Midwest Journal of Political Science* 12:550–567.

Wahlke, J. (1976) "Observations on Biopolitical Study," in A. Somit, (ed.), *Biology and Politics.* The Hague: Mouton.

Part 6
Sociology

Introduction to Part 6

For the past three to five years, a brisk debate has been underway within sociology regarding the merits, importance, and validity of a biological and/or sociobiological perspective in the study of human behavior. The origins of this contemporary debate go back at least to Pierre L. van den Berghe's 1974 article in the *American Sociological Review,* which presented a controversial biosocial theory of aggression. More recently, the question of how sociology as a discipline should respond to the new knowledge of social behavior emerging from the biological sciences received an uncommonly provocative examination by Lee Ellis. This section deals with the "Ellis debate," presents Mazur's appraisal of likely future research payoffs, and concludes with Baldwin and Baldwin's proposal for a balanced approach.

Writing in a hypothetical format, Ellis projects his view of the decline and fall of sociology during the last quarter of the twentieth century. Ellis looks back from a 21st-century point of view, saying that the immediate cause for the dissolution of the discipline was the establishment within biology of "a major new branch of science called 'sociobiology,' which rapidly engulfed the study of social behavior." He argues that because few sociologists are being trained to utilize the intellectual leads emerging from biology, there exists no possibility for sociology to sustain itself. Ellis suggests that young scholars who are interested in the study of human social behavior and who manage to receive a grounding in biological training will be absorbed eventually into departments of sociobiology rather than sociology. Ultimately, Ellis predicts, most other sociologists will associate with political science.

Of course, this rather negative scenario has been rejected by many sociologists. Responding to Ellis' position are four short articles which challenge Ellis's description of the "demise" of sociology. Barash accuses Ellis of overstating his case to such an extent that open-minded inquiry has been jeopardized. Claiming that Ellis has gone beyond the bounds of legitimate inference from animal studies, Kunkel insists that while "biochemical and genetic factors set the stage, . . . culture and history provide that script for social life." Nevertheless, he feels that with a proper focus on *human* biology, biosociology might emerge as a new subfield within sociology.

Revealing a distrust of dichotomous thinking, Lenski asks why cultural and biological explanation of human social behavior cannot be combined. "What is needed," he says, "is not a life-death struggle between sociology and sociobiology, but two disciplines that can begin to communicate and cooperate with one another and develop more sophisticated models of human societies and individual behavior than either alone could create." Lenski suggests that as a prelude to this kind of cooperation, sociologists will have to overcome their traditional prejudices and begin to study the relevant works of biologists.

As might be expected, van den Berghe is in basic agreement with many of Ellis' arguments, especially Ellis' comments about sociology's antireductionist bias. "The scientific enterprise has been a reductionist one, and sociologists show great ignorance of the history of science in making the word 'reductionism' an invective." More importantly, however, van den Berghe asserts that sociobiology might contain the germ of a new paradigm for the social science community. "Competence in the study of behavior," he says, "cannot be achieved in total ignorance of ecology, ethology, primatology, paleontology, population genetics and biochemistry. . . . " Furthermore, ". . . the intellectual framework of sociobiology is of sweepingly greater scope and generality than anything the social sciences have proposed in the last century."

To conclude this exchange, Ellis provides a brief rejoinder to his critics. Expressing a sensitivity to what others viewed as a premature burial of sociology, Ellis writes: "I hope sociology survives and emerges within the next few years as the recognized science of social behavior. . . . I still think the prospects are marginal, at best."

Two additional readings have been included to provide subject matter that goes beyond the "Ellis debate." Mazur addresses the broader question of biological explanations in sociology. In doing so, he explores evolutionary, genetic, and neurophysiological approaches to the study of human social behavior. Mazur discusses limitations in all of these approaches. Nevertheless, he finds "neurophysiological explanations of social interaction . . . particularly promising since they are capable of direct empirical test. . . ." However, he cautions that "the medical/physiological techniques that will be required for this work are outside the expertise of most sociologists, so we can expect such research to occur outside of our discipline unless there is substantial retraining within sociology."

Finally, the selection by Baldwin and Baldwin develops a rational research strategy for sociologists who are interested in pursuing biosocial theories of explanation. They develop criteria for what they call "balanced biosocial theory," balanced in the sense of integrating both genetic and environmental determinants of social behavior. They suggest a variety of studies that could be performed profitably by sociologists who are careful to follow an integrating orientation.

T.C.W.

15

The Decline and Fall of Sociology, 1975–2000

Lee Ellis

Although it was rather clearly foreseen early in the last quarter of the twentieth century that sociobiology would eventually absorb the scientific aspects of sociobiology and supplant it (Sade, 1975:263), the speed with which this occurred was remarkable. By the mid-1980s, the trends in this direction were commonly recognized, and by the end of the twentieth century, essentially nothing remained of sociology within the academic community. This paper outlines in a historical context the factors responsible for this eventuality.

Two related and interdependent assumptions retarded sociology's growth into a full-fledged science almost from its beginning. These assumptions were (1) that causal explanations of human social behavior could not be reduced to nonhuman or nonsocial levels, and (2) that human behavior was purposefully caused. Although, as will be shown, all major sciences probably originated with obvious traces of analogous assumptions, in the course of their maturation they gradually shed them. Evidence suggests that sociology was progressing toward abandonment of these assumptions, but that its overall movement was too slow for most of its practitioners to perceive the implications of numerous twentieth century biological discoveries with profound sociological implications. By the third quarter of the twentieth century, these discoveries had snowballed to enormous proportions and were ripe for the beginning of a theoretical synthesis that could account for several major forms of complex social phenomena. To assume its role in what could have been sociology's first paradigm-forming process (à la Kuhn, 1962), its "assumptional fabric" had to be modified so as to permit the incorporation of major evolutionary, genetic, ethnographic, and biochemical concepts and hypotheses. Impatiently, however, biology established a major new branch of science called "sociobiology," which rapidly engulfed the study of social behavior. Mean-

Reprinted by permission of the American Sociological Association and the author. This article originally appeared in *The American Sociologist*, vol. 12, April 1977, 56–66.

while, sociology's jurisdiction over the study of social institutions had already been largely lost to what now are called "the administrative sciences," principally political science and economics. What became of sociology thereafter, actually, was not as surprising as most science historians have held. It followed a rather logical pattern, and had at least one scientific precedent.

Antireductionism and Purposeful
Explanations in Sociology

Although sociology's founder, Auguste Comte, saw sociology rooted in biology, his concept of a hierarchy of sciences, with sociology at the summit, opened the door to a sort of "stratified segregation" of sociology from the other sciences. Thereafter, nearly all of its other early influential figures staunchly opposed any suggestion that sociological phenomena could be reduced to non-social causal explanations (Catton, 1966:303; McClintock, 1975). The position taken on this matter was most forcefully argued by Emile Durkheim, around the turn of the twentieth century; and his writings added rational substance to an approach that had already been fairly widely adopted by those affiliating with the discipline (Hatch, 1973).

By way of fortuitous political circumstances in the early 1960s, sociologists were called upon in large numbers for the purpose of finding solutions to basic social problems prevalent in major portions of North America during that period. None of the discipline's prominent theoretical explanations—or deduced remedies—for poverty, racial separatism, poor academic achievement, inadequate public health care, crime, familial instability, and perversely skewed stratification patterns went below the institutional or social-interpersonal levels. Consequently, sociologists failed to appreciate the necessity of making allowances for important biological factors in their program designs; and, of course, little or no noticeable impact could be documented in the case of most of these corrective administrative programs (Robison and Smith, 1971; Jencks, 1972; Etzioni, 1973; Gaff, 1973:553; Milner, 1973; Zigler, 1973a and 1973b; Lipton et al., 1975).

Sociology's theoretical sterility became increasingly obvious and a subject of professional concern (Willer and Webster, 1970; Freese, 1972:481; Schearing, 1973; Goldstein, 1976). Seeing antireductionism as at least part of the problem, a few sociologists suggested—some almost apologetically—that the discipline's predominant position on this matter should be critically reappraised (Catton, 1966; Friedland, 1973:514; Tarter, 1973:155; Cavan, 1976:140), but the movement remained slow. It is important to realize that at the same period, among natural scientists, reductionism had become an almost universally accepted assumption (Anderson, 1972:393). In fact, reductionism apparently even then was being perceived by a number of scientists as the main framework under which most major theoretical breakthroughs occurred (Kagan, 1972:78; Ghiselin, 1973:967; Sade, 1975:261; Fruton, 1976:332).

Purposeful explanations for phenomena usually are closely linked with antireductionism. This can be understood by noting that whereas the latter dictates where causal explanations are not to be found, the former identifies where they are to be found. Their connection was clearly conceived as far back as the writings of Dewey and Bentley (1949), who criticized the extent to which both concepts could be identified in all of the behavioral sciences during the period in which they wrote. Three stages for theory development in any science were postulated: (1) the *self-action* of purposeful stage, (2) the *interaction* or simple causation stage, and (3) the *process transaction* stage in which phenomena were viewed at the systems level, and as being composed of wholly interdependent components. This last stage translates quite well into Hardin's (1974) deceptively simple law that "You can never do merely one thing." And, it is at this last stage, of course, that the real work of science is carried out—that of continually expanding one's symbolic representation of the systems and refining one's understanding of each system's interacting elements.

The attribution of purpose to explain empirical observations can be found in all sciences during their infancies (Tarter, 1973:155). For example, Aristotle held that falling bodies accelerate because they become more jubilant the nearer they get to their earthly home. It is important to emphasize that this proposition has never been disproved; it was merely set aside as physics gradually devised alternative propositions that could be disproved. Except for occasional carelessness, statements implying intentions, purposes, aims, and goals are not found in any mature science (Kuhn, 1962:171; Skinner, 1971:6; Ghiselin, 1973:965). As alluded to earlier, sociology's antireductionism encouraged references to purposes in explaining human social behavior; and because purposeful hypotheses are not empirically disprovable sociological theory continued to stagnate.

The Emergence of Sociobiology

Because of sociology's immature assumptional framework, biologists began mounting sizable invasions into "sociological territory" in the 1970s (Gallant and Prothero, 1972; Sade, 1975:261). Those most prominently involved were the specialists in primate evolution, genetics, and finally, biochemistry. Once incursions began, two considerations led to the establishment and rapid expansion of major enclaves of study in what was then still clearly recognized as sociological subject matter. One was a swell of exciting biological discoveries beginning in the 1950s that had unmistakable social behavioral implications, and the other was the very important fact that few sociologists have ever received the academic training necessary to begin following the leads of these discoveries. By the time a number of leading sociological departments began to require graduate training in biology in the late 1980s—especially in biochemistry and genetics—the demise of sociology apparently was already too firmly established to be reversed.

Some of the specific major biological discoveries which appeared, in large part, early in the second half of the twentieth century that had profound implications for the scientific study of social behavior are summarized in Table 15.1. In no way can this table be considered exhaustive, but it does seem reasonably representative of the relative level of development in each area at that time. Most sociobiologists today will be surprised at just *how* comprehensive this knowledge really was, especially in the case of social behavior's evolutionary basis. Prior to the mid-1970s, most of the research was aimed toward documenting the evolutionary significance of complex social phenomena. Growing evidence, however, implicated genetic and biochemical factors in the etiology of human social behavior as the table suggests, and, at the same time, evidence documented the enormous extent to which social behavior in "lower animals" was responsive to environmental factors just as man's (Emlen, 1976:736). In this way, the focus of inquiry gradually, but irreversibly, turned away from disputes over *whether* human social behavior was reducible to more basic levels, to that of discovering how and to what degrees this was the case. The rapid growth in genetic and biochemical knowledge relating to social behavior also laid to rest genuine fear that the only application of sociobiology would be in the form of reviving early twentieth century eugenics (Alper et al., 1976; Sociobiology Study Group of Science for the People, 1976). As Hixson and Scott (1976:170) conceived of it near the outset of sociology's decline, "Biology is no more destiny than history is." Even in the early 1980s, the major problem for applied sociobiology was that of perfecting ways of environmentally controlling biochemical factors in conjunction with institutional factors to confront social problems.

Sociobiology insured its acceptance outside of the intellectual community when, in the mid-1980s, it began to demonstrate success with technologies to deal with major social problems, including drug abuse, poverty, and certain types of crime. Public funding (*and* regulation!) of sociobiological research increased tremendously thereafter, and continued to expand into the mid-1990s. This funding brought about the creation of many sizable academic sociobiology departments to replace sociobiology's mere representation on biology departmental faculties prior to 1980. Sociology, during the same period, began to suffer the effects of lower public funding; and younger sociologists—those who had gotten some biological training—were recruited into the many well paying and difficult-to-fill sociobiology positions about as quickly as they graduated. This continued until the mid-1990s, when sociobiology departments were producing sufficient graduates of their own.

Sociobiology's rapid elevation to a highly respected major branch of science with both a theoretical and applied base within 15 years was impressive. What has been largely overlooked by science historians is the fact that much of what was initially accomplished in the name of "sociobiology" merely involved using European mathematics developed in the 1970s (Panati, 1976) to intermesh biological theories with sociological research findings of the 1960s and the 1970s. Nevertheless, with every sociobiological advance, sociology seemed to lose more of its dwindling claim to research funds. By 1990, virtually all of its research support was being diverted to more productive (i.e., sociobiological) projects. Sociology, from then on found it very difficult to retain, and, a few years later, even to recruit, well qualified students.

Major factional disputes among sociologists erupted over the future course of their discipline. By the late 1980s, the choice seemed clear to most leading sociologists: either build "biosociology" into sociology's major branch so as to recapture jurisdiction over theory and technology lost to sociobiology, or retrench into those few areas still unoccupied either by sociobiology on the one side of the social phenomena continuum, or by the administrative sciences on the other (see Reverby, 1972:141). Continued debate without decisive action, growing embarrassment over sociology's deteriorating image within the scientific community, and impatience in the face of sociobiology's expanding share of public research funding, all contributed to sociology's withering professional influence. By 1990, membership in the major sociological association had shrunk to about a third of what it was in the late 1970s. As was already mentioned, many younger sociologists had been fortunate enough to receive some biological research and theoretical training, and were absorbed into sociobiology. Most other former sociologists obtained professional acceptance in political science.

Sociology's Regression

Those who held most tenaciously to the title of "sociologist" began to resurrect the writings of historical sociologists who had exhibited predominant tendencies toward nonreductionist and, especially, teleological explanations of social phenomena. They explained away sociobiological successes in dealing with social problems, not on the empirical basis, but by denouncing it as unnatural and immoral environmental interference with the human will. These actions attracted the support of certain public groups to whom sociology had never appealed before. Coinciding with this trend toward moral denunciation of sociobiology, some of the remaining sociologists began to call attention to what came to be called "perceptions of social essences" in the writings of teleological sociologists that they claimed could be arrayed into logical geometrical tables. Derivations by "qualified sociologists" could be made from these tables to produce what many held to be astonishingly accurate predictions. As the academic community denounced the "New Sociology" as quackery and a pseudoscience, and pressed for its ouster from institutions of

266

TABLE 15.1

Evidence of Evolutionary, Genetic, and Biochemical Influences Upon Major Forms of Human Social Behavior

Major Forms of Human Social Behavior	Evidence of the Same or Highly Similar Behavior in Nonhuman Species	Evidence Implicating Such Behavior as Contributing to Species Survival and Breeding Success	Evidence of Genetic Influences on Such Behavior in Nonhuman Species	Evidence of Genetic Influences on Such Behavior in the Human Species	Evidence of Biochemical Influences on Such Behavior in Nonhuman Species	Evidence of Biochemical Influences on Such Behavior in the Human Species
Aggressive Behavior	Scott, 1958 Calhoun, 1962 Christian, 1970 Southwick, 1972 Van den Berghe, 1974	Eisenberg and Gould, 1970 Hamburg, 1969 Trivers, 1972: 149	Scott, 1958 Guhl et al., 1960 Alland, 1967: 133 Nevo, 1969: 486 Vernon, 1969 Eisenberg and Dillon, 1971 Bekoff and Hill, 1975	Vandenberg, 1967 Maccoby and Jacklin, 1974 Van den Berghe, 1974: 780 Moyer, 1975	Peters, 1967 Edwards, 1969 Sadleir, 1969: 262 Axelrod, 1971: 605 Eibl-Eibesfeldt, 1971: 70 Sauerhoff and Michaelson, 1973 Welch et al., 1974 Sheard, 1975 Leshner, 1975	Persky et al., 1971 Williams and Eichelman, 1971 Kreuz and Rose, 1972 Eisenberg, 1973: 124 Ehrenkranz et al., 1974 Shah and Roth, 1974: 111-126 Weiss, 1974 Anonymous, 1975
Altruism and Loyalties Between Family Members	Knerer and Atwood, 1973; 1091 Kolata, 1975 Wilson, 1975	Eibl-Eibesfeldt, 1971: 60 Knerer and Atwood, 1973: 1091 Kolata, 1975 Wilson, 1975 Trivers and Hare, 1976	Eisenberg and Dillon, 1971 Trivers and Hare, 1976	Hogan, 1973: 218		
Altruism and Loyalties Within Social Groups	Struhsaker, 1976	see McClearn, 1971: 80 Williams, 1971 see Dare, 1975		Laughlin and d'Aquili, 1974		
Cooperative, Allelomimetic and Conforming Behavior	Zajonc, 1966: 39 Fox, 1967: 31 Scott, 1969: 269 Beyers, 1973: 36	McClearn, 1971: 80		Cattell, 1957		

Behavior						
Dominance and General Social Stratification Behavior	Calhoun, 1962; Stynes, et al., 1968; Wickler, 1969: 99; Christian, 1970; Le Boeuf, 1974; Van den Berghe, 1974; Schein, 1975	Sade, 1966; Milne and Milne, 1968: 69; Christian, 1970	Kolata, 1976	Cattell, 1957; Ballonoff, 1974	Leary and Stynes, 1959; Milne and Milne, 1968: 69; Siegel and Poole, 1969	
Gregariousness and Sociability	Calhoun, 1962; Fox, 1967: 28; Rowell, 1969; Singh, 1969; Hoagland, 1972; Klopfer and Klopfer, 1973: 563; Knerer and Atwood, 1973: 1091; Mazur, 1973	Wilson, 1971	Wilson, 1971	Parsons, 1967	Moyer, 1973	Moyer, 1973; Revelle et al., 1976
Sexual Selectivity and Discrimination	Fox 1967: 31; Baldwin, 1968: 298; Herbert, 1968; Wickler, 1969; Le Boeuf, 1974	Trivers, 1972: 168; Williams, 1975		Diamond, 1965: 157	Vandenberg, 1969; Johnston and Zahoric, 1975; Macrides et al., 1975; Nadler, 1975; Reinboth, 1975	Money, 1969: 230
Monogamous Sexual Pair Bonding	Milne and Milne, 1968; Chivers, 1974; Kolata, 1975	Carey and Nolan, 1975		Howell, 1972: 171		
Territorial and Hoarding Behavior	Calhoun, 1962: 250; Barnett, 1963; Klopfer, 1969; Manosevitz, 1970; McClearn, 1971: 75; Van den Berghe, 1974	Wilson and Vessey, 1968: 11; Klopfer, 1969; Carey and Nolan, 1975	Manosevitz, 1970; McClearn, 1971: 75	Calhoun, 1972: 250; Bern and Gorski, 1973	Benedek, 1952	

TABLE 15.1 continued

Major Forms of Human Social Behavior	Evidence of the Same or Highly Similar Behavior in Nonhuman Species	Evidence Implicating Such Behavior as Contributing to Species Survival and Breeding Success	Evidence of Genetic Influences on Such Behavior in Non-human Species	Evidence of Genetic Influences on Such Behavior in the Human Species	Evidence of Bio-chemical Influences on Such Behavior in Nonhuman Species	Evidence of Bio-chemical Influences on Such Behavior in the Human Species
Care and Protection of Offspring	Fox, 1967: 29 see Averill, 1968: 726 Goodall, 1969 Eibl-Eibesfeldt, 1971: 58 Hoagland, 1972 Beyers, 1973 Lancaster, 1973 Kolata, 1975	Fox 1967: 29 Eibl-Eibesfeldt, 1971: 58 Klopfer, 1971 Skinner, 1972:18; 1976: 7			Hilgard and Bower, 1966: 433 Thoman and Levine, 1970 Klopfer, 1971 Leon et al., 1973	
Normative Conduct: Ordainment, Enforcement and Compliance	Lorenz, 1966 Wickler, 1969: 104 Eibl-Eibesfeldt, 1971: 76 and 104	Huxley and Huxley, 1947 Waddington, 1961 Fox, 1967: 69 Hogan, 1973		see Dobzhansky, 1962: 102 Ghiselin, 1973: 967 Shah and Roth, 1974: 131-139 Cloninger et al., 1975		Anonymous, 1975 Satterfield and Cantwell, 1975
Linguistic Communication	Gardner and Gardner, 1969 Lang, 1970 Premack, 1970 and 1971 Rumbaugh et al., 1973 Fleming, 1974 Gould, 1975 Menzel and Halperin, 1975 Sebeok, 1975	Lang, 1970 Marley, 1970: 672	Yeni-Komshian and Benson, 1976	Kagan, 1969 Wescott, 1969 Yeni-Komchian and Benson, 1976		

higher learning, many of the laymen who supported sociology's anti-sociobiology pronouncements also were attracted to the aesthetics and logic of such tables, and by the fact that a number of "individual abstractions" could be made to help them guide their personal lives. Unwavering testimonies of the mysterious predictive and diagnostic powers of sociological "predictive tables" reached alarming proportions during the first decade of the twenty-first century among several poorly educated segments of the western hemisphere, and this trend appears to have retained some following even today as we embark upon the second half of that century.

The Significance of the Sociology-Sociobiology Dichotomy

Major developments in science are always complex, and, for that reason alone, attempts to cite historical parallels can easily be overdrawn. Nevertheless, much of what happened in the case of the sociology-sociobiology dichotomy bears a remarkable resemblance to the dichotomy between two older disciplines — astrology and astronomy. Although it is not known which of these latter two appeared first, they both aimed toward explaining the same set of phenomena (i.e., the positions and movements of heavenly bodies). In fact, throughout the Middle Ages, they constituted "a single professional pursuit" (Kuhn, 1966:92). By the eighteenth century, however, the "Copernican Revolution" had slowly driven an impregnable wedge between the practitioners of this single professional pursuit, even though Copernicus lived and wrote over a century and a half earlier (Farrington, 1961:96; Halsey, 1971:321). Copernicus proposed a disturbing concept of the universe, in which the ethnocentric notion of the earth as the center and focus of the universe was no longer defensible. Eventually, astrologers had come to associate themselves with two assumptions that astronomers rejected. First, astrologers held that the positions and movements of heavenly bodies could not be reduced to purely naturalistic-mechanical principles. Second, they believed that purposefulness (or destiny) had to be included in the ultimate understanding of stellar and planetary phenomena.

Darwinian evolutionary theory gradually created a scientific climate in which the human species could no longer be viewed ethnocentrically, although it took over a century for the intellectual community to incorporate the full implications of this assumption into its perspective of human behavior. Thus evolutionary theory exerted constant pressure upon those interested in studying social phenomena from a scientific perspective to separate themselves from those who felt that human social phenomena could not be understood if (1) reduced in considerable degree to physical, chemical, and biological elements, and if (2) considered outside the context of individual and societal purposes. The point at which sociology's jurisdiction over the scientific study of social phenomena was irreversibly lost probably lies somewhere in the latter 1970s.

References

Alland, A. (1967) *Evolution and Human Behavior,* Norwich, England: Tavistock Publications.

Alper, S., J. Berchwith, S. L. Chorover, J. Hunt. et al. (1976) "The implications of sociobiology." *Science* 192 (April 30):424-427.

Anderson, P. W. (1972) "More is different." *Science* 177 (August 4):393-396.

Anonymous. (1975) "Hypoglycemic diet yields same results as Ritalin." *Churchill Forum* 1 (3):6.

Averill, J. R. (1968) "Grief: Its nature and significance." *Psychological Bulletin* 70 (6):721-748.

Axelrod, J. (1971) "Noradrenaline: Fate and control of its biosynthesis." *Science* 173 (August 13):598-606.

Baldwin, J. D. (1968) "The social behavior of adult male squirrel monkey (*Saimiri sciureus*) in a seminatural environment." *Folia Primatologica* 9:281-314.

Ballonoff, P. A. (ed.). (1974) *Genetics and Social Structure.* New York: Halsted Press.

Barnett, S. A. (1963) *The Rat: A Study in Behavior.* Chicago: Aldine.

Bekoff, M., and H. L. Hill. (1975) "Behavioral taxonomy in canids by discriminant function analysis." *Science* 190 (December 19):1223-1225.

Benedek, T. (1952) *Psychosexual Functions in Women.* New York: Ronald Press.

Bern, H. A., and R. A. Gorski. (1973) "Long-term effects of perinatal hormone administration." *Science* 181 (July 13):189-190.

Beyers, C. (1973) "Beauty and her beasts." *Saturday Review of the Sciences* 1 (February): 34-37.

Calhoun, J. B. (1962) *The Ecology and Sociology of the Norway Rat.* Washington, D.C.: U.S.G.P.O.

Carey, M., and V. Nolan, Jr. (1975) "Polygyny in indigo buntings: A hypothesis tested." *Science* 190 (December 26):1296-1297.

Cattell, R. B., G. F. Stice, and N. F. Kristy. (1957) "A first approximation to nature-nurture ratios for eleven primary personality factors in objective tests." *Journal of Abnormal and Social Psychology* 54:143-159.

Catton, W. R., Jr. (1966) *From Animistic to Naturistic Sociology.* New York: McGraw-Hill.

Cavan, S. (1976) "Book review." *Contemporary Sociology* 5 (March):140-142.

Chivers, D. J. (1974) *The Siamang in Malaya.* Basel: Karger.

Christian, J. J. (1970) "Social subordination, population density and mammalian evolution." *Science* 168 (April 3):84-90.

Cloninger, C.R., T. Reich, and S. B. Guze. (1975) "The multifactorial model of disease transmission: III. Family relationship between sociopathy and hysteria." *British Journal of Psychiatry* 127 (July):23-32.

Dare, R. J. (1975) "Anthropocentrism and evolution." *Science* 189 (August 22):593.

Dewey, J., and A. F. Bentley. (1949) *Knowing and the Known.* Boston: Beacon.

Diamond, M. (1965) "A critical evaluation of the ontogeny of human sexual behavior." *Quarterly Review of Biology* 40 (2):147-175.

Dobzhansky, T. (1962) *Mankind Evolving.* New York: Bantam.

Edwards, D. A. (1969) "Early androgen stimulation and aggressive behavior in male and female mice." *Physiology and Behavior* 4:333–338.

Ehrenkranz, J. E., E. Bliss, and M. H. Sheard. (1974) "Plasm testosterone: Correlation with aggressive behavior and social dominance in man." *Psychosomatic Medicine* 36:469–475.

Eibl-Eibesfeldt, I. (1971) *Love and Hate*. New York: Holt, Rinehart and Winston.

Eisenberg, J. F., and W. S. Dillon (eds.). (1971) *Man and Beast: Comparative Social Behavior*. Washington, D.C.: Smithsonian Institute Press.

Eisenberg, J. F., and E. Gould. (1970) *The Tenrecs. A Study in Mammalian Behavior and Evolution*. Washington, D.C.: Smithsonian Institute Press.

Eisenberg, L. (1973) "Psychiatric intervention." *Scientific American* 229 (September): 116–124.

Emlen, S. T. (1976) "An alternative case for sociobiology." *Science* 192:736–738.

Etzioni, A. (1973) "Faulty engineers or neglected experts?" *Science* 181 (July 6):11.

Farrington, B. (1961) *Greek Science*. Harmondsworth, England: Penguin Books.

Fleming, J. D. (1974) "Field report: The state of the apes." *Psychology Today* 7 (January):31–38ff.

Fox, R. (1967) *Kinship and Marriage*. Harmondsworth, England: Penguin Books.

Freese, L. (1972) "Cumulative sociological knowledge." *American Sociological Review* 37 (August):472–482.

Friedland, W. H. (1973) "Book review." *Contemporary Sociology* 2 (September):513–514.

Fruton, J. S. (1976) "The emergence of biochemistry." *Science* 192 (April 23):327–333.

Gaff, J. G. (1973) "Book review." *Contemporary Sociology* 2 (September):551–553.

Gallant, J. A., and J. W. Prothero.(1972) "Weight-watching at the university: The consequences of growth." *Science* 175:381–388.

Gardner, R. A., and B. T. Gardner. (1969) "Teaching sign-language to a chimpanzee." *Science* 165 (August 15):664–672.

Ghiselin, M. T. (1973) "Darwin and evolutionary psychology." *Science* 179 (March 9): 964–968.

Goldstein, B. (1976) Letter to "Open Forum." *Footnotes* 4 (January):2.

Goodall, J. V. (1969) "Mother-offspring relationships in free-ranging chimpanzees," in D. Morris (ed.), *Primate Ethology*. New York: Doubleday/Anchor, pp. 365–436.

Gould, J. L. (1975) "Honey bee recruitments: The dance-language controversy." *Science* 189 (August 29):685–693.

Guhl, A. M., J. V. Craig, and C. D. Mueller. (1960) "Selective breeding for aggressiveness in chickens." *Poultry Science* 39:970–980.

Halsey, W. D. (ed.). (1971) *Merit Student Encyclopedia*. Volume 2. New York: Macmillan.

Hamburg, D. A. (1969) "Sexual differentiation and the evolution of aggressive behavior in primates," in N. Kretchmer and D. N. Walcher (eds.), *Environmental Influences on Genetic Expression*. Washington, D.C.: U.S.G.P.O., pp. 141–147.

Hardin, G. (1974) "The case against helping the poor." *Psychology Today* 8 (September): 38–43ff.

Hatch, E. (1973) *Theories of Man and Culture*. New York: Columbia University Press.

Herbert, J. (1968) "Sexual preferences in the rhesus monkey *Macaca mulatta* in the laboratory." *Animal Behavior* 16:120–128.

Hilgard, E. R., and G. H. Bower. (1966) *Theories of Learning*. New York: Appleton-Century-Crofts.

Hixson, V. S., and J. P. Scott. (1976) "On van den Berghe's theory of aggression." *American Sociological Review* 41 (February):169–170.

Hoagland, E. (1972) "Wolves and men." *Saturday Review* 55 (November 25):5–12.

Hogan, R. (1973) "Moral conduct and moral character." *Psychological Bulletin* 79 (4): 217–232.

Howell, C. (1972) *Early Man*. New York: Time-Life Books.

Huxley, T. H., and J. S. Huxley. (1947) *Touchstone for Ethics*. New York: Harper.

Jencks, C. (1972) *Inequality*. New York: Basic Books.

Johnstone, R. E., and D. M. Zahorik. (1975) "Taste aversion and sexual attractants." *Science* 189 (September 12):893–894.

Kagan, J. (1969) "A sexual dimorphism in vocal behavior in infants," in N. Kretchmer and D. N. Walcher (eds.), *Environmental Influences on Genetic Expression*. Washington, D.C.: U.S.G.P.O.

————. (1972) "Do infants think?" *Scientific American* 226 (March):74–82.

Klopfer, P. H. (1969) *Habitats and Territories*. New York: Basic Books.

————. (1971) "Mother love: What turns it on?" *American Scientist* 59 (July-August): 404–407.

Klopfer, P. H., and M. S. Klopfer. (1973) "How come leaders to their posts? The determination of social ranks and roles." *American Scientist* 61 (September-October):560–564.

Knerer, G., and C. E. Atwood. (1973) Diprionid sawflies: Polymorphism and speciation." *Science* 179 (March 16):1090–1099.

Kolata, G. B. (1975) "Sociobiology: Models of social behavior." *Science* 187 (January 10):50–51.

————. (1976) "Primate behavior: Sex and the dominant male." *Science* 191 (January 9):55–56.

Kreuz, L. E., and R. M. Rose. (1972) "Assessment of aggressive behavior and testosterone in a young criminal population." *Psychosomatic Medicine* 34:321–332.

Kuhn, T. S. (1962) *The Structure of Scientific Revolution*. Chicago: University of Chicago Press.

————. (1966) *The Copernican Revolution*. Cambridge, Mass.: Harvard University Press.

Lancaster, J. B. (1973) "In praise of the achieving female monkey." *Psychology Today* 7 (September):30–36ff.

Lang, A. (ed.). (1970) *Communication in Development*. New York: Academic Press.

Laughlin, C. D., Jr., and E. G. d'Aquili. (1974) *Biogenetic Structuralism*. New York: Columbia University Press.

Leary, R. W., and A. J. Stynes. (1959) "Tranquilized effects in the social status, motivation and learning of monkeys." *Archives of General Psychiatry* 1:499–505.

LeBoeuf, B. J. (1974) "Elephant seal as fighter and lover." *Psychology Today* 8 (October): 104–108.

Leon, M., M. Numan, and H. Moltz. (1973) "Maternal behavior of the rat: Facilitation through gonadectomy." *Science* 179 (March 9): 1018–1019.

Leshner, A. I. (1975) "Theoretical review, a model of hormones and agonistic behavior." *Physiology and Behavior* 15:225–235.

Lipton, D., R. Martinson, and J. Wilks. (1975) *The Effectiveness of Correctional Treatment.* New York: Praeger.

Lorenz, K. (1966) *On Aggression.* New York: Harcourt, Brace & World.

Maccoby, E. E., and C. N. Jacklin. (1974) *The Psychology of Sex Differences.* Stanford, Calif.: Stanford University Press.

Macrides, F., A. Bartke, and S. Dalterio. (1975) "Strange females increase plasma testosterone levels in male mice." *Science* 189 (September 26):1104–1105.

Manosevitz, M. (1970) "Hoarding—an exercise in behavioral genetics." *Psychology Today* 4 (August):56–58ff.

Marley, P. (1970) "Birdsong and speech development: Could there be parallels?" *American Scientist* 58 (November-December):669–673.

Mazur, A. (1973) "A cross-species comparison of status in small established groups." *American Sociological Review* 38:513–530.

McClearn, G. E. (1971) "Behavioral genetics." *Behavioral Science* 16 (January):64–81.

McClintock, R. (1975) "Book review." *Contemporary Sociology* 4 (May):311–312.

Menzel, E. W., and S. Halperin. (1975) "Purposive behavior as a basis for objective communication between chimpanzees." *Science* 189 (August 22):652–654.

Milne, L., and M. Milne. (1968) *The Mating Instinct.* New York: Signet.

Milner, M., Jr. (1973) "Book Review." *Contemporary Sociology* 2 (November):588–591.

Money, J. (1969) Comments reported in N. Kretchmer and D. N. Walcher (eds.), *Environmental Influences on Genetic Expression.* Washington, D.C.: U.S.G.P.O.

Moyer, K. E. (1973) "The physiology of violence." *Psychology Today* 7 (July):35–38.

———. (1975) "The physiology of violence: Allergy and aggression." *Psychology Today* 9 (July):77–79.

Nadler, R. D. (1975) "Sexual cyclicity in captive lowland gorillas." *Science* 189 (September 5):813–814.

Nevo, E. (1969) "Mole rat *Spalaz ehrenbergi:* Mating behavior and its evolutionary significance." *Science* 163 (January 31):484–486.

Panati, C. (1976) "Catastrophe theory." *Newsweek* (January 19):54–55.

Parsons, P. A. (1967) *The Genetic Analysis of Behavior.* London: Methuen.

Persky, H. K., D. Smith, and G. K. Basu. (1971) "Relation of psychologic measures of testosterone production in man." *Psychosomatic Medicine* 33:265–277.

Peters, J. M. (1967) "Caffeine-induced hemorrhagic automutilation." *Archives Internationales de Pharmacodynamie et de Therapie* 169:139–146.

Premack, D. (1970) "The education of Sara." *Psychology Today* 4 (September): 54–58.

———. (1971) "Language in chimpanzees?" *Science* 172 (May 21):808–822.

Reinboth, R. (ed.). (1975) *Intersexuality in the Animal Kingdom.* New York: Springer Verlag.

Revelle, W., P. Amaral, and S. Turriff. (1976) "Introversion/extroversion, time stress, and caffeine: Effects on verbal performance." *Science* 192 (April 9): 149–150.

Reverby, S. (1972) "A perspective on the root causes of illness." *American Journal of Public Health* 62 (August):1140–1142.

Robison, J., and G. Smith. (1971) "The effectiveness of correctional programs." *Crime and Delinquency* 17 (January):67–80.

Rowell, T. E. (1969) "Variability in the social organization of primates," in D. Morris (ed.), *Primate Ethology.* New York: Doubleday/Anchor, pp. 283–305.

Rumbaugh, D. M., T. V. Gill, and E. C. Glasersfeld. (1973) "Reading and sentence completion by a chimpanzee." *Science* 182 (November):731–733.

Sade, D. S. (1966) *Ontogeny of Social Relations in a Group of Free Ranging Rhesus Monkeys.* Berkeley: University of California.

———. (1975) "The evolution of sociality." *Science* 190 (October 17):261–263.

Sadleir, R. M. (1969) *The Ecology of Reproduction in Wild and Domestic Mammals.* London: Methuen.

Satterfield, J. H., and D. P. Cantwell. (1975) "Psychopharmacology in the prevention of antisocial and delinquent behavior." *International Journal of Mental Health* 4 (Spring-Summer):227–237.

Sauerhoff, M. W., and I. A. Michaelson. (1973) "Hyperactivity and brain catecholamines in lead-exposed developing rats." *Science* 182 (December 7):1022–1024.

Schearing, C. D. (1973) "How to make theories untestable: A guide to theorists." *The American Sociologist* 8 (February):33–37.

Schein, M. W. (ed.). (1975) *Social Hierarchy and Dominance.* New York: Halstead.

Scott, J. P. (1958) *Aggression.* Chicago: University of Chicago Press.

———. (1969) "Evolution and domestication of the dog," in T. Dobzhansky, M. K. Hect, and W. C. Steere (eds.). *Evolutionary Biology.* Volume 2. New York: Appleton-Century-Crofts, pp. 243–274.

Sebeok, T. A. (ed.). (1975) *Animal Communication.* Bloomington: Indiana University Press.

Shah, S. A., and L. H. Roth. (1974) "Biological and psychophysiological factors in criminality." in D. Glaser (ed.), *Handbook of Criminology.* Chicago: Rand McNally, pp. 101–173.

Sheard, M. H. (1975) "Lithium in the treatment of aggression." *Journal of Nervous and Mental Disorders* 160:108–118.

Siegel, R. K., and J. Poole. (1969) "Psychedelic-induced social behavior in mice: A preliminary report." *Psychological Report* 25:704–706.

Singh, S. D. (1969) "Urban monkeys." *Scientific American* 221 (July):108–115.

Skinner, B. F. (1971) *Beyond Freedom and Dignity.* New York: Bantam.

———. (1972) "Humanism and behaviorism." *The Humanist* 32 (July-August): 18–20.

———. (1976) "The ethics of helping people." *The Humanist* 36 (January-February): 7–11.

Sociobiology Study Group of Science for the People. (1976) "Sociobiology—another biological determinism." *BioScience* 26 (March):182ff.

Southwick, C. H. (1972) *Aggression among Non-Human Primates.* Reading, Mass.: Addison-Wesley.

Struhsaker, T. T. (1976) *The Red Colobus Monkey.* Chicago: University of Chicago Press.

Stynes, A. J., L. A. Rosenblum and I. C. Kaufman. (1968) "The dominant male and behavior within heterospecific monkey groups." *Folia Primatologica* 9:123–134.

Tarter, D. E. (1973) "Heeding Skinner's call: Toward the development of a social technology." *The American Sociologist* 8 (November):153–158.

Thoman, E. B., and S. Levine. (1970) "Hormonal and behavioral changes in the rat mother as a function of early experience treatments of the offspring." *Physiology and Behavior* 5:1417–1421.

Trivers, R. L. (1972) "Parental investment and sexual selection," in B. Campbell (ed.), *Sexual Selection and the Descent of Man.* Chicago: Aldine, pp. 136–179.

Trivers, R. L., and H. Hare. (1976) "Haplodiploidy and the evolution of the social insects." *Science* 191 (January 23):249–263.

Van den Berghe, P. L. (1974) "Bringing beasts back in: Toward a biosocial theory of aggression." *American Sociological Review* 39 (December):777–788.

Vandenberg, S. G. (1967) "Hereditary factors in normal personality traits (as measured by inventories)," in J. Wartis (ed.), *Recent Advances in Biological Psychiatry.* Volume 9. New York: Plenum.

Vandenbergh, J. G. (1969) "Endocrine coordination in monkeys: Male sexual responses to the female." *Physiology and Behavior* 4:261–264.

Vernon, W. M. (1969) "Animal aggression: Review of research." *Genetic Psychological Monographs* 80:3–28.

Waddington, C. H. (1961) *The Ethical Animal.* New York: Atheneum.

Weiss, B. (1974) "Food and mood: What you eat may be what's eating you." *Psychology Today* 8 (December):60–62.

Welch, B. L., E. D. Hendley, and I. Turek. (1974) "Norepinephrine uptake into cerebral cortical synaptosomes after one fight or electroconvulsive shock." *Science* 183 (January 18):220–221.

Wescott, R. W. (1969) *The Divine Animal: An Exploration of Human Potentiality.* New York: Funk and Wagnalls.

Wickler, W. (1969) "Socio-sexual signals and their intraspecific imitation among primates," in D. Morris (ed.), *Primate Ethology.* New York: Doubleday/Anchor, pp. 89–189.

Willer, D., and M. Webster, Jr. (1970) "Theoretical concepts and observables." *American Sociological Review* 35 (August):748–757.

Williams, G. C. (ed.). (1971) *Group Selection.* Chicago: Aldine-Atherton.

———. (1975) *Sex and Evolution.* Princeton, N.J.: Princeton University Press.

Williams, R. B., and B. Eichelman. (1971) "Social setting: Influence on the physiological response to electric shock in the rat." *Science* 174 (November 5):613–614.

Wilson, A. P., and S. H. Vessey. (1968) "Behavior of free-ranging castrated rhesus monkeys." *Folia Primatologica* 9:1–14.

Wilson, E. O. (1971) *The Insect Societies.* Cambridge, Mass.: Harvard University Press.

———. (1975) *Sociobiology: The New Synthesis.* Cambridge, Mass.: Harvard University Press.

Yeni-Komshian, G. H., and D. A. Benson. (1976) "Anatomical study of cerebral asymmetry in the temporal lobe of humans, chimpanzees, and rhesus monkeys." *Science* 192 (April 23):387–389.

Zajonc, R. B. (1966) *Social Psychology: An Experimental Approach.* Belmont, Calif.: Brooks-Cole.

Zigler, E. F. (1973a) "On growing up, learning, and loving." *Human Behavior* 2 (March):65–67.

———. (1973b) "Project Head Start: Success or failure?" *Children Today* 2 (November-December):2–7ff.

16

Reflections on a Premature Burial

David P. Barash

It is sorely tempting for a biologist—and a professed sociobiologist at that!—to acquiesce and even acclaim Ellis' (1977) proposed scenario for the "decline and fall of sociology." After all, interdepartmental competition for scarce university resources is likely to increase in the coming years, and my more recalcitrant colleagues could always be retrained as social workers, opinion pollsters, or perhaps (as Ellis suggests) purveyors of the occult! However, reality intervenes. Despite my distaste for the stodgy intellectual inertia of social scientists being wedded to rampant environmentalism, I confess equal discomfort with freshly converted zealots, with whom Ellis must unfortunately be numbered. There are two particular dangers to this brand of partisan enthusiasm. (1) By suggesting instant epiphanic enlightenment as the wellspring of human behavior, Ellis simply overestimates the power of an approach which is even now the subject of considerable controversy among biologists. Sociobiology may well be powerful, but it is probably not *that* powerful, and hell may have no fury like that of the aspiring sociologist who hitched his or her cart to a rising star that never quite shed the light predicted for it. (2) I fear that by overstating his case, Ellis may have antagonized sociologists, causing them to react defensively to sociobiology, rather than challenging them to study the case with the open-mindedness and perhaps even cautious enthusiasm that is more appropriate.

In fact, sociobiology deserves an airing in the social sciences, not because it threatens the professional futures of present-day sociologists, but rather because it offers a potentially powerful analytic tool in the study of human behavior. Certainly, understanding the behavior of *Homo sapiens* is an enormous task, and sociology needs all the help it can get. If evolutionary biology seems arrogant in claiming some relevance here, what of the greater arrogance of a social science that refuses proffered assistance! Sociobiology has produced

Reprinted by permission of the American Sociological Association and the author. This communication originally appeared in *The American Sociologist*, vol. 12, April 1977, 66–68.

dramatic insights into such phenomena as altruism, both in the presence (Hamilton, 1964; West Eberhard, 1975) and absence (Trivers, 1971) of genetic relatedness; strategies of spatial organization, both territorial (Brown, 1964) and social (Hamilton, 1971); mate selection (Orians, 1969); the adaptive significance of animal social systems (Crook, 1970); male-female differences in reproductive strategies (Trivers, 1972); parent-offspring conflict (Trivers, 1974); strategies of aggressive competition (Maynard Smith and Price, 1973), and parental behaviors (Barash, 1976); reproductive effort and other life history phenomena (Stearns, 1976); and behavioral predispositions as a function of genetic relatedness (Barash et al., in press), to name just a few. These findings, both empirical and theoretic, are based upon nonhuman animals, and they cry out for possible extension to the human species as well.

Accordingly, there is a particular need for sociologists to be informed in sociobiology. Indeed, rarely has so much been said by so many, about something they understood so little. Particularly disquieting was Ellis' frequent reference to book reviews (Sade, 1975), letters to editors (Emlen, 1976), and predigested accounts (Kolata, 1975; 1976), as opposed to such important primary sources as Alexander (1974), Williams (1966; 1971) and even Wilson (1975), the encyclopedic synthesis that defined the discipline and catalyzed the controversy. I have written a basic primer (Barash, 1977), accessible to non-biologists, which might assist sociologists in rushing to the attack or to the barricades, or at least, to join in the issues as well as the controversy.

Sociobiology may well represent a true "paradigmatic revolution" in the sense of Kuhn (1962). Certainly, the susceptibility of sociology to such a revolution is due to the current absence of any coherent, organizing framework for the discipline at present. The "reductionism" of sociobiology embodies both its appeal to some and its repulsiveness to others. A rational approach to human sociobiology would be to give at least "for-the-sake-of-argument" credence to evolutionary biology, and to see how much of the variance in human behavior it explains. It is no panacea, but it may well provide the soundest paradigm the science of behavior has ever had. There is considerable opportunity for sociology in this regard, especially in assessing the integration of individual versus societal benefit, in view of the evolutionary dictum that individuals ought to behave so as to maximize their inclusive fitness. And, indeed, a start has already been made (Campbell, 1975; Durham, 1976).

Curiously, if sociobiology appears reductionist to sociologists, it has an opposite aura to most biologists and psychologists. Concern with "why" an animal does what it does has usually concentrated upon such proximal issues as physiology, anatomy, characteristics of eliciting stimuli and/or the role of prior experience. Concern with distal issues—i.e., adaptive significance— seems antireductionist indeed. Reductionist or not, a sociology grounded in biology will doubtlessly appeal to many; whereas it may not be *the* wave of the future, it is likely to have some tidal consequences. Future aspirants to academic sociology may be well advised to study sociobiology, in much the same sense that physicists are obliged to know some quantum mechanics, even if their research is not in elementary particles. Similarly, familiarity with molecular genetics is *de rigeur* for biologists, even sociobiologists.

It may well be that outsiders tend to view each discipline as more substantive than its practitioners do. Thus, despite my enthusiasm for sociobiology, I very much doubt that it will *replace* sociology as the latter is currently constituted. Sociobiology may well provide substantial insight into the "deep structure" of human behavior—our gut-level inclinations and cross-cultural universals, but I am less sanguine about its power vis-à-vis more complex, emergent phenomena. These will remain the province of sociology, whether or not it is up to the task. If sociology flounders while sociobiology prospers, it will be because sociology has failed in its self-appointed role, possibly because complex human social structures are just not amenable to science, and *not* because sociobiology discovers the answers that have somehow eluded sociologists.

Finally, Ellis suggests that sociology is hampered by the twin philosophical positions of antireductionism and teleological explanations. Following Dewey and Bentley (1949), he sees these two as linked, but they are not. The essential point was foreshadowed by Norbert Wiener and his colleagues, also in the 1940s: that an automaton or an organism behaves in a goal-directed fashion does not preclude mechanistic explanation of the behavior (Rosenblueth, et al., 1943). Thermostats and guided missiles are goal-directed automatons, and a crucial aspect of sociobiology is the recognition that organisms are similarly goal-directed—the goal being maximization of individual, inclusive fitness (Barash, 1977). It is this point of view, and not the a-purposive positivism, apparently advocated by Ellis, that is most compatible with a sociobiologic perspective. Among other things, the sociobiologic approach holds the promise of explaining why people work for the goals they do; i.e., why some outcomes have a high "subjective utility." Perhaps when these sociobiologic considerations are incorporated into sociology, we will finally be able to formulate a useful theory of human society, one that may even lead to effective social action.

References

Alexander, R.D. (1974) "The evolution of social behavior." *Annual Review of Ecology and Systematics* 5:325–383.

Barash, D.P. (1976) "Some evolutionary aspects of parental behavior in animals and man." *American Journal of Psychology* 89:195–217.

———— . (1977) *Sociobiology and Behavior*. New York: Elsevier.

Barash, D.P., W.G. Holmes, and P.J. Greene. (In press) "Exact versus probabilistic coefficients of relationship: Some implications for sociobiology." *The American Naturalist*.

Brown, J.L. (1964) "The evolution of diversity in avian territorial systems." *The Wilson Bulletin* 76:160–169.

Campbell, D.T. (1975) "On the conflicts between biological and social evolution and between psychology and moral tradition." *American Psychologist* 30:1103–1126.

Crook, J.H. (1970) "Social organization and the environment." *Animal Behavior* 18: 197–209.

Dewey, J., and A. F. Bentley. (1949) *Knowing and the Known*. Boston: Beacon.

Durham, W.H. (1976) "Resource competition and human aggression, Part I: A review of primitive war." *Quarterly Review of Biology* 5:385–415.

Ellis, L. (1977) "The decline and fall of sociology: 1975–2000." *The American Sociologist* 12 (May): 56–66.

Emlen, J.M. (1976) "An alternative case for sociobiology." *Science* 192:736–738.

Hamilton, W.D. (1964) "The genetical theory of social behavior: I and II." *Journal of Theoretical Biology* 7:1–52.

———— . (1971) "Geometry for the selfish herd." *Journal of Theoretical Biology* 31:195–311.

Kolata, G.B. (1975) "Sociobiology: Models of social behavior." *Science* 187:50–51.

———— . (1976) "Primate behavior: Sex and the dominant male." *Science* 191:55–56.

Kuhn, T.S. (1962) *The Structure of Scientific Revolutions*. Chicago: University of Chicago Press.

Maynard Smith, J., and G.R. Price. (1973) "The logic of animal conflict." Nature 246: 15–18.

Orians, G.H. (1969) "On the evolution of mating systems in birds and mammals." *The American Naturalist* 103:589–603.

Rosenblueth, G., N. Wiener, and R. Bigelow. (1943) "Behavior, purpose and teleology." *Philosophy of Science* 10:18–24.

Sade, D. (1975) "The evolution of sociality." *Science* 190:261–263.

Stearns, S.C. (1976) "Life-history tactics: A review of the ideas." *Quarterly Review of Biology* 46:35–57.

Trivers, R.L. (1971) "The evolution of reciprocal altruism." *Quarterly Review of Biology* 46:35–57.

———— . (1972) "Parental investment and sexual selection," in B. Campbell (ed.), *Sexual Selection and the Descent of Man*. Chicago: Aldine, pp. 136–179.

———— . (1974) "Parent-offspring conflict." *American Zoologist* 14:249–264.

West Eberhard, M.J. (1975) "The evolution of social behavior by kin selection." *Quarterly Review of Biology* 50:1–33.

Williams, G.C. (1966) *Adaptation and Natural Selection*. Princeton: Princeton University Press.

———— . (1971) *Group Selection*. Chicago: Aldine.

Wilson, E.O. (1975) *Sociobiology: The New Synthesis*. Cambridge, Mass.: Harvard University Press.

17

Sociobiology vs. Biosociology

John H. Kunkel

My major reaction to this paper is "ouch!" I am pained by Ellis' extravagant claims for the present achievements in the human aspects of sociobiology, by the one-sided and all-too-negative view of contemporary sociology, and by some of the worst futuristic science fiction I have read in quite a while. Most of all, I am pained by the thought that many of the legitimate and useful contributions that biology can make to sociology may be disregarded by those who are put off by Ellis' paper. Here I will discuss only two topics: the present state of sociobiology and its potential contributions to sociology. I will leave the future to take care of itself, except to say that a careful consideration of these two topics reduces Ellis' views of sociology's future to whimsical phantasy.

As the very term indicates, sociobiology centers on *biology*, the social behavior of animals and its genetic and biochemical foundations. While social biology has been around for some time, the major claims of "sociobiology" are quite recent. It is interesting to note that the vast majority of data and principles derive from nonhuman species and that uncritical extrapolations to human social life abound. The human data available today allow us to go two millimeters, Wilson (1975) extends his discussion to cover two meters, while Ellis' claims cover a couple of kilometers. As today's debates among biologists indicate, it is doubtful that the combined human and nonhuman evidence allows us to go even as far as Wilson does. The examples of *human* social behavior, which is thought to be determined by biological factors, are few, overly general, and, from a sociological point of view, involve a quite unsophisticated analysis.

At the very least, social phenomena are not as simple or homogeneous as Ellis' table implies. Space limitations here allow only two examples. Wilson's (1975) discussion of altruism eventually leads him to speak of "altruistic genes." Yet the label "altruistic" is attached to a wide variety of behaviors

Reprinted by permission of the American Sociological Association and the author. This communication originally appeared in *The American Sociologist*, vol. 12, April 1977, 69–73.

which occur only in certain circumstances, depending on the observer's evaluation. Actually the data indicate only that some animals, when threatened, engage in defensive activities which sometimes result in their perishing. For example, Wynne-Edwards' (1962) famous bird studies—concerning intrinsic mechanisms for regulating the population-resource ratio—confront us with intriguing questions; the answers, however, are as yet unclear. Knowledge about the genetic and biochemical basis of altruism among humans is even more nebulous, because (1) the term covers a wide range of activities and situations whose labels depend on the observer, and (2) the behavior-context complexities are immense. Some soldiers may be altruistic, but studies of battles (Keegan, 1976) indicate that fighting (together with the associated perceived probabilities of death) was a better alternative than flight (and its associated perceived probabilities of punishment). A good psychoanalyst, moreover, can provide several arguments as to why an act which at first glance appears to be "altruistic" is, in reality, an expression of egoism, narcissism, or competition with one's father. Altruistic acts, however, are not only a matter of labeling and interpretation. As Hornstein (1976) has shown, the kinds and frequencies of "altruistic" behavior are greatly influenced by the social context and individuals' experiences within it. Hence I will continue to suspect that altruism is to be found mainly in the eyes of the beholder rather than in genes, until its biochemical determinants among human beings are demonstrated.

The word "aggression" covers a multitude of activities, and its usage depends on the actor, the recipient, and the observer. As Bandura (1973) has shown, the labeling of a behavior as "aggression" among humans is inconsistent and depends on the presumed motive of the actor (hostility or accident), the reactions of the recipient (expressions of pain or shrugging it off), the characteristics of the actor and the recipient, the nature of the situation and its historical context, and the characteristics of the observer who labels the behavior. Whether or not we view an act as aggressive or defensive, moreover, depends on our relations to the two parties and our knowledge of the situation. There is considerable evidence, finally, that "aggressive" behavior varies over time and from one situation to another, that it is learned and maintained in one context and can be greatly reduced by the alteration of the environment, such as people's reactions (e.g. Bandura, 1973; Hamblin et al., 1971). While some of the activities viewed as "aggression" may well have biological components, the questions of interest to the sociologist are: *which* "aggressive" acts have a biochemical (genetic) foundation, how do these biological factors operate, and what is the role of the social context in their expression? As the reactions to Lorenz's (1966) work and recent discussions of "aggression" in the *ASR* indicate, the answers are by no means clear and many of the determinants are as yet unknown. Present data do not allow us to say that aggression among humans is determined by genes and biological factors; instead, evidence from human studies shows that learning and the individual's context play an extremely significant role (Bandura, 1973). At the very least, we need more studies of the roles of all these elements and their possible interactions, taking into account the many different activities and circumstances that are so blithely labeled "aggression."

Similar qualifying arguments must be made for the other categories which constitute the stub of Ellis' table. The categories are so vague and general as to be practically useless, and the studies which are cited to illustrate or support a biological basis of human social phenomena concern much more specific activities and limited circumstances than are implied in the stub's categories.

If future investigations of biological aspects of social behavior proceed along lines so far established, they will probably demonstrate that genetically based biochemical factors delineate the parameters of behavioral variations while culture determines which of several possible and useful actions are learned, performed in various circumstances, and viewed as "altruism," "aggression," etc. These parameters are quite wide for most activity sets, and they vary among individuals and with age, but *their operation is yet to be specified and demonstrated*. The roles of biological restraints and preparedness in the learning process, and their effects on the formulation of learning principles, are only now being specified. The situation is certainly not as simple and our knowledge is not as great, as Ellis implies (e.g. Seligman and Hager, 1972).

That one learns, and *how*, are matters of biology and vary little among populations. But *what* one learns, and *when*, being matters of culture and history, are the proper domain of sociology. The explanation and prediction of any specific behavior, then, cannot be done without a sociological analysis. The great behavioral variations within human populations, among cultures, through historical epochs, and even within an individual's life time, demonstrate the great significance of learning and contextual determinants of behavior. When we introduce biological factors into sociology, their very nature (as known today) precludes their serving as an explanation of observed variations and potential variability. For people are selectively and inconsistently "aggressive;" they learn to be submissive or dominant as they change roles, etc. Available evidence suggests that *biochemical and genetic factors set the stage*, so to speak, *but that culture and history provide the script for social life*. Further studies are needed to specify the magnitude and influence of these several factors on particular components of social systems. The new field, then, is biosociology, with an appropriate emphasis on *sociology* rather than on the relatively constant biological basis of individuals' physical existence.

There is nothing very new or disturbing here. Sociologists have recognized and accepted the role of biological factors for decades, albeit implicitly. If humans had three arms, the average life expectancy were 150 years, adulthood were reached at the age of five, and estrus were periodic, social organization would probably be quite different from what we now experience. The fact that the sociological literature makes little of two hands, maturity at 16 and senescence at 70, does not mean that we are ignorant of these biological parameters, but only that they are simply part of the given framework of human social life.

Ellis' discussion of two factors which presumably have retarded sociology—the assumptions of antireductionism and of purpose—is overly general and again takes insufficient account of the complexities of social life. Reductionism is a matter of degree, and its utility varies with the kinds of societal phenomena under investigation. One should keep an open mind and accept particular reductions in specific areas—to the extent to which it is a valid analytical procedure that leads to demonstrably useful results. Up to now, such demonstrations have been few and hard to come by; and there may not be many for some time. On the one hand, for example, Webster (1973) argues that widespread psychological reductionism is presently impossible. I assume here that this kind of reductionism precedes the reduction of social phenomena to genetic and biochemical factors. On the other hand, Homans (e.g. 1964) suspects that there are no fundamental sociological propositions, only psychological ones. But this suspicion has not yet been subjected to systematic investigation and remains, at present, a suspicion—widely shared and attacked, nevertheless merely a hypothesis, crying out for a demonstration.

Ellis' treatment of "purpose" is equally superficial and does not indicate the extent of disagreement among social scientists; the debate continues and shows little sign of resolution (e.g. Boden, 1972). While it would be difficult to maintain that an institution has a purpose, individuals certainly have. Thus, to the extent that we "reduce" social phenomena to individualistic factors, "purpose" will creep into our analysis. People pass laws for a purpose, set up a social security system for a purpose, and most decisions individuals face involve purpose.

It is doubtful indeed that an embrace of reductionism and the elimination of purpose would make sociology more scientific, as Ellis claims, or that the wholesale introduction of biological factors would raise the status of sociology from that of "the littlest science." Biology is not the nostrum for sociology's ills, just as the disregard of biological factors has not been responsible for the failure of social programs, as Ellis implies.

While many and perhaps most programs to solve social problems have been failures, it is impossible to demonstrate that this has been due to the neglect of biological factors in their design. As Gans (1968) and others have shown clearly and convincingly, the designing and implementation of social programs usually require compromises of such magnitude—as citizens, community leaders, and various political pressures and ethical views must be accommodated—that failure is practically built into the collective effort. Furthermore, the time frames of social programs and political considerations do not coincide; the conflicting commitments of program designers and their target populations produce antagonisms; the models of man used are often invalid; and the sheer magnitude of any problem with its complex social, cultural, and historical roots precludes the success of the kinds of solutions attempted so far (e.g., Kunkel, 1975). Again, one must keep an open mind and be ready for an empirical demonstration of the ways in which biological factors might lead to social problems and be involved in their solution. Until such time, it is well to stay with what we know and attempt to overcome the hurdles just mentioned.

Perhaps the biological analysis of social problems is an unfairly difficult challenge for those who are converts to the cause of sociobiology, for it includes almost all of social life. Therefore, let it be demonstrated that the structure and operation of social organizations are significantly affected (or perhaps determined?) by biological factors. Udy (1965), for example, has summarized much of what we know about organizations, and his propositions should serve as a useful basis for a significant test of the hitherto unsupported claim that sociobiology has much to contribute to sociological analysis. The anthropologist Sahlins (n.d.), by the way, has already shown that kinship systems cannot be explained in biological terms.

Any empirical demonstration of significant sociological implications must derive from human studies, be they Udy's or anyone else's; and until human data are available, the advocates of sociobiology are just that: advocates. At the very least we must have human studies of the biochemical basis of social behavior because human beings have a great capacity to learn, communicate, and store information, and because their behaviors are more malleable and variable than animal activities. The recent history of psychology is quite instructive here. Up to about 1955 there were few studies of human learning, and principles of behavior were derived mainly from laboratory work with lower animals; most animal studies dealt with relatively few variables and concentrated on quite simple activities. During the last twenty years human studies have proliferated; they include complex activities and a host of variables. Quite apparently, the learning, maintenance, and modification of human behavior involve much more complex sets of determining factors and principles than had been anticipated in the past (e.g., Bandura, 1969).

There is little point in blithely predicting the future so as to fit one's dreams. Rather, what must be done is considerably more difficult (and useful): to demonstrate that biological factors, be they physiological, genetic, or chemical, do indeed account for a significant portion of the observed variance in social phenomena and processes. The biological factors and principles which are presumably involved must be derived from human studies, and the social phenomena which they are presumed to explain must be sociologically significant. We must be shown empirical data about humans and significant predictions about social events; and we must have an open mind to accept any proportion of variance in social behavior that is demonstrably explained by biological factors. Only then will there be a solid foundation for the new branch of our discipline: biosociology.

References

Bandura, A. (1969) *Principles of Behavior Modification*. New York: Holt, Rinehart and Winston.

———— . (1973) *Aggression: A Social Learning Analysis*. Englewood Cliffs: Prentice-Hall.

Boden, M. A. (1972) *Purposive Explanation in Psychology*. Cambridge, Mass.: Harvard University Press.

Gans, H. J. (1968) *People and Plans: Essays on Urban Problems and Solutions*. New York: Basic Books.

Hamblin, R. L., D. Buckholdt, D. Ferritor, M. Kozloff, and L. Blackwell. (1971) *The Humanization Processes: A Social, Behavioral Analysis of Children's Problems*. New York: Wiley.

Homans, G. C. (1964) "Contemporary theory in sociology," in R. E. L. Faris (ed.), *Handbook of Modern Sociology*. Chicago: Rand McNally, pp. 951–977.

Hornstein, H. A. (1976) *Cruelty and Kindness: A New Look at Aggression and Altruism*. Englewood Cliffs, N.J.: Prentice-Hall.

Keegan, J. (1976) *The Face of Battle*. New York: Viking.

Kunkel, J. H. (1975) *Behavior, Social Problems, and Change*. Englewood Cliffs, N.J.: Prentice-Hall.

Lorenz, K. (1966) *On Aggression*. New York: Harcourt, Brace and World.

Sahlins, M. (n.d.) *The Use and Abuse of Biology*. (Not yet published.)

Seligman, M. E. P., and J. L. Hager. (1972) *Biological Boundaries of Learning*. New York: Appleton-Century-Crofts.

Udy, S. H., Jr. (1965) "The comparative analysis of organizations," in J. G. March (ed.), *Handbook of Organizations*. Chicago: Rand McNally, pp. 678–709.

Webster, M., Jr. (1973) "Psychological reductionism, methodological individualism, and large-scale problems." *American Sociological Review* 38 (April): 258–273.

Wilson, E. O. (1975) *Sociobiology: The New Synthesis*. Cambridge, Mass.: Harvard University Press.

Wynne-Edwards, V. C. (1962) *Animal Dispersion in Relation to Social Behavior*. Edinburgh: Oliver and Boyd.

18

Sociology and Sociobiology

Gerhard Lenski

Lee Ellis's paper on the decline and fall of sociology is singularly frustrating. I believe he has something important to say, but it is presented in a form that confuses more than it clarifies and thus invites easy dismissal.

Sociologists need to be told—and Ellis does this forcefully—that our longstanding opposition to efforts to take biological factors into account in the study of human social systems has become an albatross. If we persist in ignoring or, worse yet, denying the powerful influence of genetic and biochemical factors, we jeopardize sociology's credibility in the scientific community. Environmentalist arguments that may have been persuasive in the 1920s and 1930s no longer wash, and the longer we persist in propounding them, the more we harm our discipline and reduce its potential. Genetic and biochemical engineering are already under way, and if we are unable or, for ideological reasons, unwilling to provide effective solutions to society's ills, very different kinds of solutions may be adopted (e.g., drug control of criminal or violent behavior, psychosurgery).

So far, so good. Confusion arises, however, when the reader tries to understand the alternative Ellis advocates. For the most part, he seems to be calling for a biological reductionism that I find as unpromising and backward looking as the antireductionism he criticizes. Occasionally he softens this with qualifying words and ambiguous phrases, but the basic scenario he develops presumes a dichotomy: sociobiology or sociology, reductionism or antireductionism, science or pseudoscience.

Long ago I developed a distrust of writers who force dichotomies on their readers. Too often these are false choices, and Ellis's "choice" between sociobiological reductionism and sociological antireductionism is a case in point. Why must we choose either? Why cannot cultural and biological explanations of human social behavior be combined?

Reprinted by permission of the American Sociological Association and the author. This communication originally appeared in *The American Sociologist*, vol. 12, April 1977, 73–75.

Ironically, Ellis attributes the demise of sociology to the growing influence of evolutionary theory, yet he seems unaware of the way the founders and leading theorists of the modern synthesis (i.e., the new evolutionism in biology) handle the very problem he raises. Distinguished evolutionists, such as Huxley (1958, 1960), Simpson (1951), and Dobzhansky (1962), have treated culture as a fundamentally new adaptive mechanism — *an emergent property* of human social systems — which, while rooted in genetics, is not reducible to genetic terms. The most obvious evidences of this are the great cultural diversity in human societies today, which exists in spite of the essential genetic unity of our species, and the revolutionary cultural changes that have occurred in the twentieth century in the absence of any remotely comparable genetic change.

The key to these apparent paradoxes is found in the new understanding of biological evolution that has developed in the last quarter century. The essence of this immensely complex process has come increasingly to be seen as *the expansion of the store of information*[1] possessed by our planet's population of living things. Genetic systems constitute the oldest and most universal method of acquiring, storing, and transmitting information. Later, this was supplemented when learning systems evolved in certain parts of the animal world. These systems provided an additional means of acquiring and storing information. Still later, some species of animals that were capable of learning developed mechanisms for signaling, or sharing learned information. And, finally, our own remote ancestors developed a capacity for symboling, which made human languages and culture-building possible.

The emergence of symbols did not mark the end of signaling, however, any more than learning marked the end of genes. The newer modes of acquiring, storing, and transmitting information have simply been added to the older ones, just as the higher centers of the human brain were added to the older, lower centers that govern metabolism, motor activities, etc. The crucial point is that human populations today employ *all four* of the basic mechanisms, using them in various combinations to cope with all kinds of complex problems. Our sexual behavior, for example, reflects the combined influence of our genes, our individual learning experiences, and communications — in the form of both signals and symbols — we receive from others. The same is true of most other areas of human life and of the social institutions we have created over the centuries.

What is needed is not a life-death struggle between sociology and sociobiology, but two disciplines that can begin to communicate and cooperate with one another and develop more sophisticated models of human societies and individual behavior than either alone could create. What we need in the years ahead are models that take account of all four of the sources of information that influence human life and the complex interactions among them.

Before this can happen, however, we sociologists will have to set aside our traditional prejudices and inform ourselves about the relevant work of biologists. And biologists, too, have a lot to learn, as the concluding chapter of Edward O. Wilson's (1975) otherwise impressive volume, *Sociobiology: The New Synthesis,* demonstrates. If Lee Ellis' paper contributes at all to this end, it will be well worth while, whatever its other limitations.

Notes

1. The term *information* used here refers to a coded record of experience that influences the subsequent actions of organisms and populations. For a more extended treatment of the compressed argument of this paragraph, see Lenski and Lenski, 1978, Ch. 3.

References

Dobzhansky, T. (1962) *Mankind Evolving.* New Haven: Yale University Press.

Huxley, J. (1958) "Cultural process and evolution," in Anne Roe and George Gaylord Simpson (eds.), *Behavior and Evolution.* New Haven: Yale University Press, pp. 437–454.

———. (1960) "The emergence of Darwinism," in Sol Tax (ed.), *The Evolution of Life: Its Origin, History, and Future.* Chicago: University of Chicago Press, pp. 1–21.

Lenski, G., and J. Lenski. (1978) *Human Societies.* 3rd ed. New York: McGraw-Hill.

Simpson, G. G. (1951) *The Meaning of Evolution.* New Haven: Yale University Press.

Wilson, E. O. (1975) *Sociobiology: The New Synthesis.* Cambridge, Mass.: The Belknap Press of the Harvard Press.

19

A Somewhat Sympathetic Response to Ellis

Pierre L. van den Berghe

Ellis' criticism of sociology's antireductionism is basically sound. The scientific enterprise has been a reductionist one, and sociologists show great ignorance of the history of science in making the word "reductionism" an invective. There is also a large residue of teleology in sociology, but unfortunately, this is also true of evolutionary thinking in biology, notwithstanding heated denials. A partial catalogue of other conceptual and methodological limitations of sociology would include a strong anti-evolutionary bias, dogmatic environmental determinism, a view of human behavior as voluntaristic and almost infinitely plastic, a heavy reliance on the statistical analysis of aggregate data far removed from actual behavior, and an almost exclusive emphasis on verbal and symbolic behavior. All these self-inflicted incapacities to reach an adequate understanding of human behavior make their contribution to the sorry state of contemporary sociology.

Though I do not share all the fervent optimism of Ellis in confidently predicting that what has recently been called "sociobiology" will pre-empt all other fields in the study of behavior, I see a distinct possibility that sociobiology contains the germ of a new paradigm. At a minimum I would say two things: (1) competence in the study of human behavior cannot be achieved in total ignorance of ecology, ethology, primatology, paleontology, population genetics and biochemistry, and (2) the intellectual framework of sociobiology is of sweepingly greater scope and generality than anything the social sciences have proposed in the last century.

These remarks must, however, be tempered by caution. As yet, there is no demonstrated linkage between any human behavior phenotype and a specific gene. There is a lot of presumptive and suggestive evidence of genetic

Reprinted by permission of the American Sociological Association and the author. This communication was published originally under the title "Response to Ellis' 'Decline and Fall of Sociology'" in *The American Sociologist*, vol. 12, April 1977, 75–76.

predisposition of certain behaviors, but so far the relationships are hypothetical, and the data on which to test these hypotheses are still quite fragmentary. Furthermore, the generality of a scientific scheme is no guarantee of its fruitfulness. Behaviorism, for instance, proved of limited applicability because (1) though very general in its concepts, it was nonevolutionary and dogmatically environmentalist, and (2) it made little allowance for genetic differences within and between species. I believe sociobiology is more promising because it constitutes the synthesis of several decades of biological research and thinking in half-a-dozen specialities, but is is definitely not the last word. No science ever can be.

Ellis' prediction of the imminent demise of sociology is most questionable because it is based on a rather naive assumption, namely, that the survival of a discipline is related to its intellectual quality. Indeed, the growth of our discipline in the last century suggests the opposite. The sociology of today is certainly no better than that of Marx, Weber, or Durkeim, and probably no better than that of Plato, Aristotle, or Ibn Khaldun. Yet, it survives. Indeed, it thrived relatively better than its sister discipline of anthropology that *did* make considerable progress in the last half-century, and that has a far better claim to scientific status in some of its specialities and a much greater intellectual and substantive scope. Intellectually, sociology has no claim to a separate existence from anthropology. The distinction between the two is largely a historical accident traceable to racism in late nineteenth-century Europe and North America: dark-skinned colonials were studied by anthropologists; light-skinned colonizers by sociologists. Sociology should, by rights, be a small specialty within anthropology: the social anthropology of western societies. Yet, it carved out for itself an academic empire of twice the magnitude of anthropology. The conclusion is not that sociology is twice as scientific as anthropology, but that white colonizers regard themselves as a far worthier object of study than dark colonials.

Should sociobiology become the new dominant paradigm for the scientific study of the evolution of behavior, then anthropology should *logically* become a subspecialty within primatology — that which studies hominids, both fossil and living — and sociology a sub-subspecialty within anthropology, the social anthropology of North American settlers and European aborigines. However, that this logical and scientific taxonomy of disciplines will prevail is highly doubtful for several reasons. (1) Our narcissistic interest in our own species will guarantee for the Sciences of Man (Persons?) a better status than that of a tiny niche within mammalogy or primatology. (2) Our ethnocentrism as representatives of Advanced Industrial Societies will guarantee the redundant survival of Sociology next to Anthropology, despite the demonstrable intellectual superiority of the latter over the former. (3) By a Parkinsonian law of academic expansion, sociobiology can grow on its own without hindering the proliferation of sociology. If it took two millenia for Latin and Greek to decline as academic subjects, and if those languages are still taught at some African universities established as late as the 1960s, there is little reason to expect the fall of sociology in a quarter of a century. (4) A Greshamian law of student selection at our populist universities will insure a steady supply of neophytes to the less intellectually demanding disciplines. If education, home economics and poultry management can survive, surely sociology has a fighting chance.

20

Rejoinder to My Critics

Lee Ellis

I appreciate the comments, and accept the validity of some, although not all, of the criticisms. I will concentrate my remarks on those issues raised that, to me, are most central to the theme of my article.

David P. Barash

The personal nature of Barash's initial remarks make them difficult for me to rebut, except in a self-serving way. I will, therefore, say only that I considered the theme of my article to be important, and that I believe it presents a conceivable outline of what could happen if sociologists do not begin very soon to incorporate evolutionary, genetic, and biochemical explanations (especially the latter two) into their theories of social behavior. Otherwise, Barash contributes some important information to several subjects barely mentioned in my paper; and his work should receive careful theoretical attention by sociologists. . . .

John H. Kunkel

In a very limited space, I can not respond to most of Kunkel's charges. I will direct my remarks primarily to his ideas about the involvement of genetics and biochemistry in human social behavior. Kunkel and I would be close to agreement on this issue in a very crucial way, provided he was serious in stating that "the questions of interest to sociologists are: *which* aggressive acts have a biochemical (genetic) foundation, how do these biological factors operate and what is the role of the social context in their expression?". . . The only qualification I would add to his statement is that sociological interests in genetics and biochemistry should not be limited just to the study of aggression. Otherwise, I could not agree with Kunkel's statement more, especially the idea

Reprinted by permission of the American Sociological Association and the author. This communication was published originally under the title "Rejoinder" in *The American Sociologist*, vol. 12, April 1977, 77–80.

that *how genetics and biochemistry are involved is of sociological interest*. The general adoption of this attitude by sociologists would represent the most important event in the historical development of sociological theory. If sociologists were to take it to heart in designing their research and formulating their theories from now on, a major roadblock to the full integration of sociology into the scientific community would have been removed.

To continue along this line, however, Kunkel and I do disagree over a) how much influence has already been documented, and b) whether or not these factors can explain many of the social behavioral differences *within* the human species. I believe that a fair reading of articles cited in Table 15.1 can only lead to the conclusion that genetic and biochemical influences upon human social behavior have already been demonstrated in several areas and strongly implicated in all. To our second point of disagreement, I will add that the evidence in the table not only suggests that genetics and biochemistry are important in explaining behavioral differences *between Homo sapiens* and other species, but also a lot of important differences *within* the human species as well. (Attempting to keep abreast of the literature in this area is a continuing effort. Upon request, I am prepared to share updated versions of the table with interested readers as substantial additions come to my attention.)

Gerhard Lenski

Lenski states very eloquently the importance of reuniting biology and sociology. Sociology's interesting, but remarkably unproductive, misadventure into the land of pure environmentalism seems to be ending. Lenski's writings have made a signficant contribution in this regard.

I yield to his criticism of my having been somewhat ambiguous in describing the type of paradigm I see emerging. [I hope] two general diagrams will clarify this issue, so that any differences between his position and mine can be discussed productively. [In Figure 20.1,] Figure 1a presents a diagrammatic sketch of what I see as the major perspective of sociology for at least the past 50 years. I would call it "purposeful environmentalism," and stipulate that it has three factorial components. Through it, behavior is seen as determined by environmental factors mediated by way of various hypothetical "rationalistic-purposeful" processes. Lenski himself has moved beyond this purely environmentalist perspective in recognizing that genetic factors interact with the environment to determine human social behavior; but, unfortunately, his various states of communication (to explain the intervening-mediating processes) still seems to me to contain vestiges of purposefulness. Furthermore, they give no recognition to the fact that learning—even the most complex learning—is, in the final accounting, purely a biochemical process which occurs predominantly in the central nervous system, and that any *real* theoretical explanations must be in those terms.

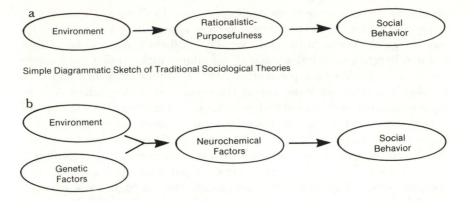

Simple Diagrammatic Sketch of Traditional Sociological Theories

Simple Diagrammatic Sketch of the Emerging Reductionist Paradigm

FIGURE 20.1

The comparable diagrammatic sketch of the approach I see beginning to unfold is shown in Figure 1b. It suggests that the two major "remote" determinants of social behavior are environmental and genetic factors, and that their influences are mediated through biochemical processes that are confined primarily to the central nervous system. This diagram, of course, would be just as appropriate for behavior in general as for social behavior, although the latter would normally be more complex (in that the social behavior of one conspecific would often be a part of the environment of another, and vice versa). In order for the actual theories to unfold under this type of paradigm, the precise environmental, genetic, and neurological factors having the greatest interacting influences will have to be specified.

Considerable progress has been made in the past decade identifying major biochemical processes whereby genetic and environmental factors interact to impose their joint influences upon behavior. Sociologists should not only be aware of this progress; they should also be contributing to it wherever social behavior is involved. Within the next few years, no course in sociology should be open to students who have not had basic training in at least genetics, biochemistry, and neurology. . . .

Pierre L. van den Berghe

I agree with van den Berghe that teleological assumptions still lurk amongst the writings of some evolutionary thinkers, especially those who slant their work toward popular audiences. Nevertheless, there are sufficient numbers of serious researchers and theorists working in the field to continue achieving significant advances in the understanding of evolutionary processes.

I accept totally the thrust of van den Berghe's remaining remarks. But by stipulating the occurrence of one additional event, I still think it is reasonable to say that sociology's development is rapidly approaching a watershed with only marginal chances of survival. Specifically, there is much to be said for van den Berghe's historical account of the ethnocentricism that has brought sociology to its Western popularity. Also, I cannot deny that much of sociology's current academic appeal (especially for undergraduates) is its reputation as one of the easiest majors on campus. I might add that this appeal is likely to spread if the competition for funds among many colleges and universities continues to be waged in large part on the basis of how many "student bodies" each institution can enroll (and keep them enrolled), regardless of talent or motivation. What better place to put such students than in a discipline which clings to theories that assume that the "right social environment" will transform anyone into anything?

Circumstances like these have increasingly segregated sociology from the natural sciences of which it should be a part. If they persist in the midst of the formation of a natural science paradigm for the study of social behavior, the chances of that paradigm catalyzing under some other name seems probable. Sociobiology is a likely candidate for assuming the catalytic function.

What is at stake is more than just the arbitrary name under which the scientific study of social behavior will be carried out. Even if the discipline has seriously compromised the academic excellence required of sociology graduates (especially in recent years, it probably has), the discipline still encapsulates an impressive reserve of creative, competent, and dedicated practitioners. Also, much of the empirical research carried out under old sociological perspectives (as well as studies done without any theoretical foundations whatsoever) actually should be very useful in sorting out a lot of the most probable theoretical formulations under the new paradigm. For these reasons, I hope that sociology survives and emerges within the next few years as the recognized science of social behavior. In part for reasons van den Berghe himself has outlined, I still think the prospects are marginal, at best.

21

Biological Explanation in Sociology

Allan Mazur

What does it mean to say that a human behavior has a "biological basis?"

To dispose of trivial answers first, let us agree that *all* human behavior is biological in the sense that it could not be performed without the genetic-physiological-morphological capacities of the human organism. No one has claimed a biological basis for cooking, yet it is clear that certain levels of brain function and manual dexterity are necessary for that task; and at least part of the cook's motivation lies in the taste buds, muscular contractions of the stomach wall, and the nutritional needs of the body. In that sense, all human activities — aggression, sex, physics — have a biological basis, but that explains nothing of interest to sociology.

Behaviors have been called "biological" to imply that they are *unlearned* and innately based on genetic information. We now know that virtually all "innate" behavior, even in one-celled organisms, can be modified through learning. Thus, there is little chance that biological explanation, in the sense of innate unmodifiable instinct, will ever have a place in human sociology.

What sort of reasonable meaning can we give to biological explanation in sociology? I suggest that we begin by looking at biological explanation in the less problematic context of biology. At least three forms of biological explanation are well accepted in biology today: (1) differences between species are explained as the result of *evolution*; (2) observable (phenotypic) differences within species — either between individuals or between groups of individuals — are explained (in part) by *genetic differences* between the individuals or groups; and (3) the structure and operation of organisms are explained *neurophysiologically* in terms of organ systems, nerve impulses, hormones, and so forth. How might these apply to sociology?

This article originally appeared in the *Sociological Quarterly*, vol. 19(4) Autumn 1978, pp. 604–613. Reprinted by permission.

Evolutionary Explanations of Human Species Behavior

It has been argued that humans have evolved a territorial nature. We tend to claim specific bounded plots of land and to defend them against intruders (Ardrey, 1966; van den Berghe, 1974). It has also been argued that human males have evolved a tendency to gather into all-male groups (Tiger, 1969), and to become aggressive when their wives commit adultery (Wilson, 1975). How are we to judge the credibility of these claims?

Visualize, if you can, a group of healthy infants raised in an environment which satisfied their basic physical, mental, and emotional needs, but in which there was no transmission of cultural information from past generations. It is difficult to design such an environment, but if we *could*, then it would be meaningful to ask how the children would behave as grownups. Would they be territorial? Would the men tend to gather into all male groups, would they choose mates, and would they become highly aggressive if their mates went to other men? Affirmative answers would support evolutionary explanations of their behaviors; negative answers would not.

For both moral and practical reasons, such an experiment is virtually impossible. What other empirical criteria might be used to decide if a behavior should be explained in evolutionary terms?

With appropriate scientific instruments, like a time machine, we could go back to primeval settings and observe the development of territoriality and so forth. Was there, or was there not, a period when our ancestors first experienced population pressure and shortly thereafter started pushing one another off specific plots of land? Did the pushers produce more progeny than the pushees, so that our ancestral line evolved a biological basis for territoriality? Lack of a sophisticated sociological methodology precludes this approach, but it serves as a useful model for an ideal method. A similar problem confronts biologists who attempt to trace the evolution of skeletal forms of various species, though they are luckier, finding occasional bones and fossils which can be dated. With these fossils, one can reconstruct the approximate evolutionary path from primitive animals to species alive today. Unfortunately, there are no fossil remains of ancestral forms of behavior.

Comparative anatomists have approached the problem from another direction, concentrating on species alive today. They can usually take the living species of any order of animals and, beginning with one species as a reference point, arrange the others as being more or less similar to it along such diverse criteria as gross morphology, development of the nervous system, and structure of protein molecules. Ratings along these dimensions usually correlate well, and we may infer that one species is more or less closely related than another to the reference species. If we happen to be working with the animal

Order of Primates, man is usually taken as the reference species, and we find that chimpanzees and gorillas are the closest of our living relatives, then certain old world monkeys such as baboons and macaques, then certain new world monkeys, then to the prosimians until we finally get to the tree shrew (which looks more like a squirrel than a monkey) as our most distant relative among the primates. Such a progression of animals, from tree shrew to man, is *not* an evolutionary sequence; we did not evolve from chimpanzees, and chimps did not evolve from present-day monkeys. (Chimps and monkeys are our cousins, not our ancestors.) Fossil evidence indicates that the earliest primate did look very much like a contemporary tree shrew, but it is still not correct to say that we are dealing with an evolutionary sequence, because each living species is the culmination of its own particular line of evolution. Still, this "quasi-evolutionary series" has some similarity to our time-machine model of a true evolutionary series, and it has the advantage of allowing comparative anatomists to study "evolution" of body tissue that has long since disintegrated from our true evolutionary ancestors. More important for our present purposes, sociologists may observe *behaviors* in these living species, and attempt to find regularities as one moves along the progression from tree shrews, through monkeys, chimps and then to man (Yerkes and Yerkes, 1935; Mazur, 1973). The method will become clearer with concrete examples.

"Blood is thicker than water" is one of many adages which indicate the basic solidarity of the nuclear family against outsiders. That is not to say that nuclear families are conflict free, for siblings fight. But when an outsider enters the fray, the sibs coalesce against him, though when he is driven off, they may return to their original squabble. Just as a person is loyal to his family against outsiders, he tends to be loyal to his community against foreigners. We have, in effect, a nested set of coalitions: Members of a nuclear family will coalesce when one is threatened by a member of the community outside the family; but these combatants, in turn, will coalesce when one is threatened by a stranger from outside the community. Can this be explained as an evolutionary development?

We may begin with our closest relative in the quasi-evolutionary series of primates, the chimpanzee. The *nuclear family* here consists of mother and offspring. (Since mating is promiscuous, and consort bonds are temporary, there is no "father.") The community consists of a loose aggregate of families and singles who know each other as individuals. It does indeed appear that chimp children aid their mothers in disputes with community members outside of the family (even when the children are grown) and that members of one chimp community will coalesce against a stranger, though the stranger may eventually be accepted into the community. Members of two chimp communities have been observed to coalesce against each other with some deaths resulting from the action (Lawick-Goodall, 1971 and unpublished). Moving down to baboons and macaques, we find the same phenomena. Primates even lower in the series have not been studied sufficiently well to know much about nuclear family solidarity, but community (troop) solidarity is present (Jolly, 1972). It appears, then, that the phenomenon of nested coalitions (nuclear family/community/stranger) exists in the primates most closely related to man, *and* it seems to exist in virtually all human societies (Geertz, 1972; Hall, 1966:163; Mazur, 1968). These two facts, taken together, suggest an evolutionary explanation for this mode of social behavior among humans.

Let us consider territoriality as a second concrete example. Do other primates obtain and defend *bounded* plots of land? There are indications that prosimians, the "lowest" primates of the series, are territorial in this sense. However, as we move along the series, through most monkeys, gorillas and chimps, we find the general rule to be absence of territoriality, with a few exceptions (Mazur and Robertson, 1972:20–21). These observations argue against an evolutionary explanation of territoriality in humans.

I doubt that we will ever make an ironclad case for an evolutionary explanation of any human social behavior but two criteria, taken together, appear to represent a plausible test. The first criterion is the one just discussed: Does the behavior, or some rudimentary form of it, appear in the quasi-evolutionary series of primates as we move from tree shrew toward man? The second criterion requires that any evolved behavior be pancultural—that is, it should appear in most known human societies. We should not require *all* societies to show the behavior since extreme environmental influences can grossly modify any characteristic, even physical features. In premodern Chinese culture, women's feet were bound to constrain their size and shape; certain African societies use stretcher plugs and scarring to alter the natural shape of ears, lips, and other body parts; circumcision is common in our own culture. It is theoretically possible to produce a society with armless and legless children by feeding thalidomide to all pregnant women. Given that extreme cultural environments can alter evolved *physical* characteristics, we must assume that any evolved *social* characteristic is also capable of significant modification, and perhaps. of total suppression. Thus, we would not necessarily expect an evolved behavior to be observable in every single society. In theory, an evolved behavior might appear in only a few societies, having been suppressed elsewhere. Thus, those who believe that territoriality is an evolved human behavior can "explain away" its notable absence in the many human nomadic societies by claiming that territoriality is culturally suppressed among these peoples. With similar reasoning, almost any behavior observed in any human group could be claimed to have evolutionary origins. The pancultural criterion, while not logically required, shifts the burden of evidence to the theorist who would explain behavior in evolutionary terms. The phenomenon of nested coalitions (nuclear family/community/stranger) satisfies the pancultural criterion and therefore, I believe, an evolutionary explanation is more plausible here than in the case of territoriality.

I do not wish to overstate the virtues of this line of reasoning; it has serious flaws. First, we can visualize behaviors that satisfy both the pancultural and the quasi-evolutionary series criteria but which are *not* evolutionary. Consider, for example, the art of tool making, which was long thought to be a solely human activity until Jane van Lawick-Goodall (1971) found chimps modifying natural objects to improve their efficiency as tools. Tool making is, of course, found in all human societies; and humans and chimps must have evolved the mental and physical abilities required to carry it out. But is tool making itself an evolved behavior? Not necessarily. Perhaps a common ancestor of chimp and man learned to make tools by accident, or by trial and error. In any case, he may have picked up the art as one discovers other new skills and then simply transmitted it to his children, and so it passed from generation to generation. Some of the present day descendants of that creature are chimps, and some are men, but they all may have learned tool making from their parents; and if so, then it is better explained as an example of cultural diffusion than of biologically evolved behavior.

On the other side of the coin, humans may have true biologically evolved behaviors which fail our quasi-evolutionary series criterion. Any behavior, like any physical characteristic, which evolved after the "human line" had split from the "ape line" would not show up in the quasi-evolutionary series. Also, as I have already noted, a behavior might have evolved among the primates but be suppressed in most human societies by cultural influences. By the tests advocated here, we would erroneously reject it as an evolved behavior.

In sum, if we are willing to accept some errors and ambiguity, we may reasonably accept or reject an evolutionary explanation of a particular human behavior if (1) it appears, or emerges in rudimentary form, as we move along the quasi-evolutionary series of primates from tree shrew toward man; and (2) it appears in nearly all known human societies. Though this reasoning has its faults, I submit that it is sounder than other forms of evolutionary reasoning that are now current. I will examine these briefly.

First, there is *reasoning by analogy* between human behavior and the behavior of one or more selected species scattered throughout the animal kingdom. For example, some writers point to the brief "imprinting" period of baby birds when they are especially prone to follow their mother or, in the absence of the mother, a substitute object. The claim is then made that human babies have a similar critical period which is crucial for the formation of later emotional attachments (Mazur and Robertson, 1972:108–14).

It is difficult to interpret the bird-human comparison. Similarities are interesting, but the differences are striking. We have vastly different gross and fine anatomy than birds; our nervous systems are barely comparable; we make discrepant use of eggs. One can always form analogies between any two species; but one cannot always tell if the analogies are meaningful, particularly when the species are widely separated on the phylogenetic tree. The difficulty is partly overcome by focusing on our phylogenetically "near" relatives, the Primate Order, which includes man. But there are still pitfalls. We cannot restrict our analogies to a single nonhuman species even if it is a primate. For example, the gibbon is a territorial primate that is closely related to man. Can we conclude, by analogy, that human defense of a section of home land has the same noncultural basis as gibbon territoriality? The gibbon, like every other species, has evolved its own idiosyncratic physical and behavioral features. By looking only at gibbons, we cannot tell if territoriality is one of its idiosyncracies or a generally evolved pattern among the higher primates. In fact, territoriality turns out to be a gibbon idiosyncracy because most other "higher" primates are not territorial. Many of the disadvantages of reasoning by analogy between humans and distantly related species, or by analogy between humans and one other species, are eliminated when we use the quasi-evolutionary series of primates. The argument for imprinting in human infants would be more impressive if imprinting could be demonstrated in the several primates most closely related to humans.

There is another weak form of evolutionary reasoning which I shall call *justification via natural selection*. The notion here is very simple. If one accepts the Darwinian view of natural selection, and if one observes that a species has some particular physical or behavioral characteristic, then one may assume that the characteristic has some relative advantage which led to its selection. One can then "explain" this characteristic by providing a plausible argument as to *why* it is adaptive and functional. Unfortunately, a reasonable selection argument can usually be constructed to explain *any* observation. Dark-skinned people tend to live in climates with strong sunshine, while lighter-skinned people live in cooler or cloudy climates. This may be explained as an adaptation to ultraviolet solar radiation, protective coloration in tropical rain forests, or optimal vitamin D production (Dobzhansky, 1962:271–73; Lerner, 1968:231–33). If Africans were *lighter* than Europeans, that could be explained by the fact that lighter skin reflects larger amounts of heat than darker skin, making light skin adaptive in a very hot, sunny climate. Wilson (1975) observes that men usually become aggressive when their mates commit adultery, and he explains this as a result of natural selection. Here are the details of his explanation:

A man who allows his mate to be fertilized by other men will waste his resources raising children who are not his own, and there will be few, if any, of his own descendants in the next generation. But, a man who acts to prevent adultery is insured that the resources he puts into child care will benefit his own offspring, and his genes will predominate in succeeding generations (Wilson, 1975:327). This mechanism is plausible — though it is rather specialized since it does not explain why women, too, object to their spouses' adultery — but I do not see how it can be tested. The explanation must remain, at best, pure speculation.

One can supply a plausible selection mechanism, indeed several mechanisms, for most kinds of behavior that are observed, as well as for most kinds of behavior that are not observed. Suppose that men, when on long trips, typically invited their brothers to copulate with their wives. We could "explain" this by saying that the husband's genetic fitness was being maximized, in effect, by the efforts of his brother, who carries most of the same genes. This is precisely the mechanism of "kin selection" which Wilson (1975:117-20) invokes to explain the evolution of altruism. If men typically pimped for their wives, this too could be explained, since the profits of prostitution would help sustain the pimp, his mate, and his offspring — all maximizing the male's genetic fitness (Mazur, 1976).

In my opinion, such arguments are wholly speculative, essentially untestable, and provide the weakest form of "explanation."

Genetic Explanations of Differences Among Humans

Natural selection has been also used to explain differences between identifiable subgroups of humans. Here is an old example:

(The negro) . . . shows complete adaptation to a tropical environment. . . . For example, the tropical environment is generally unfavorable to severe bodily labor. Persons who work hard in the tropics are . . . apt to be eliminated by natural selection. On the other hand, nature furnishes a bountiful supply of food without much labor. Hence, the tropical environment of the negro failed to develop in him an energetic nature, but favored the survival of those naturally shiftless and lazy. Again, the extremely high death rate in Africa necessitated a correspondingly high birth rate in order that any race living there might survive; hence, nature fixed in the negro strong sexual propensities in order to secure such a high birth rate (Ellwood, 1919:248-49).

Here is a new example.

Among the Jews, literally for millennia, the brightest had the best chances to marry and produce children. . . . In contrast . . . the brightest non-Jews had the least chance to have children throughout the Middle Ages. . . . (T)he priesthood attracted the most ambitious, talented, and intelligent . . . (non-Jews), . . . (but it) exacted a price: celibacy. Which meant that the most intelligent portion of the (Christian) population did not have offspring; their genes were siphoned off. . . .

Rabbinical study . . . attracted the brightest . . . Jews. . . . (R)abbis were en-
joined to marry and have children. . . . Altogether, if Jews had deliberately decided to breed children so as to maximize genetic intelligence, they could not
have done much better (van den Haag, 1969:14–17).

This is a confused and controversial topic, but much of the confusion can be
clarified with a few simple points.

1. Some of an individual's behaviors are almost certainly influenced by his
genes. Those behaviors with the most solid support for genetic influence are
performance in IQ tests, introversion-extraversion, neuroticism and tendencies toward schizophrenia. The best evidence for genetic efforts in humans
comes from two types of studies: (a) Identical twins (with identical genes),
separated shortly after birth and raised in separate families, are found to be
more similar on the above characteristics than are separated siblings (with
nonidentical genes); and (b) Children who are adopted shortly after birth are
found to be more similar to their natural than their adopted parents on the
above characteristics.

2. All human behaviors which appear to be under genetic influences are
known to be under environmental influences as well.

3. Attempts to apportion the variance in these behaviors between genetic
and environmental effects are difficult, to say the least (Layzer, 1974;
Feldman and Lewontin, 1975).

4. If we have a situation where two racial or class or ethnic groups (such as
whites and blacks) differ on (a) some observed behavioral characteristic (such
as IQ), and also on (b) cultural/environmental factors (such as opportunities
for schooling, or valuation on learning), and they also have (c) different gene
pools; then it is practically impossible to determine the extent to which the
behavior (IQ) difference is due to cultural differences as opposed to gene differences. Cultural influences and genes are transmitted along the same
pathways: within families and between friends. We have no way of separating
these factors and evaluating one apart from the other. The current
acrimonious dispute over a presumed genetic basis for black-white differences
in IQ (Jensen, 1973; Kamin, 1974) is essentially unresolvable for the near
future.

My own conclusion here is that genetic-environmental explanations of *individual* behavior are useful since we can separate the effects of genes from environment, as in twin studies. Genetic explanations of behavioral differences
between racial, class, or ethnic *groups*, though theoretically meaningful, are
essentially untestable because, as a practical matter, we cannot determine that
there is indeed a genetic effect that is separate from the environmental effect.
Therefore, I doubt that genetic explanations of groups' differences will be
useful in sociology, at least over the short run.

Neurophysiological Explanation of Social Interaction

Evolutionary explanations in sociology (and in biology) are usually not capable of direct empirical test; their acceptance depends on arguments and indirect data which make the explanations more or less plausible. Genetic explanations can be directly tested in biology where animal subjects may be selectively bred and subjected to constant environments, but these methods are unacceptable in sociology. The third form of biological explanation which I will consider—that is, neurophysiological explanation in terms of organ systems, nerve impulses, hormones and so forth—is directly testable in biology and, to a limited extent, in sociology as well. This methodological advantage gives it the potential for being the most powerful form of biological explanation in sociology.

The approach here is very close to classical scientific method: observation, hypothesis formation, experimental testing, reformulation of hypotheses, retesting, and so forth. These methods are well accepted in the study of animal behavior, and their logic is applicable to the study of humans as well. How might they work in sociology? We will look at research on emotions as an example, because these are intimately tied to social relationships.

Most attempts to relate hormones with human emotions derive from the work of Cannon (1932) who showed that animals in fearful situations experience changes associated with increased adrenaline in their blood: breathing deepens, blood pressure and pulse rate increase, reserve sugar enters the blood. Cannon pointed out that these adrenaline-induced changes are functional in preparing the animal for the emergency responses of "fight or flight," because the heart and other muscles receive increased sugar and oxygen, and waste products are eliminated more rapidly to diminish the effects of fatigue.

An obvious hypothesis at this point is that particular emotions are associated with particular hormones and some subsequent studies support this position (Funkenstein et al., 1957). Schachter and Singer (1962), however, have argued against the theory that each emotion has a particular hormone pattern. They hypothesized that two factors must be present to account for an emotion: (1) visceral sensations caused by a hormone such as adrenaline; and (2) cognitive cues to give the emotion a specific identity. Schachter told subjects that he was studying the effects of a vitamin which would be injected into them. Actually the "vitamin" was adrenaline. One group of subjects was told there would be certain side effects: shaking hands, pounding of the heart, and a warm flushed face. These are the normal effects of adrenaline, so these subjects were correctly informed of what to expect, and they will be designated the "adrenaline-informed" group. A second group of subjects was also given adrenaline but told nothing about side effects and will be called "adrenaline-uninformed." A third group was given a placebo injection which had no effect on the body and they too were told nothing of side effects, so they will be designated "placebo-uninformed."

Each subject was introduced to a stooge and told to wait with him for several minutes. When the experimenter left the room, the stooge went through a prearranged act, being either very happy in one condition of the experiment or very angry at the experimenter in another condition. The subjects were observed during this interaction, and afterward they were questioned about their emotions.

The results can be summarized as follows: Whatever the emotion of the stooge (happy or angry), the *adrenaline*-uninformed subjects were more likely to show signs of that emotion than the *placebo*-uninformed subjects. (Therefore, adrenaline contributes to two very different emotions.) Whatever the emotion of the stooge, the adrenaline-informed subjects were the *least* likely of all subjects to show signs of that emotion. (Therefore, adrenaline does not cause emotionality by itself.) These results indicate that emotions do not have single causes. The observed emotional behavior was a joint function of (1) adrenaline, (2) expectations that subjects had about the adrenaline's effects, and (3) cognitive cues (happy or angry) that subjects received from the stooge.

Our neurohormonal explanation of emotions is hardly complete. Christine Maslach of the University of California (Berkeley) has recently entered important qualifications into the Schachter theory. The relevant point here however, is that social contagion of emotions does appear to have some sort of neurophysiological explanation, and this explanation can be tested, reformulated, and retested in the laboratory.

Conclusions

Biological explanation has taken some trivial forms in sociology. At least three forms of explanation common in biology have meaningful homologues in sociology, but each has its faults.

Evolutionary explanations of human social behavior are necessarily conjectural since we have no behavioral observations of ancestral species from which we evolved. I suggest a reasonable (but not ironclad) test of such explanations, based on two criteria. First, the behavior in question should be known to occur in nearly all human societies that have been observed. Second, if we arrange living primate species into a "quasi-evolutionary series," beginning with primates most physically dissimilar from man and progressing through those which are increasingly physically like man, then we should find the behavior — or a rudimentary form of it — appearing in the species that are most similar to man. This reasoning has faults, but still seems sounder than alternate forms of evolutionary thinking current in sociology.

Genetic explanations of individual differences in behavior have a relatively sound basis in the study of identical twins raised apart, and also in the study of children reared by adopted rather than natural parents. All behaviors which appear to be genetically influenced are known to be environmentally influenced as well, so while it is relatively easy to demonstrate the existence of a genetic effect, it is exceedingly difficult to determine what proportion of the variance is explained genetically. Attempts to explain behavioral differences between cultural groups (e.g., IQ differences between blacks and whites) are almost impossible to test empirically because genes and culture are transmitted along the same pathways (i.e., within families and between friends), and it is unlikely that we can separate out these effects.

Neurophysiological explanations of social interaction seem particularly promising since they are capable of direct empirical test, though the ethics of experimentation are problematic (Barber et al., 1973). Furthermore, the medical/physiological techniques that will be required for this work lie outside the expertise of most sociologists, so we can expect such research to occur outside of our discipline unless there is substantial retraining within sociology.

Perhaps a wedding of the evolutionary and neurophysiological explanations would be particularly strong, showing specific social-physiological mechanisms operating in diverse human societies as well as in other primate species.

References

Ardrey, Robert. (1966) *Territorial Imperative*. New York: Atheneum.

Barber, B., J. Lally, J. Makarushka and D. Sullivan. (1973) *Research on Human Subjects*. New York: Russell Sage.

Cannon, Walter. (1932) *The Wisdom of the Body*. New York: W.W. Norton.

Dobzhansky, T. (1962) *Mankind Evolving*. New Haven: Yale University Press.

Ellwood, Charles. (1919) *Sociology and Modern Social Problems*. New York: American Book.

Feldman, M., and R. Lewontin. (1975) "The Heritability Hang-up." *Science* 190:1163–68.

Funkenstein, D., S. King, and M. Droletta. (1957) *Mastery of Stress*. Cambridge, Mass.: Harvard University Press.

Geertz, Clifford. (1972) "Deep Play: Notes on a Balinese Cockfight." *Daedalus* 101:1–37.

Hall, Edward. (1966) *The Hidden Dimension*. Garden City, N.Y.: Doubleday.

Jensen, A. (1973) *Educability and Group Differences*. New York: Harper and Row.

Jolly, Allison. (1972) *The Evolution of Primate Behavior*. New York: Macmillan.

Kamin, L. (1974) *The Science and Politics of IQ*. New York: Halsted-Wiley.

Lawick-Goodall, Jane. (1971) *In the Shadow of Man*. Boston: Houghton Mifflin.

Layzer, David. (1974) "Heritability Analyses of IQ Scores: Science or Numerology?" *Science* 183:1259–66.

Lerner, I. (1968) *Heredity, Evolution, and Society*. San Francisco: W.H. Freeman.

Mazur, Allan. (1968) "A Nonrational Approach to Theories of Conflict and Coalitions." *Journal of Conflict Resolution* 12:196–205.

————. (1973) "A Cross-Species Comparison of Status in Small Established Groups." *American Sociological Review* 38:513–30.

————. (1976) "On Wilson's *Sociobiology*." *American Journal of Sociology* 82:697–700.

————, and Leon Robertson. (1972) *Biology and Social Behavior*. New York: Free Press.

Ritzer, G. (1975) "Sociology: A Multiple Paradigm Science." *The American Sociologist* 10:156–67.

Schachter, S., and J. Singer. (1962) "Cognitive, Social and Physiological Determinants of Emotional State." *Psychological Review* 69:379–99.

Tiger, Lionel. (1969) *Men in Groups*. New York: Random House.

van den Berghe, Pierre. (1974) "Bringing Beasts Back In: Toward a Biosocial Theory of Aggression." *American Sociological Review* 39:777–88.

van den Haag, Ernest. (1969) *The Jewish Mystique*. New York: Dell.

Wilson, Edward. (1975) *Sociobiology: The New Synthesis*. Cambridge, Mass.: Harvard University Press.

Yerkes, R., and A. Yerkes. (1935) "Social Behavior in Infrahuman Primates," in C. Murchison (ed.), *A Handbook on Social Psychology*, Volume 2. New York: Russell and Russell.

22

Sociobiology or Balanced Biosocial Theory?

John D. Baldwin
Janice I. Baldwin

In recent years there has been a considerable reawakening of interest in animal social behavior within the discipline of sociology. There has been an increasing number of attempts to relate the social sciences to a biological base, to apply ethological principles to human social behavior, and to determine the relevance of sociobiology for sociology (Mazur and Robertson, 1972; Mazur, 1973; van den Berghe, 1974, 1975; Ellis, 1977; Eckberg, 1977). . . .

Balanced Biosocial Theory

We believe that before sociologists select any biological theories for use in the human studies, it is wise to establish general criteria against which to evaluate those theories. We suggest the following three criteria as basic features of a desirable biosocial theory.

[First,] a central criterion for an adequate theory is that it not be biased toward either nature or nurture. An adequate theory must avoid the extreme environmentalism of Watson's (1924) behaviorism or of those sociologists who refuse to acknowledge the biological nature of *Homo sapiens*, the animal. On the other hand, an adequate theory must avoid the other extreme of biological determinism, such as James's (1890) or McDougall's (1908) instinct psychology or other theories of genetically preprogramed behavior. An adequate biosocial theory must be balanced to contain an empirically defensible mixture and interaction of biological and environmental factors. This is not

Excerpts from "Sociobiology or Balanced Biosocial Theory?" by John D. Baldwin and Janice I. Baldwin are reprinted from *Pacific Sociological Review*, vol. 23 (1) (January 1980), pp. 3–27 by permission of the Western Washington University and of the publisher, Sage Publications, Inc. Footnotes have been eliminated.

easy. Although scientists have been told since the 1950s (Beach, 1955; Anastasi, 1958) to avoid extreme nature-nurture positions and to seek a balanced synthesis of both biological and environmental variables, the goal eludes many researchers and theorists.

Second, a balanced biosocial theory will have to involve multicausal models of behavior, with room for interaction effects among the numerous causes. The multiple causes fall into two main categories: phylogenetic and ontogenetic, i.e., those that shape the evolution of the species and those that shape the development of each individual from the moment of conception through the remainder of life. These two sets of causes are also known as the distal and proximal causes of behavior, since the phylogenetic causes are distant in time and the ontogenetic are proximate.

The phylogenetic causes include a multitude of factors that fall into two broad categories: phylogenetic inertia and ecological pressures, which are the primary determinants of natural selection (Wilson, 1975). A species' phylogenetic history of specialization and generalization imposes constraints on the direction and speed of its present evolution. Superimposed on this phylogenetic legacy are the mutations and genetic recombinations that produce immense variety and individuality in each new generation (Mayr, 1978). This variety, in turn, is the raw material for natural selection. Variations that are adaptive for an individual vis-à-vis the multiple demands of the current social and nonsocial environment confer competitive advantages and a statistically greater probability of surviving and leaving offspring. Differential survival and differential reproduction are the mechanisms that continuously sort the genes of a population, selecting in favor of genes that encode the information that produces an adaptive fit to the multiple ecological pressures. Thus the genetic causes of any trait reflect prior phylogenetic causes.

The ontogenetic causes of behavior shape the development of each individual from the moment the genetic endowment is fixed at conception. Whereas the genetic information represents a "blueprint" for physiological development, the environment provides the building blocks from which the developing organism is constructed. In mammals, for example, the manner in which the genotype is expressed in the developing fetus is influenced by numerous proximal causes such as the mother's diet, exposure to poisons or drugs, disease, stress, hormone titers, and anoxia. After birth, each individual interacts more directly with the environment, since it is less protected by the mother's biological systems. Postnatal physical development is shaped by nutrition, toxins, diseases, foreign chemicals (or drugs), falls, injuries, infections, parasites, exercise levels, and so forth. In addition, the hormonal and central nervous systems are structured and modified by general levels of stress and sensory stimulation, patterned sensory input, and specific learning experiences.

During the life of each individual there is a continuous interaction between genetic and environmental influences; hence a balanced biosocial theory must attempt to integrate both, including the often complex interaction effects among the multiple factors.

Third, a balanced biosocial theory must also adjust the weighting of phylogenetic, ontogenetic, and interaction effects according to the phylogenetic level of the species being studied. When analyzing the behavior of honeybees, for example, a heavy weighting must be attributed to genetic influences, a small but crucial weighting is attached to the nutrients and chemicals given to the developing larva which determine its cast as queen or worker, and a small to moderate weighting is allocated to learning. (Other weightings would be affixed to the remaining causal variables.) In contrast, an analysis of chimpanzee behavior would reveal a much reduced impact of genetic information along with increases in the weighting of ontogenetic variables, especially in the area of learning.

Since neither phylogenetic nor ontogenetic inputs to an individual's behavior are ever zero at any phyletic level, extreme nature or nurture arguments never supersede balanced biosocial theories. As sociologists expand and refine their discipline, it is only logical that balanced biosocial theories will be incorporated to guard against genetic and environmental extremes. . . .

Toward a Balanced Biosocial Science

Sociologists and other social scientists can pursue balanced biosocial research and theory in a variety of ways that avoid both the extreme evolutionary perspective and extreme environmentalism.

(1) Adhere to balanced biosocial theories. At the theoretical level, sociologists must insist that biosocial work involves a balanced integration of phylogenetic and ontogenetic variables. By expanding the task of sociology to include an interest in balanced biosocial syntheses, sociologists can take an active part in shaping the theories that will be sufficiently empirically defensible to withstand the test of time. If sociologists do not demand that biosocial theories be balanced, they only help perpetuate the current genetic theories. At present, a logical step would be for sociologists to integrate existing theory and data from the social and biological sciences, with due weighting on proximal and distal causes. This is a constructive role that will generate exemplars of balanced biosocial theories and may help guide ethologists and sociobiologists away from their current overemphasis on evolutionary mechanisms.

(2) Examine, criticize, and replicate work from the biological paradigms. Since the work of ethologists and sociologists has the potential for being biased by unwarranted genetic assumptions, sociologists can play a valuable role in biosocial research by critically analyzing the biological work, comparing it

with data on humans (and other species), and, if necessary, replicating the work with better controls. The following examples show the value of this type of work.

A key feature of sociobiology is its explanation of altruistic and cooperative behavior in terms of inclusive fitness. An altruistic animal may benefit in increased inclusive fitness if it expends effort or runs risks to help kin who share genes in common with the altruist, though the more distant the kinship, the less the effort or risk is cost effective. This genetic interpretation of altruism has led sociobiologists to think that they have the *ultimate* explanation of altruism in general; and they have begun "explaining" human altruism in purely genetic terms (Wilson, 1975; Trivers, 1971). Mussen and Eisenberg-Berg (1977) have recently balanced the picture on altruism by comparing the research from biology, psychology, anthropology, and sociology. Rather than the simplistic, single-causal-variable theory of sociobiology, Mussen and Eisenberg-Berg present a complex, multiple-factor model that weaves together biological, psychological, and social-cultural variables in a balanced manner that is well supported by data on human behavior.

The research relating sex and gender differentiation to perinatal hormones provides a similar example. When female mice, rats, hamsters, and rhesus monkeys are exposed to androgens perinatally, they tend to show masculinized behavior later in life. Biological explanations were obviously in order, and for two decades biological researchers did not consider it necessary to study the role of learning or differential social treatment of androgenized females in their theories. Studies on androgenized human females did not demonstrate the clear-cut masculinization seen in the studies of animals; however, the biological explanations were extended to "explain" human sex differences. Recently a critical review of the literature by Quadagno et al. (1977) demonstrated numerous methodological problems in the various studies, and revealed a great need for controls to test social learning hypotheses. Money's (1975:71) study of a child who was born male (thus "masculinized" perinatally) "offers nothing to stimulate one's conjectures" that biological predispositions for masculinity cannot be overriden by social learning. These critical studies help balance the field and correct the errors biological researchers frequently make.

(3) *Sociological research on biological mediators of behavior.* Because their perspective differs from that of biologists, sociologists are likely to ask different questions about the effect of biological variables on human social behavior. Thus sociologists should feel free to conduct original research on biological mechanisms either by direct manipulation or by locating natural experiments in natural social settings. Guided by different paradigms, the sociologist will not be "merely replicating" research that rightfully "belongs" to biologists, but doing legitimate sociological inquiry.

Among the biological influences on social behavior that could be studied from a sociological perspective are the sex (and other) hormones, pheromones, nutrition, parasites, genetic variables, right versus left hemisphere dominance in cortical processing, alpha rhythms, heart rate, fatigue, arousal level, physical fitness, and muscular development. Mazur (1976) has begun investigating the relationships between testosterone and male behavior, with special attention to issues of social rank, stress, and mood change. Kagan's and Klein's 1973 field study in Guatemala took advantage of "natural experiments" in nutritional and sensory deprivation to determine the impact of early retardation on later development. Money (1968, 1975), Hampson (1965), and Money and Ehrhardt (1972) have capitalized on a variety of "natural experiments" involving sex hormone and physical irregularities to evaluate the influence of biological factors on sex and gender role development.

(4) *Sociological research on animal behavior and social organization.* When it is possible to locate reliable patterns (and related causal variables) in the behavior or social organization of nonhuman species, these data can serve as a source of heuristic generalizations and tentative hypotheses about human behavior. It is unlikely that these hypotheses will generalize completely—without modification—to humans; however they offer advantages that often offset the problem of incomplete generalization.

First, animal studies can serve as a "drawing board" (Premack, 1971:186) for sketching out and analyzing simplified models of phenomena that are often exceedingly complex in humans. For example, communication and play in primates are a good deal simpler than their human counterparts, and are influenced by a smaller number of causal variables. The simplification often makes it easier to cut through the complexities that the given behavior has in humans to locate the primary causal mechanisms. Second, we stand so close to human behavior that we often cannot see the forest for the trees. We know countless rationalizations to "explain" why a given behavior under study shows unique variations in different individuals. This can sometimes be remedied by studying alien species, especially primates. From the new perspective it is often possible to see generalizations (the forest rather than the trees). The perspective, therefore, can help give insights in our study of human behavior by suggesting simple generalizations about basic underlying behavioral patterns or causal mechanisms that we share with other species. Third, it is possible to conduct multitudes of controlled animal experiments that could not be done on humans, due to practical, ethical, or financial reasons, or due to problematic experimenter effects common with human subjects. It is wise to complement laboratory experiments with field studies in order to observe how the target behavior interlocks with other behaviors in its natural context.

Since the animal studies were used as a simplification device, generalizations to humans should automatically involve a step in which one systematically builds back in special human complexities that would not have been predicted from animal data alone. Thus one would superimpose on primate generalizations a concern for relevant contributions from social learning, language, cognitive mediation, cultural influence, social sanctions, and so on. This strategy helps prevent simplistic uses of animal data and attunes the researcher to expect that the unique features of human behavior will interact with the underlying behavioral mechanisms that we share with other animals.

Generalizations from nonhuman species are strongest when they reflect consistent phylogenetic trends or stable qualities shared by most species closely related to humans. For example, Mazur and Robertson (1972) and Mazur (1973) constructed a primate series from tree shrews, to prosimians, to monkeys, to apes and humans, then compared several behaviors across the series. There were clear trends in length of preadult socialization, face-to-face interaction, ranking mechanisms, and so forth, suggesting numerous hypotheses about the observed patterns. Comparative research on exploration and play in primates indicates that the behavioral mechanisms responsible for these activities are found in all primates studied and may well be shared by humans (Baldwin and Baldwin, 1977, 1978a, 1978b). This research has humanistic implications for enhancing creativity and lifelong inquisitiveness in humans.

Summary

The rising interest of sociologists in biosocial research and theories should be directed toward a balanced biosocial synthesis of multiple-causal factors from both phylogeny and ontogeny. In order to accomplish this task, it will be necessary to avoid extreme genetic theories as well as extreme environmentalism. Social scientists can play a valuable role in the development of future biosocial theories by advocating balanced theories and criticizing and replicating work that does not reflect a balanced concern for the relevant causal variables. In addition, it is legitimate for social scientists to study biosocial phenomena from their unique perspective, since their work may well produce different findings than similar research in other disciplines.

To the degree that we succeed in producing a balanced biosocial science, we can bring beasts back in without the risks of creating beastly theories.

References

Anastasi, A. (1958) "Heredity, Environment, and the Question 'How?' " *Psychological Review* 65:197–208.
Baldwin, J. D., and J. I. Baldwin. (1977) "The Role of Learning Phenomena in the Ontogeny of Exploration and Play," in S. Chevalier-Skolnikoff and F. E. Poirier (eds.), *Primate Bio-Social Development*. New York: Garland.

_____ . (1978a) "Reinforcement Theories of Exploration, Play Creativity and Psychosocial Growth," in E. O. Smith, (ed.), *Social Play in Primates: Structure and Function*. New York: Academic Press, pp. 231–257.

_____ . (1978b) "The Primate Contribution to the Study of Play," in M.A. Salter (ed.), *Play: Anthropological Perspectives*. West Point, N.Y.: Leisure, pp. 53–68.

Beach, F. A. (1955) "The Descent of Instinct." *Psychological Review* 62:401–410.

Eckberg, D. L. (1977) "Sociobiology and the Death of Sociology: An Analytic Reply to Ellis." *American Sociologist* 12:191–196.

Ellis, L. (1977) "The Decline and Fall of Sociology, 1975–2000." *American Sociologist* 12:56–66.

Hampson, J. L. (1965) "Determinants of Psychosexual Orientation," in F. A. Beach (ed.), *Sex and Behavior*. New York: John Wiley, pp. 108–132.

James, W. (1890) *The Principles of Psychology*. Vol. 2. New York: Holt, Rinehart and Winston.

Mayr, E. (1978) "Evolution." *Scientific American* 239:3: 47–55.

Mazur, A. (1973) "A Cross-Species Comparison of Status in Small Established Groups." *American Sociological Review* 38:513–530.

_____ . (1976) "Effects of Testosterone on Status in Small Groups." *Folia Primatologica* 26:214–226.

Mazur, A., and L. S. Robertson. (1972) *Biology and Social Behavior*. New York: Macmillan.

McDougall, W. (1908) *An Introduction to Social Psychology*. New York: Methuen.

Money, J. (1968) *Sex Errors of the Body*. Baltimore: Johns Hopkins Press.

_____ . (1975) "Ablatio Penis: Normal Male Infant Sex-Reassigned as a Girl." *Archives of Sexual Behavior* 4(1):65–71.

Money, J., and A. A. Ehrhardt. (1972) *Man & Woman, Boy & Girl*. Baltimore: Johns Hopkins Press.

Mussen, P., and N. Eisenberg-Berg. (1977) *Roots of Caring, Sharing and Helping*. San Francisco: Freeman.

Premack, D. (1971) "On the Assessment of Language Competence in the Chimpanzee," in A. M. Schrier and F. Stollnitz (eds.), *Behavior of Nonhuman Primates*, Vol. 4. New York: Academic Press, pp. 185–228.

Quadagno, D. M., R. Biscoe, and J. S. Quadagno. (1977) "Effects of Perinatal Gonadal Hormones on Selected Nonsexual Behavior Patterns: a Critical Assessment of the Nonhuman and Human Literature." *Psychology Bulletin* 84:62–80.

Trivers, R. L. (1971) "The Evolution of Reciprocal Altruism." *Quarterly Review of Biology* 46:35–57.

_____ . (1972) "Parental Investment and Sexual Selection," in B. Campbell (ed.), *Sexual Selection and the Descent of Man, 1871–1971*. Chicago: Aldine, pp. 136–179.

_____ . (1974) "Parent–Off-Spring Conflict." *American Zoologist* 14:249–264.

van den Berghe, P. (1974) "Bringing Beasts Back In: Toward a Biosocial Theory of Aggression." *American Sociological Review* 39:777–788.

_____ . (1975) *Man in Society*. New York: Elsevier North-Holland.

Watson, J. B. (1924) *Behaviorism*. New York: Norton.

Wilson, E. O. (1975) *Sociobiology: The New Synthesis*. Cambridge, Mass.: Harvard University Press.

Part 7
**Biology and the Social Sciences:
Problems and Questions**

Introduction to Part 7

The previous chapters on anthropology, economics, political science, and sociology have attempted to illustrate how the life sciences might have an intellectual impact on those disciplines and how new, expanded conceptualizations of human nature might influence the course of future scholarship. In all of the individual social sciences, serious questions are being raised about the advisability of proceeding in these directions. Many of these analyses and critiques are included in the literature of the present volume.

This final section deals with several more broadly conceived arguments, problems, and questions relating to a biological emphasis in the social sciences. Chapter 23, by Piotr Fedoseev, a Marxist theoretician, has been included to demonstrate the character of a dialogue that could emerge if biosocial science were viewed as challenging certain preconceived ideological positions. Following Marx, Fedoseev asserts that it is an "indisputable thesis" that human "social consciousness is determined by social, not biological, factors." He goes on to "categorically reject the biologisation of social phenomena because it is *social* laws that *fully* determine the 'behavior' of classes, nations, and all social groups in general" (emphasis added). Nevertheless, Fedoseev insists that more research is required to demonstrate a relationship between biological factors and *individual*-level behavior. Here he recognizes that human beings are a part of nature, and he argues that scholarship must take this into account; but he clearly rules out on ideological grounds the prospect of demonstrating relationships between social behavior and biological variables.

Although many critiques of the now voluminous sociobiological literature have been cited and discussed in previous selections in this book, an article by Lewontin has been included here to illustrate the types of fundamental questions that can be raised by biologists themselves regarding the application of sociobiology to the study of human social behavior. Lewontin attempts to demonstrate that "human sociobiology so vulgarizes natural selection and the theory of adaptation that it does not have a claim to be a serious form of scientific investigation." He develops his case by arguing that each of what he considers to be the three basic elements of sociobiological theory—description, heritability, and adaptive story—has its own peculiar methodological difficulties. According to Lewontin, much of the work in human sociobiology has simply ignored the work of anthropologists, psychologists, and evolutionary morphologists. Many human sociobiologists, for example, have treated analytical categories such as territoriality, aggression, and dominance "as if they were natural objects of unquestioned status, rather than as historically and ideologically conditioned constructs."

In spite of these strong criticisms, especially of what he calls the "imaginative reconstruction" of evolutionary adaptiveness, Lewontin feels that there might be an intellectual role for a sociobiological perspective in the study of social behavior. For such a development to take place, however, sociobiologists must adopt much more modest goals and become more frankly explicit about their own methodological and epistemological problems.

This section closes appropriately with an article by Peterson and Somit that raises a number of methodological issues that social scientists and human ethologists must confront and address with some success if rigorous interdisciplinary scholarship is to be pursued. After discussing the basic conceptual assumptions of modern ethology, Peterson and Somit examine some of the general methodological problems encountered in animal studies. They discuss such issues as observer effect, measurement, recording, sampling, reliability, and species identification. All of this is a prelude to their careful exposition of problems associated with applying ethological perspectives to the study of human social behavior. These difficulties include the impact of human culture, biases of individual researchers, the difficulty of scholars in accepting new ideas, problems of experimentation with humans, and concerns regarding cross-species comparisons. In spite of these many problems, Peterson and Somit conclude that "ethology may prove most fruitful as a means of sensitizing us to man as a biological as well as a social animal."

T.C.W.

23

A Marxist View of Biology and the Social Sciences

Piotr Fedoseev

. . . It has become fashionable to speak of the convergence of biological and social research known under the names of "social biology" and "sociobiology." It was for the specific purpose of effecting such integration that the *Journal of Biosocial Sciences* was started in 1969. Over the last few years, courses in "social biology" have been gaining increasing popularity in British colleges, universities and higher forms of secondary schools. The programmes of most of the courses in social biology include, besides biological subjects, such sections as social psychology, human behaviour, the basic sociological concepts, social structure and organisation, the cultural evolution of man, and the problems of crime.

The well-known journal *Science* has published a special article on what "sociobiology" is all about. The article begins with these words: "Altruism, faithfulness to one's mate, parental sacrifices for the young and other similar behavioral patterns occur in many species ranging from social insects to mammals" (Kolata, 1975:50–51). The social behaviour of specimens, the author of the article continues, is aimed at maximising their genetic contribution to the following generation; this is a kind of "genetic imperative." On the other hand, he asserts, the methods of studying the social conduct of animals should influence the study of the social behaviour of man.

The article goes on to give a brief description of the various types of relationships between animals, insects, etc. — "altruism," mutual help, "territorial aggression," conflicts between parents and their offspring, sexual conflicts — and draws the conclusion that all these relationships have obvious analogies in human conduct. The author does say at the end, however, that many social scientists are worried by such an extension of sociobiology. They

Published originally under the title "On the Problem of the Social and the Biological in Sociology and Psychology," in *Social Science Information,* vol. 15 (4–5), 1976. Reprinted by permission of the publisher and the author. The format of the citations has been revised and footnotes have been eliminated. Large portions of the article have not been reprinted.

are worried, in particular, by the fact that theories in sociobiology have proved to be flimsy and superficial, that these theories aspire to explain everything but in fact explain nothing. Nevertheless, the author of the article concludes, social biology will change the trend of research in the field of the social sciences.

Thus we see an obvious attempt to synthesise or combine biological and sociological research — an attempt which, despite all reservations, ignores the specific social laws that determine social phenomena. For example, M. Argyle (1969:25), a social psychologist well known in the West, writes plainly that "social interaction is to a great extent pre-programmed by innate neural structures which result from natural selection, and by cultural norms, which represent past collective solutions to the problems of interaction."

Sociology is in effect being replaced by biology under the guise of convergence. Such attempts have a history of more than a hundred years, but they proved to be vain because they lack a scientific basis and fail to accord with the basic principles of the scientific method requiring concrete research in every specific field.

Marxists have been lucidly expressing their negative attitude towards such attempts since their inception.

We shall cite only a few examples.

In the 1860s the German philosopher and sociologist F. A. Lange advocated the biological interpretation of social phenomena. He placed the whole history of society under the Darwinian law, belonging to natural science, of the "struggle for life" and combined it with the Malthusian theory of overpopulation. Karl Marx resolutely denounced such a concoction and wrote of Lange's concept: "So, instead of analysing the 'struggle for life' as represented historically in various definite forms of society, all that has to be done is to translate every concrete struggle into the phrase 'struggle for life,' and this phrase itself into the Malthusian 'population fantasy.' One must admit that this is a very impressive method — for swaggering, sham-scientific, bombastic ignorance and intellectual laziness."

Lange is known to have asked Marx and Engels to collaborate in his publications. In his letter to Lange, Engels explained the fundamental difference in their theoretical views and conclusions. "For us," Engels wrote on behalf of himself and of Marx, "so-called 'economic laws' are not eternal laws of nature, but historical laws."

In the 20th century, Bogdanov, the Machist, set out to "rectify" and "develop" Marx's doctrine by supplementing it, in part, with allegations that social forms belong to a common classification of biological adaptations.

Lenin trenchantly criticised all such attempts quietly to substitute biological analogies for the analysis of social phenomena. Recalling Marx's criticism of Lange's biologistic exercises, Lenin most convincingly showed a wide gap to exist between Marxism and the "biological" Machist jackstraws. "The transfer of biological concepts *in general* to the sphere of the social sciences is *phrase-mongering*. Whether this transfer is undertaken with 'good' intentions or for the purpose of bolstering up false sociological conclusions, the phrase-mongering nonetheless remains phrase-mongering," said Lenin (vol. 14:329).

Biologism in the social sciences is a profoundly erroneous "methodology" primarily because it takes no account of the universal structure of being, of the material world as a whole, and the historical differentiation of that structure. Overcoming the problem of the biological and the social relies on philosophical interpretation of the *unity* of the world and the *qualitative distinction* of the various levels, manifestations and spheres of this unified material world. The various levels and spheres of being are subject to *universal* laws expressing the unity of the world, and at the same time *specific laws* operate at every qualitatively distinctive level of being. Thus, between the different spheres or levels of being there is a similarity, continuity, connection, and also a qualitative distinction.

This general philosophical tenet enables us to understand, for instance, that the role of physicochemical laws are exceptionally important in determining biological phenomena, and that at the same time this is a qualitatively new phenomenon which cannot basically be reduced to physicochemical processes. Physics and chemistry are necessary but insufficient for understanding life. In the same way we may say that a knowledge of physiological and in general biological laws is absolutely essential for understanding psychological processes. Yet the psyche, consciousness and thinking are qualitatively new phenomena which are determined by more complex, specific laws that can by no means be reduced to physiological laws.

In the evolutionary development of the organic world, the human organism represents the highest level of biological organisation; it differs from purely biological objects of living nature by the presence of more developed structures and processes with a far greater number of new socially mediated ties and relations.

With the emergence of man, the development of the world assumes an entirely new property — social life. "The human essence," wrote Marx, "is not an abstraction inherent in each single individual. In its reality it is the ensemble of the social relations" (Marx and Engels, 1969:14). Society is quite a new, qualitatively distinctive form of development of the objective world. The specific laws here are precisely social laws which, whatever biologism may say, cannot be replaced or dominated by biological laws.

The social, having emerged and taken shape historically on a biological basis but under the impact of social relations, has become the leading and determining aspect of the development of man; it has become his essence.

The biological and the social, notwithstanding their interdependence, are in many ways different spheres of being, each having specific laws.

Denial of the qualitatively distinctive phenomena, levels and spheres of being is as inconsistent and dangerous as an incomprehension of the unity of the world, of the interconnection of all phenomena, of the continuity and reciprocal transformations of the different forms of movement of matter. Outside this continuity the development of the world in its unity is altogether impossible.

· With reference to the biological-social problem, this means that it is necessary to find, in reality itself, that concrete *mode of interaction* of the biological and the social by virtue of which the two, firstly, would not be identified with each other, and, secondly, would not be separated from each other. In other words, what has to be done is to bring out the *specific nature* of each of these two spheres of being, as well as their *continuity*, interconnection and their reciprocal transformations. This should be done in relation to all aspects of the multifaceted and complex biological-social problem. We have in mind, above all, the case where the combination of the biological and the social comes out in some form of relationship in certain facts of human behaviour.

We categorically reject the biologisation of social phenomena because it is social laws that fully determine the "behaviour" of classes, nations and all social groups in general.

However, this does not rule out the necessity to investigate the relationship between the biological and the social *in man as an individual*. In this case too we do not accept any form of social Darwinism or biologism. For us it is a truism that man is created by society, that man is a social creature, that his social conditions determine his development, conduct, etc. But we are also against the oversimplified notion that man is completely separated from nature. Man is a social as well as a biological creature, for he is part of nature. As Engels said, he has a bodily existence.

In general, we believe it is an irrefutable truth that man has left the animal world far behind. It would be naive to think, though, that people have completely overcome everything that is natural and inherent in the human being as a biological creature.

The human organism is born, takes shape and develops in accordance with socially mediated laws of biology. The mediation of the biological by the social takes place mainly through the central nervous system, which performs, on the one hand, the function of reflecting the surrounding world in the form of notions, concepts and judgements, and, on the other, the function of uniting, regulating and coordinating the processes inside the organism and in its interaction with the external, primarily social, environment. The mechanism and structure of the interaction between the social and the biological are discerned by the methods and means of different sciences, each revealing one aspect of the problem or another.

Considering all these varied aspects of the problem, we realise that science is faced with a most complex task — to reveal that concrete and universal *mode or "mechanism" of interaction between the biological and the social* which makes for (1) the specific nature, the non-identity, and also (2) the continuity, the interconnection of both these spheres of being in the development and conduct of man.

This basic type of interaction between the biological and the social has been defined by Marx (vol. 1:173) as follows: while changing external nature in the process of labour, man changes his own nature. In other words, the very *nature* of man is a product of *history*. This classical precept of Marx overcomes in principle each and every variety of the dualism between the biological and the social in man. In the course of his social activity man does indeed *change*, and does not destroy, the natural, the biological in himself. Owing to this, the interconnection, the continuity of the biological and the social, far from disappearing, develops historically. Genuine unity, but not identity, of the two exists primarily in work, i.e., in the social *activity* of people.

It is this initial fundamental proposition of Marx that underlies a number of investigations of this problem.

For instance, on the basis of this proposition the Soviet psychologists S. L. Rubinshtein, B. M. Teplov, B. G. Ananyev and others have fruitfully elaborated the problem of the formation of abilities (musical, sensory, etc.) and the problem of man's psychological development in general. On the same basis they have devised one of the key methodological and philosophical principles of Soviet psychology — the principle of the unity of consciousness (the psyche in general) and activity. According to this principle, psychological processes and characteristics (abilities in particular) not only manifest themselves but also *take shape in activity* — in work, study, communication, etc. Human abilities are not something like a finished product before their manifestation. At every stage of socially useful joint activity, as new socially significant results are obtained in the process of this activity, man rises to a qualitatively new stage of his psychological development, i.e., the development of his abilities, character, etc. The psychological development of man therefore constitutes a true organic, indissoluble unity of the biological and the social in the process of activity.

To exemplify this let us look at yet another aspect (somewhat unexpected at first glance) of the social-biological problem. This aspect is connected with the sensational question: "Can a machine think?"

Genuine (i.e. human) thinking is a living unity, reciprocal transformation, continuity of the biological and the social. This means that thinking is simply impossible without the brain and outside society. In other words, any separation of the biological from the social, any violation of their unity and interconnection makes thinking impossible.

On the other hand, as a result of the epoch-making achievements of cybernetics, e.g., the general theory of automata, many scientists are being increasingly convinced that machines can and will think (or are already thinking). A stormy dispute broke out over this problem in the late 1950s and is still continuing.

Some philosophers and psychologists have reason to reject the thesis that machines can think. The number of opponents of this thesis is growing. For instance, Academician P. K. Anokhin in the last years of his life very convincingly criticised the attempts to create the so-called "artificial intellect" (see, for example, Anokhin, 1973). This group of philosophers, psychologists and physiologists has been joined by some mathematicians. For instance, N. N. Moiseev, Corresponding Member of the USSR Academy of Sciences (1975:8), writes: "I am convinced that now and twenty years hence, as was the case twenty years and twenty centuries ago, the discovery of new laws . . . will be accomplished at the cost of strenuous creative activity, at the cost of an incredible expenditure of *human* intellect and spirit. No amount of *machine* time spent will replace these; the electronic computing machine only makes this process easier by performing more and more *routine* procedures."

The thesis that the machine can think transcends the boundaries of the proposition on the indissoluble unity of the biological and the social in man, in his thinking activity. The automatic machine is a product of human activity in which *immediately* there is *nothing biological*, nothing living, since it consists of artificial materials only. Consequently, in itself the machine is devoid of *immediate living* unity and continuity of the biological and the social. Such a violation of this unity makes independent, creative thinking impossible, although with the further development of science and technology man will hand over more and more mental functions to the machines created by him and operating under his control.

The Marxist thesis that human nature is a product of history constitutes the only possible philosophical basis for overcoming the afore-mentioned erroneous extremes in the study of the biological-social problem. On the one hand, there is no truth in the sociologistic assertion that man is but a concentration of economic effects or a "socium" entirely devoid of anything biological, organic, of anything natural altogether. On the other, we firmly reject the directly opposite, biologistic assertion of Freud, Lorenz and others that *animal* lusts and instincts underlie the behaviour (in particular, the "aggressiveness") of man. As a matter of fact, as we have seen from evidence given by Marx and modern science, something innate does exist in man: it by no means disappears in the course of history, but undergoes significant change and development in the process of the anthropogenesis and the subsequent social progress of mankind. Hence the historically moulded requirements of man cannot be reduced to those of animals.

When speaking about these two erroneous extremes (biologistic and sociologistic), we have to bear in mind, of course, that they seldom appear in pure form. They are usually interconnected. Both extremes rather appear as definite tendencies of reductionism (in biology or sociology). And we have to bear in mind that the term "environment" itself is understood in terms of the biological as well as in the sociological aspect. So if research focuses on the role of the external environment in human development, this does not mean that this particular line of research is sociologistic rather than biologistic, because the external environment can be understood in the sociological as well as in the purely biological sense, and also as a totality of physical states. This versatile interpretation of the external environment once again shows how complex the relationships between the biologistic and sociologistic tendencies can be.

For instance, one of the leaders of contemporary behaviourism, B. Skinner, is a zealous representative of the more biologistic extreme even when he deals with the most acute social and philosophical problems of our time. In his article entitled "The steep and thorny way to a science of behaviour," he writes: "I must begin by saying what I take science of behaviour to be. It is, I assume, part of biology" (1975:42). It is primarily from such biologistic positions that he examines the problem of man, particularly of his freedom, responsibility and dignity. That is why in his famous book *Beyond Freedom and Dignity* (1971:173), he opposes freedom of the individual to the survival of the human race and comes to this conclusion: "If it, Western civilisation, continues to take freedom or dignity, rather than its own survival, as its principal value, then it is possible that some other culture will make a greater contribution to the future."

He writes of the aims of his book: "My book is an effort to demonstrate how things go bad when you make a fetish out of individual freedom and dignity." Skinner was in a large measure right when he sharply criticised the individualism of bourgeois society. But the trouble is that in effect he identifies individualism with individual freedom in general. In an attempt to save the capitalist system from the anarchy of bourgeois individualism, Skinner in fact almost denies personal freedom and dignity. Personal freedom, responsibility and dignity are, in his opinion, something like thermogen and phlogiston in prescientific physics. Preservation of freedom and dignity is incompatible with the "survival of Western civilisation." Hence Skinner's desire to turn man into an obedient automaton by means of "behavioural engineering."

Such is the result of Skinner's pragmatic-biologistic methodology. The conclusion he draws in his book is this: survival is the only value by which civilisation will ultimately be judged, and any practice substantiating survival possesses this value by its very definition.

So however intricately the biologistic and the sociologistic approaches to the problem of society may interact, or however far apart they may be, they remain unpromising for the study of man.

But admission of the one-sidedness of these two approaches still does not lead to the truth. The well known "left-wing" philosopher, Erich Fromm, rejects the biologistic and the sociologistic approaches, but he himself flounders vainly in the jumble of psychoanalysis.

In a recent book called *The Anatomy of Human Destructiveness* (1973), he asserts that man is dependent neither on nature nor on society; man is possessed by the passions rooted in his character. One group of passions he calls the "syndrome of maintaining life," in which he includes love, solidarity, justice and reason. The other group he calls the "syndrome of destroying life" — greed, cruelty, sadism, egoism and the like. The behaviour of every person is determined, according to Fromm, by a combination of these syndromes in him.

Fromm (1973:438) notes that malignant passions are encouraged by the poor organisation of the sociocultural space which surrounds man and penetrates his inner world. The creation of tolerable material and housing conditions for a man does not save him from possible outbursts of his own aggressiveness. He sees the solution in the self-perfection of man, in the inner changes of the human personality, in the saturation of the human soul with love for life.

In a word, under the guise of innovation Fromm comes to the old ideological dogma of self-perfection, which denies the necessity to change radically the social conditions of human life.

Thus, both points of view (the sociologistic and the biologistic), though they seem to oppose each other, and also the psychoanalytical concept "towering" above them, are erroneous for one and the same reason. They ignore the key fact, generalised by Marx, that by changing external nature man changes his own nature (i.e. the nature of man is a product of history).

The major fact is that they all fail to recognise the class character of social consciousness, class psychology, i.e. the impact of the class structure of society on the formation of the consciousness and behaviour of people belonging to different classes and social groups.

Social psychology, far from remaining unchanged, develops together with, and on the basis of, transformations in social life. In bourgeois society proletarian psychology is essentially, according to Lenin's definition, the psychology of class struggle against the exploiting classes and their state (vol. 19:506). After the Socialist Revolution new conditions are created, the psychology of the builders of the new life, of a new labour discipline is formed; millions of people are educated and at first hand learn to manage the state and social production (Lenin, vol. 28:426).

As the foundations of social life are radically transformed, the national psychology changes and a new psychological climate is created in the relationships between people of different races and nations.

Racial traits are biologically determined, but relations between the races are not determined by biological causes. Racist behaviour is of a purely social origin. It is not true that the white man is genetically ill-disposed to people of the yellow or black races. Such hostility can only be the result of a social system that is based on the exploitation of man by man. With the elimination of this system racism is uprooted. New social relations create the basis for the development of new views and new rules of conduct in regard to people of other races. We are against dividing tribes or races, as if some are characterised by lofty human qualities and a lofty morality and others by wicked or harmful inclinations.

But it would be an oversimplification if, while seeing the determinative significance of social conditions, we ignored the biological characteristics of man, thus barring the investigation of human biology genetics.

If we take, for instance, *personal* conduct, a special analysis is required which takes account of both the social and the biological (and natural, in general) conditions, for they interact to form the general determinants of personal conduct. We must, in particular, consider the inborn inclinations of the person, for they affect, in one way or another, the development of his *abilities* when he engages in labour activity. Marx, Engels and Lenin never said that all people are equal in their abilities. By equality Marxism means social equality, not biological equality, not equal abilities.

Developing the basic Marxist principles of scientific socialism and communism, Lenin repeatedly explained the interconnection and the distinction between the socioeconomic equality of people under socialism and their inequality as regards abilities, requirements, etc. He wrote: ". . . Economic equality means nothing other than the *abolition of classes*. . . . The abolition of classes means placing *all* citizens on an *equal* footing with regard to the *means of production* belonging to society as a whole. It means giving all citizens equal opportunities of working with the publicly owned means of production, on publicly owned land, in publicly owned factories, and so forth" (Lenin, vol. 20:145, 146).

The problem of equality is tackled in a different way when it concerns the abilities, requirements, etc., of individuals.

With the situation in tsarist Russia in mind, Lenin wrote (vol. 20:145): "Individual members of the nobility are *not* equal in physical and mental abilities any more than are people belonging to the . . . peasant class. But in *rights*, all nobles are *equal*, just as all peasants are equal in their lack of rights."

In other words, among the noblemen, among the peasants, and in the other classes there are people with different abilities, inborn inclinations, etc.; but the whole trouble is that the members of different classes live in different socioeconomic conditions, which may either speed up, or slow down, or altogether distort the development of human abilities. Socialism and communism create the most favourable conditions for the physical development of all working people. But, as Lenin wrote, "It is absurd to expect *equality* of strength and abilities in socialist society. In brief, when socialists speak of equality they always mean *social* equality, equality of social status, and not by any means the physical and mental equality of individuals" (vol. 20:146).

This general fundamental principle as to differences in the inborn inclinations and abilities of people, and, consequently, as to the definite but not fatal role of natural inclinations in the development of human abilities, is elaborated and given concrete expression in a number of pieces of research carried out by biologists, psychologists, etc. For instance, Academician N. P. Dubinin considers the existence of "genetic distinctions as to a person's physical disposition, inclinations, talents, special abilities, etc." (1972:79) to be an irrefutable fact. Paying due regard to this fact, he works out the problem of what he calls "social inheritance," i.e. the problem of the continuity from generation to generation, of the social and cultural acquirements of mankind.

Thus, the dominant role in the formation of the views, the manners and customs in any society is played primarily by the social conditions. But if we take individuals from one and the same society, from one and the same class, from one and the same group, we must not ignore the biological, psychophysiological and other distinctions between them.

For example, it would simply be ridiculous to look for the roots of crime in human biology; yet we must bear in mind that a number of facts point to the necessity to take some of the above-mentioned individual distinctions into account. Lenin emphasised that "the fundamental social cause of excesses, which consist in the violation of the rules of social intercourse is exploitation of the people, their want and their poverty. With the removal of this chief cause, excesses will inevitably begin to 'wither away' . . . " (vol. 20:464). Some of these excesses, however, may occur even under communism, when all the social roots of crime will have been eliminated. The possibility of these excesses may be connected with, among other things, individual biological and psychophysiological differences among people, since these differences can influence the development of a certain disposition towards a particular conduct.

So while the "behaviour" of classes, nations and social groups is socially determined, in determining the conduct of a particular individual we must take account of the very complex interaction between the social and the biological.

On the whole, in principle we cannot help acknowledging that the formation of a person's *abilities* and *character*, which develop in the course of his labour *activity* under a definite set of socioeconomic and class conditions, is somewhat influenced by *natural* factors (inborn inclinations, etc.). That very many more concrete questions (how exactly the influence of inborn inclinations takes place, and other issues) remain unanswered, is a different matter. It will take more than one decade of systematic research to solve them. This should all the more be emphasised since the relevant section of biological science—the biology of development (the ontogenesis of animals and man)—has been far less studied than other sections of biology, such as the chromosome theory of heredity and the evolutionary theory of the formation of species. As the late Academician B. L. Astaurov (1972:67) wrote, in the field of "the biology of development we are wandering in the total darkness of an incredible amount of established facts, special laws and their elaborate fragmentary explanations, without possessing an adequate theory and while still gazing at the development of chickens in eggs as if this were a real miracle."

With the further development of biology (genetics, physiology, etc.), psychology, sociology and other allied sciences, increasingly deep research will be carried out into the very mechanism of interaction between the biological and the social in man, in the individual, in the personality.

The general thesis that the development of man is the development of a social being stems, in the final analysis, from the conviction that his social consciousness is determined by social, not biological, factors. But notwithstanding this general and indisputable thesis, for us all it is an equally indisputable fact that we cannot wholly discard the impact of biological, natural factors. Little is known as yet as to where the boundary of this impact lies and as to what its mechanism is like. Experimental data on this question seem to be inadequate as yet. The history of mankind and the evolution of man and human society provides a wealth of material for this general thesis, whereas a great deal still has to be clarified as regards the mechanism of interaction between the biological and the social, particularly in the field of psychology.

Genetic conditionality and biological influence in general seem to vary at different levels of development. For example, the genetic conditionality of anatomical and purely physiological characteristics of man differ significantly from the far more complex, more indirect and largely unknown genetic conditionality of certain psychical peculiarities of man. Among the latter, too, we apparently have to differentiate psychical functions of a varying degree of complexity, since their genetic prerequisites may be highly varied. . . .

At present an increasing number of sciences are ever more successfully beginning to study the human being, who poses the most difficult and yet the most exciting of all scientific problems. Some scientists have proposed devising a special composite science for the study of man, but this is hardly possible. Man poses multifaceted problems; he is studied not by one science, but by a complex of sciences (anthropology, genetics, physiology, psychology, sociology, ethics, aesthetics, ethnography, etc.)

Of course today both the integration and the differentiation of the sciences are conspicuously expressed (this is especially true of the sciences that deal with various aspects of the problems of man). But any such integration of knowledge implies not the fusion or mutual dissolution of the sciences, but their interaction and mutual enrichment for the sake of the joint solution of complex problems. In this respect we may say that there are no composite sciences, but there are composite problems (and each is studied by a particular science in one aspect or another).

It is this cooperation of various "independent" sciences for the joint study of the complex problems of man that can yield fruitful results.

References

Anokhin, P. K. (1973) "The Philosophical Meaning of the Problem of Natural and Artificial Intelligence." *Voprosy Filosofii* 6:83–97.

Argyle, M. (1969) *Social Interaction*. Chicago: Aldine.

Astaurov, B. L. (1972) "Theoretical Biology and Some of its Immediate Tasks." *Voprosy Filosofii* 2:61–74.

Dubinin, N. P. (1972) "Today's Natural Science and the Scientific World Outlook." *Voprosy Filosofii* 3:76–87.

Fromm, E. (1973) *The Anatomy of Human Destructiveness*. New York: Holt, Rinehart and Winston.

Klineberg, O. (1971) "Race and IQ." *UNESCO Courier*, Nov.: 5, 13, 32.

Kolata, G. Bari.(1975) "Sociobiology (1): Models of Social Behavior." *Science* 187 (4171):50–51.

Lenin, V. I. *Collected Works*. Moscow.

Marx, K. *The Capital*. Vol. 1. Moscow.

Marx, K. and F. Engels. (1969) *Selected Works*. Moscow.

Metress, J. (1974) "The Biological Concept of Race: An Issue in Social Biology." *Biology and Social Affairs* (2):34–35.

Moiseev, N. N. (1975) "Preface," in T. Naylor *Computer Simulation Experiments with Models of Economic Systems*. Moscow (Russian edition).

Nebylitsyn, B. D. and G. Grey (eds.).(1972) *Biological Bases of Individual Behaviour*. New York, London: Academic Press.

Penrose, L. S. (1971) "Ethics and Eugenics," in W. Fuller (ed.) *The Social Impact of Modern Biology*. London.

Reuchlin, M. (1974) *La Psychologie Differentielle*. Paris.

Skinner, B. (1971) *Beyond Freedom and Dignity*. New York: Knopf.

———— . (1975) "The Steep and Thorny Way to a Science of Behavior." *American Psychologist* 30 (1):42–49.

24

Sociobiology as an Adaptationist Program

R. C. Lewontin

A strain that has been growing in evolutionary theory in the last 25 years has been the search for principles of optimization that will be broadly applicable to a wide range of evolutionary phenomena. For the most part, the formal theories of population genetics and population ecology have been purely kinematic descriptions of the changes in genetic composition or species numbers that occur as a result of differential rates of reproduction. But this has seemed unsatisfactory to theorists of evolution because of its purely formal nature and they have sought to replace these kinematic descriptions with some principles equivalent to the Principle of Least Action, or the minimization of potential energy in physics. Fisher's (1930) Fundamental Theorem of Natural Selection and Wright's (1931) formulation of changes in gene frequency as a kind of potential function have both been interpreted as guaranteeing that in the course of evolution by natural selection, the average fitness of individuals in a population will be increased in some absolute sense, although these formations do not, in fact, allow such an inference (Li, 1955; Cain & Sheppard, 1954). In ecology the search for an optimizing principle has led to models of the minimization of resource wastage (MacArthur, 1969). But no attempt so far to produce maximization, or equivalently, minimization, principles that flow rigorously from the kinematics of population biology has succeeded at any general level. It simply has not yet been possible to replace the purely kinematic description of evolutionary changes with a rigorous alternative optimality principle.

An alternative to searching for a formal optimization principle flowing from the kinematic equations of population biology has been to assume that evolution of species and communities does, in fact, lead to adaptation, high fitness, maximum population size, maximum intrinsic rate of increase or some other

Reprinted from *Behavioral Science*, Volume 24, No. 1, 1979, by permission of James Grier Miller, M.D., Ph. D., editor.

attribute of the population related to reproductive success of individuals. Given this assumption, the task of the evolutionary theorist becomes to show what characteristics of the organism would be, in fact, optimal, given the state of the environment. In this tradition are Lewontin's (1961) attempt to analogize evolution with the "game against nature" and to provide methods for determining the optimal mixed strategy for the species, Levins' (1968) fitness sets for solving the problem of optimal strategy in the face of a changing environment, and Maynard-Smith's (1972) Evolutionarily Stable Strategies (ESS) for predicting the optimum behavioral strategy based on Nash equilibria. All of these general approaches have in common that they isolate certain problems to be solved by organisms and regard evolutionary change as the acquisition of these solutions as the consequence of natural selection. The procedure has both a forward and a backward form. In the forward form, the problem is set by the investigator a priori, based on some evaluation of the life history pattern of the organism, and the organism's morphological, physiological or behavioral phenotype is searched for the solution, or one is predicted for a hypothetical organism. For example, Leigh (1971) assumed that efficiency of food gathering is a problem for a sponge which filters particles out of water and should therefore expel already processed water as far as possible, and he then showed by a hydrodynamic analysis that sponges were an optimal shape to solve this problem. In the backward form of the program, a particular aspect of the organism is assumed to be a solution and the problem is searched for. An example is the explanation of the dorsal plates of the dinosaur, *Stegosaurus*, as heat regulation devices, allowing the animals to be active at very high ambient temperatures.

I call that approach to evolutionary studies which assumes without further proof that all aspects of the morphology, physiology and behavior of organisms are adaptive optimal solutions to problems *the adaptationist program*. It is not a contingent theory of evolution or hypothesis to be tested since adaptation and optimality are *a priori* assumptions. Rather, it is a program of explanation and exemplification in which the purpose of the investigator is to show *how* organisms solve problems optimally, not to test *if* they do. In this sense, such studies are much more akin to engineering than they are to physics.

Sociobiology is one manifestation of the adaptationist program, concentrating on the behavioral aspect of the phenotype. Despite the prefix "socio-," the subject is by no means restricted to the behavior of integrated groups and includes, for example, the behavior of individual parents and children towards each other (Trivers, 1974). In fact, the central analytic concepts, kin selection and extended fitness (Hamilton, 1964), are used in sociobiology in the form that relates the relative advantage of an individual to its behavior toward another individual of a given degree of genetic relationship. Sociobiology is held together by the concentration on behavior and by a commitment to the adaptive program. It is these two elements that account for the virtually unanimous and uncritical popularity that greeted the first self-conscious announcement of the field in Wilson's *Sociobiology: The New Synthesis* (1975a), for it is universally recognized that behavior, in animals at least, is a critical element in their evolution, and optimality arguments have been the dominant mode in evolutionary theory for the last ten years (see, for example, the table of contents of *The American Naturalist* for the last decade). Sociobiology then suffers from a number of serious methodological and epistemological problems that it has in common with all manifestations of the adaptationist program, and in addition has many of its own methodological problems that arise when behavior, and especially human behavior, is the subject of inquiry. In particular, I will try to show that human sociobiology so vulgarizes natural selection and the theory of adaptation that it does not have a claim to be a serious form of scientific investigation.

The general form of sociobiological argument is the following. The behavioral phenotype of a species is described. As for any other aspect of the phenotype, this description cannot be exhaustive, but is framed in terms of those elements that seem significant to the observer. It is then to be demonstrated that this phenotype has been established in the species by natural selection. To do so requires, first, an adaptive story to explain the circumstances that would cause individuals of that phenotype to leave more offspring than individuals of other phenotypes, and, second, an argument that phenotypic differences with respect to the trait are or were heritable. Evolution by natural selection requires genetic differences, or else the differential rate of reproduction of phenotypes can have no effect on population composition in future generations. Each of the three elements of sociobiological theory, description, heritability and adaptive story, has its own deep methodological problems that have not been faced, or apparently even been considered, by the practitioners of the program when applied to humans.

Description

What is immediately striking to the reader of Wilson's *Sociobiology* or of books by Dawkins (1976), Lorenz (1966) and others, is the total lack of consideration of the problems of correct description of behavior. While anthropologists have agonized for years over problems of ethnocentrism and, more recently, of sex bias, in the descriptions of human culture, while behaviorist psychologists have concerned themselves with anthropocentrism in studies of rats, while evolutionary morphologists have questioned the relationship between growth processes and commonly identified units of morphology, human sociobiologists in particular seem to have no consciousness of the fundamental problems of the description of behavior. They treat categories like slavery, entrepreneurship, dominance, aggression, tribalism, territoriality, etc., as if they were natural objects of unquestioned status, rather than as historically and ideologically conditioned constructs. Yet any argument about the evolution of entrepreneurship depends critically upon whether it has any existence outside the heads of modern sociologists and historians. There are four forms of error of description committed by sociobiologists and all require serious study if the field is to become serious science.

Arbitrary agglomeration. One of the most vexing problems of evolutionary theory is to decide how the organism is to be cut up into parts in describing its evolution. What are the "natural" suture lines for evolutionary dynamics? What is the topology of phenotype in evolution? All of these are ways of asking the question that anatomists as well as sociobiologists must pose. For example, is it proper to speak of the evolution of the hand? To do so implies that the hand is a level of description relevant to genetic and developmental changes and also to forces of natural selection. It implies an intensity of interaction in development or the determination of fitness such that we cannot study the evolution of each finger separately, or of each joint of each finger. Yet for the hand this is an unsolved problem still and some functional anatomists have considered the evolution of the thumb, rather than the hand as a whole.

Another example is the problem of the evolution of the chin. The morphological evolution of *Homo sapiens* seems describable as a process of neoteny since there is a much greater similarity between human and lower primate fetuses, and between human adult and human fetus, than there is between human adults and adults of other primates. The exception to neoteny is the chin, which becomes more pronounced in humans and less in primates during development. The answer to the paradox of the chin seems to be that it does not exist! There are two growth fields, the alveolar holding the teeth, and the dentary, making up the jaw bone. Both show neoteny, since both are getting smaller in human evolution, but the alveolar has regressed slightly faster than the dentary, resulting in a chin.

If the problem of an appropriate decomposition of the morphology of an organism is serious, how much more so is the decomposition of behavior. The topology of central nervous function, especially memory, has an unknown relation to morphological parts. Specific memories are not stored in specific parts of the cerebral cortex, and integrated cognitive functioning is totally mysterious in its structure. Yet sociobiologists seem to experience no difficulty in discussing the evolution of culture.

Reification. Related to arbitrary agglomeration is the erroneous confusion of metaphysical categories with real objects. Only real material things, not mental constructs, can be the subject of evolution by natural selection. We must be careful here not to confuse this with the problem of epiphenomenalism. Mental constructs can only arise from the sensuous activity of physical objects, human beings, and these mental constructs can, in turn, influence physical events as when men kill each other for ideological reasons. So, although the ability to create mental constructs is a consequence of evolution and although mental constructs may even alter the future course of evolution (more of the evolution of insects and plants than of our own), specific mental constructs are not real objects. Moreover the way in which knowledge about the world is organized is historically and culturally conditioned. The possession of property, for example, as defined in modern law, was unknown in the thirteenth century, when the legal relationship was between persons, i.e., feudal relations, rather than between a person and a thing which could be alienated (see for example Tigar & Levy, 1977). To suppose that the modern law of real property is somehow to be evolutionarily derived from animal territoriality is to suppose that property or territoriality are real objects capable of evolving, rather than mental constructs, made up as ways of talking about or organizing the world. In fact the relation between a person and a thing which we call ownership is a legal fiction masking a social relation between persons, a social relation that is only a few hundred years old in Europe. The problem of reification is a cloud hovering over all the sociobiological descriptions of human behavior, which is not to say that all sociobiological descriptions are reifications, but only that the status of "more entrepreneurial than" is not the same as "heavier than," although sociobiologists seem not to understand that.

Conflation. Human sociobiology makes use of many descriptive categories that we originally derived from human social relations, then applied, sometimes a very long time ago, to animals, and are now seen by sociobiologists as derived in humans from those animal states. In the process of transfer from humans to animals, however, they necessarily lost their specific historical and cultural content and became transformed into descriptions of quite other phenomena by a process of metaphor. When these metaphors are reintroduced into arguments about human society, they carry with them their derived, animal significance and become erroneously conflated with the original human concept. The clearest example is the idea of aggression. Originally meaning simply an unprovoked attack of one person on another, it came also to have a political meaning as the aggression of one state against another. In its first sense, it was taken over into animal behavior to describe a wide range of agonistic behaviors. Some sociobiologists now wish us to believe that human political aggression and human individual aggression are transformations of the same phenomenon, general animal aggression. Thus, war becomes a manifestation of human nature, the inbuilt aggression in all of us that must be artificially controlled if the species is to be at peace. But a few moments' reflection shows that people do not march off to wars because they feel aggressive toward each other, although governments attempt to instill such feelings after the fact as a tactic in war. They do so because they are drafted and threatened with imprisonment or death if they do not kill the enemy, or because they are paid mercenaries, or because they are told that their lives will be unbearable if the other side wins. Political aggression derives from political and economic causes, not from gut feelings of territoriality, xenophobia and aggression. The conflation by sociobiologists of the two meanings of aggression in a single explanatory attempt is obfuscating. The same conflation exists between the animal and human meanings of territoriality and hierarchy. Although Wilson, for example, has been more careful with the concept of caste and slavery (1975a), the danger of conflation in the use of these terms for utterly unrelated phenomena in ants and humans is great, since it tends to mask the commodity nature of human slavery and its use for the production of economic surplus rather than for subsistence.

Confusion of levels. While sociobiology is meant to be an adaptive explanation of social behavior, it deals, ironically, with individual behavior. This is necessarily so because sociobiology attempts to explicate the specific content of human actions as flowing from the genotype which is a quality of individuals. That is, sociobiology treats human social phenomena as if they were nothing but collections of acts of individuals. So, war, a social and political phenomenon, becomes nothing but the collective manifestation of the individual aggressivities of single human beings. Educational and political systems and the creation of ideologies become nothing but the collective manifestations of individual drives for conformity and indoctrinability (Wilson, 1975a). The basic philosophical error is the confusion of properties of sets with properties of members of sets. The basic methodological problem is that beginning with a biological determinism of the behavior of individuals as primary and social behavior as consequential on individual behavior, it is simply impossible to deal with uniquely social properties. There is no way, for example, that sociobiological theory can deal with human social institutions that might be universal despite genetic variation within the population, or social changes that occur on a time scale much more rapid than population genetic changes, or with social institutions that may remain constant despite genetic change. That is because sociobiology sees human institutions as the direct consequence of human genotypes and therefore cannot deal with the dynamics of social properties that are not dynamically linked to genetic changes. Now it may be argued by sociobiologists that no such social properties exist, that individual gene-mediated behavior is indeed primary and that all manifestations of human group behavior, as for other animals, are simply the collection of individual behaviors, although reactive to each other. But one should be at least suspicious of such an explicit claim if it is ever made because it will be making a virtue of necessity. Moreover, sociobiology does not make such an explicit assertion for the human species, which would be exceedingly difficult to defend, but simply commits the elementary fallacy of composition, that what is true of each individual element is true of the collection.

Heritability

In order for a trait to evolve by natural selection it is necessary that there be genetic variation in the population for such a trait. Thus, although I might argue that the possession of wings in addition to arms and legs might be advantageous to some vertebrates, none has ever evolved a third pair of appendages, presumably because the genetic variation has never been available. Not only is the qualitative possibility of adaptive evolution constrained by available genetic variation, but the relative rates of evolution of different characters are proportional to the amount of genetic variance for each. These considerations make both retrospective and prospective statements about adaptive evolution extremely uncertain unless there is evidence about genetic variation. For example, it is common in adaptive theory to try to explain life-history patterns (life-history strategies, as they have come to be called by adaptationists) by asserting that the particular pattern of reproductive rates and longevity exhibited by a species has evolved because it is optimal. Codfish lay millions of eggs, each of which has virtually no chance to survive, while the eelpout, *Zoarces*, has very few offspring and bears them alive, rather than laying eggs. Why such a contrast between two marine fish? The adaptationist program attempts to give an answer solely in terms of the relative advantage of increasing egg numbers, as opposed to increasing investment in survival of each egg (see Lewontin, 1965, for a numerical argument of this kind). But such an argument is illegitimate for it can only be correct if the available genetic variance for fecundity and maternal care are equal. It may simply have been that codfish ancestors had much more genetic variance for fecundity whereas the ancestral line of *Zoarces* had much more genetic variance for developing a broad pouch. Knowledge of the relative amounts of genetic variance for different traits is essential if evolutionary arguments are to be correct rather than simply pausible.

For prospective studies it is possible, at least in principle, to assay additive genetic variance for different characters in present populations of animals. What is required is that individuals of different degrees of relationship be raised under controlled environmental conditions so that genetic and environmental components of variance can be distinguished. It is not necessary to make controlled matings, provided natural relatives of different degrees, especially parent-offspring, full-sib and half-sib combinations, are available. It is essential, however, that genetic similarity not be correlated with environmental similarity or else genetic and environmental components of variance will be totally confounded. Unfortunately there is no way in human populations to break the correlation between genetic similarity and environmental similarity, except by randomized adoptions. Such adoptions do not exist as large groups and as a result we have no way of estimating genetic variances in human populations except for single-gene traits in which environmental variation is trivial, e.g., blood groups. The consequence of this methodological difficulty is that we know little or nothing about the genetic variance for any human metric trait, even including height, weight, metabolic rate, skin color, etc., except that there is clearly some heritable component. For human psychological traits absolutely nothing is known, because adequate random adoption studies do not exist. It is simply not possible to state whether there is any genetic influence at all on an individual's degree of xenophobia, dominance, entrepreneurship, conformity, indoctrinability, fear of incest, homo- or heterosexuality or any of the myriad psychosocial traits with which human sociobiology deals. Although a list of such traits is given by Wilson (1975a) as having moderate heritability, he appears to have depended on secondary sources for his information. Studies of the heritability of psychosocial traits are virtually all parent-offspring or identical-twin correlation studies, neither of which gives estimates of genetic variance unconfounded with environmental variances. Indeed the highest parent-offspring correlations known are for political party and religious affiliation (Fuller & Thompson, 1960). Nor is there any likelihood that methodologically adequate studies will be made in the foreseeable future.

The problem of retrospective studies is that to argue about the evolution of present day human populations it would be necessary to get information about genetic variance in the past. Evidence for genetic variance in the present, even if it were available, would be of little help because evolution by natural selection destroys the genetic variance on which it feeds. It is a fundamental theorem of population genetics that as natural selection proceeds, additive genetic variance is used up and eventually disappears. Thus, if present human populations show no genetic variance for, say, entrepreneurship, it can be claimed by sociobiologists that there used to be such variance, but it was used up by selection for the trait. On the other hand, if there were some variance at present, sociobiologists could point to it as evidence for the heritability of entrepreneurial activity. There is no conceivable observation about genetic variance at present that could disprove the contention of past evolution of the trait.

What is so distressing about sociobiological theory is not that adequate estimates of genetic variance are lacking, since that is a problem that plagues all of evolutionary reconstruction, but that the problem is either totally ignored or recognized and glossed over. Genes for conformity, xenophobia, and aggressiveness are simply postulated for humans because they are needed by the theory, not because any evidence for them exists (Wilson, 1975a).

Especially if characteristics are social rather than individual, the postulation of specific genes is inappropriate.

Human sociobiologists sometimes say that they do not really envisage specific genes for warfare or tribalism, but only human genotypes that make these social manifestations possible, given appropriate environmental circumstances. But this argument throws out the baby with the bath water. All manifestations of human culture are the result of the activity of living beings and therefore it follows that everything that has ever been done by our species individually or collectively must be biologically possible. But that says nothing except that what has actually happened must have been possible. If human sociobiology is to accomplish its program, it must do better than that. It must state what human society cannot do and what it must do and why, or at the very least provide probability statements or descriptions of human norms of reaction for psychosocial traits.

The *norm of reaction* is the basic concept of developmental genetics (Lewontin, 1974). The phenotype is the unique result of development of a given genotype in a particular environmental sequence. There is, in general, no one-to-one correspondence between genotype and phenotype, but a function that relates phenotype to the particular combination of genotype and environment. The norm of reaction of a genotype is the enumeration of phenotypes that will arise from various environments. Obviously, the complete norm of reaction of a genotype cannot be specified since that would involve specification of every possible environmental sequence during development. In practice, norms of reaction are determined for specific ranges of particular environmental variables like temperature. There are no generalizations about the shape of norms of reaction and they must be determined experimentally for each genotype and environmental variable. Norms of reaction have not yet been determined even for human anatomical traits, because of the lack of control of human developmental environments. For social traits, the question of what is prohibited by the human genotype becomes a problem of extrapolating social behavior from historical social organizations to unknown future social institutions. Thus, there is no sound scientific basis for statements such as: "Thus, even with identical education and equal access to all professions, men are likely to continue to play a disproportionate role in political life, business and science" (Wilson, 1975b). Even if domination of women by men were a compositional trait, simply the collection of individual behaviors, it is impossible to say what the manifestation of genotypes relevant to this character, if any, will be in the most egalitarian society.

In summary, both retrospective arguments which attempt to rationalize the current state of a species as adaptive, and prospective arguments which attempt to predict the future evolution or social manifestation of current genotypes, require absolutely that there be information on the kinds of genetic variance available to species and on the norms of reaction of genotypes. The absence of such information, as in humans, makes the adaptive program an exercise in plausible story-telling rather than a science of testable hypotheses.

The easiest part of the adaptive program is the creation of a plausible story explaining why the observed traits of a species are optimal. There are two methods, depending upon the degree of specification of the trait. The first, an experimental one, can be used for extant species where traits and environment are measurable. I will call this method *progressive ad hoc optimization*. A particular aspect of the organism's life history is isolated as a problem to be solved. By an engineering analysis, the optimal solution is deduced, subject to certain constraints about the nature of the species, and then the species is measured to see whether it has provided the optimal solution. If it has, then a plausible argument is made that the trait examined has in fact arisen as an optimal solution to the posed problem. If, on the other hand, the solution appears not to be optimal, one can try again with a different problem, or what is more usual, a second additional problem is proposed for which the trait must also be optimizing so that the organism is really optimizing both simultaneously. In general a maximum of a function of N dimensions cannot be found by maximizing sequentially in each dimension. This procedure can be extended until a satisfactory fit is obtained. Often the added problems are not stated quantitatively, but added heuristically to rationalize the lack of optimality under the original criterion. Such a progressive *ad hoc* procedure, especially when only one variable is experimentally determined, is guaranteed success, so nothing is tested.

An example of progressive *ad hoc* optimization is Orians and Pearson's (1978) attempt to show that food gathering behavior in a central place forager is optimal. If a bird searches for food particles and brings them back to a central place before they are consumed, the net energy reward to the bird will depend on its food searching behavior. If it takes only very large particles, it may take so much search time and energy that the round trip is not paid for by the food. On the other hand, if the bird takes the first particle it comes across, that one may be so small as to make the round trip a waste of time. There is an optimal distribution of food particle sizes taken that depends on the available distribution of food sizes in space. Orians calculated the optimal feeding pattern for a bird in nature, based upon his actual observation of available food, and found that indeed birds did not take food at random, but were biased toward the optimal size. However, they did not fit the optimal solution either. He then rationalized the lack of fit by postulating that nesting birds cannot stay away from the nest too long, or their offspring will remain unprotected against predators. The actual behavior was then said to be a compromise between (measured) food particle size optimization and (unmeasured) protection of the young.

The second method, a nonexperimental, nonquantitative method, I call *im-*

aginative reconstruction. In this method one simply thinks about a species, past or present, and literally invents a reason why a certain trait should have been favored by natural selection. All of human sociobiological explanation is of this kind. Some such explanations are no doubt correct, but others are not, and in the absence of experimental falsifiability there is no way to tell which is which.

The possibility of plausible imaginative reconstruction has been immensely enhanced by Hamilton's (1964) principle of extended fitness. Hamilton developed a suggestion by Haldane that natural selection could increase the frequency of a trait even if the possession of the trait was at a selective disadvantage, provided the trait increased the fitness of close relatives because close relatives also may carry the gene. So altruists may give up their own reproduction to enhance the reproduction of, say, sibs and the result would be an increase in the frequency of the altruistic genotypes, if any. A paradigm example of the application of this principle in sociobiology is an imaginative reconstruction of the evolution of homosexuality (Wilson, 1975a). It is first postulated that homosexuality is genetic, although there is no evidence on this point and, of course, the manifestation of homosexuality is strongly dependent on history, culture and class. Second, it is asserted that homosexuals themselves leave fewer offspring than heterosexuals. While this must be true for persons who are exclusively homosexual, there is no information whatever on the reproductive rate of persons engaging in mixed homosexual and heterosexual behavior. Given the two unsubstantiated assumptions of heritability and lower fitness, there is clearly something to be explained since natural selection should have eliminated homosexuality. The answer given is that homosexuals may have devoted their energies to helping their sibs raise children, since they had no children of their own to feed, and thus by the principle of extended fitness increased the frequency of the genes for homosexuality.

The principle of kin selection does not cover every contingency, however. What are we to make of altruistic acts performed toward unrelated individuals? To handle this problem Trivers (1971) has introduced the concept of reciprocal altruism, according to which individuals will benefit from altruistic acts toward others, if the recipient remembers the altruistic act and reciprocates at a future time. Genotypes that lead to such reciprocation will be selected for.

By combining arguments of individual advantage, kin selection and reciprocal altruism, an imaginative reconstruction can be made for any observed behavior. In this way the underlying assumption, that all traits are adaptive, is always confirmed and can never be falsified. In the case of homosexuality, it is explained by kin selection in a socially organized species like *Homo sapiens*. But what about insects? The courting of males by other males is extremely common in *Drosophila*, a completely asocial fly. How could this possibly be adaptive? My own imaginative reconstruction is as follows. In nature unmated females are very rare, showing that females are fertilized very soon after emergence. There is also resistance to multiple insemination. It is of great advantage, then, to a male to be the one who gets to the female first. The reproductive cost to a male of passing up the rare unfertilized female is much greater than the cost of wasting some energy courting another male. Therefore natural selection will favor males who court indiscriminately since they are much more likely to get the unmated females than are males who are too circumspect. Whether or not this story is correct, it is at least plausible, is based on known facts about natural populations of *Drosophila* and took me no longer to construct than the physical time required to write the words. It has the virtue that certain measurements of energy and time expenditure might be made in natural populations to actually test the assertion of costs of homosexual courting. If those measurements should contradict the hypothesis, a substitute reconstruction would be called for, and could be produced with fair ease. Given the assumption of the adaptive program, it is hard to conceive of an impossible case.

Alternatives to Adaptation

An examination of the dynamical theory of natural selection, of the effects of stochastic variation in gene frequencies and of the facts of development shows that there are a number of evolutionary forces that are clearly nonadaptive and which may be the correct explanations for any number of actual evolutionary events.

First, natural selection does not necessarily lead to adaptation. A mutation which doubles the fecundity of individuals will sweep through a population rapidly. If there has been no change in efficiency of resource utilization, the individuals will leave no more offspring than before, but simply lay twice as many eggs, the excess dying because of resource limitation. In what sense are the individuals or the population as a whole better adapted than before? Indeed, if a predator on immature stages is led to switch to the species now that immatures are more plentiful, the population size may actually decrease as a consequence, yet natural selection at all times will favor individuals with higher fecundity.

Second, there are multiple selective peaks when more than a single gene is involved in influencing a character (Wright, 1931). The existence of multiple peaks means that for a fixed regime of natural selection there are alternative paths of evolution and the particular one taken by a population depends upon chance events. Thus, it is not meaningful to ask for an adaptive explanation of the difference between two species that occupy alternative peaks. For example, there is no adaptive explanation required for the existence of the one-horned rhinoceros in India and the two-horned rhinoceros in Africa. We are not required to explain why two horns are better in the west and one in the east. Rather, they are alternative outcomes of the same general selective process.

Third, the finiteness of real populations results in random changes in gene frequency so that, with a certain probability, genetic combinations with lower reproductive fitness will be fixed in a population (Wright, 1931). If fitness differences between genotypes are small, there is a very high probability of the loss of favorable genes. This is especially true during times of restriction of population size, which is precisely when environment is likely to be changing, and selective pressures for new genotypes are most likely to appear. Even in an infinite population, because of Mendelian segregation, a new favorable mutation has a probability of only $2s$ of being incorporated into a population, where s is the selective advantage. Thus, natural selection often fails to establish more fit genotypes.

Fourth, many changes in characters are the result of pleiotropic gene action, rather than the direct result of selection on the character itself. The yellow color of the Malphigian tubules of an insect cannot itself be the subject of natural selection since that color can never be seen by any organism. Rather it is the pleiotropic consequence of red eye pigment metabolism, which may be adaptive.

Fifth is the common phenomenon of allometric growth of different body parts. In cervine deer, antler size increases more than proportionately to body size (Gould, 1973) so that larger deer have more than proportionately large antlers. It is then unnecessary to give a specifically adaptive reason for the extremely large antlers of large deer. All that is required is that the allometric relation not be specifically maladaptive at the extremes.

Sixth, there is an important random or noise component in development and physiology. The phenotype is not given by the environment and genotype alone, but is also subject to random noise processes at the cellular and molecular level. In some cases, as for example bristle formation in *Drosophila*, variance from developmental noise may be as great as genetic and environmental variance (Lewontin, 1957). All individual variation, especially in human social behavior, is not to be explained deterministically and cannot be taken as demanding specifically adaptive stories.

If sociobiological theory is to make a lasting contribution to our understanding of evolution, it must abandon the naive adaptationist program that now characterizes human sociobiology and become very much more explicit about the epistemological and methodological difficulties that face it. To do so will require that sociobiologists abandon their claim to universal explanation of all human social phenomena and accept a much more modest goal of providing well founded explanation of, say, caste formation in social insects, a difficult enough task and one requiring much serious experimental, natural historical, and theoretical work. By being less grandiose in its project, sociobiology may become more fruitful in its outcome.

References

Cain, A. J., and P. M. Sheppard. (1954) "The Theory of Adaptive Polymorphism." *American Naturalist* 88, 321–326.

Dawkins, R. (1976) *The Selfish Gene*. Oxford: Oxford University Press.

Fisher, R.A. (1930) *The Genetical Theory of Natural Selection*. Oxford: Clarendon.

Fuller, J.L., and W.R. Thompson. (1960) *Behavior Genetics*. New York: John Wiley & Sons.

Gould, S.J. (1973) "Positive Allometry of Antlers in the 'Irish Elk', *Megaloceros giganteus*." *Nature* 244, 375–376.

Hamilton, W.D. (1964) "The Genetical Theory of Social Behavior." *Journal of Theoretical Biology* 7, 1–52.

Leigh, E. (1971) *Adaptation and Diversity*. San Francisco: Freeman, Cooper & Co.

Levins, R. (1968) *Evolution in Changing Environments*. Princeton: Princeton University Press.

Lewontin, R.C. (1957) "The Adaptations of Populations to Varying Environments." *Cold Spring Harbor Symposium Quantitative Biology* 22, 395–408.

_____ . (1961) "Evolution and the Theory of Games." *Journal of Theoretical Biology* 1, 382–403.

_____ . (1965) "Selection for Colonizing Ability," in H. Baker (ed.), *The Genetics of Colonizing Species*. New York: Academic Press, 77–94.

_____ . (1974) "The Analysis of Variance and the Analysis of Causes." *American Journal of Human Genetics* 26, 400–411.

Li, C.C. (1955) "The Stability of an Equilibrium and the Average Fitness of a Population," *American Naturalist* 89, 281–296.

Lorenz, D.Z. (1966) *On Aggression*. London: Methuen.

MacArthur, R.H. (1969) "Species Packing, and What Interspecies Competition Minimizes." *Proceedings of the National Academy of Sciences* 64, 1369–1371.

Maynard-Smith, J. (1972) *On Evolution*. Edinburgh: Edinburgh University Press.

Orians, G., and N. Pearson. (1978) "On the Theory of Central Place Foraging." In D.J. Horn, R. Mitchell, and G. R. Stairs (eds.), *Analysis of Ecological Systems*. Columbus: Ohio State University Press.

Tigar, R., and M. Levy. (1977) *Law and the Rise of Capitalism*. New York: Monthly Review Press.

Trivers, R. (1971) "The Evolution of Reciprocal Altruism." *Quarterly Review of Biology* 46, 35–57.

_____ . (1974) "Parent-Offspring Selection." *American Zoologist* 14, 249–264.

Wilson, E.O. (1975a) *Sociobiology: The New Synthesis*. Cambridge, Mass.: Harvard University Press.

_____ . (1975b) "Human Decency Is Animal." *New York Times Magazine*. October 12.

Wright, S. (1931) "Evolution in Mendelian Populations." *Genetics* 16, 97–159.

25

Methodological Problems Associated with a Biologically Oriented Social Science

Steven A. Peterson
Albert Somit

Introduction

The publication of Edward O. Wilson's *Sociobiology* has sparked a controversy which shows little sign of abating. A resolution condemning sociobiology (the study of the genetic bases of social behavior) as racist, sexist and elitist was proposed — though defeated — at the 1976 American Anthropological Association meeting in Washington, D.C., and, at the 1977 Eastern Sociological Association meeting in New York, similar hostility was evident (Committee Against Racism, 1977).

The criticisms have been as much ideological as scientific in nature (Emlen, 1976; 'Letters', 1976; Wade, 1976). Perhaps the most vigorous assaults on Wilson have come from the Sociobiology Study Group, a radically oriented collective of scientists, who argue that to explain human behavior in biological terms is to rationalize and justify the political *status quo*. Sociobiology is not the only target of this type of attack, for other recent efforts to explain human behavior in biological terms have also aroused angry discussion in which science and political polemic have become hopelessly intertwined. Essentially similar animadversions have been directed at the work of Jensen and Shockley on race and intelligence, and at Lorenz, Tiger, Ardrey and Morris for their emphasis on the genetic components of human behavior.

These debates have served, *inter alia*, to further stimulate an emerging interest among social scientists in exploring the possibility that biological factors may significantly influence human behavior, an interest already manifest in

Reprinted with permission from the *Journal of Social and Biological Structures*, January 1978, Vol. 1, pp. 11–25. Copyright by Academic Press Inc. (London) Ltd.

several disciplines. While these several efforts have looked to somewhat different areas of the life sciences, ethology has been the major source of inspiration (cf. Tiger & Fox, 1966, 1971; Somit, 1972, 1976; Mazur, 1973; Campbell, 1975). Up to this point, a 'biologically oriented' social science has been one heavily influenced by ethology and we will use these two terms interchangeably, although ethology is but one of the major subfields of the larger discipline.

The political controversies noted above have essentially precluded a reasoned discussion of the methodological problems associated with biologically oriented explanations of human social behavior. Since we find an increasing number of social scientists drawing upon ethology, such assessment seems overdue. Those who utilize ethology should be more fully aware than is often the case of the methodological problems endemic within that discipline and should better understand the limitations of the research techniques employed by ethologists. Simply put, ethological data are frequently extraordinarily 'soft,' even by the relatively undemanding standards of social scientists.

In this essay, then, we delineate the methodological pitfalls of which ethologically oriented social scientists should be aware. First, we identify some of the conceptual issues from which these methodological problems often stem. Next, we describe those methodological problems generally encountered in the ethological study of behavior. Finally, we turn to the special difficulties which arise when *Homo sapiens* becomes the object of investigation, difficulties which must be addressed *in addition to*, rather than in place of, those encountered in dealing with other species.

The Basic Assumptions of Modern Ethology

Before we examine the issues, however, it may be useful briefly to summarize the assumptions underlying contemporary ethology. Ethologists seek to explain animal behavior in terms of the interplay among four factors: (1) genetically transmitted behavioral tendencies acquired over literally millions of years; (2) learned behavior; (3) the external environment in which the species functions; and (4) the varied experiences of the individual throughout its unique developmental history.

Axiomatic to contemporary ethology are the following propositions.

1. The behavior of every living species is influenced to a significant degree by its genetic inheritance.
2. This genetic inheritance is the product of natural selection. For behavior to be 'selected,' it must have a greater survival value than alternative modes of behavior.

3. Survival value is to be understood solely in terms of reproductive success.

4. Natural selection works in terms of adaptation to environmental conditions and environmental competition. This means that the behavior manifested by a given species can be best understood in terms of the environmental challenges with which that species has had to cope and to which it has had to adjust.

5. No behavior has any inherent value other than as it contributes to survival. No species has any inherent value other than as it manages to survive.

6. Adaptation is likely to be a modification of previous behavior rather than a total substitution of new responses for old. Species are likely, therefore, to retain residual aspects of earlier behavioral traits (as well as of earlier physiological mechanisms or structures).

7. Selection is an opportunistic process. Evolution is interested in only one outcome—survival. Any means toward this end may be selected for, including the capacity increasingly to utilize culture and learning.

Does this general formulation hold true for *Homo sapiens*? Practically every ethologist would answer in the affirmative, although there are disagreements as to the degree to which genetic tendencies and learning account, respectively, for different types of behavior. Man is the product of the evolutionary process which fashioned all other species; we are subject, therefore, to the same biological principles operative on all other forms of life.

The Conceptual Basis of Some Methodological Issues

As noted earlier, some of the methodological problems encountered in ethology have their roots in conceptual disagreements which still beset the field. Two of these require at least summary mention.

Instinct vs. *Learning*

The old nature/nurture debate is still around, although in somewhat more subtle form. Wilson asserts that the contemporary debate should be viewed more as a matter of differing emphases rather than completely opposed perspectives, since there are assumptions common to both camps (Wilson, 1975). However, ethologist John Alcock points out that this is *not* a 'pseudo-question,' but one involving different assumptions, emphases and philosophical viewpoints (Alcock, 1975). This is an issue with far-reaching research ramifications. Before commenting on the consequences of accepting one contention against the other, we should briefly summarize the respective positions.

Instinctive (or innate) behavior is usually characterized as nonlearned, under genetic control, not subject to environmental control, stereotyped (occurring in the fixed form whenever the behavior is elicited) and normally activated when an appropriate stimulus impinges upon the animal's proper sensory receptor(s). Thus, a male robin will begin an aggressive action against another male robin upon sight of the second bird's orange breast feathers. This reaction is typical of 'all' male robins, satisfying still another criterion for innate behavior.

From the developmentalists' stance, even such seemingly innate activities emerge in stages and, at each stage, are affected by the organism's experience with the environment. Behavior unfolds, they maintain, as a function of the continuing interactions of genes and experience. The DNA of the individual determines the probability that, in a given environment, its development will proceed along certain pathways. Species-typical behavior (i.e. a fixed behavior pattern which characterizes the species and occurs in the same form throughout that species) occurs only when the development of an animal takes place in a species-typical environment. If the organism does not encounter the environment and experiences appropriate to its species, its behavior may well deviate from the species-typical pattern.

How might one resolve this debate? Instinct theorists stress the value of deprivation experiments (Lorenz, 1965; Eibl-Eibesfeldt, 1970), arguing that the only sources of information for the animal's behavior are either environmental (learning) or genetic (innate). If the animal is raised in isolation and still exhibits species-typical behavior, it is then reasonable to assume that particular mode of behavior is innate. The developmental theorist contends, however, that the animal has not been isolated from itself, and that experience can still play a major role. Gilbert Gottlieb's experiments with isolated Peking ducks show, in fact, the effects of experience on behavior (Gottlieb, 1971).

The study of imprinting illustrates how the two opposing perspectives shape research design *and* methodology. Instinct theorists focus on the lasting effects of imprinting and the relative inflexibility of the critical period; developmentalists examine the effects of various experiences and conclude that imprinting is reversible and the critical period is *not* fixed. Divergent theoretical views thus lead ethologists to study the phenomenon in different ways and, in some cases, to place different interpretations on the same data. Each perspective suggests different questions to study, different types of 'experiments' and this, in turn, leads to different findings.

A second major conceptual disagreement is that between those who advocate naturalistic field observation and those who see laboratory experimentation as an equally useful, or even better, method of studying animal behavior; for decades proponents of these two basic techniques have argued about which is preferable. Today, there is an increasing rapprochement between the two camps as ethologists have come to realize that each method meets a real need and that, used together, they can provide a more complete understanding than either alone. Furthermore, the dividing line between field observation and laboratory experimentation has blurred as elements of the one are incorporated in the utilization of the other. Still, for simplicity of presentation, we will treat the longstanding disagreement in 'either-or' terms.

Some questions about a species' behavioral repertoire—e.g., natural food preferences, eating habits, seasonal and daily variations in behavior, social structure, response to predators, intergroup relations, and the interactions among individuals, the group and the environment—can best be studied in the field under 'natural' conditions (Carpenter, 1964; Dolhinow, 1972). On the other hand, this type of research has some inherent disadvantages. One can only make inferences about causal mechanisms (e.g. the impact of hormones on behavior). Furthermore, the observer must select and record data while a complex array of events takes place and important information may be lost in the process (we will return to this later). Third, observer bias may lead to perceptual distortions of what is actually occurring. While this can also happen in the laboratory, it is much more likely under field conditions where it may not be feasible to arrange a convenient separation between 'fact' and interpretation. As William A. Mason, a leading primatologist, has said (Mason, 1968:401):

> The fieldworker must be able to accept solitude, physical discomfort, and frustration as normal parts of his daily routine. He is heavily dependent on his own resources in collecting and evaluating his findings and must be able to tolerate a high degree of complexity and ambiguity in his data, particularly in the early phases of research. The neat temporal separation between fact and interpretation, which is usually possible in the laboratory, is often unattainable in the field where the process of formulating, checking and revising interpretations goes on continuously and is an inseparable and essential part of gathering information.

Experimental studies have the great advantage of control, since one can isolate with some precision the effects of different variables on behavior. But experiments often abstract one particular mode of behavior from an animal's complete repertory and carry the risk that the richness of the organism's survival strategy, and the interaction between different behavior patterns and the environment, is missed or not fully appreciated.

Finally, the experimental animal is (normally) taken from its natural environment and studied in a 'strange' setting. Under these circumstances, behavior may well be altered. For example, it was once believed that female prosimians were sexually receptive all year round. However, this seems to have been an artifact of captive conditions for, in the wild, there is apparent a clear birth season. In some experimental settings in fact, 'natural' behavior may not occur at all. Some species, to take a familiar instance, will not mate under laboratory conditions, making a study of their reproductive behavior impossible.

General Methodological Problems Encountered in Ethological Research

We turn now to a consideration of more specific problems associated with ethological observation and experimentation which must be considered: observer effect, measurement, recording sampling, reliability and identification.

Observer Effect

The mere awareness of being observed may affect an animal's behavior. The physical presence of the observer, a leading ethologist warns, can produce reactions in some primate species which eclipse normal reaction patterns (Carpenter, 1964; see also Hutt & Hutt, 1970). Jane Goodall's study of chimpanzees in Tanzania provides a case in point. To secure better observing conditions, she made food readily available near her camp. This attracted chimps who came to feast upon her bounty. Regrettably, the unusual abundance of bananas seems to have triggered increased aggressive interactions among the animals and disrupted their normal social patterns. Later, Goodall realized that the feeding station, intended to facilitate observation, had actually functioned to distort the chimpanzees' natural behavior (van Lawick-Goodall, 1971). This difficulty is not limited to field studies alone; awareness of the observer(s) may produce nontypical behavior in a laboratory setting as well.

Measurement

The basic question here might be phrased: how does the researcher know that *what* he is measuring is what he wants to measure? Robert Plutchik, a primatologist, surveyed the analytic schemes employed in observational studies of the higher apes and found that a bewildering profusion of classificatory devices has been used to describe behavior, with each observer tending to create a unique set of categories. For example, in a field study of rhesus monkeys, one researcher utilized a checklist of 56 'socially significant' behavior patterns. No rationale was given for selecting these behaviors and there was no attempt to organize the discrete acts (including such manifestations as 'hold tail erect' and 'ignores') into broader groupings (Plutchik, 1964). The problem of the metric(s) to be employed is not restricted to observational studies. The experimenter in the laboratory must also find some satisfactory solution to this issue.

Recording

Although closely related to measurement, there are some special aspects which make recording a separate problem. Under laboratory conditions, this is not particularly troublesome given the availability of instruments (film, tape, etc.) which can automatically record the animal's behavior. Although the same equipment could, in principle, be deployed in the field, realistically this is often of limited practicality. As Bramblett notes (Bramblett, 1976:282):

> The main liability of such systems is equipment failure. This is a particular problem in the field, where humidity or dust may cause breakdowns and repair service may be nonexistent. Only those who have experienced such breakdowns can appreciate the frustration and even heartbreak caused by discovering a failure to record only after the event.

The ethologist may thus be left with the task, taking the example mentioned above, of simultaneously observing and recording data—on a 56-item checklist. Regrettably, there is a significant loss of information when data are recorded by hand. The Altmanns estimated that they could record only about 20 percent as much by hand as by instrument (Altmann & Altmann, 1970).

Sampling

There are at least four aspects to the sampling problem faced in animal behavior: (1) an adequate number of individuals and groups must be studied; (2) observations must be made over a sufficient period of time; (3) observation, whether of individuals or groups, should be intensive; and (4) individuals and groups should be studied over the full environmental range inhabited by the species (Carpenter, 1964).

The first item is self-explanatory. It is hazardous to generalize about a species if one has not studied enough individuals or groups, a difficulty encountered in both observational and experimental studies. It is also risky to generalize about all animals on the basis of data drawn from a handful of species. The proverbial visitor from Mars would certainly be struck by the bias toward mammals in general, and rats in particular, reflected in the comparative psychology literature of recent decades. The inconvenient fact is that different species behave differently (Beach, 1950; Breland & Breland, 1961; Bitterman, 1965).

The second and third points suggest the importance of long-term, in-depth studies. Some behaviors are periodically recurrent (reproductive cycles in many species) or seasonal (e.g., migration) and can readily be missed if one observes the species for only a relatively brief period. Thousands, rather than hundreds, of hours of painstaking observation are needed before behavior patterns can be described with any degree of confidence. Presently, in looking at those paragraphs in research reports describing the methods employed to gather the data, one is often struck by the relatively low number of hours of observation.

The importance of studying a species in different settings across its naturally occurring range can hardly be exaggerated. Many animals inhabit a variety of environments and behavior may differ markedly from one setting to another. The savanna baboon, for example, displays basic continuities in social behavior but there are also important differences from one group to another which seem related to environment. If we were to study the savanna baboon in only part of its habitat, we could mistakenly conclude that a given set of behavior patterns is typical of the species when, in actuality, there is considerable variation. Ethologists have, in fact, postulated a general relationship between environment and social behavior (Crook & Gartlan, 1966). Although the impact of the environment on social behavior is clear, the patterns are not as clear-cut and predictable as Crook & Gartlan hypothesized.

Reliability

Unfortunately, until recently, ethologists have not been overly concerned with reliability data. All too often, no information is provided on the level of agreement among independent observers using identical categories to record behavior (Plutchik, 1964; Bramblett, 1976). In many investigations, particularly where the observer works alone in the field, this shortcoming is literally built into the research design. An almost classical instance of the difficulties which can arise because of this is to be found in studies of savanna baboons conducted by Hall and DeVore in several areas of Africa. They reported a form of social spacing adopted during troop movements (DeVore & Hall, 1965). Just a few years later, however, the Altmanns studied some of the same troops in Kenya and did *not* observe this structure (Altmann & Altmann, 1970). Manifestly, these findings could be evaluated more adequately if reliability data were available.

Reliability is less of a problem in laboratory-based research. Recording can be automatic and readily checked after the event by other persons; given control of the experimental situation, the basic measures employed can be more readily defined, standardized and operationalized.

Identification

Identification has two aspects, i.e., individual and taxonomic. Individual identification is critical for observation if one is interested in social behavior. If we wish to study the dominance hierarchy in a specific primate society, we would have to begin by identifying individuals in order to note interactions.

This can be most difficult, especially when the primates live in trees with dense foliage.

A second aspect of identification might not seem so obvious, but it is significant. There must be proper identification of the species under investigation. For example, one common classification scheme assigns the savanna baboons to the same genus but to four different species: *Papio anubis, P. ursinus, P. papio* and *P. cynocephalus* (e.g., cf. Napier & Napier, 1967). Presumably, then, variations in behavior among the four species might be due largely to phylogenetic differences. However, not all primatologists agree that there are, in fact, four separate species. Buettner-Janusch argues that on morphological grounds, all four are really races of *one* species (Buettner-Janusch, 1966). This is not a trivial dispute. Should behavior vary across the total population of baboons and if there are, in fact, four separate species, one might adduce phylogenetic adaptation as an explanation. If, on the other hand, we are dealing with a single species, this explanation is not likely to be correct and we might be better off pursuing adaptive modification as an explanation (cf. Kummer, 1971, for further discussion of phylogenetic adaptation vs. adaptive modification).

Special Problems Encountered in Conducting Ethological Research on Human Social Behavior

Introduction

The methodological problems met in studying the behavior of any organism or any society of organisms are compounded by another layer of difficulties when *Homo sapiens* becomes the object of inquiry. This additional layer arises from three factors. To begin, in analyzing human behavior, we must take into account not only the interplay among genetic programming, learning and experience but, no less important, the role of culture. This socially transmitted legacy serves simultaneously to provide humans with a repository of approved behavioral models and, at the same time, to preclude the consideration of other models which are prohibited or may not have even been recognized by that particular culture. To what extent, and under what circumstances, does culture determine our individual and social behavior? In seeking an answer to this question, we must cope with methodological problems far more complex than those encountered in the study of any other species. We should be aware, further, that some eminent scholars hold that human culture may have become emancipated from direct genetic influence (cf. Dawkins, 1976; Sahlins, 1976). To the degree that this has occurred, we may find that cultural norms can and do override genetically influenced predispositions (cf. Campbell, 1975).

Second, the ethological study of man requires that a scientist, functioning with the intellectual equipment shaped by natural selection, be able to comprehend and describe precisely the behavior of his conspecifics *and* the extent to which that behavior has been molded by the same process of natural selection. It is not unthinkable that the cognitive limitations and predispositions produced by the latter render extremely difficult, if not actually impossible, the attainment of the former. To this point we subsequently return.

Third, neither the scientists undertaking the investigation nor the peers to whom the findings are presented enter upon their respective roles with what Locke would call a *tabula rasa*. The myth of scientific objectivity notwithstanding, we bring to our professional labors a set of commitments — disciplinary, theoretical, political, ethical, religious, etc. — of which we are, at very best, only partially aware. These commitments are normally of little practical moment when other animal species are being studied, since the findings in such cases are not likely to affect social policy. They may have profound consequences, however, when we study *human* behavior and the results are perceived as bearing on current public policy issues. Obviously, these ineluctable biases pose great methodological difficulties; any perceived linkage to public policy virtually guarantees controversy over the merits of the research design and the validity and proper interpretation of the data.

Sociology of Science

The acceptance of a new theory, historians of science are aware, is not necessarily a speedy or automatic process determined solely by the inherent validity of the idea itself (Ziman, 1968; Kuhn, 1970; Blissett, 1972). In many cases, the new conceptualization may be rejected by a significant number of those in that particular discipline; the discipline may be deeply divided for years — or decades — over the merits of alternative ways of explaining reality. The eventual resolution of the dispute may be as much a matter of generational succession as it is of the explicit abandonment of the older, and endorsement of the newer, formulation.

There are several reasons why acceptance may come slowly. Few scientific theories, particularly in their earliest versions, are so powerful that they provide an adequate answer for all the questions to which they are addressed. There may be some phenomena for which they do not seem to account or for which a rival theory appears to afford a more plausible interpretation. In principle, such issues can be decided by so-called critical experiments; in practice, this may be impossible. The theories may be stated in such a fashion that they cannot be tested; experimental results may be inconclusive, especially to those holding contrary views; or, as is often the case, the experimental technology of the day, or the ingenuity of the experimental scientist, may simply be inadequate to the task.

Theories, moreover, are born into a world populated with already accepted orthodoxies. It may be extraordinarily difficult for the existing scientific establishment to admit, even to itself, the superiority of a new concept. To do so could be tantamount to a confession of scientific error; the value of previous discoveries and achievements based on the older formulation, might come under question; and status, prestige and reputation jeopardized.

The point here, of course, is that for a half-century most social scientists have taught and conducted their research on the assumption that human behavior is almost totally learned and that our genetic makeup contributes little, if anything, to our behavior. The ethologists' contention that human behavior, like that of all other species, is significantly shaped by our genetic legacy flies directly in the face of this tradition. It is hardly surprising, then, that many social scientists trained in the conventional wisdom have given a chilly reception to the Neo-Darwinian approach in general and to its specific applications (as, for example, the suggestion that there is a genetic component to both aggression and altrusim in particular).

This normal disciplinary resistance to change is compounded by the fact that, in the latter part of the nineteenth century, social philosophers and biologists alike sought to apply to human behavior Darwinian concepts which they often did not fully understand and which, in any event, were inadequate to the task. The result, predictably enough, was disastrous. By the turn of the century, Social Darwinism of all varieties was on its way into disrepute, carrying with it into scientific obloquy the notion that biological factors played any meaningful role in human behavior, and was soon succeeded by the still prevailing theory of cultural determinism.

Memories of the earlier intellectual debacle linger and constitute yet another obstacle to be overcome (cf. Hofstadter, 1955). Ethological research on human behavior can expect extraordinarily painstaking (read 'hostile') methodological scrutiny and inconclusive or ambiguous experimental results are almost certain to elicit a knowing 'aha!'

Technical and Moral Limits of the Experimental Method

The difficulties encountered in seeking to study individual and social behavior mount as we turn to organisms capable of wider and wider diversity of response to environmental challenges. Even with animals below the primate level, extraordinary resourcefulness is required to devise experiments by which to ascertain the mechanisms underlying behavior. This is especially troublesome if one wishes to discern the relative contribution to a given behavioral pattern of genes, on the one hand, or learning, on the other. Still, many of these technical difficulties are, in principle, soluble so long as the species under scrutiny is one on which experiments may properly be conducted.

When we turn to *Homo sapiens*, the research problems take on another magnitude of complexity. No one has yet been able to devise an experiment which will tell us, for instance, whether xenophobia—almost universal among human societies—springs primarily from man's genetic makeup or whether it is fundamentally cultural in origin. To date, scientists have been no more capable of devising that kind of test than they have been in structuring one which will establish the relative merits of rival theories which would tell us how people should live their own lives, for example, with respect to child rearing, sex, duty, self-indulgence, etc. So far, this problem has eluded solution; we have had to rely upon inference, analogy and laboratory attempts which seek to simulate real life conditions—all methodologically unsatisfactory.

But this is only half the story. Even if we were able to overcome the methodological difficulties, there would remain profound moral (as well as legal) barriers to such experimentation. The Judaic-Christian tradition emphasizes that man is to be treated as an end in himself, not as a means to some 'higher' end. The mainstream of Western religious, moral and ethical doctrine rejects the notion that humans may properly be the subject of any experiment to which they do not willingly lend themselves or which demeans their humanity. Memories of the 'research' conducted in the German concentration camps are an appalling reminder that the extension of knowledge should not be the ultimate criterion by which our conduct is to be determined. It has been and, we hope, will continue to be unthinkable among civilized people that humans would be subjected to the kinds of experiments conducted, say, by Harlow and his associates upon infant rhesus monkeys. Sound as this moral prohibition may be, it necessarily circumscribes the kind of investigations which can be undertaken and will demand methodological creativity of the highest order.

The Comparative Method

Given the limitations on human experimentation, many researchers have turned to the comparative method as a means of inferring the evolutionary basis of human behavior. This carries with it a new set of difficulties. Since this topic has been dealt with in more detail elsewhere (cf. Peterson, n.d.), we will present only a brief summary of the subject. The two basic modes of comparison are homology and analogy. Homology is any resemblance between two (or more) species which can be explained by their evolutionary descent from a common ancestor who possessed that trait. Analogy, on the other hand, is resemblance in some trait between two or more phylogenetically unrelated species (cf. Atz, 1970; Lorenz, 1974). An obvious risk in the comparative method is mistaking an analogy for a homology; another is that, by their very nature, comparisons tend to be essentially inferential.

Robert Ardrey's treatment of human territorial behavior nicely illustrates one of the pitfalls to be avoided. Ardrey examines territoriality in many species (including man) and then, *inter alia*, suggests an innate human territoriality (Ardrey, 1966). However, analogy does not establish that these continuities across species are caused by similar mechanisms. Thus, his conclusion remains suspect.

Through analogy, one can draw inferences about the survival value of behavior. If different species have similar behavior patterns, one might theorize that congruent selection pressures have led to this convergence. For example, if we find that a large number of unrelated species display more rigid dominance hierarchies in impoverished environments than they do in lusher settings, we might infer that this type of social structure is an adaptation to harsher ecological conditions and serves to increase the survival chances of the species. In this fashion it is possible to develop hypotheses about the survival value of behavior. However, these are only hypotheses to be tested — a difficult empirical task.

Political Problems

Attempts to apply ethological concepts to humans, as we have seen, have evoked considerable criticism. The objections have often been politically motivated. This is understandable, since ethological evidence suggesting that differences among human subpopulations are fundamentally genetic rather than environmental could conceivably be used for political purposes. After all, it was not too long ago that some of the Social Darwinists justified their opposition to social welfare legislation on the grounds that the poor were 'naturally unfit' and that efforts to help them would be both pointless and contrary to nature's grand design.

Some of the political opposition to Neo-Darwinism has focused on the validity of the evidence, and the inferences which may be legitimately drawn therefrom; the main attack, though, has been aimed at the research itself, rather than at the empirical data. The issue has become not one of scientific merit but, instead, whether this type of investigation should even be permitted. The situation is not without irony. In pleading the perils of ethological research on human behavior, left-wing ideologists have adopted, with appropriate terminological modernization, the basic arguments against scientific inquiry employed by conservative theologians of almost all denominations over the past half dozen centuries.

Irony notwithstanding, we can anticipate that the radical left, possibly supported by elements from the opposite end of the political spectrum, will be on the alert for any inquiry into the genetic basis of human behavior. To the degree that such studies rely on public funds — or funds from sources sensitive to political pressures — research design may be as much influenced by the desire for protective camouflage as by the quest for methodological rigor.

Level of Analysis Problem

In principle, the level of analysis problem can occur in any branch of science; in practice, it has been particularly troublesome in the social sciences (cf. Waltz, 1959; Singer, 1961; Eulau, 1974). The caveat to be observed is that conclusions based on observations taken at one level of behavior do not necessarily apply to behavior which occurs at higher or lower (i.e., more or less complex) levels. For example, data derived from the study of individual behavior may not afford a valid basis for generalizations about the type of behavior which would be manifested by collectives of these same individuals (i.e., social groups); similarly, data derived from the study of small groups may not predict very accurately the behavior of much larger groups — or of individuals. To offer a trivial illustration, manifestations of consistent altruistic behavior within the family does not warrant the conclusion that the same individual (or individuals) will behave benignly in a labor union, or industrial firm, setting.

Other things being equal, it is easier to study a) individuals rather than small groups; b) small, rather than large, groups; and c) large, rather than very large, groups. The research strategy employed, however, must be determined by the level at which the inquiry is directed. This requires the investigator to determine beforehand just what phenomena he wishes to analyze and to make sure that his research design yields data directly from observations taken at that level.

The use by many ethologists of the comparative method makes this point even more important. As Thelma Rowell explains (Rowell, 1967:300):

> Comparison of human with other primate societies can be misleading, but it would be unreasonable to ignore them altogether. . . . The main source of confusion seems to be that there is no nonhuman equivalent to what is broadly thought of as 'society' in industrialized countries: monkey social groups can be compared only with human more or less extended family groups, perhaps in some cases with the isolated farming hamlet.

This difficulty is often not adequately addressed by practitioners of the comparative approach. For example, Willhoite compares dominance behavior in baboon troops with human societal stratification systems (Willhoite, 1976). Since the two phenomena are not really at the same level of analysis, one must remain sceptical about the conclusions drawn.

The Limitations of the Inquiring Mind

We suggested earlier that the human brain (i.e., our cognitive capabilities) may have been so fashioned by natural selection that we could be designed 'by nature' to be unaware of critical aspects of our own behavior—and possibly that of our conspecifics (Alexander, 1975). Pursuing a parallel line of reasoning, a leading sociobiologist has suggested that natural selection may well have operated to produce in us a 'natural tendency toward selfishness, cheating, cowardice and amoralistic aggression, to mention only some of the possibilities' (Trivers, 1971:35–37).

Seeking to explain one of the most pervasive and least attractive aspects of human behavior, Arthur Koestler has argued that an unfortunate miscarriage of natural selection left *Homo sapiens* devoid of the genetically transmitted prohibition against killing each other which characterizes most other predator species (Koestler, 1968). Conceivably, comparable flaws (or limitations) have been built, by the same process of natural selection, into our cognitive and intellective faculties (Stent, 1975). There is some evidence that the human brain may perceive that which does not exist; that it may ignore that which does exist; and that it may often misinterpret its perceptions (McGeer, 1976). Are we, in this sense, literally incapable of designing the type of scientific inquiry which will enable us to understand ourselves? As with a classical Greek paradox, no answer seems possible. Although the query is unanswerable, it poses a question which we should not cavalierly brush aside.

Conclusion

Formidable conceptual and methodological problems must be solved, it is clear, if the marriage between ethology and social science is to be successful. Ethology may hold promise for enabling us to better understand man's nature but, as one of the authors has argued elsewhere, that promise may be a long time in fulfillment (Somit, 1972). Nonetheless, certain short-run benefits may justify the enterprise. The ethological trust may lead social scientists, willingly or otherwise, to reconceptualize their approach to social behavior to take cognizance of the possibility that some social phenomena are related in some measure to our general biological evolutionary heritage.

In the final analysis, ethology may prove most fruitful as a means of sensitizing us to man as a biological as well as social animal. Second, and hardly less important, it may induce social scientists to turn again to a type of research they have too often tended to ignore—the study of actual human behavior. If either, let alone both, of these gains are accomplished, biology will have significantly enriched the social sciences.

References

Alcock, J. (1975) *Animal Behavior*. Sunderland, Mass.: Sinauer Associates.

Aldrich-Blake, F.P.G., T.K. Dunn, R.I.M. Dunbar, and P.M. Headley. (1971) *Folia Primatologica* 15, 1.

Alexander, R.D. (1975) *Behavioral Science* 20, 77.

Altmann, S., and Altmann, J. (1970) *Baboon Ecology*. Chicago: University of Chicago Press.

Ardrey, R. (1966) *Territorial Imperative*. New York: Atheneum.

Atz, J.W. (1970) "The Application of the Idea of Homology to Behavior," in L. Aronson et al. (eds.), *Development and Evolution of Behavior*. San Francisco: W.H. Freeman.

Bateson, P.P.G. (1977) *Animal Behavior* 25, 247.

Beach, F.A. (1950) *American Psychologist* 5, 115.

Beer, C.G. (1975) *Animal Behavior* 23, 957.

Bitterman, M.E. (1965) *American Psychologist* 20, 396.

Blissett, M. (1972) *Politics in Science*. Boston: Little, Brown.

Bramblett, C.A. (1976) *Patterns of Primate Behavior*. Palo Alto, Ca.: Mayfield Publishing Company.

Breland, K., and M. Breland. (1961) *American Psychologist* 16, 681.

Buettner-Janusch, J. (1966) *Folia Primatologica* 4, 288.

Campbell, D.T. (1975) *American Psychologist* 30, 1103.

Carpenter, C.R. (1964) *Naturalistic Behavior of Non-human Primates*. University Park, Pa.: Pennsylvania State University Press.

Clutton-Brock, T.H. (1974) *Nature* 250, 539.

Committee against Racism. (1977) *Sociobiology: The New Racism*. Leaflet distributed at Eastern Sociological Association meeting, New York.

Corning, P.A. (1971) "An Evolutionary-Adaptive Theory of Aggression." Presented at American Political Science Association meeting, Chicago.

————. (1976) "Toward a Survival Oriented Policy Science," in A. Somit (ed.), *Biology and Politics*. Paris: Mouton.

Crook, J.H., J.E. Ellis, and J.D. Goss-Custard. (1976) *Animal Behavior* 24, 261.

Crook, J.H., and J.S. Gartlan. (1966) *Nature* 210, 1200.

Davies, J.C. (1970) *Western Political Quarterly* 23, 611.

Dawkins, R. (1976) *The Selfish Gene*. New York: Oxford.

DeVore, I., and K.R.L. Hall. (1965) "Baboon Ecology," in I. DeVore (ed.), *Primate Behavior*. New York: Holt, Rinehart, and Winston.

Dolhinow, P. (1972) "Introduction," in P. Dolhinow (ed.), *Primate Patterns*. New York: Holt, Rinehart, and Winston.

Eibl-Eibesfeldt, I. (1970) *Ethology: The Biology of Behavior*. New York: Holt, Rinehart, and Winston.

Eisenberg, J.F., N.A. Muchenhirn, and R. Rudran. (1972) *Science* 176, 863.

Emlen, S.T. (1976) *Science* 192, 736.

Eulau, H. (1974) "Some Aspects of Analysis, Measurement and Sampling in the Transformation of Micro- and Macro-level Unit Properties." Presented at Conference on Design and Measurement Standards for Research in Political Sciences, Delevan, Wisconsin.

Fields, C.M. (1976) *Chronicle of Higher Education* 13 (December), 5.

Gottlieb, G. (1970) "Conceptions of Prenatal Behavior," in L. Aronson et al. (eds.),

Development and Evolution of Behavior. San Francisco: W.H. Freeman.

———. (1971) *Development of Species Identification in Birds*. Chicago: University of Chicago Press.

Hall, K.R.L. (1968) "Experiment and Quantification in the Study of Baboon Behavior in the Natural Habitat," in P. Jay (ed.), *Primates*. New York: Holt, Rinehart and Winston.

———, and I. DeVore. (1965) "Baboon Social Behavior," in I. DeVore (ed.), *Primate Behavior*. New York: Holt, Rinehart and Winston.

Hamilton, W.D. (1964) *Journal of Theoretical Biology* 7, 1.

Hofstadter, R. (1955) *Social Darwinism in American Thought*. Boston: Beacon Press.

Hutt, S.J., and C. Hutt. (1970) *Direct Observation and Measurement of Behavior*. Springfield, Ill.: Charles C. Thomas.

Klopfer, P., and J. Hailman. (1967) *An Introduction to Animal Behavior*. Englewood Cliffs, N.J.: Prentice-Hall.

Koestler, A. (1968) *The Ghost in the Machine*. New York: Macmillan.

Kuhn, T. (1970) *The Structure of Scientific Revolutions*. Chicago: University of Chicago Press.

Kummer, H. (1971) *Primate Societies*. Chicago: Aldine.

Kuo, Z.Y. (1967) *The Dynamics of Behavior Development*. New York: Random House.

Lehrman, D.S. (1970) "Semantic and Conceptual Issues in the Nature-Nurture Problem," in L. Aronson et al. (eds.), *Development and Evolution of Behavior*. San Francisco: W.H. Freeman.

Lorenz, K. (1965) *Evolution and Modification of Behavior*. Chicago: University of Chicago Press.

———. (1974) *Science* 185, 229.

Mason, W.A. (1968) "Naturalistic and Experimental Investigations of the Social Behavior of Monkeys and Apes," in P. Jay (ed.), *Primates*. New York: Holt, Rinehart and Winston.

Mazur, A. (1973) *American Sociological Review* 38, 513.

McGeer, P.L. (1976) "Some Effects of the Biological State of Brain on Values Associated with Mind." Presented at International Conference on the Unity of the Sciences, Washington, D.C.

Montague, M.F.A. (ed.). (1973) *Man and Aggression* 2nd ed. New York: Oxford.

Napier, J.R., and P.H. Napier. (1967) *A Handbook of Living Primates*. London: Academic Press.

Petchesky, R. (1971) "Biological Engineering as a Social Control Device." Presented at American Political Science Association meeting, Chicago.

Peterson, S.A. (n.d.) "Comparative Ethological Analysis of Politics: an Appraisal." Unpublished ms.

Plutchik, R. (1964) *Folia Primatologica* 2, 67.

Rowell, T.E. (1966) *Journal of Zoology* 149, 344.

———. (1967) "Variability in the Social Organization of Primates," in D. Morris (ed.), *Primate Ethology*. Garden City: Doubleday Anchor Books.

———. (1969) *Folia Primatologica* 11, 241.

Sahlins, M. (1976) *The Use and Abuse of Biology*. Ann Arbor: University of Michigan Press.

Schneirla, T.C. (1966) *Quarterly Review of Biology* 41, 283.

Singer, J.D. (1961) *World Politics* 14, 77.

Somit, A. (1972) *British Journal of Political Science* 2, 209.

———— (ed.). (1976) *Biology and Politics*. Paris: Mouton.

Stauffer, R. (1970) "The Role of Drugs in Political Change." Presented at International Political Science Association. Munich.

Stent, G.S. (1975) *Science* 187, 1052.

Struhsaker, T.T. (1969) *Folia Primatologica* 11, 80.

Tiger, L., and R. Fox. (1966) *Man* 1, 75.

————. (1971) *The Imperial Animal*. New York: Holt, Rinehart and Winston.

Trivers, R. (1971) *Quarterly Review of Biology* 46, 35.

van Lawick-Goodall, J. (1971) *In the Shadow of Man*. Boston: Houghton Mifflin.

Wade, N. (1976) *Science* 191, 1151.

Waltz, K. (1959) *Man, the State and War*. New York: Columbia University Press.

Willhoite, F.M., Jr. (1976) *American Political Science Review* 70, 1110.

Wilson, E.O. (1975) *Sociobiology*. Cambridge, Mass.: Harvard University Press.

Ziman, J. (1968) *Public Knowledge: The Social Dimension of Science*. Cambridge: Cambridge University Press.

Index

Index

Abortion, 159
"Absolute Idea of Freedom," 219
Acheulian tradition, 108
Activity preference, 67, 70
Adaptation. *See* Biology, and
    adaptation; Culture, and
    adaptation; Ecology, and
    adaptation; Economic behavior,
    optimization through choice;
    Individual, and adaptation;
    Sociobiology, adaptionist
    program
Administrative sciences, 262, 265
Adopted children, 306, 309, 342
Adrenaline, 307–308
African Genesis (Ardrey), 95
Aggression, 25, 48, 56, 59, 71, 89–90,
    91, 110, 215, 217, 218, 238, 278,
    282–283, 295, 300, 322, 323, 328,
    338, 339–340, 363
Aging, 235
Agriculture, 109, 232
Alchian, A. A., 151, 153, 154, 155
Alcock, John, 95, 351
Alexander, R. D., 62, 81, 104, 107,
    120
Alland, Alexander, 151
Alleles, 21, 174
Allometric growth, 347
Allotropy, 134
Alpha rhythms, 315
Altman, J., 111
Altmann, J., 355
Altmann, Stuart, 355
Altruism, 21–22, 46–47, 71, 85, 86,

159–160, 166–167, 169, 171,
    178–181, 183, 218, 278, 281–282,
    283, 323, 345
animal, 71
fitness, 85, 86, 305, 314
reciprocal, 62, 160, 161–162, 345
transactional, 38
unilateral, 38, 40, 96, 107, 109
American Anthropological Association,
    349
American Naturalist, The, 337
American Sociological Review (ASR),
    259, 282
Analogy, 360–361
Ananyev, B. G., 327
Anatomy, 108, 300, 338
Anatomy of Human Destructiveness, The
    (Fromm), 330
Androgens, 314
Animal behavior. *See* Ethology
Anokhin, P. K., 328
Anthropocentrism, 34, 337
Anthropology, 13–14, 119–123, 129,
    188, 214, 337
biological, 37–38
British school, 15
cultural, 55–57, 59, 66, 68–70,
    214, 237
and cultural evolutionism, 13. *See
    also* Cultural evolution
medical, 56, 91
physical, 55, 57, 121
social, 121, 292
and sociology, 292
structural, 205